The Life and Times of
Sir George Cornewall Lewis, Bart.

The Life and Times of
Sir George Cornewall Lewis, Bart.
A Radnorshire Gentleman

by RWD Fenn
President of the Radnorshire Society
President of the Cambrian Archaeological Association 2004–5

in association with

Sir Andrew Duff Gordon, Bart

Logaston Press

LOGASTON PRESS
Little Logaston, Logaston,
Woonton, Almeley, Herefordshire HR3 6QH

Published by Logaston Press 2005

ISBN 1 904396 29 1

Printed in Great Britain by
Bell & Bain Ltd., Glasgow

*Front cover illustration: Sir George Cornewall Lewis
by George Richmond (© National Portrait Gallery)
(Rear cover illustration © The Bridgeman Art Library)*

Contents

Acknowledgements

The authors' sincere gratitude is due to the Librarian and staff of the National Library of Wales into whose care the Harpton Court papers were deposited on loan. They have since been scheduled in five volumes. Mr WL Banks, CBE, has given free access to the Banks Archives and has willingly given of his time to discuss relevant aspects of 19th-century English politics. Mr JB Sinclair has been of great assistance in maintaining the momentum of the enterprize, besides being a constant help in keeping wayward computers, printers, and scanners to heel. Dr Phillip Cleland of the Kington Surgery gave us access to some of the more obscure aspects of Victorian medicine. We have also been helped by Mrs MC Curthoys, Archivist, Christ Church, Oxford; Mrs P Hatfield, Archivist, Eton College; Mr John Harnden; the Revd Dr David H Williams; and Mr Laurence Smith for allowing use of photographs by WH McKaig and for photographing some of the portraits. The suggestions of Andy Johnson of Logaston Press were consistently to the improvement of the text.

Our thanks are due to those, especially members of our respective families, our friends, and fellow members of the Radnorshire Society, who over the last five years have so persistently kept on asking when was it all going to be finished. This more than anything kept us going.

Lastly, the book would not have been completed were it not for the professional skills of Dr S Willoughby, her colleagues of the County Hospital, Hereford, and the medicinal properties of Aspirin.

RWDF
ADG

Preface

In his much praised biography of Gladstone, Roy Jenkins made a passing reference to 'the somewhat forgotten George Cornewall Lewis'.[1] Jenkins himself remembered him as a solitary grumbler when Gladstone presented his 1859 budget:

> But as he had as Chancellor in 1855-8 been largely responsible for the build-up of the deficit, and was also manifestly sour at himself being not again in the office, he did not cut much ice.[2]

What little is remembered about Lewis here is not necessarily accurate. There is nothing particularly sour in Lewis's own record of events in his diary, where, if there was any bitterness, one would expect to read of it:

> I received a note from Ld Palmerston informing me that Ld J[ohn] R[ussell] took the Foreign Office, & asking me to be Chancellor of the Exchequer. I afterwards went to his house by appointment ... My name was put down for Ch of Exch, but I stated that I did not wish to make any claim to it, in case Gladstone decided to have it.[3]

But this is the fate of the 'somewhat forgotten', the detail, though there, is overlooked. Even the date of Lewis's premature death in April 1863 was 'somewhat forgotten' and Jenkins makes his short life a year shorter by placing its sudden end in 1862.[4] It was the forgetfulness of biographers he had to fear rather than their indiscretions, which he thought added 'a new terror to death'. Lewis had generous obituary notices and a full entry in *The Dictionary of National Biography*. A memorial in Westminster Abbey, a statue in the forecourt of the Shire Hall at Hereford, and a monument in New Radnor were all set up in his honour. It was not the intention of his contemporaries that he should be forgotten.

The monument at New Radnor, reminiscent of the Martyrs' Memorial at Oxford, stands in a state of dignified decay, and few reading its inscription: Radnorshire: to her most distinguished son, unless they made the effort to read the rest of its weathered message, would know the identity of this most distinguished son. This becomes all the more remarkable when it is remembered how few distinguished sons can be claimed by the diminutive county of Radnor. The choice is very limited.

Making much use of Cornewall Lewis's diaries which cover the years 1846-63 and the other Harpton Court papers at the National Library of Wales, together with the diaries of Lady Duff Gordon, Lewis's aunt, now partially at the National Library and partially at Downton House, together with the resources of the Banks and Duff Gordon Archives, we have tried to make Cornewall Lewis less forgotten. A picture has emerged of a well-connected member of the Radnorshire gentry, who was a scholar of European reputation, and a statesman of promise and distinction, who found time and energy to attend the meetings of the governors of John Beddoes' School in Presteign, meetings of the county magistrates, of whom he was one, the county agricultural societies of both Hereford and Radnor, and the Kington Friendly Society. The Herefordshire Bow meeting could gather on the lawns of Harpton Court and politicians and scholars in its library.

However, rescuing, hopefully, Cornewall Lewis from partial oblivion is one thing; we have found getting to know him, especially the inner private man, as opposed to the public persona, a quite different and far more difficult task.

The *Oxford Dictionary of National Biography* was published in 2004, after this manuscript had passed the point of no return with its publisher. Readers, however, are referred to D.A. Smith's very informative entries in the *Dictionary* on Sir George Cornewall Lewis and Lady Theresa Lewis.

RWDF
ADG

Lewis Pedigree[1]

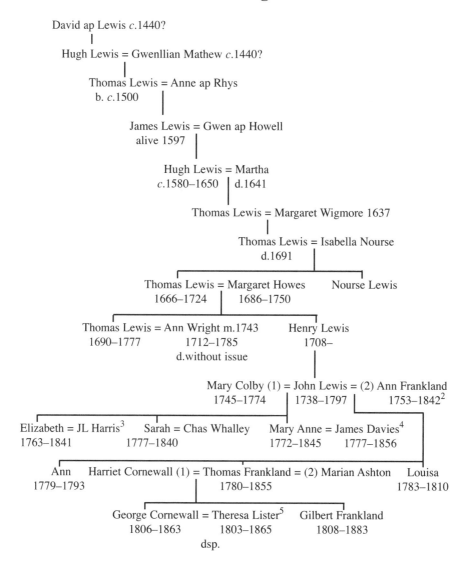

David ap Lewis *c*.1440?
|
Hugh Lewis = Gwenllian Mathew *c*.1440?
|
Thomas Lewis = Anne ap Rhys
b. *c*.1500
|
James Lewis = Gwen ap Howell
alive 1597
|
Hugh Lewis = Martha
c.1580–1650 | d.1641
|
Thomas Lewis = Margaret Wigmore 1637
|
Thomas Lewis = Isabella Nourse
d.1691
|

Thomas Lewis = Margaret Howes   Nourse Lewis
1666–1724 | 1686–1750

Thomas Lewis = Ann Wright m.1743   Henry Lewis
1690–1777   1712–1785   1708–
d.without issue
|

Mary Colby (1) = John Lewis = (2) Ann Frankland
1745–1774 | 1738–1797 | 1753–1842[2]

Elizabeth = JL Harris[3]   Sarah = Chas Whalley   Mary Anne = James Davies[4]
1763–1841   1777–1840   1772–1845   1777–1856

Ann   Harriet Cornewall (1) = Thomas Frankland = (2) Marian Ashton   Louisa
1779–1793   1780–1855   1783–1810

George Cornewall = Theresa Lister[5]   Gilbert Frankland
1806–1863   1803–1865   1808–1883
dsp.

1. Derived from *Archaeologia Cambrensis*, X, 1864, pp.29-39.
2. She married, secondly, the Revd Robert Hare, of Herstmonceaux, Sussex, in 1811
3. Of The Moor, near Kington.
4. Of Moor Court, Pembridge.
5. Sister of the 4th Earl of Clarendon.

Chapter One:
Childhood, Education, and Early Career

George Cornewall Lewis was born on 21st April 1806 in London, perhaps at 8 Portugal Street, Piccadilly, an address at which Boyle's *New Fashionable Court and Country Guide and Town Visiting* lists his father Thomas Frankland Lewis as living in January that year.[1] Thomas Frankland Lewis, aged 25, had in March 1805, married Harriet, fourth daughter of Sir George Cornewall, Bart., of Moccas Court, in Herefordshire. The country seat of the Lewis family was at Harpton Court in the parish of Old Radnor on the Welsh side of the border with Herefordshire. Thus Lewis himself was born of Anglo-Welsh stock, a fact he never admitted. Radnorshire, however, was not only the smallest of the Welsh counties, it was also the poorest, and Lewis no doubt in his English schooling heard the jibe often enough:

> Alas! Alas! Poor Radnorshire,
> Never a park, nor even a deer,
> Never a squire of five hundred a year,
> Save Richard Fowler of Abbey Cwmhir.

It was made all the worse because it was Richard Fowler of Abbey Cwmhir, rather than Frankland Lewis of Harpton Court, who was named as Radnorshire's sole squire worth five hundred a year.

Moccas Court had been built 1775–81 to the designs of Robert Adam. Though austere without, it was 'restrained and refined' within, and no doubt moved Thomas Frankland Lewis to bring in John Nash to give Harpton Court a gracious frontage and elegant interiors, altogether appropriate for his new wife. Nash was active at Harpton *c.*1805–12, and the result, in the opinion of Samuel Lewis, was 'a handsome mansion situated in grounds tastefully laid out',[2] and in recent times the architectural historian Thomas Lloyd judged it to be 'the best of the very few classical houses of the county'.[3]

Gilbert, George's younger brother, was born at Tyberton Court, another house of taste, designed by John Wood in 1728, and part of the Moccas estate. The fact neither boy was born at Harpton may have been due more to the house being rebuilt at the time than to coincidence. How much attention their father was able to give to Nash when the latter was working at Harpton is uncertain, for in December 1803 he was commissioned as a Lt-Col in the Royal Radnorshire Militia and was second in command to Lt-Col Richard Price of Norton Manor. He held this commission until 1815 when the regiment was disbanded on the conclusion of the Napoleonic wars.

Gilbert Lewis recollected that George's boyhood was spent divided between Radnorshire and London and that

> his frame was strong, and, at this period of his life, his health was good, with this single exception, that he frequently suffered from severe headache.[4]

The headaches remained with him for life,[5] but Gilbert was later to recollect George's 'eager pleasure' in reading as the only point of distinction between his behaviour and that of other young boys:

> The *Arabian Nights*, two translations of Portuguese romances, *Amadis de Gaul*, and *Palmerin of England*, were among the books that gave especial entertainment, and were in continual requisition.[6]

According to Gilbert, George mastered the usual rudiments 'with facility' before leaving Harpton

> to take his place among the forty boys at the school of Monsieur Clement at Chelsea (who contrived by some means to make his pupils talk French and to work at their business whether they liked it or not).[7]

Monsieur Clement held his school in Durham House in Chelsea's Paradise Row, demolished in 1906 to make way for the Chelsea Embankment. In 1805 a Monsieur Ouiseau had set up a school in this large house which enjoyed the benefit of having behind it what was deemed to be 'one of the finest playgrounds in or about London'. His pupils were the 'sons of or nearly related to the nobility'. The school's reputation, however, was really established by the next proprietor, Monsieur Clement:

a French gentleman, of very considerable merit who, by his indefatigable zeal and perseverance succeeded in placing it on a respectable footing and in rendering it an establishment of unrivalled pretensions for the acquirement of the French language and for the attainment of the Classics certainly not surpassed by any. Mr Clement met with the reward due to his constant and honourable labours and withdrew to a more tranquil state of life.[8]

A fellow pupil was Sir John Walsham of Knill Court, just within Herefordshire, who was later to speak of him as 'the inseparable companion of his childhood, and the steadfast friend of his whole lifetime', recollecting

the old schoolroom at Chelsea, visions of the playing fields at Eton, and visions of their wanderings about the hills and valleys and woods.[9]

It was at Chelsea that George Lewis acquired the basis of what was to become his prodigious knowledge of Latin, Greek, and Ancient History. His father had little interest in such matters. He had gone up to Christ Church from Eton as a gentleman commoner, matriculating in 1798, but he took no degree.[10]

A Radnorshire contemporary of Thomas Frankland Lewis at Christ Church was Walter Wilkins, Junior, of Maesllwch, the son of Walter Wilkins, who made a fortune in India, bought Maesllwch and was MP for Radnorshire from 1792 until his death in 1828.

Walter Wilkins, Junior matriculated in February 1797, and unlike Thomas Frankland Lewis did graduate. But much of his time and money at Oxford was occupied by horses, and in this his behaviour was by no means unusual. A Herefordshire contemporary at Christ Church, Thomas Foley of Newport, Almeley had a mishap with Lewis's mare which he had borrowed from him in his absence.

Mr Foley had your mare but a few days after you left Oxford but by some accident or other he strained one of her fore legs in the sinue [*sic*]. I have sent her to grass ever since she his a great deal better and by the time you return to College she will be as sound as ever I hope.[11]

Cyril Jackson, the Dean of Christ Church did his best to encourage his undergraduates to embrace their studies with some enthusiasm, but Walter Wilkins and his circle were obdurate:

> It gives me great pleasure to inform you that Fisherman was the winning horse, by which I pocket 10 guineas. Sir Watkins' *Alexander the Great* was the ugliest devil I ever saw and was handsomely beaten by Lord Grosvenor's. The Dean put up a *Moneo* against going, so I conclude I shall get a handsome rowing at Collections which will have very little effect.[12]

Owing then little to his father and everything to Monsieur Clement for the sound foundations of his classical education, on 14th January 1819, aged twelve, he entered Eton,[13] as his father had before him. His tutor was the Revd Edward Craven Hawtrey, who had joined the staff in 1814 as a young man of twenty-five. An Etonian himself, and whose family connections with the school extended back nearly 300 years, he was to have a profound influence on Lewis. He infused new vigour into the school's academic life, helped to found the school library, contributed several volumes from his own valuable collection, and encouraged the emergence of school magazines like *Apis Matina* and *The Etonian*.

The Head Master at this time was the Revd Dr John Keate, who, like Hawtrey, was a distinguished classical scholar. Already an assistant master, he was elected Head Master in 1809. From his previous experience he knew that school discipline was bad and that the staff were too few to give him sufficient support. He himself was expected to control 170 boys or more in one room, and was subjected by his pupils to frequent indignities.[14]

> He was little more (if more at all) than five feet in height, and was not very great in girth, but in this space was concentrated the pluck of ten battalions. He had a really noble voice, and this he could moderate with great skill, but he had also the power of quacking like an angry duck, and he almost always adopted this mode of communication in order to inspire respect.[15]

From the first Keate set himself to repress turbulence and disorder and on one occasion flogged more than eighty boys on the same day.[16] His courage, however, combined with genuine kindness, made him popular with the boys, who, apparently, cheered him after the great flogging. Cornewall Lewis seems not to have shared in this respect for Keate. Thus in April 1820 after a boating accident in which a boy drowned, boating on the Thames was voluntarily abandoned by the boys, something which, Cornewall Lewis informed his mother

> Keate would not have done with all his slang.[17]

4

When the Duke of Wellington talked about the battle of Waterloo being won on the playing fields of Eton he had in mind not games but fighting, and in this respect the Lewises were no exception:

> My cousin Fitzharris had a most dreadful battle the other day with Buccleugh; I do not believe either of them were the worse for it, as the only claret that was spilled was by one of them slipping and on his nose, which made it bleed.

Lewis's pugillistic cousin was James Howard Harris, third Earl of Malmesbury. In July 1777 his grandfather had married Harriet Mary Cornewall, half sister to Cornewall Lewis's mother.

Though, apparently, 'never very studious', Harris was to become Foreign Secretary 1852–55 in Lord Aberdeen's Tory administration and again in 1858 in Lord Derby's second cabinet. His ministerial career was to be intertwined with that of the Liberal Cornewall Lewis. Buccleuch, the other combatant in this 1820 engagement, was Walter Francis Scott, who in 1819 became the fifth Duke of Buccleuch and seventh Duke of Queensberry.

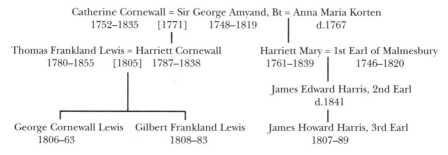

Catherine Cornewall = Sir George Amyand, Bt = Anna Maria Korten
1752–1835   [1771]   1748–1819 | d.1767

Thomas Frankland Lewis = Harriett Cornewall   Harriett Mary = 1st Earl of Malmesbury
1780–1855   [1805]   1787–1838   1761–1839 | 1746–1820

James Edward Harris, 2nd Earl
d.1841

George Cornewall Lewis   Gilbert Frankland Lewis   James Howard Harris, 3rd Earl
1806–63   1808–83   1807–89

NB Sir George Aymand, Bart assumed the surname Cornewall on his marriage to Catherine Cornewall of Moccas in 1771.

Lewis, seems not have enjoyed school life at Eton:

> I am very glad the holidays are so near, for this has been the most stupid time I ever passed: the only thing that it is possible to do is to play at fives, but that is entirely prevented by the rain, there are hardly ever two hours together but what some falls.[18]

The academic supervision was poor and Lewis complained to his mother:

> I have not been looked over a single exercise in school for more than a fortnight, and since I have been read over by Knapp, he

> has only looked [over] one copy of lyrics and a theme of mine,
> so that I have no chance of being sent up this time.[19]

But despite being neither encouraged nor inspired during his early days at Eton, Lewis's precocity continued. He writes to his mother, at some length, about the subject prescribed for his Latin verse: Avarice. He turned to the work of the clerical poet Edward Young for inspiration, but found it lacking. Young, Rector of Welwyn for thirty-five years, was thought in his day to be witty and brilliant, and in 1820 his *Night Thoughts* were still immensely popular, though, one would have thought, hardly inspirational to a thirteen-year-old. Lewis would have, perhaps, agreed with the opinion that whilst Young's poetry has earned him a place in almost every dictionary of quotations ever published, it has also kept him out of most anthologies.[20]

> Our subject for verses was *Avarice*, which, of all subjects, is the worst. Young does not think proper to ascend from tolerable to good, but makes a grand bathos, and goes from middling to horribly bad. It is a miserable, narrow, cramped, and confined subject; no poetical idea, and the verses are consequently as niggardly as the subject.[21]

Perhaps there are echoes of Hawtrey here and it may have been the same when Lewis moved on to consider the works of Shakespeare:

> I have read *King Lear* and *Hamlet*, and have begun *As you Like it*. *King Lear* is a most wonderful thing, it leaves such a striking remembrance on one's mind. The fool and the king are such a good contrast; the scene on the heath is a most surprising effort of genius. *Hamlet* is not so striking; I must own that altogether I was rather disappointed with it, the plot flags so much after the first two acts; but there are some beautiful passages in it. However, one does not look back to it with so much wonder and admiration as the other.[22]

In 1823, when Lewis was in the Sixth Form he was placed 12th out of 73[23] and some of the characteristics which became prominent in later life are already apparent in the adolescent Lewis. Amongst these are his reluctance to say or to do things for the sake of their being said or done, which was later to give him a reputation for coldness:

> Pray read this letter to Gilbert, for I have nothing to tell him which I have not said in this letter, and it is not the slightest use to copy this out for his inspection.[24]

Related to this was his emotionally detached, objective interest in events, even when they concern himself. This shows itself in his account of the drowning of a fellow pupil:

> He fell in about one o'clock. However, although they went on dragging the whole of that and the next day, they were unsuccessful; but, about eight o'clock in the morning of Wednesday, they dragged out his body about a quarter of a mile down the river, in a deep hole of dead water close to the bank. The hooks caught round his leg below the knee. When he was first brought out, his face was quite red, so that it is supposed that from having pulled up against a strong stream and being very hot, being suddenly plunged in very cold water, drove all the blood into his head and caused an apoplexy; so that if they could have dragged his body sooner it would have been of no avail. He was immediately brought on a hurdle to his tutor's house, where, I believe, his body now is, but he is not to be buried here.[25]

The unfortunate youth was the seventeen-year-old John Angerstein, whose father John Julius Angerstein, MP, was a philanthropist, art connoisseur, Lloyd's underwriter, and pioneer of the idea of the state lottery. Lewis's detached, clinical interest in medical symptoms remained with him all his life. It was the same thirty-five years later when, now Chancellor of the Exchequer, he describes his own symptoms and his diagnosis to Gilbert:

> I have been plagued during the last week by a severe pain in the back of my head & I have staid at home since Thursday, in order to take care of it. I am better today, but not well. I cannot satisfy myself as to the cause of it, but it seems to be of a rheumatic character, though complicated with torpor of the liver.[26]

Lewis's facility and interest in languages were nurtured further at Eton by Hawtrey, who, it was said, whilst he was an assistant master, learnt so many languages that 'he was known in London as *the English Mezzofanti*. Ancient and modern literature became alike familiar to him, and his translations into German and Italian were admirable'.[27] Lewis himself became proficient not only in Latin and Greek, but also fluent in French, German, and Italian, and had a working knowledge of Spanish, Provençal, and Anglo-Saxon.

Gilbert Lewis, who was two years behind George at Eton, recollected that his brother wrote elegant and correct Latin verse with great facility. Gilbert drew upon this skill in the preparation of his own exercises, even when George had left Eton for Oxford:

My dear Gilbert,
I have not time to fill up all the empty places in this copy, which
you with the help of *Gradus* will do more easily than me. There
wants a word after '*marisque*' like *faciem* or *aequor, sinus* I believe
won't do. There is some particular word to come in before
seconda which I quite forget, and for *firmata* something like
refecta or *levata* is wanted ...
Yr affnate brother
G Lewis.[28]

These exercises were corrected in haste, but not without thought,
and later the same day George wrote again to Gilbert, warning him to
be aware of some mistakes, which he does not bother to point out
himself. No mention is made of the subject of the exercsie, but it gets
no more approval from George than did Hawtrey's choice of *Avarice*
six years earlier:

The verses have been done in a great hurry and on reading
them over I see one or two mistakes, however I believe they are
sufficiently good to shew up to Hawtrey, particularly on such a
disgusting subject. Aunt Gordon[29] has let her house & is coming
here for a short time. How does yr Algebra go on, I hope you do
a little now and then so as not to forget it.
Yr affnate brother
G Lewis.[30]

One skill, for which Hawtrey himself was famed, that of conversation, Lewis failed to learn from his tutor. His obituary notices spoke
of his 'slouching gait, the uneasy manner, the hesitating speech.'[31] But
when Lewis left Eton in December 1823 Hawtrey, writing to his father,
found many virtues and achievements to catalogue:

My dear Sir, I have great pleasure in assuring you that your son
has left Eton with great credit to himself as a scholar, and that
in all other respects he stands deservedly high in the good
opinion of all who know him ...
    In Latin he has certainly read much more than most boys
of talent have done at his age; in Greek, I think, as much. And
his taste and habit of observation in both are such as give every
reason to expect that his success at Oxford will be as gratifying
as it has been at Eton.
    His good sense and right feeling appear to others, as well as
to myself, to have corrected those defects in manner which were
the only impediments to his progress. His success during the last
six months is a convincing proof that this has been the case.

> I have only to add, that I have parted with him with very
> sincere regret, and shall ever feel the warmest interest in his
> future.[32]

Cornewall Lewis and Hawtrey became lifelong friends, the pupil outliving his master by only a year. In 1846 Lewis is found proof reading Hawtrey's article on Eton which he had written for JR McCulloch's *Statistical Account of Great Britain*.[33] Two years later Hawtrey, headmaster of the College since 1834, was seeking Lewis's Parliamentary help, as MP for Hereford, in the College's fight against the Great Western Railway.[34] The Great Western duly abandoned its plans in 1834 for building a branch to Windsor from its main line at Slough in the face of the violent opposition of Eton College. The proposed line would have to cut through Eton property and would have been, in the opinion of the College authorities, both a moral and physical danger to the boys in their care.

The matter came up again in 1848 and though the railway company was successful this time all manner of provisions were inserted to the act for the protection of the College and its pupils. Screens or planting were to be provided to ensure the privacy of the Bathing Place; the Thames Bridge was to have a clear waterway to the satisfaction of the Provost and Head Master; the Provost and all Masters were to have free access to the station to find any scholar, 'whether on the Foundation or otherwise'. There were to be police along the line to prevent access of scholars, in default of which the College was empowered to appoint two at the expense of the Company; all such bridges as the College may require for passage to bathing places or other places of amusement and to carry flood water were to be provided; no intermediate station or buildings were to be erected or passengers or goods taken up without consent of the Provost and College under their common seal; and special constables were to be appointed during construction to control workmen subject to the orders of the College.[35]

The branch was opened for traffic in October 1849 and no doubt Lewis and his wife used the station when they travelled down to Eton from London in June 1853:

> Kent House. Went to Eton with Theresa & had luncheon with
> Dr & Mrs Hawtrey. I went over the Provost's lodge with him,
> which he now occupies. I saw the interesting collection of
> pictures of Eton men. Returned in the afternoon.[36]

Earlier in the year Lewis had congratulated Hawtrey on declining an invitation from King's College to migrate to Cambridge. Lewis had been editor of the *Edinburgh Review* since December 1852, and, perhaps hoped to persuade Hawtrey to become a contributor.[37] Hawtrey's days at Eton, however, were drawing to a close, and in 1854 he was inducted as Vicar of Mapledurham. On the Thames, near Reading, this Eton College living was worth £878 *pa*. In the following year, 1855, Lewis dedicated his *Enquiry into the Credibility of the Early Roman History* to him.

After Eton, Lewis travelled on the Continent, mainly in Switzerland and northern Italy. Lausanne did not impress him, but provoked one of his rare touches of humour:

> Friday last was the great fast and holiday of the Swiss, both Catholic and Protestant, and everything was shut up as close as Edinburgh on a Sunday.[38]

It was a time of serious sight-seeing in which Lausanne came out badly:

> Lausanne is a dirty, steep, irregular town, famous for nothing, one can hardly spin out a day of real sight-seeing.[39]

The cathedral[40] and the university[41] both escaped his notice. The public library had little in it worth seeing and all in all French Switzerland compared poorly with German Switzerland. It rained continuously and Mt Blanc resisted their every attempt to view it. Something he saw did meet with his approval and he thought it worth while to tell his father about it. Thomas Frankland Lewis, who since 1812 had been MP for Beaumaris, had an interest in Irish affairs, sitting on the commission to inquire into the Irish revenue in 1821, and in 1825 was to join the commission on Irish education:

> There is an English church both at Geneva and Lausanne, and a regular clergyman who is paid by subscription. The service here is read in a Roman Catholic church, and the altar, and candlesticks, and images, and pictures, are separated by a low curtain. What a good example for the Irish, I think that you had better mention it to Sir Abraham Bradley King.[42] The Catholics are earlier risers than we are, and they have their prayers in the morning, and leave clear room for us at half-past eleven.[43]

Even more interesting, as far as Lewis was concerned, was the introduction of regular steam boat services on Lakes Geneva and Constance, the result of American enterprize:

> There is a steamboat of ten-horse power that performs its journey from here to Geneva, thirty-six miles in six hours, set up by a Mr Church, an American; the engineer used to work in the Liverpool packets. The Geneva People have just launched an opposition boat of greater power; the same Mr Church has just set up one in the lake of Constance.[44]

Lewis and his friends met other English tourists at Lausanne. There were, for example: Mr and Mrs Henley Eden who were also disappointed not to see Mt Blanc because of the rain. Eden was a lawyer and a commissioner of bankrupts, becoming a Master in Chancery and MP for Fowey in 1826.[45] There were also Mr Fazakerley,[46] Mr Vaughan,[47] and Mr Fox, with whom Lewis hoped to go on to Vevey, the Castle of Chillon, the Great St Bernard, and make a second attempt at seeing Mont Blanc.[48]

When Lewis entered Christ Church in the Michaelmas term of 1824, the college had no more than 150 undergraduate members.[49] The serious minded Lewis, with memories of his experiences at Eton behind him, makes no mention of the riots which from time to time disrupted college life. In 1823, when Lewis was in his last year at Eton, there was prolonged rioting in Christ Church, in consequence of which William Stewart, Lord Castlereagh's son, was sent down. Attempts to stiffen discipline resulted in more disorder, with bonfires, red paint, and cabbages in the quad. When Charles Wellesley, the Duke of Wellington's second son, was to be rusticated for his part in one of these disturbances, the Duke intervened and sent both his sons to Trinity College, Cambridge. Lord Conyers Osborne died 'in a wine-party frolic', having, in the words of Martin Tupper, another contemporary of Lewis, 'been back-broken over an arm-chair by the good-natured but only too athletic Earl of Hillsborough'.

The College authorities appeared temporarily to be in danger of losing control and in Michaelmas 1824, the term in which Lewis entered the college, Dean Smith considered there were more undergraduates in residence than the authorities could manage. During the summer of 1825 this situation caused Charles Lloyd, Professor of Divinity, to be 'in expectation of what the University has not often seen, a positive rebellion'. Rowdy late-night supper-parties were seen as the source of much of the trouble, but in Dean Smith's opinion 'young men' were at the University 'to be taught the use of their liberty and must abide by the consequences'. On the other hand, Lloyd thought that such parties should be stopped, for they were incompatible with 'academical pursuits'. In June that year there was a demonstration at the founder's dinner against the college authorities, and eighteen undergraduate Students were brought before the Dean and Chapter to be admonished. One of them was required to prepare a Latin Epistle to the Dean and Canons acknowledging the offence and asking pardon for it, and to it read out in the Chapter House in the presence both of Dean and canons and of the other reprimanded Students. By the end of the year rustications and expulsions had restored calm to the college.[50]

But Christ Church included the diligent as well as the idle in abundance, and amongst the honours men there was not merely the rigour but also the sense of intellectual excitement which would be regarded today as one hallmark of an effective university.[51] Thus Lewis was surrounded by intellects equal to his own, some of whom would contribute to the Oxford Movement, the seeds of which were soon to be planted in the Senior Common Room of nearby Oriel College to shake the life of the Church of England and revive an awareness of its pre-Reformation traditions. Prominent amongst these was Charles Lloyd, mentioned already, a skilled teacher who was in succession lecturer at Christ Church in mathematics, tutor, and censor. He was, whilst Lewis was in residence, Professor of Divinity, occupying the chair from 1822–27. He then became Bishop of Oxford. His graduate lectures were attended by Froude, Pusey, Newman, and Oakley, all of whom became prominent in one way or another in the Oxford Movement. Edward Bouverie Pusey overlapped Lewis both at Eton, and at Christ Church. Like Lewis he also took a first in Classics. Lewis, however, was to use the term Puseyite as one of consistent contempt, whereas Gladstone, who also overlapped Lewis at both Eton and Christ Church, became a firm Tractarian and with great respect for Pusey.

Other contemporary influences on Lewis were Short, Longley, and Gaisford. Thomas Vowler Short was Tutor and Censor 1816–29, and college Librarian from 1822. He worked for the reform of the University's examination system, and in a way was one of the progenitors of the Oxford Movement. Pusey was Short's pupil, Keble his friend, and he examined Newman for his degree. In 1841 he was consecrated Bishop of Sodor and Man, and was translated to St Asaph in 1846. Thomas Gaisford was Tutor and Public examiner 1809–11, and in 1812 became Professor of Greek. He declined the bishopric of Oxford in 1829 and became dean in 1831. Lastly, and most important, there was Charles Thomas Longley, who was Lewis's tutor. He was appointed Reader in Greek at Christ Church in 1822, and was an examiner in the Classical Schools in 1825 and 26. 'A man of learning, of cultivated intellect, of courteous manners, and an even temper', he became Headmaster of Harrow 1829 and then, by way of the sees of Ripon, Durham, and York, he arrived at Canterbury in 1862.

The teaching at Christ Church was in the hands of six classical tutors and one mathematical lecturer. Each tutor was responsible for all his pupils' work, except for divinity, which was taught by the senior censor, and the lectures given to the whole college by the Greek and Rhetoric readers. One tutor was solely responsible for mathematics. Under this system a good deal of private tuition was necessary. The first two terms went in preparing for Responsions and for these there were lectures in arithmetic and the first two books of Euclid; and lectures in Greek and Latin with one's own tutor. Responsions negotiated, there followed at the Examination Schools Mods and Greats.[52]

Whilst Lewis was up at Oxford the first Oxford and Cambridge cricket match took place in 1827 and the first boat race in 1828. In both of these innovations, his Christ Church contemporary and fellow classicist, Charles Wordsworth, later Bishop of St Andrews, was instrumental. But Lewis was neither oarsman nor batsman, and was none too secure on the back of a horse. But when it came to the Schools, or Finals, he was successful and took a first in Classics, but was disappointed with a second in Mathematics:

> No lack of will, no lack of intellect interfered; but an unhappy failure of health. One morning when he awoke his pillow was stained with blood; a vessel in his lungs was ruptured; care and rest were prescribed as necessary. But as the bleeding from the lungs continued, by the advice of his physician he lived for a year on a vegetable diet and spent winters in the south of France and Italy.[53]

Convalescence was not inactive and in 1828 John Murray, with whom Lewis had a life long professional relationship, published anonymously a translation from the German of Augustus Böckh's *The Public Economy of Athens*,[54] the first of what was to become a very substantial list of publications. In the opinion of a modern commentator no work produced during this period by an Oxford tutor outmatched that of Cornewall Lewis who at twenty-two, in his translation of Böckh, broke new ground, for Oxford was still an insular university in which few of its senior members knew German.[55] Lewis, with befitting modesty, published his translation anonymously, but his achievement did not go unrecognized, and in June 1828 Dean Smith nominated Lewis to one of the 101 Christ Church studentships:

> Dear Sir, I am happy to have it in my power to express my approbation of your diligence and good conduct during your residence at Christ Church, and the sense I entertain of the distinction you have obtained in the university, by nominating you to a studentship.
>
> It will be necessary that you should come to Oxford on Tuesday or Wednesday next, as I shall propose you for election to the chapter on the 25th or 26th, and you will be admitted on the day following.
>
> I am, dear sir, very faithfully yours,
> S Smith.[56]

Besides the academic prestige of a Christ Church studentship which was similar to a fellowship at other Oxford colleges, it also carried with it a modest stipend and dining rights at high table.

In June 1828 Lewis entered the Middle Temple and became a pupil in the chambers of Barnes Peacock, who was four years his junior.[57] Legal studies, however, did not entirely engage Lewis's attention. London at this time was more open than Oxford to continental scholarship and there was a growing interest, in which he shared, in the political significance of ancient history. Lewis's next publication, however, was philosophical rather than historical, and in 1829 he published *An Examination of some Passages in Dr Whately's Elements of Logic*. Richard Whately became Principal of St Alban Hall in 1825, during Lewis's time at Oxford, and was elected Drummond Professor of Political Economy in 1829. Two years later, in 1831, he was enthroned as Archbishop of Dublin. He has been described as:

> a philosopher of sufficient eminence to be reviving the study of logic in Oxford; more ingenious than profound, but the hardest head in the university; with rough manners and huge frame, eating vast helpings at high table, smoker of many pipes, wearing hairy untidy garments, utterly unclerical in appearance and caring nothing for convention. Whately never read books. He evolved his meditations round five or six favourite authors, and was a dialectician battling his ideas out of the rough and tumble of militant conversation.[58]

For many years Whately's *Elements of Logic*, first published in 1826 and into its ninth edition by 1848, was a standard text-book. Whilst not laying 'posterity under permanent obligation', its logic 'unquestion-ably marked, if it did not make, a new epoch in the history of the science'.[59] So, why did it engage Lewis's critical attention? Was he uncertain as to whether his career after Oxford was to be as a lawyer or a philosopher? Later he was to share in Whately's opposition to the Tractarians and they had certain mannerisms in common. But more important than these considerations was the fact that Lewis shared Whately's concern with language and the meaning of words, and both men fought against illogicality and ambiguity in argument and debate. Indeed, the American scholar CF Mullett believes that Whately influenced Lewis as a young man more than any one else,[60] even more than John Austin, whose lectures on jurisprudence Lewis attended in 1830 at the newly founded University of London.[61]

John Austin, after a brief a military career, was called to the bar in 1818. He married in 1820[62] and settled in Queen Square, Westminster, where their garden overlooked that of Jeremy Bentham. Other close friends were James and John Stuart Mill and it was in this circle that Utilitarianism was born. The political philosopher, Thomas Carlyle, and Sydney Smith, the witty canon of St Paul's, whose description of Lewis in Hades saw him as 'for ever and ever bookless, essayless, pamphletless, grammarless', Henry Bickersteth, and John Romilly, who succeeded each other as Master of the Rolls, were other welcome visi-tors to the Austin household. So, too, of course, was George Cornewall Lewis, who was to become related to the Austins when Lucie Austin married Lewis's first cousin, Sir Alexander Duff Gordon, the third baronet. Lewis was also to engage him as his secretary in 1855[63] on his own appointment as Chancellor of the Exchequer.

Lewis maintained his interest in Classical History whilst preparing for the bar and in 1830 joined with his contemporary at Eton and Christ Church, Henry Tufnell, 1805–1854, in translating from the German Karl Ottfried Müller's *The History and Antiquities of the Doric Race*.[64] Tufnell was then a student at Lincoln's Inn. In the following summer, that of 1831, in the course of his legal training, Lewis accompanied Sir John Vaughan, 1769–1839, as his marshal, whilst that judge was presiding over the assizes on the Northern Circuit.[65] His duties, as he informed his father, writing from York, were social rather than legal:

> We have got through three of the public dinners of the judges;
> that of yesterday was given to a select party of forty-five barristers;

the remaining forty-five dine today. People are very venisonivorous, as I have experienced by carving a haunch of venison one day and a neck another.[66]

Lewis also tells his father about the skills and the fees of the advocates and his own financial expectations as a marshal:

> There are about 120 causes on the cause-list at this place, which is considered a small number. Pollock has the most business here; it is said that he sometimes makes £1,000 at York alone. John Williams is the second fiddle, and he does his business extremely well. He is a better speaker than Pollock, though he is not, I suppose, so good a lawyer. My brother marshal informs me that the marshal's fees sometimes amount to more than £200 on this circuit; this time, however, they will not be so much.[67]

Jonathan Frederick Pollock was a sadler's son from the London parish of St Martin's-in-the-Fields, and educated at St Paul's School and Trinity College, Cambridge, where he graduated in 1806 as senior wrangler.[68] A college fellowship followed and in 1809 he was called to the bar. Elected FRS in 1816, he took silk in 1827 and when Lewis observed his performance in court in July 1831, he had recently been returned to Parliament as the Tory member for Huntingdon.[69]

There were other things, besides the talents of his professional colleagues, to interest Lewis in York. In February 1829 Jonathan Martin, an incendiary with a strong antipathy to the Church of England, set fire to York Minster. The roof was destroyed from the central tower to the east end of the chancel, as well as the choir stalls and the organ. Martin was arrested within a few days, but in his trial at York was found not guilty on the grounds of insanity. He was confined in St Luke's Hospital, London, where he died in 1838.

> All the building part of the Minster is completed; the inside woodwork alone remains, which has been done very cheaply by some foreign workmen who came over to carve wood for the interior of Buckingham House, and were dismissed when the works were stopped.[70]

Lewis then turned in his letter to Parliamentary matters. His father was now the member for the county of Radnor. He had become a Privy Councillor and Vice-President of the Board of Trade in 1828, and Treasurer of the Navy in 1830. The matter of the day was the passing of the Reform Bill and Earl Grey appealed to the electorate after the defeat of his bill in April 1831. Both Frankland Lewis and Richard Price of Norton Manor, the member for the Radnor boroughs, had voted with the Tories against the bill. This action enjoyed considerable approval amongst the small number of free-holders in Frankland Lewis's constituency, and at a public meeting at Presteign he was assured of their continuing support in the forth-coming election:

> We the undersigned Freeholders of the County of Radnor, approving ... the Parliamentary conduct of ... Thomas Frankland Lewis, take this mode of publickly announcing ... the continuance of our cordial support at the ensuing election.[71]

The 175 signatories included the Kington lawyers Richard Banks, James Davies, and EW Cheese, and the Ven Richard Venables of Llysdinam. Frankland Lewis had opposed the bill on its second reading, and explained his reasons in an open letter to the 'Gentlemen, Clergy, and Freeholders of the County of Radnor':

> The point on which the schism between Parliament and His Majesty's Ministers immediately took place, was the refusal of a Majority of the House, to accede to a large reduction in the number of English Members of Parliament. Great Statesmen have on former occasions proposed to reform Parliament by adding to its members. Though the wealth, territory, and busi-ness of the country have greatly increased it is now, for the first time, proposed not only to extinguish a portion of our repre-sentatives but to change the proportions fixed at the unions with Scotland and Ireland. The only argument urged in support of this measure has been, that the numbers were so large as to be *inconvenient*; this is the only reason assigned. I confidently state that the real though not the avowed reason is, that the reduction in the numbers of our representatives has a tendency to increase the influence of the Crown. It does so in this obvious way, the members who hold office in connexion with Government are about Fifty, who are in constant attendance, their weight and influence would necessarily be increased by diminishing the number of those by whom that influence is counterbalanced.
>
> I distrust a measure which at once blows hot and cold, which purposes by its general character to restrain the influence of the Crown, and by other arrangements is meant to increase

it. I distrust the measure because I find it popular in places where bribery habitually, systematically and shamelessly prevails, amongst Electors with whom the receipt of money for their Votes has not been confined to the low or the needy. The provisions of the bill not only do not provide an efficient remedy for this species of Corruption, they tend I fear very materially to increase it.

I refrain from enlarging on the remaining provisions of the bill, but whoever will examine them will find so much error and confusion, as to render correction a tedious and difficult task. It was stated by Lord Brougham[72] in one of his Speeches to the Electors of Yorkshire that he would effect four objects: He would reform the Representation of Scotland: He would give Members to the great Towns by transferring from decayed or corrupt Boroughs: He would disfranchise non-resident Freemen: He would provide the means of diminishing the expense of popular Elections. Had any measure for accomplishing these objects been submitted to Parliament, it should have met with my willing support. To the proposed annihilation of Sixty English members of Parliament, connected as it was with a most extensive and important change in the right of voting in Cities and Towns in Ireland, I entertain the strongest objection.[73]

The Bill passed the Commons in September 1831 after a session of three months. It was rejected, however, by the Lords, and did not reach the Statute Book until June 1832, after a protracted and bitter national debate. Cornewall Lewis was writing from York to his father when the debate in the Commons was at its height, but that is not the Parliamentary matter upon which he comments:

I rejoice that ministers succeeded on the wine duties.[74]

The Wine Duties Bill, equalizing the duty on French and Portuguese wines, occupied sporadic Parliamentary attention from July to September 1831.

Lewis himself was called to the bar on 25th November 1831, and joined the Oxford circuit, but his energies were far from committed to his legal duties. In December he was at the Worcester Quarter Sessions, intending to call, on his way back to London, on his Oxford friend Edmund Walker Head. Lewis retained his Studentship at Christ Church until 1839 and this helped to sustain his academic interests. Head at this time was a Fellow and Tutor of Merton College and both men were involved in the fortunes of the short-lived Cambridge-centred *Philological Museum*. This publication first appeared in 1832, with the object of promoting 'the knowledge and the love of ancient literature'. Julius Charles Hare and Connop Thirlwall were the editors.

Lewis, in the convoluted pattern of kinship which existed amongst the early 19th-century gentry, was related by marriage to Hare. His grandmother Ann Frankland was John Lewis of Harpton's second wife. She married again in 1811, after some years of widowhood, the Revd Robert Hare who was the incumbent of the family living of Herstmonceux in Sussex. He occupied it until his death in 1832 when it passed to his nephew, the Ven Julius Charles Hare. Ann Hare died at Cheltenham in 1842 and was long remembered as a benefactor to Old Radnor parish church. The clock in the tower was her gift, made in 1798, presumably in memory of her first husband, John Lewis, who died in the previous year.[75] In 1841 she offered to give £10 towards building an infant school room at Walton besides taking a sustained interest in the school at New Radnor.[76]

Connop Thirlwall was Bishop of St Davids and learned Welsh, acquiring 'the language so perfectly as to use in public within a year of his appointment.'[77] He insisted upon Lewis's clergyman brother Gilbert making more adequate pastoral arrangements for his parishioners at Gladestry during his repeated absences. Lewis, however, had some doubts about Thirlwall's scholarship, so it is surprising that he was prepared to entrust nine articles to the pages of the *Philological Museum* in the course of two years:

> in the first place, his citations of authorities are insufficient; and in the next place, his views are scarcely expressed with distinctness. He always seems … to exercise his ingenuity in evading a decision of the question.[78]

Hare are also had eccentricities in his scholarship, systematically, for example, using 'preacht' for preached, and the same form in similar cases. He maintained this principle in an essay in the *Philological Museum*; and it was also used for a while by Thirlwall.

But Lewis was keeping company with some distinguished contributors in the *Philological Museum*: William Wordsworth, for example, published a translation of part of the first book of the *Æneid*, as did his nephew, John Wordsworth. He also seems to have been acting both as some kind of agent or assistant to Hare in editing the new journal, and as Head's mentor:

I am sorry that I did not at once send you my copy of Buttman,[79] as it would have saved you much trouble; but I have carefully looked over your article, and found nothing to correct except clerical errors. There are, however, several points on which I still entertain considerable doubt; so much so, that if you think that you are not likely to write an article in the spring number, I would ask you to keep it back for a time, that I might have an opportunity of looking into some of the points with you; for to discuss it on paper would be endless ... Hare writes me word that he has matter for 160 pages at Cambridge, which is the reason why I have not sent your article to him. Till I hear from you, I will do nothing.[80]

Head eventually had two essays in the *Philological Museum*'s 1833 volume, and one wonders how the none too robust Lewis managed simultaneously to carry out his legal duties as a barrister, supervise the research of his friends, and pursue and write up his own scholarship. Besides contributing nine articles to the *Philological Museum* in the years 1832–33,[81] he also published in 1832 his *Remarks on the Use and Abuse of some Political Terms*.[82] The *Museum* did not flourish and in November 1832 Lewis reported to Head that 'Thirlwall is in distress for matter' which spurred the two men to send more material to Cambridge for publication. But in July Lewis told Head:

I see no advertisement of the *Philological Museum*, and therefore conclude that Thirlwall's attempts to get money from the delegates [*ie* the university authorities] have failed.[83]

Lewis retained his capacity for almost ceaseless intellectual activity throughout his life and its practice was based upon his belief in the Protestant Ethic. At some time and somewhere in his childhood, Lewis had subconsciously become a Calvinist, at least to the extent that he accepted the teaching of Calvin that it was one's duty and responsibility to be successful through hard work. This was long before Weber wrote of *Die protestantische Ethik*,[84] and it was a not value shared by his parents or his brother. Gilbert recollected that

So earnest was [George's] desire to elucidate, to remember, and to record, that from his youth he thought that to be doing nothing amounted to a crime. 'Read,' he has often advised me, 'when you have plenty of time at command; write in the shorter spaces when your time is broken up; this is the way to employ yourself to the best advantage: you will forget what you read in fragments of time, what you write in them will not be lost.' And this was the practice that he followed. He also in his younger days provided against the waste of any fragments which circumstances might cause to be lost to him, by either learning by heart or repeating in these intervals. I think that I remember my father telling me that once in Italy, when travelling after dark with George, he repeated to him a great part of the third book of the *Aeneid*; and I well recollect, when on one occasion I was waiting with him in the ante-room of a Physician, he took a Horace or Virgil from his pocket, and gave it to me, that I might hear him say a portion of its contents by heart, and he had repeated a large number of lines before he was summoned to his interview.[85]

In the Autumn of 1832 Lewis went to the south of France, accompanied by his mother, for his health's sake. But Cannes did not commend itself to him:

Today, I am happy to say, is the last day of our captivity, and tomorrow we shall be released from this execrable fishing village, where meat appears to be almost unknown, and fish, sparrows, and roasted chestnuts are the staff of life.[86]

In comparison with Nice, Hereford was 'lively and active',[87] and they soon moved on to Italy. Then, the winter over, they were back in England where one of the issues of the day was reform of the provision for the nation's poor.

Since the reign of Queen Elizabeth I the care of the poor was a responsibility of the parish in which they lived. Each year an Overseer of the Poor was appointed at the Easter Vestry, subject to the approval of the magistrates. The office was unpaid and one's expenses were not reimbursed. The Overseer, however, had authority to raise a poor rate for the support of the parish poor and to apprentice poor orphans to local householders, however reluctant.

To be eligible to claim relief the claimant had to be settled in the parish from which the claim as made. The magistrates could instruct the overseer to return a claimant to the parish of their origin for their relief and this was a source of resentment and contention between parishes. Many left the parish of their settlement to work in the new manufacturing centres. When, however, they were laid off, the local overseer could refuse their relief and return them to become the responsibility of the parish of their origin. Consequently, there was often considerable acrimony between all concerned in the local administration of the poor law, and there was ample scope for jobbery and corruption, made worse by appeals to the magistrates at the Quarter Sessions and litigation. Rural poverty was further aggravated by farmers paying their labourers as little as they thought feasible in the belief that their labourers' wages would be made up to an acceptable subsistence level by parish relief. This could result in ruinous charges being made upon the property of the landowners. Matters were brought to a head when the desire amongst agricultural workers for a living wage caused agrarian disturbances in 1830. Two years later a Commission was set up 1832 to consider the reform of the Poor Law.

Of the Commission's nine members the most important and most influential was the political economist Nassau Senior, 1790–1864. The son of a clergyman, he had experienced the evils of misdirected charity in his father's Wiltshire parish. Believing

> it is as difficult to elevate the poor as it is easy to depress the rich. In human affairs it is much easier to do harm than good,[88]

he was committed to Poor Law reform. He became a member of the Political Economy Club in 1823 and was the first to hold the chair of political economy, established at Oxford in 1823. Lewis and Senior shared several friendships and both men had an affection for classical literature and history.

They met in Paris in October 1832 and Lewis wrote afterwards to his father:

> I saw Senior to-day, who is come here for about a fortnight partly on a speculation about French charities. He showed me a long and very able letter he has written to Brougham (privately) about the results of their investigations. Brougham, it seems, wishes to bring forward some measure on the subject. Senior's principal suggestion is to take away the controlling power of the magistracy, and to vest it, together with the duty of revising and auditing the accounts, in paid local authorities, who might also be employed for other purposes. Everything, I think, now shows that some thing is wanted in the rural districts more efficient than the amateur services of the justices. He says that their returns show that over the greater part of England and Wales (particularly North Wales) things are in a much worse state than he imagined; and you know that he did not think very highly of the condition of the labouring poor.[89]

Senior was largely responsible for the Commission's report and most of its recommendations were incorporated into the Poor Law Amendment Act of 1834. The system of 'outdoor' relief or allowances for able-bodied paupers was to be abolished and replaced by work-houses run by unions of parishes. Conditions in these workhouses, which were not to be confused with almshouses, were intended to deter all but the genuinely destitute. The Poor Law unions would be run by elected Boards of Guardians which would be answerable to a central authority consisting of three commissioners, Thomas Frankland Lewis, John George Shaw-Lefevre,[90] and George Nicholls.

> It has to be admitted that the three men to whom this task was jointly committed were not badly chosen. The senior, Thomas Frankland Lewis, who acted as chairman, was a man of fifty-four, a Welsh country gentleman who had sat in the House of Commons for twenty-two years as a member of the Tory party, had served on various Commissions and Committees of Inquiry, and had for three years held non-Cabinet office, but with the rank of Privy Councillor, in the successive administrations of Canning, Goderich, and Wellington. He had long been inter-ested in the problem of Poor Relief.[91]

It was also through the influence of Senior, a familiar figure at Harpton, that the Commissioners appointed Edwin Chadwick as their secretary, but he enjoyed only their half-hearted support. A Benthamite in his sympathies, and though 'tactless, impetuous, and cocksure', he was, nevertheless, the Commission's driving force. Senior, in fact, had recommended Chadwick, along with Frankland Lewis, as a Commissioner, for in his opinion Chadwick was:

> the only individual among the candidates, perhaps I may say in the country, who could enter into the office of commissioner with complete prearranged plans of action.[92]

In an adroit juxtaposition, Cobbett spoke of 'two thousand a year [Frankland] Lewis, penny a line Chadwick'.[93]

Then, in November 1833, with a deft touch of nepotism, Cornewall Lewis was appointed as an assistant-commissioner to inquire into the condition of the Irish poor. Lewis the scholar had become Lewis the civil servant.[94]

The appointment was not entirely inept. Irish matters were often discussed at the Harpton dinner table. Thomas Frankland Lewis represented Ennis in County Clare from 1826–28 and served on two of the 114 commissions set up to investigate matters relating to Ireland between 1810 and 1833. Irish matters were often covered in his letters to and conversations with his son:

> You have often heard me talk of the Poor Law Committee, of which Sturges Bourne[95] was the chairman, and know how anxious a part I took in all the proceedings. Nothing of importance passed which I was not acquainted with during the sitting of the committee. And when the bills were passing which resulted from our recommendations, though the committee sat no longer, I continued in constant communication with Sturges Bourne on the subject of their provisions.[96]

Cornewall Lewis's particular responsibility was to inquire into the condition of Irish labourers in the industrial towns of England and Scotland. Despite having once described an Irishman as 'potato-headed', Lewis set about his task with sympathy and diligence visiting the Irish communities in Birmingham, Bristol, Leeds, Manchester, and Bristol. Then came Glasgow and Edinburgh, followed by Paisley, Greenock, Portpatrick 'and so to Ireland'.

He found that the Irish were largely ministered to by English Roman Catholic priests who were against the trades unions and supported the masters. They were a separate and rejected caste, like the Jews under the Romans, their children ostracized even by their fellow Sunday School pupils:

> Most of the priests on this side of the water are English. Out of three priests at Birmingham, one was Irish, educated in Portugal. Of the eight (I think) at Liverpool, one only was Irish, educated at Maynooth; and I must say that he is a very respectable man, and gave very fair and candid evidence. Here out of about six priests there are two Irish Maynoothians;[97] and though one whom I have seen is, in my opinion, an insincere man, yet I hear a very high character of him on all sides, and among persons quite above suspicion of interest or caprice. The priests have taken a very decided part against the Trades Unions, and all societies bound by secret oaths; and I believe that their influence has in many instances had great effect. They dissolved the union of the Irish bricklayers' labourers in Manchester this autumn; and it has never been formed again. Altogether, in the contests between the masters and workmen (which are the conservative and destructive parties of these manufacturing districts), they have sided with the former, and that in the most open and uncompromising manner. The Irish occupy so low a

place in the scale of society in the large English towns, that it is difficult to imagine that the most enthusiastic or far-sighted among them could ever entertain the project of supplanting the English on their own soil. If they are like the Jews a *separate*, they are also like the Jews a *rejected* caste; they are emphatically in this country what Tacitus says of the Jews among the Romans, '*despectissima pars servientium*', the most degraded of the working population. The Irish do not associate with the English, not because they dislike the English, but because the English dislike them. They are glad to perform their drunken orgies with any Englishmen who will descend to their level, and herd with them. All the reluctance is on *our*, not *their* part. The very children in the mills complain of being put to work next to an Irish child; and in the Sunday-schools the English move from them.[98]

In Lewis's estimation the Irish did better than the Welsh amongst whom he lived, and about whom he shared the sentiments of his friends. George Clive, born 1805, of Perrystone Court in south Herefordshire, and MP for Hereford 1857–69 and 1874–80, once ended a letter to Edmund Head with what the latter described as a 'pious and benevolent ejaculation':

That the devil would fly away with this miserable race of Celtic savages.

Head, related this to Cornewall Lewis with approval, adding:

I need not say how heartily I repeat 'Amen' to the above petition, reckoning of course that Wales begins just beyond New Radnor. The gradual action of Boards of Guardians, railroads, and other opportunities of intercourse, may civilize them in about three centuries.[99]

Lewis agreed, despite the fact his father had once stated with pride to a meeting of his tenantry:

that he stood on ground which had never been bought or sold, a boast which could be made but by a few of the highest aristocratic families in the kingdom.[100]

These Harpton ancestors were Welsh speaking patrons of the bards, and Lewis himself had mastered Provençal, no less a minority language than Welsh:

George Clive is, I have no doubt, quite right in his opinion of the intelligence of the Welsh. And how that intelligence is to be raised, while they retain their villainous Celtic language, it is not easy to see.[101]

Parliament, it is said, despite its commissions and committees, acquired its knowledge of the Irish problem at second hand. Hitherto few people travelled in Ireland and saw Irish conditions for themselves,[102] but from 1830 there followed period of 'reform by critical strangers'.[103] Lewis was one of these critical strangers.

The Irish Church Temporalities Act of 1833 attempted to rationalize the position of the established Church of Ireland which suppressed ten of the twenty-two Anglican dioceses, the revenue thus saved being distributed amongst poorer Irish livings, of which there were many. The Irish Ecclesiastical Commission was set up to supervise the revenues released by the reform for Irish charitable or educational purposes. Disestablishment was now a future possibility. Many High Churchmen saw this as a serious example of Erastianism whereby the will of Parliament was imposed upon the Irish Church, thereby setting a precedent which later could be applied to the Church of England. One consequence was John Keble's 1833 assize sermon before the University of Oxford on the theme of 'National Apostacy' from which the Oxford Movement, Tractarianism, and Puseyism were to stem. They enjoyed the consistent and systematic disapproval of Cornewall Lewis who, as has been mentioned already, had been well aware of the High Church sympathies of several members of the Oriel College Senior Common Room whilst he himself was an undergraduate at nearby Christ Church.

In August 1834 Lewis, having gone to Ireland to investigate the condition of the poor, was appointed a member of the commission to inquire into the state of Church property and Church affairs in Ireland. One of the other Commissioners was Thomas Henry Lister, whose widow, Maria Theresa Lister, Lewis was to marry in 1844. Lewis also continued with his inquiries into the condition of the Irish poor, his opinion being there was no alternative to reform by critical strangers, such as himself. In August 1834 he informed his father, in confidence, from Dublin:

> I have therefore nearly two months clear for the Poor Inquiry; and although it may be troublesome, I am, on the whole, glad that I have not withdrawn my neck from the yoke. For in the first place, these people would have abused me, and have attributed the ill results of their own inefficiency to the desertion of their assistant commissioners; and secondly, there is such a want of any person who can reckon up to twenty without a fault that I hope to be serviceable to them, however thankless the service

may be … The reports received are, moreover, as far as I can learn, mere waste paper. Of course you will not mention any of this private history, as it is not fitted for the world at large.[104]

In the event Lewis dissented from the *First Report of the Irish Poor Inquiry Commissioners* in 1836, confessing to his lifelong friend Head he had made few friends amongst his Irish colleagues:

The Irish Commissioners would probably send over a detachment of Whiteboys to dispatch me if they found out that I criticised their performance in so insidious a manner. I flatter myself that I have made a complete smash of them, but of this you will judge when I show you in the country what I have written. Their utter misconception of the entire subject, both the state of Ireland and the English poor law, is less provoking than the impudent way in which they beg the question while professing to argue it.[105]

The Commission, whose findings led to the passing of the 1838 Act for the More Effectual Relief of the Destitute Poor in Ireland, reported that 2,385,000 people in Ireland were in need of relief from poverty. The Act divided Ireland into 130 unions, each of which had a workhouse run by an elected board of guardians on the English system.

But in Lewis's opinion:

Adopt what plan you will the question always recurs, how are you to strike at the root of the evil, the improvident habits of the people with regard to breeding?[106]

And he wrote to Head:

You will doubtless have seen, and perhaps have attempted to read, the Irish Poor Report in the newspapers. It sins both in excess and defect; it does NOT contain an account of the state of the people, the causes and extent of their poverty, and the effects which it produces on them; and it *does* contain all kinds of absurd projects which I hope that no sane Government will ever think of introducing.[107]

In the previous October he began his work with the Irish Church Commission, and found things better than they were with the Poor Law Commission:

Today I went to the Church Commission and found the commissioners preparing to start, in general well pleased with their instructions and making no difficulties. One benefice near

Dublin was examined on Saturday containing six parishes; there were only fifteen Protestants in it. Hitherto, the number of Protestants has turned out to be very small, smaller than was anticipated.

... Our great object has been to make the commissioners as much automatons as possible, to leave nothing to discretion, as we have some men who want to show up the Protestants and others who want to show up the Catholics. My notion is that we shall make such a damning case against the Church as must in the end produce an entire remodelling of its ministers and revenues.[108]

He wrote in a similar vein to his friend Mrs John Austin:

For the last six months I have been in Dublin, demolishing the Church. Our proper style and title is the Public *Instruction* Commission, which the friends of the Church in this country changed into Public Destruction Commission. It is a mere statistical inquiry, and proceeds very satisfactorily, but, as you say, proves only what everybody knows. Nevertheless it is something to establish disagreeable truths beyond the power of contradiction. Whately[109] is supposed to have said that the clergy had been long revelling in the *Book of Job*, but that now they were forced to take a spell in the *Book of Numbers*.[110]

In January 1834 Lewis was elected a Fellow of the Geological Society of London, founded in 1807 as the first specialist society devoted to the exploration of the mineral structure of the globe. The fortnightly discussions, which followed the reading of papers before the assembled Fellows in the Society's rooms at Somerset House, were hailed as the most exciting in scientific London and often went on into the small hours of the morning. The Society 'possessed all the freshness, the vigour, and the ardour of youth in pursuit of a youthful science'.[111] Lewis's proposers were RI Murchison, Henry Thomas de la Beche, William Rowan Hamilton, John Taylor, Charles Daubeny, Charles Lyell, Edward Turner, and William Buckland. Few can have been proposed for the Fellowship of the Society by a more illustrious collection of names.

Roderick Impey Murchison with the careers of a soldier and a country gentleman behind him, and influenced by Sir Humphry Davy, had embarked upon a new career, that of a geologist in 1825, the year in which he was admitted as a Fellow of the Geological Society. In the following year, 1826, he was elected FRS and appointed secretary of the Geological Society.

Murchison had come to Harpton in the summer of 1831 in the course of his geological investigations which resulted in the publication of his *opus magnum, The Silurian System* in 1839. Lewis, with his father, was amongst the Radnorshire landed proprietors who signed an address to Murchison urging him to publish his work in a book rather than in the *Transactions* of the Geological Society:

> and knowing that the cost of such a publication (when illustrated with maps, drawings, sections, & the figures of many organic remains) must be considerable, and being desirous that the author should not be exposed to pecuniary loss, do hereby agree severally to subscribe for a copy of a book to be delivered to each subscriber at a price commensurate with the actual cost of the publication, provided that it does not exceed the sum of five guineas each copy.[112]

Sir Henry Thomas de la Beche, after a short military career became a Fellow of the Geological Society in 1817. He is remembered as the father of the Geological Survey and founder of the Museum of Practical Geology in Jermyn Street. He was President of the Geological Society in 1847. Sir William Rowan Hamilton, was a mathematician, and John Taylor a mining engineer. Elected a Fellow of the Geological Society 1807, Taylor was treasurer from 1816 to 1844. In 1825 he was elected FRS, and was one of the founders of the British Association in 1832, and its treasurer till September 1861. He was also one of the founders of University College, London. Charles Giles Bridle Daubeny, though trained for medicine, was a chemist and botanist. A FRS, he became Professor of Chemistry in 1822, and Professor of Botany at Oxford in 1834. He took part in the first meeting of the British Association and was its president in 1856. The geologist Sir Charles Lyell, had been a Fellow since 1819 of both the Linnean and the Geological Societies, and his *Principles of Geology*, 1830–33, had begun to cast doubts on the inerrancy of the biblical story of creation. Edward Turner, FRS, was the first occupant of the chair of chemistry at the University of London. Lastly, William Buckland, FRS, was the future Dean of Westminster, and the leading Oxford geologist, seeing his subject, as many clerics did in his day, as the handmaid of natural theology. His influential *Reliquiae diluvianae* was published in 1823.

Both Buckland and Daubeny saw the utilitarian implications of their respective disciplines, and were at their academic prime whilst Lewis was up at Oxford. Taylor and Turner were both connected with the infant University College, London whilst Lewis was attending

Austin's lectures there. Lewis's basically radical sympathies, developed in the days when he moved in Austin's London circle in the early 1830s, remained with him in Ireland, so that he published his thoughts on the Irish Church Question in October 1836 in the *London Review*, a journal of philosophical radicalism, which amalgamated with the *Westminster Review*.[113] Substantially expanded into a 458 page volume, it was published in 1836 as a study *On Local Disturbances in Ireland, and on the Irish Church Question*. Sales, however, disappointed him:

> My book on Ireland has not sold much; there is no market for books on Irish subjects unless they are full of religious bigotry.[114]

His Irish experience, however, did alter some of his thinking.

> Before I went to Ireland I had very strong opinions as to the influence of race on the Irish character. But when I came to look at things more nearly, and to see all the demoralising influences to which they have been and are subjected, I asked myself whether a people of Germanic race would have turned out much better; and I really could not answer in the affirmative … *Ceteri paribus*, I would sooner have a German than a Celt, and a Protestant than a Catholic; but I have no doubt that a peasantry of Catholic Celts may be so governed and placed under such moral influences as to be peaceable, industrious, and contented; and I have no doubt that a peasantry of Protestant Germans might, if properly oppressed and brutalised, be made as bad as the Irish.[115]

Irish affairs, however, did not entirely engage his attention, and in October 1835 Lewis found respite from Ireland in Germany, visiting Frankfurt, Weimar, Leipzig, Dresden, and coming home by way of Hamburg. He had already shown his fluent command of German in his translations of August Boeckh's *Public Economy of Athens*, 1828, and Müller's *The History and Antiquities of the Doric Race*, 1830, both of which also reflected his fascination with the transformation of historical studies which was taking place in German universities. Happily for Lewis the classicist, the emergence of the scientific study of history began with ancient rather than modern history and the work of BG Niebuhr, August Boeckh, and Carl Ottfried Müller was to influence him profoundly in his own writing.

In April 1836 he found time to write a piece on the La Roncière case, a French *cause célèbre*. La Roncière was found guilty of assaulting a young lady in her third floor bedroom to which he had gained access from the outside by a ladder. He was found guilty and sentenced to twelve years' imprisonment, but the justice of the verdict was disputed. Lewis was invited to write the article by Abraham Hayward, QC, who enjoyed the approval of JS Mill and was the editor of the *Law Magazine, or Quarterly Review of Jurisprudence*.[116]

> I have written an article for Hayward on La Roncière. It is a stupid affair, but having once undertaken it, I was bound to finish. The evidence is nearly balanced, and it is difficult to make out anything with certainty; so that one wants the exact words, and the report I had was so loose that one could affirm nothing with confidence. The story is in truth a marvellous one; the only result I have arrived at is that both La Roncière and the lady are mad, or as good as.[117]

At the same time Lewis took up the study of Sanskrit and Buddhism, learning to his surprize that there were nearly three times as many Buddhists as Christians in the world. His tutor was Friedrich August Rosen, Professor of Oriental Languages at University College London 1826–30 and 1836–37 who probably found some relief in having Lewis as his pupil from 'giving practical elementary lessons in Persian, Arabic, and Hindustani, to students at the college'.[118]

It was also suggested in 1836 that Lewis should join John Austin, who had been appointed as a commissioner to inquire into the administration and government of Malta, as an unpaid and unofficial member of the commission. Austin was tubercular and it was thought that Lewis could deputise for him when he was ill, and offer his friend companionship and counsel. Lewis, however, was unprepared to accept so passive a role and complained from Harpton to Nassau Senior, who had joined the Poor Law Commission in 1833.

> How would it be possible for me, if I were to go merely as Austin's friend, to take part in the business? My presence would be an impertinent intrusion. What could I say to the authorities of the place? That I had taken upon myself to institute inquiries into the state of the island and its government? It seems to me that I might as well seat myself on the bench in a court of law, and say that I was come to assist the judge in trying causes. It is very true that I would be there with Austin's consent; but what would that matter to the persons whose conduct might be called into question? They would say that I was come into the island as a volunteer spy, as a self-appointed inquisitor; that their cause was tried *coram non judice*.[119]

Though Senior was familiar with Lewis's uncomfortable relationship with his fellow commissioners in Ireland, he wanted him to go to Malta[120] and in the event Lewis won the argument and went on his own terms. On 10th September 1836 he was appointed a joint commissioner with Austin. They travelled through France to Marseilles and Lewis could not help but notice that 'Nothing can exceed the look of comfort among the peasantry. It is a terrible contrast to Ireland'.[121] They sailed from Marseilles for Valetta in the Royal Navy's largest frigate. The voyage took ten days and Lewis was not a good sailor:

> I found it quite a mistake to suppose that there was no motion in large ships; a small vessel has, moreover, this advantage, that it is worked without there being a crew of four hundred and fifty men to walk over one's head during the chief parts of the night.[122]

Lewis thought Valetta, with its resemblance in some respects to Edinburgh, the most striking and beautiful town he had ever seen. But the dinner-giving, where one met the same people again and again, was all too reminiscent of Dublin. He told his father:

> The people here, I am sorry to say, remind me of the Irish. They have in common mistrust and mendaciousness among the upper classes, and superstition and prolificness among the lower, and its consequence, over population.
>
> In this island it is quite a singularity to have less than ten children: the place is a perfect human warren, and with regard to the numbers of families, the upper classes are just as bad as the lower. Starving nobles with fine sounding titles, and a couple of hundred pounds a year, marry at twenty, and begat twelve or fourteen children.[123]

He did not see the English at their best and soon concluded that:

> If an Englishman is to preserve any vestige of sympathetic feelings towards his own countrymen as such, he should certainly never see them out of England.[124]

What some saw as administrative vigour and energy, was for Lewis no more than a system of driving and kicking mankind into obedience, and in the long run, mischievous and absurd.[125] As in Ireland, the clergy in Malta advocated early marriage as a remedy for lust, but unlike many Protestant critics of the Roman Catholic clergy, the Malthusian Lewis did not ascribe this teaching to clerical greed:

> The world, always ready to find bad motives for every action, attributes this doctrine in Ireland and elsewhere to the desire of the clergy to augment their fees. In my opinion, their advice is perfectly disinterested; and is founded on a sincere conviction (however mistaken) that they are discharging an imperative religious duty. I am not at all clear that Protestant clergymen would not give just the same advice, if the practice of confession afforded them the means of enforcing it.[126]

There was in 1837 an outbreak of cholera, which killed 2,000 of the teeming population of 120,000 in five weeks. Lewis was on the island's soup committee,[127] but he found some relief from his public duties by selecting a donkey for a friend of his father. He was quite pleased with his choice of animal: 'a finer one I will undertake to say never ate an English thistle', though at £50 it was not cheap. Nor was it a good sailor, and it died on the voyage to England. Lewis, however, was a true son of Radnorshire, and having expressed his regrets to his father on hearing of the animal's demise, went on to warn him:

> I will send you, by next post, an account of what I paid. There is his keep for some time, besides the crib, and the payment for his food when on board.[128]

Lewis did not enjoy colonial experience and it made him remind his brother Gilbert and his friend Edmund Head that there was a fate worse than living on the Welsh Marches. Gilbert was now rector of Monnington on Wye, which though a Cornewall living of little ecclesiastical consequence, was much to be preferred to the bishopric of Calcutta.[129] Head, who was now an assistant Poor Law Commissioner for Brecknockshire, lived in adjoining Herefordshire at Monnington Rectory with Gilbert, still both bachelors, in what Lewis described as 'a joint-stock ménage'. Lewis reminded him from Malta:

> There is doubtless, a great deal to be said against Brecknockshire and Herefordshire, but I think you have had a great escape in not plunging into a colony.[130]

Lewis had discovered that though the girls attending the island's charity boarding schools were taught to read and pronounce Italian to perfection, they could not understand or speak a word of it. Then the thought struck this descendant of the patrons of the Welsh bards:

> I hope this is not the way in which English is taught in Welsh schools.[131]

In their report Lewis and Austin recommended the abolition of these schools. They also recommended freedom of the press, an idea not well received in London, an improved tariff to relieve trade and industry, and the relaxation of restraints imposed by military governors. They also began the codification of the laws for the island.

In March 1838 the Colonial Office directed them to wind up their commission as soon as possible, and Lewis left Malta on the 27th April. George Fisher Russell Barker, the prolific contributor to the *Dictionary of National Biography*, and author of its article on Lewis, said of the work of Lewis and Austin in Malta:

> No commission ever did its work more carefully, and its reports to the colonial office are remarkable papers, dealing with great ability and thoroughness with some of the most important questions of political economy and jurisprudence.

Lewis arrived in London in the summer of 1838, just after the bustle of the Queen's coronation, which he was, no doubt, happy to escape. In August his mother, Harriet Lewis, died, aged fifty-one, and in October 1839 Frankland Lewis, taking John Walsham's advice that he should not allow himself 'to brood over private afflictions', remarried.[132] His second wife was Mary Anne Ashton, daughter of Capt John Ashton of the Royal Horse Guards. George Lewis, then living at Hertford Street, the Mayfair home of his cousin Sir Alexander Duff Gordon, was a party to the marriage settlement. But neither the death of his mother nor the re-marriage of his father is mentioned in any of Cornewall Lewis's surviving correspondence.

In January 1839 Lewis succeeded his father, wearied by his 'troublesome office',[133] as one of the three principal Poor Law Commissioners for England and Wales. This was an arrangement which had been envisaged in 1833 when Lewis had been offered the post of Assistant Poor Law Commisioner, but now, confronted with its reality, he was at first inclined to reject the offer when it was made to him by Lord John Russell in August 1838,[134] even though his friend John Walsham thought his great mental powers well qualified him for the position.[135]

Chapter Two:
Poor Law Commissioner

The 1834 Poor Law Amendment Act was intended to be a five years' experiment, but the Commissioners found it hard to stay the course. In September 1838 George Nicholls was sent to Ireland to superintend the introduction of Poor Law reforms there, and he made his home in Dublin, not returning to London till November 1842. Thomas Frankland Lewis, it will be recollected, resigned as chairman of the Commission in 1839, and by 1841 the severe work of reorganising the poor-law system had taken its toll upon Shaw-Lefevre's health, and he moved to the Board of Trade as joint-assistant secretary. Moreover, the rigour and bureaucracy with which the Commissioners exhausted themselves were so unpopular that the Whigs merely renewed the measure for another year in 1839 and again in 1840. Sydney Smith in his Somerset Rectory wrote to Lewis, expressing his concern for him:

> You appear to be awkwardly situated, both as respects your future colleague, and the duration of your office.[1]

The awkwardness was that, when in 1841 Russell proposed to continue the Act until 1851, the extension was, in the event, limited to six years, until 1847 and a new Commissioner had to be found to replace Shaw-Lefevre. The new Commissioner would have to be capable of standing up to Chadwick, whose aim, in Thomas Frankland Lewis's opinion, had been to control and overawe the Commissioners.[2] He told his son that feared the new appointment would be a political one.[3]

It was at this stage that Cornewall Lewis and Nassau Senior published anonymously their influential pamphlet *Remarks on the*

Opposition to the Poor Law Amendment Bill, by a Guardian. The Webbs, in their authoritative history of the poor law, noted the extent of pamhlet's influence:

> This remarkable *apologia* entirely convinced both Whig and Tory statesmen, the successive committees of both Houses of Legislature, and the relatively small class of influential people outside, among whom these documents were diligently circulated, not only of the essential wisdom of the commissioners' administration, but also of the skill and prudence with which they had performed their arduous task.[4]

Thomas Frankland Lewis's anxieties were exaggerated, and Shaw-Lefevre's place was taken by Sir Edmund Head, who for the last five years had been languishing in Herefordshire as an assistant Poor Law Commissioner. Lord Normanby, the Whig Home Secretary 1839–1841, had shrunk from promoting him for party reasons. It was Sir James Graham,[5] who, despite his reputation for being 'so little conciliatory in manner and so rash in utterance', and to Lewis's delight, laid aside such considerations and gave Head the appointment. Lewis wrote from his Chester Street London home, where he was now living, to his father in Rome:

> On the whole I consider the prospects of the Poor Law Commission much brighter now than they were this time last year. Graham has been very kind to me, and I like him as a man of business. I need not say anything of Head as a colleague.[6]

All the same, Lewis found there was little time for himself:

> There is something perpetually stirring in Parliament about Poor Laws, a question, or a return, or some small matter. But sufficient (with the current business) to occupy my time so completely that I have been barely able to read or do anything for myself, except correct the proofs of the reprint of my translation of Boeckh.[7]

Even so, he was obviously putting what little time he had to himself to good effect. The affairs of the Poor Law Commission did not entirely keep him from his books or those of his friends. George Grote's library was especially useful:

> I return two out of the several books of yours in my possession. If you are by chance sitting in your own room, pray send me the volume of Seneca the philosopher, which contains a treatise

styled *Apocolocyntosis*. If you are sitting upstairs, pray put it out for me to-morrow, and I will send again.[8]

In 1839 Lewis published *A Glossary of Provincial Words Used in Herefordshire and some adjoining Counties*. The publication of glossaries was in vogue, and he listed those of other workers in this field which he consulted. Several were recently published. Lewis felt he has supplying a need, and doing so economically:

> The only collection of the provincialisms of Herefordshire which has been hitherto made is that inserted in Duncumb's topographical work on the county. As this list is meager and imperfect, and as it is contained in a scarce and expensive book, it seems worthwhile to form a new collection, and to print it separately.[9]

Lewis defined provincial words as being those which, though not used by educated persons, nonetheless formed part of the common vocabulary. He claimed that the words included in his Glossary were at that time generally current in Herefordshire, and in parts of the contiguous counties of Brecknock, Radnor, Monmouth, and Gloucester. He used some of them himself, surely one of the most educated of men, and thereby invalidating his claim that provincial words were not used by the educated. Thus, writing in 1832 to his father from Cannes, he tells how long the ten mile journey took by cabriolet from Cannes to Grasse:

> Lest Gilbert should think that the Hereford horses have a monopoly of *the slows*, let him be assured that I was three hours in going and two and a half hours in returning, having *baited* there nearly two hours.[10]

Even the *Sporting Magazine* spoke of *the slows* in 1826 to describe slow-paced horses,[11] whilst Lewis notes in his Glossary that *bait* is 'a meal taken by a labourer in the middle of the day'.[12] The expression is still used In Herefordshire and Radnorshire.

It is surprising that Lewis identified so few Welsh words in use in Herefordshire in 1839, despite the survival of Welsh place-names and the Welsh language in the county:

> It was because of the persistence of the Welsh language in his diocese that the bishop of Hereford (as well as the Welsh bishops) was enjoined by parliament in 1563 to see that copies of the Welsh Bible and Common Prayer Book were placed in

those churches where Welsh was the language of the people. In some Herefordshire parishes near the Welsh boundary, like Welsh Newton and Kentchurch, Welsh was spoken in the eighteenth century. In Ewyas the language survived in to the nineteenth century and it was not until 1883 that the last Welsh speaker of Cloddock died at Garn Galed in that parish.[13]

Nearer to Harpton, when Hester Sayer endowed her school at Kington in 1733, she specified that it was to be an *English* school, the implication being that there was much Welsh still being spoken in the area. Likewise an advertisement in the *Hereford Times* for a solicitor's clerk for a Kington lawyer at this time required that he should be able to speak Welsh. Worship at Glascwm, a parish contiguous with those of Old Radnor and Nant Mellan, was in the 18th century still bilingual, despite its proximity to the English border, only six miles away. In 1745 the bishop of St Davids was assured that there were a folio Bible and Common Prayer Books in the parish church there, both in English and Welsh. Two years earlier the parishioners had petitioned the bishop because their vicar, Walter Meyricke, had dropped the Welsh part of their bilingual services. They wanted the Second Lesson read in Welsh every Sunday and a sermon in Welsh every other Sunday. They later complained that though the vicar could neither speak nor understand Welsh, he insisted on reading the Second Lesson himself.

Mullett noted that 'once Lewis published a book he apparently forgot about it, for though he referred in his letters [and in his diaries] to what he was doing, he seldom referred to what he had done'.[14] In this the *Glossary* was an exception. He was still collecting his provincialisms after its publication, sending a copy to an Assistant Poor Law Commissioner working in Shropshire who in return sent him a list of Shropshire and Sussex provincialisms

With Herefordshire's provincialisms behind him, Lewis had to find time for more social activity. He now lived in Wilton Place, off Belgrave Square, and in May 1840 he attended the wedding at Kensington Old Church of his cousin Alexander Duff Gordon to Lucie, the daughter of his friend and colleague John Austin. His brother, the Revd Gilbert Lewis performed the ceremony, and Lewis himself was a trustee for Lucie's marriage settlement. There were several of his friends among the guests and he was able to discuss with them his plans to translate Müller's *History of the Literature of Ancient*

Greece and to write, with his experiences in Ireland and Malta to draw upon, *An Essay on the Government of Dependencies*, which was published in London in 1841.[15]

Lewis's relations with Chadwick at this time were less stressful than they were to be with his fellow Poor Law Commissioners. They shared a Benthamite perspective, and Lewis may have met Chadwick in earlier days at Bentham's house where Chadwick lived. Even so, he was careful to distance himself safely from any unpleasant consequences of Chadwick's reforming notions falling on his own shoulders:

> Chadwick is writing a long report on the means of preventing disease by drainage, cleansing, &c. It contains a great deal of good matter, and, on the whole, I prefer it to anything else he has written. We shall present it shortly as his report, without making ourselves responsible for it.[16]

Head's presence at the Commission's London office was useful for Lewis whose health, especially in the winter, was no better in the long term, despite the respite offered it by Malta:

> [GJ]Guthrie is now attending me for a slight cough, which I made worse by my journey to Cheltenham. I shall stay in the house for a day or two, and leave the office to Head, by which means I shall avoid all risk.[17]

Besides trouble with his chest, Lewis seems to have suffered from migraines as well:

> I have this evening reached the *crapula*[18] of a headache; which, though more or less unpleasant, is a far better thing than the headache itself.[19]

Nicholls, the third Poor law Commissioner, returned to London from Dublin in November 1842. The task of implementing the provisions of the Irish Poor Law Act of 1838 proved very difficult, and his efforts were hampered by opposition and criticism. Early in 1843 Lewis was back in Dublin and complained to George Grote:

> Everything in Ireland is carried on with such a hubbub and noise, and there is so much insincerity in a vast deal that is said, that there is no finding out the truth except by coming to the place and selecting one's informants.[20]

By the autumn of 1843 Lewis's health was failing and he went for some weeks to Leamington Spa for a cure. The skills and financial success of his physician, Dr Jephson, impressed him, and he commended them to the ailing Edmund Head:

> I shall probably come to London in about a fortnight. My health has got so much out of order, that I found it necessary to do something for it, and I have derived very decided benefit from the strict regimen upon which Dr Jephson has put me, and which I have now pursued nearly three weeks. I should not be surprised if he could do good in your case; his chief skill lies in chronic disorders of the digestive organs. People come to him from far and wide; he makes at least £16,000 a year, which is an extraordinary provincial income.[21]

On 26th October 1844, at the age of thirty-eight, Lewis married Lady Maria Theresa Lister, three years his senior. She was the widow of Thomas Henry Lister, by whom she had a son and two daughters.[22] Mention has already been made of Lewis's meeting with Lister in Ireland in 1834 in connection with the Royal Commission on Church Property, and two years later he was appointed as the first Registrar-General of England and Wales. Remembered as 'a refined, accomplished man', he wrote several novels, which are now seldom read. Like so many in Lewis's circle, Lister suffered from tuberculosis and when Lewis heard the news of a relapse in March 1842 wrote to Grote with a misplaced degree of optimism: 'Lister has had a severe pulmonary attack, from which he is slowly recovering'.[23] He died later that year.

The wedding took place at Watford parish church, subsequently restored in 1848. It then lost its box pews which Cornewall Lewis regretted:

> Grove Mill. Went to Watford church, which has been repewed. Open seats, with low backs. The appearance of the church is improved, but the sitting is less commodious.[24]

The Grove just outside Watford, became the seat of the Earls of Clarendon in 1776, and it was from here that, by licence, Theresa Lister was married. She was given away by her elder brother, the Earl, and the ceremony was performed by another brother, Henry Montague Villiers. He was the evangelical rector of St George's, Bloomsbury and in 1856 was Palmerston's choice for the bishopric of Carlisle. He was translated in 1860 to Durham where he died a year later. The witnesses were the Earl of Clarendon, the Earl of Verulam, Thomas Frankland Lewis, Thomas Villiers Lister, Cornewall Lewis's twelve-year-old step-son by the marriage, and Lord Grimston who was to succeed his father as the second Earl of Verulam in 1845.

In Lady Duff Gordon's opinion, for Theresa Lister:

> Her heavy losses had been too much for her in early life. Her health had a severe blow, when Lord Ellesmere, then Lord Francis Leveson,[25] threw her over she had a paralytic seizure, then her fondly loved two brothers Hyde[26] & Edward Villiers[27] died, then she was engaged to Lord Holland,[28] and that his brother prevented taking place.[29] Then she married Mr Lister. I then much lost sight of her, but I believe she liked him & valued him. But they were poor. I know nothing about how she felt his death.[30]

Lewis now forsook Wilton Place for Kent House in Knightsbridge. This substantial mansion, overlooking Hyde Park, and famous for its extensive gardens, belonged to Thomas Lister's kinsman, the Earl of Morley, John Parker, FRS, who was ennobled as the first earl in 1815. Theresa Villiers, Lister's wife, was the earl's niece. The arrangement continued under the second earl, who with his wife, mother, and three children inhabited one part of the house, and Cornewall Lewis, with his wife, mother-in-law, Charles Villiers, his brother-in-law, and their three step-children, the other part. The Lewises were assisted in the mundane affairs of everyday life by a butler, valet, two coachmen, lady's maid, cook, nurse, two housemaids, and a nursery maid.

Described as a fascinating hostess, clever, agreeable, and accomplished, Theresa Lewis was to become a considerable asset to Lewis's political career. A new dimension was now also added to Lewis's cultural life in the form of music. Lewis was not musical, but Theresa's musical meetings engaged the attention of *The Times* and of Lady Duff Gordon.

> Miss Clara Loveday, this clever pianist gave a matinee musicale yesterday at the residence of Lady Theresa Lewis of Kent House Knightsbridge which was attended by a numerous and fashionable audience. Miss Loveday has for some years resided in Paris. She had acquired a considerable reputation as an elegant and practised pianist of the modern school. Her execution is exceedingly brilliant and sure.[31]

Lady Duff Gordon and her daughters, however, were unaccompanied by the correspondent of *The Times* when they went to Kent House some years later to listen to the music:

I went to Theresa Lewis's Morning Music which was really very good. Miss Trehearne sang very well and a great deal single parts in Choral music and about 14 others, young & middle ages, and when all was over Miss Thellingson acted one thing, the loss of Balaclava [Tennyson] and then the Widow's Son.[32]

Domestic pleasure, however, was progressively outweighed by professional friction in the Poor Law Commission. 'The board was attacked on all sides, and while the local authorities protested that it interfered too much, the philanthropists declared that it did too little. The difficulties of the board, moreover, were intensified by the want of a representative in parliament'[33] and Lewis complained to George Grote:

> For my part, nothing but a consciousness of the impossibility of resigning would have induced me to hold my office even to the present time. To be exposed to the insults of all the refuse of the House of Commons without the power of defending oneself, and to have one's chief opponent as the secretary of the board of which one is a member, without the power of dismissing him, is a position which nothing but necessity can render tolerable, and which I only submit to for the present because I have no alternative.[34]

The Secretary of the Board, who the Commissioners could not dismiss, was still Edwin Chadwick, whom Thomas Frankland Lewis thought had done his best to exhaust them out. Aware of his son's physical fraility, he urged him, when 'sufficiently disembarrassed from the cares of office' to come down to Harpton.[35]

Prominent amongst 'the refuse of the House of Commons' was William Busfeild Ferrand, Esq., of Harden Grange, near Bingley, in Yorkshire, MP for Knaresborough.[36] It was said that his speech on Sir Robert Peel's Corn Law Bill in February 1842 was delivered with great force, and his exposure of the Truck System of paying wages in grocer's commodities and at public houses was complete.[37] He also enjoyed some approval outside Parliament, inspiring such pamphlets as *The Manufacturers, their System, and their Operatives. A letter to W. Busfeild Ferrand, Esq, MP, confirming the statements he made in his recent speeches in the House of Commons,* 'by a factory operative of twenty-five years experience'.[38] The Tory minded *Blackwood's Edinburgh Magazine* described him as:

> the fearless member for Knaresborough, a man most ill-used, even abandoned by the very party he so signally serves; yet who is never slow to chastise the cur which snarls whilst it crouches before him.[39]

He was an accomplished self-publicist and his parliamentary speeches on the Corn Laws and the Poor Law went through several editions. In 1842 there was an inquiry into the affairs of the Keighley Union in general, and the Bingley Workhouse in particular, which was in Ferrand's constituency and over which as a local magistrate and chairman of the local Board of Guardians he would have had some influence and responsibility. The Assistant Commissioner responsible was Charles Mott, who had conducted the inquiry into the workhouse at Eye in Suffolk in 1838 whilst Frankland Lewis was still a Commissioner,[40] so he enjoyed the confidence of both father and son.[41] He enjoyed, too, the confidence of Nassau Senior, and in September 1841 Lewis asked him, with another Assistant Commissioner, to enquire into 'the destitution of the working classes in the manufacturing districts'.[42] A few weeks later, however, along with his colleague Col À Court, he incurred the displeasure of James Graham for writing letters to the papers.[43]

In February 1842 Lewis wrote to Mott, asking him to investigate an alleged example of what had come to be seen as a classic abuse of the Poor Law by local Guardians who had factories and worked the system to enable them to pay their employees low wages which were made up from the poor rates:

> It has been represented, *in a confidential manner*, to the Commissioners that great abuses with respect to the payment of wages out of the rates, exist in the Keighley Union. It has been stated to them that the manufacturers in the Board combine for the purpose of lowering the wages of their workpeople, & making them up from the rates which are mainly levied upon the agricultural classes.
>
> I should be glad if you would take an early opportunity of visiting this union, & inquiring into the system of relief practised there, without creating suspicion, or assuming the appearance of making a special investigation, and should be glad if you would communicate to me the results of this inquiry. Pray let me know whether the union has any & what workhouse & what the Guardians make of it.
>
> The Commissioners have moreover heard a report that in many or some, of the manufacturing unions in the West Riding of Yorkshire & Lancashire, there exists an intention of electing Guardians pledged to abstain from acting. Pray let me know if you have heard anything of the existence of such an intention. Do you know how the electors at Manchester & Liverpool are

likely to turn out, and will it be necessary that the Commissioners should take any preparatory or precautionary steps with reference to them?[44]

That Mott should have been chosen for this inquiry was later thought to have been significant:

> Mr Power, it seems was the regular inspector for Keighley; but he not being pliable enough was not employed, being superseded on this occasion by the redoubtable Mott.[45]

Power certainly had experience and the Commissioners' confidence for he was one of the three who had served under the Poor Law Inquiry Commission 1832–34 and was then re-appointed at £750 pa.[46]

So why was Mott chosen? It may well have been that, in Lewis's eyes, Mott had proved useful in similar difficult situation involving the Poor Law Guardians of the Bolton Union. In October 1841 Sir James Graham had given his approval to Lewis's communications to Mott respecting the proposed visit of Sir John Bowring, MP for Bolton, to his constituency.[47] Graham unexpectedly referred to Mott's subsequent report on the affairs of the Bolton Union in answering Bowring in the Commons, and thereby 'extinguished the poor polyglot doctor'.[48]

Since the information leading to Mott's inquiry had been given in confidence, Mott wanted to know from Lewis whether his report should be private or public. In April Lewis in response advised him somewhat conspiratorially that

> We think it desirable that you should make a *public* Report on the Keighley Union. You can begin it by stating that you ascertained the facts in one of your regular visits.[49]

Since Mott was not the regular inspector for Keighley, this strategy would certainly have raised eyebrows, and Mott himself did little to allay suspicions:

> Down came our Special Commissioner Mott to Keighley, and in no very good humour; for it comes out in the evidence of Mr Hulbert, Vice-chairman of the board before the select committee of the Keighley Union, that 'when he came into the room [of the board of guardians] he appeared, from the first words he uttered, to be in a bad temper, before he saw anything'.[50]

Mott's report was far from favourable, and was 'commented upon in every newspaper in the kingdom'. It alleged that the proceedings of the Keighley Guardians were entirely at variance with the provisions of law and the directions of the Commissioners. Relief was given by supplementary wages and rents were paid on behalf of applicants to what was seen to be an alarming extent. It was alleged that at the workhouses both at Bingley and Keighley 'all the errors of the old Poor Law were followed'.[51] Ferrand himself was singled out for disfavour for

> jobbing as a guardian by giving encouragement to lawyers to create legal disputes, and sanctioning such proceedings in his capacity as a magistrate.[52]

A few weeks later, another Assistant Commissioner inspected the Keighley Union. This was Sir John Walsham, Bart[53] of Knill Court, and a near neighbour of Lewis. He went at the request of Sir James Graham to verify Mott's account and found it to be substantially true.[54] Ferrand thereupon demanded and received an immediate explanation from John Hartley, the Union's medical officer:

> I forward a correct account of the Bingley workhouse. I have made particular inquiry of the relieving officer and Whitley [the master of the poor house], and being in the habit of giving daily attendances myself, can satisfactorily answer all your questions.
>
> No inmate ever slept in the same bed with a corpse, neither do they sleep in the same room.
>
> The beds are not improperly crowded, never exceeding two in each, except they be young children.
>
> The sexes are not improperly mixed and seldom mingle together. Their food is both sufficient and wholesome.
>
> The vicar has not attended the workhouse for some time, in consequence of the dissenting ministers being permitted to preach. He refused to attend unless they were dismissed: and as people of different denominations were inmates of the house, the authorities refused to grant his request.
>
> The number of inmates is 51. Ten children from 1 year to 16; 12 from 16 to 40; six from 40 to 60; 23 above 60.
>
> The workhouse is very clean and wholesome.[55]

On 17th June 1844, Ferrand questioned Sir James Graham in the House. By coincidence, at least in the opinion of *The Times*, Mott's report had already got into Sir James Graham's red box in some mysterious way, to be ready to extinguish Mr Ferrand on the first convenient opportunity … Sir James Graham immediately arose to reply, and produced Mr Mott's red-hot shot, as he had formerly produced the Bolton document for the edification of the learned member for that place. By this report the Keighley Union was charged with sundry acts of misconduct and malad-ministration, … To clinch the matter Sir James declared that he was quoting from a document prepared by one of a class of men 'whose reports, he for one, speaking from experience' was ever anxious to rely upon with confidence.[56]

By another strange coincidence the reports of both Mott and Walsham, though dated 23rd April and 9th June respectively, arrived at Keighley on the same day, 26th June. An extraordinary meeting was called for the next day and the Guardians wrote to assure the Poor Law Commissioners that:

the master of the Keighley Poor-house is well known to this board as a very intelligent and humane man, and they have closely examined him touching the general state of the bedding in the poor-house and the condition of the inmates, and although it can not be denied that Sir John Walsham's state-ment is generally in substance correct as to the want of classifi-cation and discipline, nevertheless his observation 'of the dead companioning the living' must not be understood to mean that the living is placed in the same bed with the dead, as such has not been the case.[57]

A Select Committee of the House Commons examined both Mott's and Walsham's reports and concluded they were 'substantially true'.[58] But the iron had entered into Ferrand's soul and he was not prepared to let matters rest. In June 1844 he published a pamphlet: *The great Mott question, or the Mystery unravelled in a letter to Sir J Graham*,[59] which was reviewed by *The Times*:[60]

We have here a most plain-spoken and unshrinking exposure of the crooked paths which 'men in high office' when defending evil deeds, are compelled to take: and of the startling lengths to which the present Ministers have gone in order to crush, if possible, the opposition now surging against the cruel Poor Law, both in and out of Parliament.

Mott's 'plain-spoken and unshrinking exposure' did him little good, and in the words of *The Times* he was 'cashiered'. This was not strictly true, rather he had 'been reduced to the ranks' by being appointed an Auditor on an annual salary of £379, as opposed to the £500 he received as an Assistant Commissioner. He made Lewis aware of his financial embarrassment:

> From the first circular issued by the Board with reference to the Salaries of the Auditors I was led to believe that the Government grant was intended to pay the half year's salary due *Lady day last*, and not to operate retrospectively. As regards the Salary due 29th Sept last, acting on this belief, coupled with my pecuniary difficulties with which you have been made acquainted (brought on I regret to say through my importunate connexion with the new Poor Law), I expended the half year's salary paid to me in April last.[61]

Ferrand over the last two years had become progressively more convinced that the events leading to Mott's demotion in consequence of his mishandling of his inquiry into the affairs of the Bolton Union were also related to his inquiry into the Keighley Union, the board of which Mott was the chairman:

> The case of Mott, the now cashiered Poor Law Commissioner ... Sir James Graham and his Ministerial friends contrived to involve it in somewhat of a mist. That mist, however, Mr Ferrand has now dispelled by virtue of this very explanatory epistle to the Home Secretary. No one who reads this letter can be ignorant of what Mott really has been and is. He appears in his true colours:
> 'that tool
> Which knaves do play with, call'd a fool'.[62]

Ferrand alleged that Sir James Graham, who found the former's hostility to the new Poor Law a Parliamentary nuisance, had used Mott to produce a false report on the activities of the Keighley Union to crush him and ruin his political career. But in the Spring of 1844 Ferrand took matters further and alleged in a speech at Leeds that not only was Mott's report false but that Graham had been joined by Cornewall Lewis, in his capacity of a Poor Law Commissioner, in conspiring to obtain it. This was censured in the Commons as 'unfounded and calumnious accusation'.[63]

Sir John Walsham now returned to the fray, having, in the cosiness of the Windham Club, apparently just read Ferrand's pamphlet on *The great Mott Question*. In a letter to Ferrand of 3rd June 1844 he says he is driven to conclude that:

> 1st That you allege that, in June 1842, I drew up a report on the Keighley Union, which has been proved to be false; and
> 2nd that you further allege, in reference to this report, that I was sent down to the Keighley Union, previously to the debate of the 27th June, 1842, for the special purpose of getting up a statement to be used against you in the House of Commons.

But, in case his interpretation is incorrect, he continues:

> Before, however, I determine what steps it will be proper for me to take in vindication of my conduct two years ago, now unexpectedly assailed, I would request you to inform me whether I have correctly apprehended your meaning. If I am mistaken you will doubtless see the propriety of pointing out in what respect I have misunderstood that portion of your letter to Sir James Graham which appears to affect my character.[64]

Ferrand replied to Walsham next day from the Carlton Club:

> I have only to inform you that the remarks upon your public conduct as an Assistant Poor Law Commissioner, which appear in my letter to Sir James Graham on the Great Mott question, were made by me, and published in *Hansard's Parliamentary Debates*, and the public newspapers, *nearly two years ago*; and that the question now at issue is between myself and Sir James Graham, with the *chief*, and not with the *subordinate*.[65]

Walsham was not to be put down so easily and replied the same day by return of post:

> I am quite aware that the remarks which appeared in your letter to Sir James Graham have reference to my public conduct as an Assistant Poor Law Commissioner, and that similar remarks were stated to have been made by you in your place in Parliament, *previously* to the report of the select committee appointed by him to inquire into the truth of the allegations contained in my own and Mr Mott's report on the Keighley Union.
>
> I wish, however, to observe, that remarks reported in the newspapers to have been made by you in your place in Parliament on the public conduct of a public servant, are a totally different matter from remarks published by you in a pamphlet, with a view, apparently, of repeating in your individual capacity, and in the teeth of the conclusions arrived at by the select committee, your former Parliamentary charge against me of having drawn up a false report.

Had I at once questioned your observations in the House of Commons upon my conduct, I should have committed an unjustifiable breach of privilege, for the same Parliamentary report which circulated these remarks announced also Sir James Graham's offer to you to second a motion for a select committee 'to inquire into all the circumstances connected with the management of the Keighley union, as set forth in the report of Mr Mott and Sir John Walsham'.

But, with regard to your remarks as to the avowed author of a printed pamphlet, you must allow me to consider myself entitled to, and to renew my request for, a distinct answer to the questions which in my yesterday's communication I submitted to you in terms free, I trust, from the slightest tinge of discourtesy.

You are, of course, perfectly at liberty to apprize me, that in the exercise of your discretion you must decline to answer these questions. I shall then know how to proceed. But if in attacking a Secretary of State you think it proper to introduce the name of so unimportant a person as myself, it is not sufficient to tell me (in answer to my request for exact information respecting the meaning which certain passages relating to my conduct are intended by you to convey) that the question now at issue is between Sir James Graham and yourself.

Permit me, moreover, to suggest to you, antitheses to be effective should be appropriate. I have the greatest respect for Sir James Graham, and the high office he fills. But, officially, he is not my *chief*, nor is he responsible for any of my acts, as for those of a *subordinate*. I owe my appointment to the Poor Law Commissioners, and hold it at their pleasure.[66]

The Times was unimpressed: 'If the worthy baronet had studiously considered how he should make or show himself ridiculous, he has by his long-delayed publication very completely effected that purpose'.[67] Ferrand, for his part, went on to reiterate the same charges had made against Graham and Lewis in Parliament, in two letters to *The Times*, published on the 8th and 10th of August 1844. Lewis was now able to seek recourse at law, but was slow to do so until events pressed upon him in 1845.

Colin McDougal, the Master of the Andover Workhouse, had a reputation for inhumanity. Bone crushing was a normal occupation for paupers, and involved the bones of horses, dogs and other animals (and there were hints that some from local graveyards) being crushed for fertiliser for local farms. In 1845 the Andover paupers, it was reported, were so hungry that they were eating the rotting bones brought in to be crushed. Alone amongst the Andover Guardians, Mr Hugh Mundy, a member of the borough council and a prosperous farmer, protested. Mundy was a man of some humanity and in December 1837 had written to the Poor Law Commissioners for permission to give all the Andover inmates a Christmas dinner. His request was refused:

> The Poor Law Commissioners for England and Wales regret that they do not feel justified in assenting to the proposition contained in your letter of the 18th instant that, the paupers in the Union Workhouse should be regaled on the ensuing Christmas day with a good Dinner & Beer, to be provided at the expense of the Guardians & others willing to contribute by voluntary subscriptions.
>
> The Commissioners consider that this proposition is directly at variance with the principles upon which the efficacy of the Workhouse System depends (namely) that the condition of the pauper inmate of the Workhouse should not be desired or envied by the independent person; and the Commrs therefore cannot consent that the inmates of the Workhouse should be supplied with indulgencies which too many of those who support themselves without parochial aid are obliged altogether to forgo.[68]

Munday's complaints about the bone crushing were unheeded by his fellow Guardians and he eventually took them to Ralph Etwall, MP for Andover. Just before the summer recess Etwall's Parliamentary colleague John Wakely, MP for Finsbury, asked whether it were really true that the Andover paupers were relieving their hunger by gnawing bones. Graham dismissed the story as being absurd, part of a 'mere workhouse squabble', but the Poor Law Commissioners hurriedly sent one of their nine assistants, Henry Walter Parker, down to Andover to investigate. He arrived on August 3rd 1845 and conducted a Public Inquiry in the Town Hall. The revelations which followed were reported in a series of twenty-nine articles in *The Times*.

Parker's conduct of the inquiry did him little credit; partial and impudent, he offered excuses for McDougal, the workhouse master, whenever he could, and interrupted and bullied the witnesses. When McDougal decided to retire to avoid the shame of public dismissal, Parker recommended the former master of the workhouse at Oxford who had just resigned for the same reason, *ie* to avoid dismissal, on being accused of inhumanity.[69] TF Lewis wrote to his son of Parker's distressing conduct, but then pointed out that Shaw-Lefevre, who had left the Commission in 1841, was his patron.[70]

The Commissioners lost little time in asking for Parker's resignation, whilst assuring him that they did so with the utmost reluctance, and acknowledged the zealous and efficient services which he had on various occasions rendered to the Commission.[71] They could hardly do otherwise, for as Lewis was to admit later:

> they removed Mr Parker from his office because he had lost their confidence; because they believed him to have conducted the enquiry unskilfully and partially; and because he showed an unwillingness to act upon their instructions, although *they were responsible for all he said and did in his official capacity.*[72]

In the following month, November 1845, the Commissioners prohibited the crushing of bones in workhouses. Parker himself felt aggrieved at his treatment by the Commissioners, and published all the letters and replies which had passed between himself and the Commission. He also petitioned the House of Commons praying that his case should be investigated. Others agreed, though for other reasons, and on 5th March 1846, it was ordered that:

> a Select Committee be appointed to inquire into the Administration of the Poor Laws in the Andover Union, and also into the Management of the Union Workhouse; and into the Conduct of the Poor-law Commissioners, and their late Assistant Commissioner, Mr Parker, in reference to the two Investigations held at Andover; and into all the Circumstances under which the Poor-law Commissioners called upon Mr Parker to resign his Assistant Commissionership.

Ferrand, of course, saw the Andover inquiry as an opportunity to revive interest in the affairs of the Keighley Union, and in May, Peel, the Prime Minister, was conferring with Lewis about Ferrand's recent questions in the House respecting the Bingley workhouse.[73]

The inquiry's chairman was William Reginald Courtenay, eldest son of the tenth Earl of Devon and MP at that time for South Devon.[74] The committee conducted its business in public, and one of the witnesses examined by John Wakeley was Charles Lewis, a labourer whose children had survived on raw potatoes and scraps that the master of the Andover workhouse threw to the chickens:

Evidence of Charles Lewis, a labourer, when examined by Mr Wakeley.

What work were you employed about when you were in the workhouse?

I was employed breaking bones.

Were other men engaged in the same work?

Yes.

Was that the only employment you had?

That was the only employment I had at the time I was there.

Was the smell very bad?

Very bad.

Did it appear to affect your health?

It did a great deal mine, and appeared to affect the others.

How many men were so employed?

Whether it was nine or ten boxes round the room, I don't recollect.

Was it a close room or shed?

It was a very close room.

How did you break them?

We had a large iron bar to break them with.

Something like a rammer?

Yes.

Had you no other employment at all?

No, not while I was there, but breaking the bones.

What sort of bones did they appear to be?

All sorts.

During the time you were so employed, did you ever see any of the men gnaw anything or eat anything from those bones?

I have seen them eat marrow out of the bones.

You were not examined before Mr Parker, the Assistant Commissioner?

No.

Have you often seen them eat the marrow?

I have.

Did they state why they did it?

I really believe they were very hungry.

Did you yourself feel extremely hungry at that time?

I did, but my stomach would not take it.

You could not swallow the marrow?

No.

Did you see any of the men gnaw the meat from the bones?

Yes.

Did they use to steal the bones and hide them away?

Yes.

Have you seen them have a scramble and quarrel amongst the bones?

I do not know that I have seen them scramble, but I have seen them hide them.

And when a fresh set of bones came in, did they keep a sharp look-out for the best?

Yes.

Was that a regular thing?

While I was there.[75]

With such evidence before him it is difficult to understand how the radical Cornewall Lewis was able to claim that:

If any one would calmly and dispassionately look to the facts as they now appear, he will not be surprised if it should turn out (as it is pretty certain to do), upon the publication of the evidence, that the case against the poor-law or the commissioners, which was blown out into a fictitious importance by the London press, shrinks up into very small dimensions.[76]

It is easier to understand how Greville in his *Memoirs* described Lewis as 'cold blooded as a fish, totally devoid of sensibility'.[77] In August Lewis was attacked in Parliament by Wakeley in a manner which Frankland Lewis considered to have the character of persecution, though he felt no permanent stigma would attach itself to Lewis's character.[78]

Thomas Frankland Lewis followed events closely: had he not been a Commissioner and it was surely, at least partly, on his advice that his son Cornewall Lewis had followed in his footsteps? By July, and on 12th July Lewis appeared before the Andover Committee,[79] Frankland Lewis was concerned about Cornewall's health and was suggesting that he should at least winter in a warmer climate. He evaluated witnesses' evidence: what Nicholls had said must have been very injurious to the Commission, whereas that of Head was very effective, Coode's[80] examination did him great credit; and Frankland Lewis himself was prepared to appear before the Committee. The triumphalist attitude, however, of *The Times* so disgusted him he that he wrote to cancel his subscription, though he still wanted a copy on the days when reports of the Andover Committee appeared,[81] partial and garbled they may be.[82]

In October 1846, anticipating a hostile report from the Select Committee, and urged on by the fact that a powerful attack on the Commissioners, generally attributed at least to Chadwick's inspiration, appeared in the *Westminster Review* for October 1846 under the title of 'Patronage of Commissions'; and was separately published and widely circulated under the title of *The Poor Law Commission*,[83] Lewis set about a measure of damage limitation. He spent two days at Harpton writing an article on the Andover case for the *Hereford Times*, a copy of which he sent James Davies of Moorcourt, the Kington lawyer and banker.[84]

It appeared anonymously on Saturday, 10th October, and claimed to be 'a correct outline of the case':

> The guardians of the Andover union appear to have misman-
> aged the workhouse. They kept in office, as master of the work-
> house, a man who was alleged not to be sober in his habits, to
> have probably insulted some of the female inmates, and to have
> certainly behaved with cruelty on two or three occasions to indi-
> vidual paupers. This man resigned his office after the enquiry
> instituted by the poor-law commissioners in the autumn of last
> year. The books of the union were, moreover, not properly kept
> by the officers, and the inspection of them was not regularly
> performed by the guardians.

But Lewis, under the cloak of anonymity, then goes on to claim that since the Commissioners were not informed of the Andover situation by their subordinates they could do nothing about the situation for which, by implication, they were hardly to blame:

> The instances of local irregularity and abuse, which occurred in
> the Andover union were not reported to the poor-law commis-
> sioners, and therefore could not have been rectified by their
> interference.

Lewis's defence is consistently that of ignorance: for what the Andover Guardians did not inform the Commissioners they, the Commissioners, could not be held responsible:

> Certain irregularities and abuses prevailed in a single union in
> Hampshire; these abuses were owing to the defective control of
> the guardians; they were not discovered by the assistant commis-
> sioners, and were not reported to the commissioners. As soon as
> they were disclosed and made known to the commissioners
> measures were taken for rectifying them.

Besides Mr Parker, another casualty was William Day. As a young Sussex squire he was keenly interested in Poor Law administration, and became Vice-Chairman of the Uckfield union. In 1836 he was offered and he accepted office as an Assistant Commissioner; and he is found, for the next few years, putting the Act in operation in the Western Midlands and Wales. He seems to have been an energetic but not always subordinate official, and in 1844 the commissioners removed him from office. This was at the time of the Rebecca Riots, and 'they did not consider him well fitted for the inspection of the Welsh district at that period'. This, however, was the same Mr Day who in 1840 gave Lewis some assistance in compiling his *Herefordshire Glossary*,[85] but in this case Lewis forgot old debts and asked anonymously through the pages of the *Hereford Times*:

> If amongst your readers there are any members of the boards which were under his inspection, perhaps they may not be inclined to agree with the committee in thinking that Mr Day ought to have been retained in his office.[86]

In November 1843, according to TF Lewis, Day had complained that in the Pembrokeshire workhouses the use of soap was not permitted.[87] Perhaps this was his misdemeanour, but be this as it may, his removal was due apparently to the representations of Robert Henry Clive, and William Cripps, two of TF Lewis's fellow Commissioners on the Commission inquiring into the causes of the Rebecca riots.[88]

The complaint of the Select Committee, however, in respect of Mr Day was not so much that the Commission dismissed him, but the manner in which he was dismissed. Chadwick had often complained that the Commissioners by-passed him, though he was their officially appointed Secretary. Lewis admits that there was truth in Chadwick's complaint, but then dismisses it as being of no consequence:

> The [Select] committee attempt to found a charge of arbitrary and illegal conduct against the commissioners upon the fact that in calling for the resignation of Mr Parker and Mr Day, the wish of the commissioners was intimated by a private letter, written by the chief commissioner, and not by an official letter, signed by the secretary. Upon that slight and technical point a grave accusation was based.
>
> No attempt was made by the committee to attack the several orders of the commissioners, by which alone their administration of the law, and their exercise of the powers confided to them, could be fairly tried. However, they produced

the secretary of the commission, Mr Chadwick, who having quietly held his office for 12 years, came forward to charge his official superiors with transacting their business in a manner different from that prescribed by law. This charge was distinctly denied and disproved by the commissioners, and yet the committee expressed no opinion upon it.

Mr Chadwick's principal complaint against the commissioners seems to have been that they had arranged their proceedings so as to transact all their business with little or no assistance from him, their secretary, except writing his name at the bottom of their letters.

It was the considered opinion of Frankland Lewis, who as a Poor Law Commissioner had had five years experience of Chadwick, that he was 'an able man, but … as unscrupulous and as dangerous an officer as I ever saw within the walls of an office'.[89] On the other hand, since the reputation of his son was at stake, one might say 'he would wouldn't he'. In the opinion of Cornewall Lewis and his fellow commissioners Chadwick had got above himself by daring to query the behaviour of his 'official superiors'. But truth to speak, it was the Commissioners, and not Chadwick, who had got above themselves, or indeed had been unscrupulous and dangerous. The retrospective judgement of the Webbs, for example, was that Mott was diligent but tactless and indiscreet.[90] So forced resignation was the reward for diligence, and an idividual's tactlessness and indiscretion the qualifications for becoming a convenient scapegoat.

Likewise, that the inmates of the Andover workhouse had to gnaw bones for their marrow should be dismissed by Lewis as a matter which had been blown out into 'a fictitious importance' casts a dark shadow on his humanity darkened further by having these thoughts published in the *Hereford Times* anonymously. Again, one wonders why a man of Chadwick's ability was appointed as a secretary and then not allowed to discharge his accepted responsibilities. Lewis claimed the Commissioners did not know about the malpractices going on in workhouses because no one told them which is, of course, a serious condemnation of the manner in which the Commissioners conducted their business. As Commissioners *they should have known*.

The Select Committee, therefore, found serious fault in the conduct of the Commissioners and 'what had begun as the trial of a workhouse official ended in something like a trial of the Poor Law Commission itself'.[91] Thus, in 1847 the Poor Law Commission, established in 1834, came to an end. Its dissolution being brought about in part by disagreements between Chadwick and the Commissioners who were undone by Chadwick's unloved zeal and his own impatience with those who shrank from carrying out his drastic plans of reform.

Lewis confided in George Grote, who shared his interest in the workings of democracy, his fear that the Poor Law Commissioners would always be the scapegoats for the inadequacies of the Poor Law though these had been legislated by Parliament:

> If it should be found on experience that the direct representation of the Poor-Law Commission in Parliament leads to the abandonment of some wholesome regulations which are now in force, and renders the administration less impartial, this change for the worse must be imputed to our parliamentary constitution, and not to the Poor-Law department or the existing administration. Parliament is supreme, and we cannot be better governed than Parliament is willing to govern us. It is vain for a body of subordinate functionaries to attempt to enforce, on such a subject as Poor Laws, opinions which are repudiated by the majority of the sovereign legislature.[92]

In 1847 the Poor Law Commission was replaced by the Poor Law Board, and Lewis was invited to be its secretary.[93] He heard this from the Earl of Clarendon, his brother-in-law, and, until a few weeks ago, President of the Board of Trade.[94] He told Lewis this as the result of an interview he had with the Duke of Bedford who, in turn, had seen *his* brother Lord John Russell, then Prime Minister, about matters. This it seems is how things were done. Lord John Russell wanted to retain Lewis's talent in some other post, but Lewis feared that it was really with the reformed Poor Law that he wanted to retain his services. Lewis noted in his diary:

> Ld J's message was friendly, & he offered, if I desired it, to consider how some employment not connected with the PL Office might be provided for me.[95]

On the next day Lewis wrote to Clarendon, stating that he wished there to be no misunderstandings about the matter, but he considered his connexion with the Poor Law Commission to have terminated. He was anxious, however, that his retirement from the Commission should not be interpreted by anyone, perhaps with Ferrand in mind, as a sign that through the discharge of his official duties as a Commissioner he had lost the confidence of the government. Then, hedging his bets, he continued that as to any offer, he left the matter entirely to the discretion of the government.[96]

> Friday June 25. I gave my letter to Clarendon, when he informed me that Ld John had revised the offer to [John] Lefevre, but he had already told Ld John that I had no wish to be the Secretary to the new PL Commission. I thanked him for having done so, & requested him to confirm what he had said.

> Saturday June 26. Wrote to Lefevre, informing him that I had quite made up my mind to retire finally from the PL Commission, and that with respect of any views of a future connexion with the Dept which he might entertain, he may consider me as entirely out of the question.

A month later, on Monday July 26th, Lewis's connection with the Poor Law Commission ended, and he made his final journey from Kent House to his office, where he had ruled as one of the so-called Somerset House Three for seven years:

> At the office for the last time. Received gratifying letters from Mr Lumley & from all the Clerks, expressing their regret at my quitting the department.

Chadwick became a commissioner to inquire into the health of London, and on the recommendation of Prince Albert was created a CB in 1848, in which year the first Board of Health was formed, with Chadwick as one of the commissioners. Lewis's hope that there 'he may remain quiet'[97] was unduly optimistic. His star, at least, was still rising.

Though Lewis now no longer had any official connection with Poor Law administration, there was still some related unfinished business to be completed. This was the matter of Mr Ferrand's alleged libel. He first sought the professional advice of Sir David Dundas, of the Middle Temple and MP for Sutherland. In 1847 Russell made him Solicitor General. Dundas, whose chambers in King's Bench Walk were famous for their library, shared Lewis's scholarly interests, but declined to act as his counsel because the Andover report would be coming before him as an MP.[98] His second choice was John Meadows White, of Lincoln's Inn Fields, an eminent parliamentary solicitor and an authority on the Poor Law. He was working on the case by the end of August 1846.[99]

A key figure in any litigation between Lewis and Ferrand would be Mott, and White wanted to interview him. Mott, who was auditing on the Isle of Man, was concerned as to why White wished to see him and was worried as to the confidentiality of their conversations:

> Perhaps you will give me an intimation of the subject upon which you wish to see me in order that I may if necessary refer to my memorandum to refresh my memory.
>
> We have heard so much of the violation of private communication that I am afraid to imply any privacy but I should certainly decline communicating in that way. I believe private explanations through a respectable Solicitor are held sacred even in Courts of Law and in this way I should have no hesitation in communicating personally with you.[100]

Meadows White replied reassuringly by return of post:

> I quite concur with you as to the hazard of any communication being called 'confidential' in the present day. Indeed we ought instead of marking our letters 'private' to mark them 'public, being on private affairs'. Nevertheless communications from and to Solicitors are still I believe considered as privileged where certain relations exist between parties, and I do not recollect in the recent breach of confidence cases, that any Solicitor was caught in that delinquency. My object in seeing you is simply this: Mr GC Lewis is advised that in vindication of his official position which has been so coarsely and falsely attacked by Mr Ferrand he should take proceedings in the Court of Queen's Bench next term. The libels complained of are in his letters, published in *The Times* on the 8th and 10th August last. They refer to the Keighley Union in which case your Report and name are so much mixed up and there are some points as to your being retained, or rather directed by Mr Lewis to visit that Union to which it is desirable and necessary you should depose. On these I wish to see you personally that I may prepare the requisite Affidavit. Hence if you can come hither, say, on Friday the 9th October, I shall be glad to see you, and of course will readily meet your expenses. You will see that this is a straight forward matter of business, and has no character of privacy about it except that which all professional men are bound to use in discharging their duty to their Clients. So in this case Mr Lewis is my Client not the Poor law Commissioners whose Solicitors are Messrs Sharpe & Field. I must therefore in accordance with that wholesome rule beg you to consider this communication as confidential on the above footing.[101]

On Friday 2nd October Meadows White came down to Harpton, where, as Lewis noted in his diary, 'he dined & slept and gave me the proposed brief in Ferrand's case'. Mott was still nervous about confidentiality, and Meadows White repeated earlier reassurances:

I can only repeat in reply to your remarks about confidential communications that all professional communications given in confidence are sacred. I say 'are' when perhaps it would be more correct to say 'ought to be'. The two ought to be identical, but in these days are not, so as I said in my former letter I do not wonder at your precaution. As regards Mr Lewis or myself, all I request is the ordinary precaution of not divulging what may pass so as to frustrate the very object which I desire to attain, namely, a legal investigation of the charges against Mr Lewis made by Mr Ferrand, as far as you are concerned they are that Mr Lewis instructed you to make a false Report, and that you having made one Mr Lewis knowing it to be false, placed it in Sir James Graham's hands, for the purpose of deceiving the legislature and the Country. Now the fact I wish deposed to by you, always supposing that it is the fact, is that you received no instructions to make a false report, that you did not make one, and that your Report was a true and faithful Report on the evidence before you. These are simple points and do not appear to me to require any great extent of confidential communication between us and I presume that for the sake of truth and justice if such be the facts, you not only would not object, but would desire to aid in elucidating the truth, and promoting the ends of justice by making an Affidavit setting forth what you know on the subject.[102]

Meadows White saw Mott in London on 19th October, and in reporting to Lewis shows that he was not without some anxiety about the case, urging Lewis to 'unlock his memory':

I had 4 hours conversation with him on many points & especially of course on this case ... his recollection was unshaken as to the accuracy of his report according to the statement he had sent to you & the affidavit prepared from the statement he was prepared to make with some additions negativing altogether any knowledge of Mr Ferrand until he saw him in the Keighley Union Committee room when his report was declared substantially true.

Mr Mott since questioning had searched some papers at Chelsea, not before looked at, & among them he found, I am glad to say, the original letter of which I also send a copy as of his reply. It explains the whole matter & shews that the Commission had received private information about Keighley & therefore ordered the investigation, & as you wrote to him privately it accounts for his asking you whether his report should be private or publick & your direction it should be the latter shews that there was no substantial concealment contemplated ...

It now seems to me of great importance that with these keys before you, you should unlock your memory so as to recollect by whom the private information was given. Mr Ferrand will swear it was Sir J Graham. I have no doubt it was either Mr Ellis or some other of the Keighley Guardians.[103]

Barnes Peacock was engaged as Lewis's counsel. Though not yet a QC, he had made his name in 1844 as counsel for Daniel O'Connell in the latter's successful appeal to the House of Lords against his conviction for creating discontent and disaffection amongst the Queen's Irish subjects.[104] On 26th October Meadows White sent Lewis an outline of Peacock's proposed argument against Ferrand:

The fact that Sir James did not know of Mr Mott's visit to Keighley, & his Report till after they were made, are stated by Sir James himself, for this you will see in the libels themselves, for Mr Ferrand fastens his attack on you upon your saying that Sir James suggested Mr Mott should go to Keighley, which he observes is in direct opposition to what Sir James had himself declared. I assume that a rule *nisi* for a criminal information will be granted upon these affidavits, & it will then be for Mr Ferrand to answer them. If he do not, then the rule will be made absolute & proof of the handwriting & publication will be required on your part when the case comes on for trial. He may of course put any facts in issue by his pleading, but I do not see how he can prove his main allegations of your motives & intentions.[105]

Lewis's diary records the continuing progress of the case:

Saturday Oct 31. K[ent]H[ouse]. Swore my affidavit in Ferrand's case. Office [at Somerset House[.

Monday Nov 2. KH. Office. Obtained a recte nisi for a criminal information against Mr Ferrand.

A Rule *Nisi* was made in favour of Lewis on 2nd November 1846, and he was to illustrate that he had cause of complaint against

Ferrand on 24th of the same month. Meadows White encouraged Lewis as to the justice of his cause, as one might expect. He felt that though Ferrand's Counsel and Solicitor would probably advise him to retract: 'Mr Ferrand is of too obstinate a character to listen to rational advice'.[106] He then went on to underline the fallacies in Ferrand's allegations. In his first letter to *The Times*, of 8th August 1846, Ferrand admitted that a Committee of the House of Commons had found his charge against Sir James Graham that he 'took steps to procure a report which was false' to be 'calumnious and unfounded'. He also admitted this in his second letter, of 10th August, thereby, in the opinion of Meadows White, confessing that he was, by his own admission, a convicted calumniator in respect of the very charge he was making against Sir James Graham. This, however, did not prevent him from making 'a like charge in the grossest terms against Mr Lewis'.

In Meadows White's opinion the key to all Mr Ferrand's attacks was Mott's Report on the Keighley Union of 23rd April 1842:

> This Report alleged by Mr Ferrand to be false, a Committee of the House of Commons by their Report ... found to be '*substantially true*'. Mr Lewis in his Affidavit speaks of it as being in all its material statements & allegations true. Sir James Graham deposes to having suggested that Sir J Walsham should test its truth by an investigation of Keighley, and Sir J Walsham refers in his Affidavit to his Report where he states that he went to verify that of Mr Mott which he finds to be substantially true, and also states that the Poor Law Commissioners deemed it advisable that he should go to Keighley for that purpose. But Mr Mott speaks to its being true whilst the Committee of the House of Commons and the other Affidavits speak in a more qualified tone.
>
> The inference may be drawn that if only substantially true it is not wholly so & so far as it is not substantially true it must be false, whilst the precaution of Sir J Graham & the Poor Law Commissioners in verifying Mr Mott's Report may support the inference that its accuracy was doubted.[107]

Whilst the convolutions of this argument may seem arcane to those inexperienced in the subtleties of jurisprudence, their fallacy was plain to Meadows White:

> The reply is obvious, that this anxiety to verify the report forbids the other inference that either Sir J Graham or Mr Lewis desired to procure a false one, or to palm it off if false as true

on the legislature and the Country. And the Committee of the House of Commons, if their Report be examined, will be found to have declared it true so far as the facts are concerned though wrong in some of its inferences as for instance when he refers to the order to employ the Attornies in turn, the fact was so but the inference that it was 'a Job' is negatived by the Committee.[108]

Finally, there was the important consideration, at least in Meadows White's eyes, that Ferrand's conduct was indisputably unbecoming of a gentleman:

Surely for a member of Parliament to vent his slanderous attacks against a functionary of no ordinary importance in the public prints, to raise the popular cry against him in his character of a public officer charged with a high and onerous duty by the state, to charge him with malversation of Office and appeal to the House of Commons against him, the only tribunal which has the power by an address to the Crown to remove him from an office of high trust and emolument, is so gross and scandalous offence that the libeller ought not to protect himself by accidental mistakes or discrepancies on comparatively trifling points on the part of the Complainant or to be allowed to shirk from producing the proofs of which he makes so vaunting a boast in his letters to the Editor of *The Times*.[109]

But Meadows White concludes that Lewis need have no anxieties with Barnes Peacock at the helm:

The case is however left with perfect confidence in the hands of Counsel, by whom no doubt its great importance to Mr Lewis both individually & as an Officer of the State will be fully appreciated.[110]

Meadows White was right and on 24th November Lewis noted in his diary that the 'Rule against Mr Ferrand was made absolute by the Queen's Bench'. All was now set for the great confrontation, for which Lewis was still not completely at ease despite the best endeavours of Messrs Barnes Peacock and Meadows White, and he had to admit to his father: 'All the press is with Ferrand.'[111] This was certainly the case with *The Times*.

A new cloud, however, appeared on Lewis's horizon, and once again it was connected with Mott. The day before Lewis had his Rule *recte*, Mott wrote to Meadows White from Rochdale. His mood was solemn:

The facts which I am about to name to you are, in my opinion so serious, that extreme caution is desirable. I should not have recurred to them now, but, that I know that efforts will be made to bring them before the public. I considered the particulars of such importance, that I named them to Mr Coode with a request that they might be confidentially named to the Commissioners by him. I understood that he brought the matter privately under the notice of 2 of the Commissioners, who did not, I believe, consider them deserving of notice. There I should have let the matter rest. But finding that Mr Coode had named them to Mr Chadwick, and that Mr Chadwick had mentioned the subject to Mr Parker, and Mr Parker, when I met him in London, in October last, having stated that he should inquire into the subject in order to bring it before a Committee of the House of Commons, I thought it right to name it to you, in order that Mr Lewis may if he thinks proper enquire into the transaction.

The following are the particulars:

In the summer, I think of 1843, Capt Britten, whom I had known from having purchased a Freehold property of his family, who lives, or did live, at St John's Wood, whose brother is a respectable wine merchant in the City, called on me one day, when I happened to be at Somerset House; and stated that he wished me to give him some information respecting the salary and other allowances of the Assistant Poor Law Commissioners: after I had satisfied his enquiries, I asked him for what purpose he wanted the information; when he informed me, it was about purchasing an appointment of Assistant Poor Law Commissioner, I asked him if he was aware of the serious consequences of such a proceeding; he said, yes, but he had managed it so that no person would know anything about it. The only difficulty, he felt he saw was, as to raising the money which was stipulated to be £2400. I think he said he could manage £1600 or £1800, and he thought he should be able to get the difference of his brother. He then left, and said he would see me again in a few days; accordingly, about a week after, he called again in Somerset House, when I again saw him. He then informed me that he thought he should be able to manage it; and in reply to my enquiries he stated, that the money [the £2400] was to be placed in a Banker's hands in the names of the contracting parties, to be drawn out by their joint signatures as soon as his appointment was gazetted. I left London for Lancashire soon afterwards, and heard no more of it.[112]

Meadows White seems to have taken the matter up with George Coode who, in turn, referred it to Lewis as a Commissioner, who, it seems, once again had difficulty in 'unlocking his memory':

> I am much obliged to you for your information about Capt Britten. The circumstances must certainly have made very little impression upon me at the time, for I cannot say that I have the slightest recollection of it. It is to be regretted that the matter was not cleared up during Capt Britten's life, as I fear it may now be difficult or impossible to get at the truth. We shall, however, take such steps as are now in our power for investigating the origin of the statement.[113]

There is no further mention of the late Capt Britten's attempts to buy a public office in the Lewis Papers. Nor is there any mention of Mr Jenkin Jones and his involvement in the same activity. *The Times*, however, in August 1846 dwelt upon the matter at length. Jenkin Jones had been appointed as an actuary in the Poor Law Office in 1836 at a salary of £200 pa. In 1842, being hard up, he asked an old friend to lend him £130, for which in return he would find the friend's friend a position as a clerk in the office. Unfortunately, the friend's friend 'was subsequently found to be incompetent and was discarded'. Jones embarrassed by the way things had turned out returned the £130 he had loaned. In December 1843, 15 months after Jones himself had left Somerset House, he was visited first by Hugh Owen,[114] a clerk at Somerset House, and then by Cornewall Lewis who, according to the account in *The Times*:

> personally examined him twice on this transaction, without telling him he intended to found upon it a charge of misdemeanour. At the end of the second interview when Mr Lewis had pumped out of him all that he wanted, he astonished the unfortunate statist with the question; 'Now, Mr Jones will you join the Commissioners in the prosecution?' *ie*, we presume 'Will you, to save yourself, turn Queen's evidence against your old friend?'

Jones, having considered his predicament, went to see George Coode, and then applied unsuccessfully for another interview with the Commissioners. This moved him to write to Sir James Graham himself at the Home Office:

> He pointed out that Mr Lewis, as well as the other Commissioners, had been in the constant practice of violating

that provision in the act of Parliament which required that nothing should be done except by a board consisting of at least two Commissioners, and to exercise all the powers of the Commissioners, giving directions, conducting correspondence, and issuing various orders under seal of the board, with his own name affixed at the time, and the name of another Commissioner fraudulently added. Having then explained to Sir James the charge brought against himself, he compared the two, and intimated, clearly enough, that he would take reprisals if he found himself hardly used.

There was, of course, nothing new in these allegations, and one can see the shadow of Chadwick cast over them, for he himself, as has already been seen, had made similar accusations. *The Times* was well aware of the folly of Jones's actions:

Of course, Mr Jones, having once assumed so hostile a position, ought to have kept the enemy at arm's length, and done nothing without his lawyer at his elbow.

There was another interview with Coode at the Poor Law Office, at which Hugh Owen was also present, and Coode informed Jones:

Unless you are determined to go to trial, I am authorized by Mr Lewis to state to you that it was far from the wish of the Commissioners to injure you, and that they would not press the matter further if you would agree to withdraw your plea of not guilty, and plead guilty.

At the end of the interview, Owen, 'his personal friend' congratulated Jones 'on his escape from an embarrassing position', and informed him that he could withdraw his plea of not guilty, and substitute one of guilty without any publicity, and he could rest assured he would not be brought up for judgement. Jones accordingly pleaded guilty, despite the efforts of his lawyer to dissuade him from doing so 'and having called him a "madman" for trusting Mr Lewis and the Commissioners'.

A week later, on 14th June 1844, Owen called on Jones to tell him that there that there appeared to be some mistake in his memorandum of the interview of the 7th June, as he there supposed he would not to be brought up for judgement, and that Coode wanted to see him on the subject. Accordingly, on that same day Jones called on Coode, who explained that the Commissioners did not mean, in their authorized message of the 7th June, that he was not to be brought up for a judgement, but that a judgement of some slight sort would be passed upon him.

The Times went on to explain things:

> What the commissioners were working at was, of course, that Mr J Jones should resign himself wholly into their hands and accept the fullest measure of punishment with so entire a resignation as to disqualify him for the disclosures he had threatened. They were in his power either if they made no terms whatever with him, when of course he would be under no obligation, or if they let him off so entirely that he would be able to boast the victory which he had won over their consciousness of their own bad case. To avoid both those courses, to punish him severely with his own forced or cheated consent, was their design, and for the present they succeeded. They cajoled him into surrendering his case point by point, and then having bound him hand and foot, they delivered him to the executioner.

Jones submitted another statement for Coode's approval which 'Owen returned to him with notes in pencil, *suggesting the omission of Mr Lewis's name as the sender of the authorized message, and of Mr Owen's name as present at the first interview between him and Mr Coode*'. (Italics of *The Times*.)

On the 23rd November, the same day on which Jones filed his affidavit, '*he was brought up for judgement, and sentenced to 12 months' imprisonment*'. (Italics of *The Times*.) According to *The Times*, at Jones's trial the Attorney-General[115] addressed Jones's solicitor to this effect:

> *The Commissioners do not wish the case to go on; the Attorney-General does not wish it to go on; but Sir J Graham does, that man is a brute.*

In May 1845, a petition, 'numerously and respectably signed by merchants and other persons of influence in the city' was unsuccessfully presented on Jones's behalf at the Home Office. On the 10th July following Jones informed Coode:

> The matter cannot and shall not rest here; I hope to hear from you by Tuesday at the latest. If I do not, I shall consider that I have nothing to expect from the Commissioners.

The Times considered that:

> The opinion of her Majesty's present Attorney-General on the subject will be read with peculiar interest. Though an extra-judicial judgement, it is very decisive, and it would be difficult to

show that the facts do not bear it out. Happily, however, for Mr J Jones the game had been carried a little too far; so far as to release him of all obligation. He was now at liberty to say what he chose. Accordingly he repeated to Mr Secretary Coode in a few simple and emphatic words the threat he had administered to Sir James Graham, and *he was immediately liberated*.[116]

The episode had not, of course, escaped Ferrand's attention, though it was sometime before he was able to bring it to the attention of the House:

> Sir James Graham ... then defended himself from having dealt unfairly with the case of Jenkin Jones. In that case he had acted under the advice of the then law-officers of the crown, Sir F Pollock[117] and Sir F Thesiger. He knew not what had passed between Mr Jenkin Jones and the Poor Law Commissioners. He only knew as Secretary of State that Mr Jones had pleaded guilty to the charge of selling public office, and that he had been sentenced in consequence to a year's imprisonment; and he should have been guilty of a dereliction of his duty if he had remitted his punishment until he had suffered an imprisonment of some duration.[118]

It is not surprising that Frankland Lewis advised his son to contend for himself and not fight Graham's battles.[119] Lewis could also rely upon support in the House from his brother-in-law, Charles Pelham Villiers, MP for Wolverhampton, 1835–98:

> Mr Villiers observed that the able and manly manner in which Sir J Graham had met this charge precluded any other person from entering into it. He defended Mr Lewis from the charge of entrapping Mr Jenkin Jones into a plea of not guilty, and applied some provocatory language to Mr Ferrand for making that charge, which in other times would have called down the animadversion of the Speaker.[120]

The matter, however, of the *Queen v Ferrand Esqre MP* was due to be heard in the Hilary term of 1847 and on 15th January Lewis 'entered into recognisances to prosecute Ferrand'.[121] So Ferrand knew Lewis was now in earnest, though other things interested Lewis equally, and two days later he noted in his Diary: 'My article on Quarantine [appeared] in yesterday's *Economist*'. *The Times*, however, once again spoke out in defence of Ferrand, suggesting that Lewis had entered into this action 'for the purpose of intimidating the defendant in the discharge of his duties as a Member of Parliament'.[122] Meadows wrote to the solicitors of *The Times*, admitting there had been substantial delays in the matter coming to court, delays which he considered to have been unavoidable. He was going to make no attempt 'to refute the charge of attempting to intimidate, which you as a professional man must know to be utterly groundless', for in his opinion the boot was on the other foot and he was writing:

> to complain of the attempts to intimidate our Client and ourselves by some articles which have appeared in *The Times* since the rule was made absolute ... That *The Times* should adopt such a course, forgetting the wholesome and acknowledged rule that the power and influence of the press should never be used to intercept the course of justice, is both a cause of surprize and affords ample grounds for complaint.[123]

Indeed, *The Times* itself had been responsible for some the delay by its tardiness in supplying evidence of identification as to the authorship of the two letters complained of, *ie* of the 6th and 10th August 1846:

> And as all we ask is the ordinary fair play of letting the case take its due course, we trust to your influence with *The Times*, as your Clients, to secure this for us. We assure you as regards the case, Mr Lewis is now in the hands of his Counsel, and the case will neither be accelerated nor retarded by extraneous pressure.[124]

On 28th January Ferrand spoke again in the Commons on the matter and next day *The Times* in its editorial gave him the support he was denied at Westminster:

> The Devon Commission attained a hitherto unexampled success. It produced three very thick folios, which produced in their turn nothing, or worse than nothing. The Andover Union Committee produced two stupendous folios, and there it stops, or there it would stop if nobody came forward to push on the matter. It seems to be considered as much the function of a committee to make a huge report as it was the work of a Pharaoh to build a pyramid. In fact, the report is to be the tomb of the subject. The Poor Law Commissioners and their illustrious chief hoped to rest under the load of monumental paper. Indeed, it requires no small heart for a man to set about disinterring the crimes of the Commission under so vast a pile. Happily, however, we possess in the hon. Member for

> Knaresborough a man who makes nothing of a mass consisting of a thousand documents, and some thirty thousand questions and answers ... On a subject which would overpower most men, he is able to secure for several hours the full attention of a full House to an impassioned speech charged with laborious detail and bold accusation.[125]

Again, this made little impact upon Lewis, who simply recorded in his Diary:

> Thursday 28th January, Kent House. Debate on Ferrand's motion.

Little sleep, it seems, had been lost. A fortnight after Ferrand's motion, its contents came to the notice of Sir John Walsham, who had been, hitherto, too busy to read newspapers. However, he was not now too busy to write to Cornewall Lewis:

> I yesterday read the report published in the *Times* Newspaper of the 29th *ulto* of Mr Ferrand's speech in the House of Commons on the preceding evening (which I had not previously had leisure to do); and I find that, in this speech, Mr Ferrand is represented to have stated, *inter alia*, that 'Sir John Walsham was employed to go to town, at the suggestion of the late Secretary for the Home Department, to visit the [Keighley] Union, that he got instructions to draw up a report as to the horrible state in the workhouses, which was to be handed to the Secretary for the Home Department, and that he was to come down upon him [Mr Ferrand] with another slashing attack which he did.
>
> ... The object I have in view in troubling you with this letter [is] once more for about the tenth or twentieth time, to give the flattest contradiction possible in decent language, to Mr Ferrand's pertinacious recitation of his absurd story about my having been sent down to Keighley 'to draw up a flaming report', in order to enable Sir James Graham 'to crush an independent member of parliament' when in this identical 'flaming report' it is shown, if I mistake not, distinctly, that I inspected the Keighley and Bingley poorhouses solely in consequence of a statement made to me by the parishes themselves, and not at all in consequence of any instructions from the Commissioners ....[126]

This, of course was in contradiction to Sir James Graham's deposition that Walsham went to Keighley at the suggestion of Graham and with the approval of the Commissioners.[127] Unfortunately Walsham had not filed the relevant paperwork to prove the matter:

> When a person receives yearly above 5000 letters, reports, and official documents, and knows that his own reports are registered and filed, he will possibly discover, as I did, at the end of two or three years, that no particular advantage is to be gained by filling trunk after trunk with papers of which nine tenths are practically useless.[128]

Though it had been Ferrand's expressed hope in the January debate that 'as Sir J Graham and Mr Lewis were now both pledged to enter the witness-box, … the trial would take place immediately',[129] there were still delays and it was not until 20th March that Lewis's lawyers received Ferrand's plea.[130] In May Lewis was assuring Abraham Hayward, QC, 'whose dinners in his chambers at the Temple were famous for choiceness of fare and distinction of company'[131] that any conspiracy beween himself and Graham to injure Ferrand existed only in the imagination.[132] A few days later Sir James Graham was congratulating Lewis that the recent 'satisfactory vote in Parliament is a very strong demonstration in favour both of the Poor Law itself and of the past administration of it'.[133] The vote concerned the introduction by Sir George Grey, the new Home Secretary, of the bill which became the Poor Law Board Act. But still matters tarried, so that when in July Ferrand lost his seat in Parliament and Lewis began his Parliamentary career, the latter sought the advice of Sir Frederick Thesiger, FRS, DCL, the Attorney General 'who advised me to persist in the proceeding against Mr Ferrand'.[134]

Towards the end of August Lewis 'received a letter from Hayward relative to the Ferrand prosecution and answered it'.[135] Abraham Hayward was perhaps suggesting that Ferrand was prepared to retract his letters. Certainly, when Lewis met Hayward at the Athenaeum in early November, he was told that

> Ferrand was willing to retract his letters, & to express his regret they had been published. He said that Ferrand. had promised to instruct his counsel to this effect, & he authorized me to make this communication to Thesiger.[136]

Thesiger thought a retraction by Ferrand would be much more satisfactory than a successful prosecution,[137] and Lewis recorded the subsequent course of events in his Diary:

Thursday, November 11th. Received a letter from Thesiger approving of accepting Ferrand's apology.

Friday November 12th. Received from Hayward proposed form of Ferrand's apology.

Wednesday November 17th. Saw Meadows White & Hayward & made the final arrangement of the insertion of Ferrand's retraction in the newspapers.

Ferrand's resolve had cracked, and on the following day, 18th November, there appeared this statement in *The Times*:

We are authorized to say that the matter has been arranged through intervention of friends: Lord John Manners acting for Mr Ferrand and Mr Hayward for Mr Lewis; and the charges in question have been withdrawn.

The following is the form of withdrawal definitively agreed upon by Lord John Manners[138] and Mr Hayward, on behalf of the parties respectively:

Memorandum

Mr Ferrand withdraws the letters which constitute the alleged libels in this case, and also the pleas pleaded in justification of them. Both letters were written under feelings of considerable irritation and excitement, when Mr Ferrand was suffering from illness, and had no opportunity of consulting with his friends. Before writing the first [of August 6th 1846] he had received information, which at that time, and for sometime afterwards he saw no reason to distrust, leading him to conclude that Mr Lewis had co-operated with Sir James Graham to lower him in public estimation; and he wrote the second letter [of August 10th 1846] under a *bona fide*, though erroneous impression, that the mistake into which Mr Lewis fell in his evidence, and which was the sole cause of the second letter being written, was an intentional mis-statement. On full and calm inquiry, and after consulting with his friends, Mr Ferrand is now convinced that he acted hastily and without accurate information in both instances. He therefore withdraws the charges contained in the letters so far as they affect Mr Lewis, who will stand precisely as if they had never been written; and Mr Ferrand regrets that he ever wrote and published them.

In his time Ferrand worked hard for the Ten Hours Factory Act of 1847, the abolition of the Truck System, and for the reform of the

New Poor Law. He supported Disraeli's Young England party, and sought to restore the influence in politics of the squirearchy of which he was part. He was a pioneer of field-garden allotments and in 1844 established a Cricket Club in his constituency at Cottingley Bridge. He tried unsuccessfully to re-enter Parliament in 1851 by standing for Aylesbury, but did represent Devonport 1863–66. He doggedly persevered in all his undertakings, strenuously supporting the agricultural interests, and opposing the manufacturers who turned the River Aire into a sewer, giving evidence in Leeds in 1866 to the Commission of the Pollution of Rivers. That same year he was elected the inaugural President of the Bradford Working Men's Conservative Association. He died in 1889 when his will was unsuccessfully contested on the grounds that he was of unsound mind at its execution.

The Ferrand episode, however, did little to diminish Lewis's intellectual energy, and in between consultations with his lawyers, and his duties as a Commissioner, he worked on articles for the *Edinburgh Review* and the *Economist*. Since 1829 the *Review* was edited by Macvey Napier, FRS, and Carlyle, JS Mill, Thackeray, and Nassau Senior were amongst Lewis's fellow contributors. The *Economist* was founded by James Wilson, a politician and political economist, and first appeared in September 1843. Its consistent advocacy of the repeal of the corn laws, and its belief in free trade were entirely consonant with Lewis's own sentiments.

Lewis's diary shows that both Napier and Wilson ran their respective journals with enviable efficiency and no problems of peer review:

> Saturday December 5th 1846. Sent to Macvey Napier my article on Local Taxes for the *Ed Rev*.

> Monday December 14th 1846. Returned proof of my article to Macvey Napier.

> Monday January 11th 1847. Sent to Wilson an article for the *Economist* on Quarantine.

> Sunday January 17th 1847. My article on Quarantine in yesterday's *Economist*.

Lewis took pride in his writing and was not slow in letting his friends know of his latest publications. He had new responsibilities as well in the form of his three step-children, and he told George Grote about both:

> There is an article of mine on Local taxation in the last number of the *Edinburgh Review*. We have taken Villiers Lister from Mr Youldon's and sent him to Harrow this school time. He seems very happy at the change.[139]

Villiers Lister was now fourteen and Lewis himself took him to Harrow to enter him on 20th January 1847. The school was convenient by train both for Kent House and Grove Mill, near Watford, and since 1844 had been undergoing a renaissance under its new headmaster, Charles John Vaughan. On Vaughan's arrival there were only sixty or so pupils on the roll and the discipline was weak. But within two years, it is said, he had raised the numbers to over two hundred, and poured fresh life into the studies and discipline of his pupils. During Villiers Lister's stay at Harrow few schools enjoyed greater academic prestige, and Vaughan 'in his dealings both with boys and masters he happily joined firmness with consideration, and no headmaster, Arnold excepted, gathered round him a more gifted band of scholars or colleagues'.[140] All this would have met with Lewis's approval, though other aspects of Vaughan's regime, had he known of them, would not, Vaughan's relationships with his so-called 'doves' lacking the innocence expected of schoolmasters.

Events, especially the Ferrand affair and public and parliamentary debates, in which Ferrand played a prominent part,[141] on reforming the Poor Law, did, however, take a toll on Lewis's health, as his diaries show:

> Saturday February 6th 1847. In bed till late in the evening from illness.
>
> Sunday March 16th 1847. Headache.
>
> Tuesday March 30th 1847. Staid at home on account of cough.

Chapter Three:
Parliament

The general election, which in 1847 saw Ferrand's departure from Parliament, saw Lewis's arrival. Kedgwin Hoskins, who, as a Whig, had represented the County of Hereford since 1831, now, at the age of 72, announced his intention of not standing in the forthcoming general election and Lewis, jobless, discussed his own prospects of winning the seat with Sir George Clive of Perrystone Court, who had been an Assistant Poor Law Commissioner 1836–69.[1] Politics were a prominent part of the Lewis family tradition, going back to 1547 when Thomas Lewes (*sic*) of Harpton became MP for the Radnor boroughs. Lewis's father, Thomas Frankland Lewis, was MP for the County of Radnor 1828–34, becoming a Privy Councillor, Vice-President of the Board of Trade, and Treasurer of the Navy. Frankland Lewis, however, was a Tory and his son George offered himself to the constituents of Herefordshire as a Liberal. This involved no dramatic change of political sympathies, and he moved in radical circles in London before he joined the Poor Law Commission. It is significant, too, that his Tory father was appointed chairman of the Poor Law Commission in 1834 by a Liberal administration.

The decision to stand made, at least Lady Duff Gordon was taken by surprize. She learned the news at Kent House where she was attending a happening arranged by Lewis's mother-in-law, Lady Theresa Villiers:

> We went for a short time to Lady Theresa, who had a Child's Ball and all Herefordshire assembled! I understand that George is going to stand for Herefordshire in the place of Kedgwin Hoskyns![2]

The week following his meeting with Sir George Clive, John Murray published Lewis's pamphlet justifying the Poor Law Commissioners: *Letters addressed … to the Secretary of State respecting the Transaction of the Business of the Commission.*[3] Two days later he was in his office discussing his election plans with Frederick Bodenham, the Hereford solicitor, who lived in St John Street, and who was to act as his agent.[4] Besides being a solicitor, with his offices in the High Street, he was also treasurer of the county of Hereford. Lewis had other matters in hand as well, and it being a holiday at the office on 25th May he felt that was an appropriate occasion to begin an article on Homer. The following Sunday he kept holy by writing to his publisher John Murray about a *Dictionary of Ancient Physics*, then on Thursday next he wrote an article for the *Economist* on the Poor Law.[5]

On Friday, loyally assisted by his brother Gilbert, who was Rector of the family living of Monnington on Wye, Lewis spent a day at Kent House writing electioneering letters to his constituents and to the Hereford papers, and on Saturday it was back to working on his article for the *Economist* on the Poor Law.[6]

Lewis told Head:

> The number of voters for the county exceeds 7,000, and it is difficult to make much impression on so large a body without giving some time to the work … The yeomanry of the county are numerous and independent, and are a good deal under the influence of the small proprietors. Fortunately, however, there is no subject on which they feel strongly.[7]

On the 28th July Lewis with wife Theresa and step-daughter Alice travelled down to Hereford by train and coach and settled in at the Green Dragon where he dined with his agent Bodenham, the High Sheriff and his Chaplain joining them. This made it quite a family occasion, for the High Sheriff was his cousin, Sir Velters Cornewall, Bart, of Moccas Court. A man of violent temper which eventually gave way to insanity, Velters Cornewall died, unmarried, in a private asylum in 1868. The Sheriff's Chaplain was Lewis's brother, Gilbert.[8] Next day he attended the Assizes and served on the Grand Jury, with Sir Hungerford Hoskins, of Harewood, as Foreman, to decide which cases should proceed to trial, and afterwards dined with the Judges.[9]

Using the Green Dragon as his base, Lewis made himself known to the magistrates, the bishop at the palace, and the farmers at the market. He went to the cathedral and All Saints' church, not only to worship, but to meet congregations as well. He canvassed in Kington, Leominster, Ledbury, Bromyard, and Ross, attending on fair days to meet more people, and in the outlying villages.

Despite his own clerical connections, the local clergy tended to look upon Lewis askance. One of these was the Revd Joseph Barker, MA, the long serving Chaplain of the County Gaol and the Infirmary, and who lived at Moorfield Place.[10] He wrote to Lewis expressing the opinion that the course taken by Peel in his Maynooth Endowment Act,[11] by which the Roman Catholic Church in Ireland would considerably benefit, was both sinful and dangerous, and he wanted to be acquainted with Lewis's views upon the matter.[12] Lewis in his reply argued that the fact that the government helped different denominations financially did not necessarily mean it agreed with their teaching. He assured Barker that there was no immediate prospect of the Roman Catholic clergy in Ireland being endowed, but went on to express his conviction that they should, nevertheless, be assisted from local funds. This was because the position of the Roman Catholic clergy in Ireland was different from that of English dissenting ministers, since the former were the clergy of the great majority and the latter were not.[13] This did not satisfy the Protestant Mr Barker who replied that because of Lewis's latitudinarian principles, he had to decline to give him his electoral support.[14]

Canvassing caused a resurgence of what Lewis called 'his ancient pulmonary enemy' and in his diary he records how, at morning and night, he had symptoms of haemorrhage from the lungs. He put it down to the heat and standing in the sun whilst he canvassed, and refused to have a doctor, whilst admitting he would have to do less, perhaps for a week. In a way all this effort was quite unnecessary: the county was represented by three members and there were only three candidates, though it was rumoured that the Chartist leader Feargus O'Connor and factory reformer Richard Oastler, both old opponents of his, were going to stand against him.[15]

The other candidates were Francis Richard Haggit, and Joseph Bailey, junior. Haggitt lived at Belmont and was the only son of an Anglican clergyman who was chaplain to George III.[16] He assumed the surname of Wegg Prosser in 1849, and a year later he married Lady Harriet Catherine Somers-Cocks, a granddaughter of Earl Somers of Eastnor Castle. Wegg Prosser relinquished his career in politics in 1852, embraced Roman Catholicism, and it was largely by his generosity that the Benedictine abbey at Belmont, near Hereford, was built. Its foundation stone was laid in 1854 and both church and its attendant monastic buildings were completed in 1858. There were further extensions in 1860 and 1882. Lewis's aunt, Lady Duff Gordon, seems to have shared the views of the Revd Joseph Barker, and was not entirely convinced that Belmont abbey was a good thing when she saw the new buildings in 1859:

> Went to see the outside of the Roman Catholic Church & College & School House building by Mr Prosser at Belmont. Very handsome, a most unfortunate Building for this neighbourhood, for evidently there are more pounds than his expended on it, & no doubt wily Jesuits are concerned in it, and many Roman Catholics will be brought about the Neighbourhood.[17]

Lewis's sympathies with Roman Catholics were broader than those he felt for Anglican Tractarians and Puseyites, and this, before long, was to influence the course of his political career in Herefordshire.

Joseph Bailey, junior, of Easton Court, was the eldest son of Sir Joseph Bailey, Bart, of Glanusk Park, Breconshire. Educated at Brasenose College, Oxford, he unsuccessfully contested Monmouthshire in 1835 and 1837, the due reward perhaps for being precocious, but he was successful at Sudbury in Suffolk, which he represented from 1837–41. He was a member for Herefordshire from 1841 until 1850, when, aged 38, he 'died after a long-suffering illness'. Though a strong protectionist, Lewis thought him 'a perfectly honourable and straightforward colleague'.[18]

On Wednesday 4th August 1847 Lewis got his reward for all his electioneering:

> I went with my father & Lady Lewis, Gilbert & Mr Davies[19] to join the meeting of my supporters at the Whitecross. Rode from thence to the County Hall for the proceedings for the election of 3 members for the County. There was no opposition, & no other speech delivered. The return was declared and afterwards I was chaired round the town, & in the afternoon dined at a public dinner of my supporters at the Green Dragon.[20]

Next day he wrote to Head:

> My election passed off quietly yesterday, notwithstanding the alarms of Feargus O'Connor and Oastler. Nothing could go off better or more peaceably than the whole affair.[21]

But the Poor Law was still in his blood and he hoped Head would continue to champion his cause:

> I hope you will write the Settlement article in the *Edinburgh Review*. I see no necessity for making it very long. *You might begin with a reference to my article* [our italics] on Local Taxation, at the end of which the subject is adverted to.[22]

Exhausted, Lewis was confined to the Green Dragon for the next three days with headaches, but visited the inmates of the County Gaol before returning to Harpton. Lady Duff Gordon, down from London for her annual tour of Herefordshire enjoying in turn the hospitality of her many local kinsmen, thought her nephew looked remarkably well:

> Tuesday August 9th 1847, Harpton. George, Theresa, & little Alice Lister came from Foxley,[23] all their duties duly performed to attending the last Election Dinner at Hereford yesterday. George very well & very comfortable in his new MPship.

At Harpton there was rejoicing on two accounts, for Lewis's father, Thomas Frankland Lewis re-entered Parliament in 1847 as MP for the Radnor boroughs. He too was unopposed and there now lived under the same roof at Harpton two MPs, father and son, but of opposing parties, a fact which seemed to do little to disrupt domestic harmony.

Lewis attended New Radnor church on Sunday morning, 15th August, and on his return home found a letter waiting for him from the Prime Minister, Lord John Russell, announcing his intention of offering him a Secretaryship in the Board of Control before the new session.[24] In November Lewis informed George Grote that he had not yet completely made up his mind to accept it, though it was obvious the fact it was not very laborious was in his eyes a favourable consideration:

> The Government have offered me one of the Secretaryships of the Board of Control, and I have virtually accepted it, but I have not yet been up to London to see Hobhouse.[25] I do not apprehend that the office is a very laborious one. I hear that Jones Loyd[26] was favourable to the Government interference with the Bank, but I have still to learn how bankrupt merchants are to be made richer by more bits of paper.[27]

He was still more a philosopher than a politician, and that his parliamentary duties were not too laborious influenced his decision to accept them. Even so he thought he should gain a better knowledge of his constituency, and where better than on the local race course?:

> Tuesday Aug 24. Left Harpton, & travelled to Hereford. Found Villiers & Therese who had arrived on the same day from London, at the Green Dragon.
>
> Wednesday Aug 25. Attended at the Hereford Races, as steward with Mr Haggitt as my colleague. Afterwards presided at the ordinary, & went to the play in the evening.[28] Slept at the Green Dragon.
>
> Thursday Aug 26. Attended again at the races & at the ordinary where Haggitt presided. Afterwards at the Ball. Slept at the Green Dragon.

Lewis was opposed to protectionism and approved of the repeal of the Corn Laws in 1846. His constituency was, of course, predominantly agricultural, and he felt the need to mend his fences before taking his seat in the new session. The harvest brought with it agricultural shows which the county's new MP assiduously attended and Lewis told Grote:

> A short time ago I made an excursion into Herefordshire to attend some agricultural societies, and to deliver my sentiments on subjects of which I was considerably ignorant.[29]

The first society to hear his sentiments upon such subjects was at Bromyard, followed by Leominster:

> Wednesday Oct 13. Went in train with Theresa from Grove Mill to Worcester & thence in a fly to Bromyard. Slept at the Falcon Inn.
>
> Thursday Oct 14. At Bromyard. Visited the cattle show & dined with the Agricultural Association. Mr J Hopton in the chair.[30] Returned thanks when my health was drunk. The attendance was large; above 100 persons sat down to dinner. The farmers are all in good humour: chief grievance the failure of the hops.
>
> Friday Oct 15. In the morning at Bromyard. Called on Mr Cooke, the vicar.[31] In the afternoon to Leominster. Slept at the Lion Inn.
>
> Saturday Oct 16. At Leominster attended the cattle show & the dinner of the Agricultural Society. Afterwards went to Monnington, & slept there.

> Sunday 17th October. At Monnington attended Monnington Church. Gilbert preached a sermon on the Thanksgiving for the Harvest & the collection for the distressed Irish.[32]

From Monnington Lewis moved on to Garnstone. Castellated and vast, set in its deer park, and built by Nash, it was the home of another of Lewis's kinsmen, the peppery Daniel Peploe Peploe. From here Lewis went to Hereford to attend yet another Cattle Show, this time at in a field at Moorfield Place, and to dine with the Agricultural Society.[33] By the end of the week he had left Garnstone and was back at Watford, where at Grove Mill House he got down to reviewing the recently published third and fourth volumes of Grote's *History of Greece* for the *Edinburgh Review*. The work, though, proceeded slowly:

> My mind is not in the blank paper state, but in a state much worse, that is, a number of confused blots and scratches have been made upon it ...[34]

Much of the trouble, apparently, was 'this abominable meeting of Parliament' which deranged him in every way,[35] though the new session was not in fact due to open for another month. With all thoughts of his constituency and its needs banished from his mind, he returned to a subject upon which he had been working since 1844:

> At present I am writing on a subject on which I had previously collected some notes, a subject not strictly of logical science but connected with it, viz. *the legitimate province of authority in matters of opinion and practice.* The problem is to determine the cause in which we can properly believe anything, not on appropriate evidence, understood by us, but merely because another person thinks so and so. It opens a great variety of questions connected with ethics and politics, which have never been looked at from this point of view, and it interests me to pursue the various threads of speculation. I have, however, very much lost my faith in the advantage of abstract speculation on morals and politics in the present state of knowledge and opinion, and I write it rather for my own sake than from any idea of being useful. It seems to me that there is too little consensus about elementary facts in the moral sciences for any abstract treatment to be of much avail; and I have come to the conclusion (particularly after reading your four volumes) that an enlightened commentary upon historical data, well ascertained, is the best form in which instruction on such subjects can be presented to the public. A series of good histories would be the

best foundation and preparation for a really scientific treatment of politics and morals.[36]

With the Parliamentary session begun, Lewis, installed in the Board of Control, found life much more to his taste than it had been in the Poor Law Office:

> During the last few months I have much changed my mode of life, having commuted a very laborious office into one with little labour, and having besides had to attend in Parliament. India is a very interesting subject from its magnitude, but the government is mainly in the local authorities and the Court of Directors, and the Board of Control is, as its name imports, merely a controlling body. It originates very little, and all the preliminary work is done at the India House. However, it is the link with Parliament, upon which everything ultimately depends; and since the abolition of the trading functions of the Company, the Court of Directors is assuming more and more the character of a sub-department of the Government.[37]

With characteristic thoroughness he applied himself to acquiring the necessary background knowledge for the post by reading Edward Thornton's six volume *History of British Empire in India*.[38] He also found leisure enough to go to the British Museum to search 'for dates relative to the domestic history of the Earl & Countess of Denby'.[39] This was in pursuit of his wife's family history, she being a Villiers. William Fielding, who became the first Earl of Denby in 1622, married Susan Villiers, daughter of Sir George Villiers of Brookesby, Leicestershire. He is remembered as 'the plain country gentleman who had the good luck to marry Buckingham's sister in the days of her poverty'. By this match he is said to have made his fortune.[40]

Lewis, however, was distracted from reading his Thornton and writing up his wife's family history by constituency matters. William Leader Maberley, Secretary of the General Post Office, had written to him about the suitability of a candidate for the position of Receiver of Letters for Staunton on Wye. This was a matter of information rather than patronage, though there may have been some undertones of controversy here. Maberley's sustained opposition to the Post Office reforms proposed by Rowland Hill is alleged to have caused the loss of some millions of public money. Lewis wrote from Grove Mill to Gilbert, whose parish of Monnington on Wye was on the opposite bank of the river to Staunton, for advice:

My dear Gilbert,

The letter from the treasury merely asks me to recommend a fit person to be appointed as a Receiver of Letters at Staunton on Wye, but does not mention whether the appointment is a new one, or intended to fill up a vacancy. I will however write to day to Maberley,[41] & ascertain the point, and will let you know the result.

We go to town on Friday & on the following Thursday hostilities commence. There will be a long fight about taxation, I take for granted, but the Jew bill is the first question. I hear that the protectionists have entirely discarded G Bentick,[42] on the ground of his vote on the Jew question, & that he is not now considered as their leader. Inglis[43] seems to me to be the fittest man for them.[44]

In the beginning of February Lewis was again dealing with postal matters. This time it was to appoint a sub-distributor of stamps for Leominster. There were two candidates, James Valentine Chilcott, 'printer and publisher; general newsagent; and Agent for the General Life and Fire Insurance Company', of Broad Street, Leominster, and John Went, junior, son of 'Francis Went, printer, bookseller, stationer, and postmaster', of Leominster High Street. They came up to London to be interviewed by Lewis on a Saturday morning at Kent House, and John Went was the successful candidate. The Staunton on Wye appointment was also still to be made and Lewis then went over to the General Post Office to discuss the matter with Maberley, '& thence to the office'.[45]

Lewis's earlier forecast to his brother that there would be a long fight over taxation when Parliament reassembled proved true, but Edward Horsman's proposal for graduated income tax gave it some interest. Horsman was something of political malcontent of Liberal sympathies and it was said that to his political cave of Adullam 'he invited everyone who was in distress, and everyone who was discontented'. Lewis thought on this occasion:

Horsman[46] spoke well, but his argument was weak, & he afforded materials for criticism by bringing forward a detailed plan.[47]

But his real interest of the day lay not in the proceedings of Parliament, but of the breakfast table. Here he was joined by the historians Macaulay, Milman and Hallam, and the lawyer Charles Austin:

> I breakfasted with Macaulay & met Milman, Hallam, & Charles
> Austin. Much conversation about the French revolution, & we
> agreed that the general character of the new govt was *Socialist,*
> & that it was impossible to anticipate the events which a short
> time might produce. There is no sympathy with the king, but a
> general feeling among men of sense that the violent change of
> govt was a wanton act, not prompted by any reasonable
> motive.[48]

Louis Philippe abdicated 24th February 1848 and came to
England as an exile. A republic was proclaimed in France and there
were fears that the presentation to Parliament of the third Chartist
petition, planned for Monday 10th April would bring with it serious
unrest, if not revolution itself. Lewis described these anxieties to
Edmund Head whose departure in October 1847 to Canada as
governor of New Brunswick, had deprived him of a close friend:

> A threatened movement of the Chartists, which was to take
> place on Monday last, and to bring about an English revolution,
> was completely frustrated by the preparations of the
> Government and the voluntary organisation of the upper and
> middle classes. There was more genuine alarm in London on
> that day than I ever remember to have existed. People hardly
> doubted of the event, but they feared a bloody conflict in the
> streets.[49]

He recorded the events of the day in his diary in detail:

> Today was the day appointed for the great Chartist procession
> from Kensington Common to the House of Commons to
> present a petition. Preparations on a large scale were made by
> the govt. & the inhabitants generally had taken measures for
> defending their property & preserving the public peace. The
> public offices were supplied with arms & provisions, & several of
> them were garrisoned with soldiers & marines. Cannon were in
> readiness in the neighbourhood of the Houses of Parliament.
> The preparations made were so ample, & the Chartists were so
> decidedly outnumbered by the civil force opposed to them, that
> the leaders abandoned the project of a procession, & Fergus
> O'Connor called at the Home Office at 1 o'clock to announce
> the change of purpose. The petition was brought unostenta-
> tiously to the House of Commons in hackcabs, & deposited on
> the floor, where I saw it soon after 4 o'clock. It was presented by
> O'Connor, without any remark, & read by the clerk at the table.

> I was at the office between 12 & 1 o'clock, the streets were then quite quiet. There was a crowd of spectators in Parliament Street, but nothing more. The people who had attended the meeting at Kennington Green dispersed about 12 o'clock, & many of them passed over Westminster Bridge. These were turned by the police in the direction of Trafalgar Square. It began to rain about 3 o'clock & the rain lasted more than an hour. This helped to disperse the crowds. There was no rioting or disturbance in the evening, as was expected. The House of Commons was crowded from an early hour. There was much curiosity, & a strong feeling in consequence of the events of the day, but no undue excitement.[50]

On 1st May Lewis went up to London from Watford by an early train to keep an appointment with the Prime Minister, Lord John Russell, who offered him a move to Home Office as an Under Secretary. In the privacy of his diary Lewis confided that he 'had no desire to make the change, but acquiesced in the proposition'.

Lewis assumed his new office on Monday 15th May 1848. A fortnight later Sir George Grey, the Home Secretary, sent for him[51] and they discussed another Chartist procession. Its intention this time was to secure the release of one of their imprisoned leaders, John Mitchel, an Irish nationalist awaiting transportation for sedition:

> Was sent for to the office by Sir G Grey in consequence of a Chartist procession which had marched from the East of the town to Leicester Square, apparently with the intention of surrounding the House of Commons. Their object was declared to be the liberation of Mitchel.[52] They were stopped at Charing Cross by the police, & turned up the Strand, the column then marched eastwards and dispersed peaceably, without having done any damage. Their number was reported to be 2 or 3 thousand. Whitehall was perfectly quiet all the night.[53]

Relief from the Chartists was offered by a well-attended dinner of the Herefordshire Society, founded in London 'in or about the reign of Charles I'. Its purpose was the clothing and apprenticing in London of the children of poor natives of Herefordshire to provide them with a trade.[54] The dinner took place at the Freemasons Tavern, Lewis responding when his health was proposed as a County member. It had been a full day, for he had already been at the office and was 'early at the House'. But there was time enough to recover the next day, for the House did not sit 'on account of the Derby'.[55]

At the end of June Lewis wrote an account of his duties at the Home Office in response to a letter from Edmund Head in New Brunswick. It had taken him two months to reply:

> I have delayed answering it for some time in consequence of the incessant occupation of my day as well as night, which my present office combined with Parliament produces. The business is not of any great importance. The Home Office is a sort of central point for an immense number of offices and officers, commissions, lord-lieutenants, magistrates, &c.; all their correspondence with the Treasury and other departments, and all their applications for instructions or money, pass through or are made to the Home Office. It is also a house of call for numbers of people who wish to receive information, or to communicate it. Then there is a great deal of routine parliamentary business, arrangements about returns, and the like. The time of the Secretary of State is very much occupied with Cabinets and interviews; and it is only by constant attention on the part of the Under Secretaries that at a moment of pressure, such as has been lately caused by the Chartists, the routine minor business of the office is kept going. The Home Office is likewise a Colonial Office for the Channel Islands and the Isle of Man; and although these are not large communities, each of them has a governor and a little government complete in itself, which gives rise to the various questions which a separate government invariably creates. On the whole, although the Home Office subjects are more familiar to me, and I feel that I am more in my proper place, I regret on many accounts the easy life which I had at the Board of Control.[56]

The easy life at the Board of Control had made Lewis somewhat dilatory over matters which demanded rather more prompt attention. Elected in July 1847, it was not until the end of September 1848 that he got round to formally thanking his agent Frederick Bodenham:

> Sent a silver tankard to Bodenham, with this inscription: To Fd Bodenham, Esq. The gift of Mr Cornewall Lewis, in memory of his kind & friendly assistance at the Election for Herefordshire in 1847, together with a letter of thanks. Bodenham managed the whole of my Election gratuitously.[57]

It was perhaps surprising that Bodenham got his tankard even then, because Lewis spent all of September at Grove Mill working on

Sir George Cornewall Lewis by H. Weighall
(© National Museums & Galleries of Wales)

The north front of Harpton Court in 1784 (watercolour),
before Frankland Lewis's substantial alterations

Harpton Court from the south-east c.1840 (pencil and chalk)

Harpton Court from the south-east (watercolour), by Lady Head

Harpton Court painted by Gertrude Jekyll (1843–1932)
(© Surrey County Record Office)

*Standing by the gate to Harpton Court in the early 1900s are Len and Susie,
children of then butler, Jack Standen. The gatehouse was part of the
rebuilding carried out in 1857 by Thomas Nicholson of Hereford*

*Harpton Court with its croquet lawn.
Both photographs on this page are by W.H. 'Billy' McKaig*

*The Rt. Hon Sir Thomas Frankland Lewis (father of George Cornewall
Lewis) 1780–1855. Drawing by Eden Upton Eddis, 1840*

Rev. Sir Gilbert Lewis, brother of George Cornewall Lewis,
by Rannie Swinton, 1843

*Detail from an oil painting of
Theresa Lewis, wife of George
Cornewall Lewis*

*An oil painting of Lady Theresa
Lewis, wife of George Cornewall Lewis*

*Lady Caroline Duff Gordon, oil
painting by G.F. Watts, O.M., R.A.*

*Memorials to Sir George
Cornewall Lewis, 1864
Above: Statue in bronze by
Baron Carlo Marochetti in front
of Hereford's Shire Hall.
Right: Memorial by John Gibbs
in New Radnor*

his *Essay on the Influence of Authority in Matters of Opinion*. Then in October he and his wife set out for Herefordshire and the annual round of race meetings and agricultural shows and dinners. Bromyard came first, the Lewises staying at Gaines with John Freeman, a local magistrate. Haggitt, his fellow MP for the County, joined him as steward on a wet and windy race-course, and there were only twenty at the dinner afterwards. After another night at Gaines it was Belmont with Haggitt before going, on using his brother Gilbert's carriage, to Foxley and Sir Richard Price. The two men went to the well-attended dinner of the Herefordshire Society at Hereford, and then next day it was back to Bromyard where Lewis lightened the proceedings of the Agricultural Society with 'some remarks on the probable price of corn & prospects of agriculture', when returning his thanks for his health being drunk.[58] He also addressed himself to the problem of Herefordshire roads:

> This part of the country had not undergone so much change in respect to the introduction of railways as other parts had of late years, and therefore the turnpike trusts of the district had not been so much deranged by their operation as elsewhere. He trusted, however, that in the next session of Parliament Sir George Grey would be able to introduce the bill for making an improved arrangement with regard to highways, and that they might see some advance made next session towards a more improved and systematic management of our highways.[59]

Lewis's father once recollected in a much quoted anecdote that as late as 1848 when the Kington-Leominster road was under repair the mud was so bad that it was said it would cost little more to have the road navigable and have a canal. The leader of a team of sixteen horses bringing stones for the road fell into the mud and it required the strength of the remaining fifteen to get him out, so unrecognizable as a horse that the people of Kington came to see the spectacle. Sir Frankland Lewis was something of an expert on roads and well qualified to express an opinion on them. For besides being a Turnpike Trustee, in 1843, as a response to the Rebecca Riots, he was one of the three commissioners appointed by the government to look into what caused them and the part played by the turnpike system. Consequently, the trusts were abolished in Wales in 1844. It was, perhaps, partly because of his informed background that in 1849 the Home Secretary Grey delegated to Cornewall Lewis the responsibility for introducing the bill he had promised the Bromyard farmers the previous Autumn. As usual Edmund Head was informed about things:

> I have introduced as a Home Office measure a bill altering the entire management of the roads, abolishing turnpike trusts, and placing all roads under the control of a county board of magistrates and the Board of Guardians. It is opposed by the Tory country gentlemen, because they are sulky about the price of corn, and by the clerks of 1100 trusts, so that I am not very sanguine of its success, but it has a good deal of support.[60]

A few weeks later Lewis was working at the Home Office writing a report on turnpike trusts for the bill's committee stage, whilst his fellow MPs went off to the Derby.[61] Lewis was right about its prospects and it had to be withdrawn:

> The General Roads Bill was defeated by the opposition of the clerks to trusts, who are nearly all attorneys, and their influence with members, particularly as there was at Easter some expectation of a Protectionist dissolution, was irresistible. We were forced to withdraw it, and the question must now be settled in some other way.[62]

He was still trying to do something about the roads six months later, concluding that the turnpike trusts, rather than the actual highways were the real problem.[63] But no other positive way *was* found, and in England the trusts were left to slip steadily into decline. The affairs, for example, of the Kington Turnpike Trust, of which Lewis's attorney kinsman, James Davies, was for many years the Clerk, were wound up in 1877. The duties of the few other surviving trusts were finally taken over by the County Councils when they were set up in 1888.

But to return to that 1848 Agricultural Society dinner at Bromyard, his constituency duties were then done, and there was no need to linger in Herefordshire longer, so the Lewises set out for Watford next day. Travelling by way of Worcester, they stopped to see the cathedral, which amazed them more than Chamberlaine's china manufactory:

> There is nightwork in it for burning the china, & employment of children, both boys & girls, for various subordinate functions. The boys are worked about 10 hours a day.[64]

At Grove Mill, Lewis immediately resumed work on the *Essay* and continued at it until the 19th December when he turned to Auguste Comte and his six-volume *Cours de philosophie positive*[65] which occupied him throughout the twelve days of Christmas. He had an enthusiasm for Comte, recommending the four octavo volumes of his *Traités de Législation* to Edmund Head because:

> It contains the best and truest account of the savage state of society and mode of life which I am acquainted with, and I should be glad to know what you think of it.[66]

There was a short visit to Hereford at the beginning of February, staying at Gilbert's rectory at Monnington on Wye, mainly to preside over a dinner of the Agricultural Society. One suspects he thought it was hardly worth his trouble:

> About 40 persons attended. Few gentlemen. I spoke on the prospects of Agriculture & on the chance of obtaining a railway for the county.[67]

What really concerns Lewis in his diary is his progress with the *Essay*. He had sent the first six chapters to the press the day before he and Therese set out for Hereford:

> All these have been composed from a sketch more or less complete, since the end of last session. The same was the case with the tenth chapter. The 7th, 8th, & 9th chapters & the appendix were written in the last months of 1846, & have been revised & completed during the last recess.[68]

It was the same back in London, even the Sabbath was broken on its behalf:

> Sunday 11th February. Kent House … Sent today to the press the three first sheets of my *Essay*.
>
> Monday 19th February. Kent House. Office. Returned the sixth sheet of my *Essay* to the press …
>
> Monday 4th March … Kent House. Returned sheet O to the press. The printing of my *Essay* has proceeded at the rate of 3 sheets a week.[69]

A month later he sent the last proofs to the press[70] and whilst he awaited its publication, diverted his thoughts by a visit to the British Museum to see the Nineveh marbles, his recent connection with the affairs of India whilst he was at the Board of Control gave one of the exhibits a particular interest:

> There is a very curious small obelisk with bas relief, evidently representing the submission of representatives of an Indian territory, with Indian animals & products as tributes, to the Assyrian king.[71]

At last, on Thursday 19th April 1849 he was able to write in his Diary: 'My *Essay* published today'. Now for the reviews which appeared promptly, and he was soon to write in his Diary:

> In the *Examiner* of yesterday is a notice of my *Essay on Authority* by a competent critic (perhaps John Mill). The judgement is favourable to the book, but does not go into details.[72]

The *Athenaeum*[73] also gave a favourable review as did some newspapers, but most satisfactory of all, for Lewis was always commercially minded:

> nearly 200 copies have been sold, which, as the subject is not a very attractive one, and the mode of treatment is not intended to be popular, is quite as much as I could hope for I had considerable difficulty in dealing with the question of Church authority; and I am glad to find that Milman approves of my chapter, who is an excellent judge in the matter.[74]

Contact with the constituency, or at least a section of it, was maintained through the Herefordshire Society which had an annual dinner in London at the Freemasons Tavern, at which the MPs for city and county were guests. Lewis used the dinner as an excuse for not attending the House, and with Haggitt in the chair Lewis was joined by Sir Richard Price and Henry Morgan Clifford of Perrystone.[75]

Next day was Derby day and so the House did not meet, so Lewis spent the day writing a report on Turnpike Trusts for a parliamentary committee,[76] though there were other ideas circulating at the back of his mind. It has been said that once Lewis published a book he apparently forgot about it, for though he referred in his letters to what he was doing he seldom referred to what he had done.[77] Another one was now gestating:

> Since Easter I have sketched a plan of work upon the *Methods of Reasoning in Political Science* & have during the last fortnight written portions of a chapter upon Political Causation. If I am

able to complete this work, I expect that it will occupy several years & that it will form two volumes.[78]

Lewis sent Head a personal prospectus which gives some insight to the former's character and self-estimation. It was not tempered by anything like modesty or self-doubt:

> The work which I have in my mind, if I could execute it properly, is an organon[79] for the use of the political enquirer - a manual of rules for the guidance of the historian or politician in the method of conducting his investigations. A work of this kind would dispose of nearly the whole body of political speculators, from Plato downwards, without refuting their conclusions separately, by showing that their methods were unsound, and could lead to nothing but error, except, indeed, by accident.[80]

August interrupted the work with race meetings at Leominster and Hereford to be seen to. Lewis's sojourns in Herefordshire were brief and it was a matter of getting back to Grove Mill as quickly as possible for work on the *Treatise*. A further interruption came with the necessity to attend a county Bow Meeting at Whitfield before eventually arriving at Harpton Court. There, after church, he discovered to his satisfaction that 'an article on the Grand Style of Government, written by me, is in yesterday's *Examiner*'. This gave him impetus for another day working on the *Treatise*.[81] At the end of the month there were the races at Hereford, a ball, and the Three Choirs Festival to be endured. Lewis was not musical and staying at the Green Dragon he began a paper for the Prime Minister on the re-siting of London's Smithfield in the interests of public health:

> I have been working lately at a commission on the subject of Smithfield and Newgate Markets: the latter being the market for the sale of *dead* meat. The magnitude of the business transacted at these two markets is enormous. The value of the stock sold at Smithfield is estimates at seven millions a year. Both of them are far too confined and ought to be removed.[82]

The problems of the Smithfield so preoccupied him that he excused himself from attending another Bow Meeting, this time at Eywood, sending Theresa and her brother Villiers, and her two girls instead. He did, however, go to a church bazaar the next day, where Lady Lewis had a stall, whilst managing to send off his memorandum on Smithfield to Lord John Russell.

Lewis went to two sessions of oratorio during the Festival, staying at the palace as the guest of the new bishop, Dr Hampden, who was submerged in controversy. First it was to *Elijah* in the Shire Hall, and Lewis was reluctant to pass judgement on the performance:

> Went to the Oratorio. *Elijah* by Mendelssohn. I understand it to be considered by competent judges second only to the *Messiah*.[83]

Next day, still at the palace, he went again to the oratorio, but its name slipped his memory, perhaps because the performance was after dinner with the Archdeacon of Hereford, Lord Saye & Sele, and was followed by a ball. He left Hereford next day after lunch, and made his way back to Watford and the *Treatise*.[84] He found time, though, to give his friend Head in New Brunswick an account of his doings. He had been unable to reply to Head sooner:

> partly in consequence of a series of duty *gaieties* which I have been going through for my constituents. I have already attended Leominster and Hereford races, two days of each, and have been to a bow meeting, and have a music meeting in prospect.

Lewis was a great railway traveller, a serious rival to Kilvert in this respect, and his classical background provoked the remark: 'What grand railways the Romans would have made if they had been invented in old times!'[85] But in 1849 the railways were getting a bad press mainly due to the disastrously extravagant speculations of George Hudson, Tory MP for Sunderland. Known as the Railway King there was a time when he was a favoured house guest amongst the influential and wealthy and 'not to know him was to argue oneself unknown'. Those days were now over and Lewis continues in his letter to Head:

> ... The excitement of the railway speculations has done much harm; and having been driven up by unsound competition far above their proper height, they have now been as unfairly depressed by the exposure of Hudson's proceedings, which has made people think that *no* railway management is to be trusted. It was very unlucky for Herefordshire that it did not get a railway before the tide turned. It will be several years before railway speculation will revive, and then it will assume a much more sober form.[86]

Back at Grove Mill, work on the *Treatise* was soon interrupted:

> Received a communication from Ld J Russell, stating that he adopts my suggestion of an unpaid commission for enquiring into Smithfield market, & intends to put me on it, with Sir James Duke, F Byng, & Professor Owen, & a fifth person to be added. I wrote consenting to serve.[87]

Even so, a few days later Lewis, still at Grove Mill, was able to write in his diary:

> Since I went to Herefordshire I have written a chapter on Prediction in Politics for my *Treatise*.[88]

He was back in Hereford in October for the Cattle Show and when he presided at the Agricultural Society's dinner he found that the farmers were in the worst of humours on the subject of prices.[89] Next morning, Saturday, he left the Green Dragon early for Gloucester on the *Mazeppa* stage coach, where he caught the train to London, arriving 'at the office before four'.[90] It was his capacity to start work at the office on a Saturday afternoon after a long journey by coach and train which overfilled his time-table. Consequently we find him a few weeks later sitting for his portrait on three successive days. That it 'had remained unfinished since 1845' is in itself surprising, but all the more so when it is recollected that the artist was Sir Francis Grant, the most fashionable portrait painter of his day. Queen Victoria, Prince Albert, and Lewis's fellow politicians Lord John Russell, Sir George Grey, and Lord Palmerston all sat for him. This time the portrait was finished and brought home,[91] 'greatly improved ... both as a portrait and a painting'.[92]

There was at this time a revival of nationalism in Wales which showed itself in a growing pride and interest in the Welsh language and in the nation's history and culture. But Lewis had no interest in this renaissance and his lack of sympathy for the Welsh and their language, despite his own Welsh ancestry, showed itself in December 1849 when he was invited to take the chair at a meeting of the short-lived Cambrian Literary Institution at the Clarence Hotel in Aldergate:

> I was in the chair & stated the objects of the Society. Made some remarks upon the evils arising to Wales from the use of the Welsh language. Several other persons addressed the meeting.[93]

There were others, however, who lived on the Welsh border who did not share his attitude. There was, for example Lady Elizabeth Brown Coffin, the only child of William and Elizabeth Greenly of Titley Court, near Kington, and almost a neighbour to Harpton. She was a confirmed *eisteddfodwr*, and was conspicuous for her enthusiasm for things Welsh. She shared this enthusiasm with her friend, the eccentric Augusta Waddington whose marriage to Benjamin Hall of Llanover she attended in 1823. Later, as Lady Llanover, Augusta Hall was to perpetrate the myth that Welsh women should all look like Mother Goose and dress in a red cloak over a petticoat and bedgown and wear a tall black hat. Despite Augusta and Benjamin Hall's determination to revive the Welsh language, culture, and crafts, they spent the first three years of their married life at Newport House, Almeley. In 1832 she attempted to kindle Lewis's interest in the Celtic renaissance, by quoting Edward *Celtic* Davies and articles in the *Cambrian Quarterly* on the druids and the bards which she was happy to lend him. She hoped thereby that Lewis would give the ancient literature of his country a higher grade in his estimation than it then possessed.[94] She was unsuccessful.

The *Treatise* kept Lewis occupied to the end of the year, working on it on Christmas Eve and on Boxing Day. By 8th December he had written three chapters on 'observation, experiment & history' and was now turning his attention to the chapters on 'political causation'. But with the New Year he was beginning to have some doubts about the venture:

> I have been writing my *Political Logic*, which, if it is ever finished, few people will read. I shall nevertheless do my best to complete what I fear may prove a somewhat thankless labour.[95]

In 1850 Lewis found that concerns with law and order were not limited to his duties at the Home Office. In April Lewis informed his friend Edmund Head:

> My father is in very good health now, but he was a good deal annoyed by a burglary which took place in the house at Harpton while he was there at Easter. The thieves broke in on the ground floor, and carried away a silver inkstand and plate to the value of about eighty pounds. They were probably Birmingham thieves and had no connection with the neighbourhood.[96]

Lewis was correct in his surmise that the burglars came from Birmingham, but they had inside information, which led them to believe that the proceeds of Lady Day rents would be in the house. In fact rent-day had been postponed. Radnorshire had an appeal for Birmingham burglars and two years later, the last man to be sentenced to transportation at the Radnorshire assizes was Henry Russ of Birmingham. Described as an experienced house-breaker, he broke into a house near Presteign and was eventually captured after a violent struggle at a public house near Birmingham. He had a previous conviction and was sentenced at the Spring Assizes of 1852 to transportation for life.[97] Then in May Lewis had to go down to Grove Mill one Sunday to discuss the prosecution of the housemaid for theft.[98]

All the same, by snatching at whatever opportunities that came his way to escape from the office to visit the British Museum[99] he was able to tell Head:

> I have made considerable progress with my book, at which I employ all my odd hours.[100]

On May 30th, after an early session at the Home Office, Lewis went to a morning sitting of the House of Commons in its new chamber. He was not impressed:

> Morning sitting in the new House which seems to me utterly unfitted for its purpose, & bad for hearing. It will, if used, alter the character of the debates in the H of C.[101]

On July 1st Lord John Russell offered Lewis the office of Secretary to the Treasury. He accepted the invitation for it satisfied both his political and his financial ambitions:

> It is considered a superior office to that of Under Secretary, & the salary is higher.[102]

It was not long before Lewis was informing Head of events which took the form of a parliamentary version of musical chairs. Henry Tufnell, the present Secretary to the Treasury, who had collaborated with Lewis in translating Karl Gottfried Muller's *History and Antiquities of the Doric Race* in 1830, wanted early retirement. William Hayter, MP for Wells, was his successor, and Lewis followed him, Edward Pleydell-Bouverie, MP for Kilmarnock stepping on to the lowest rung on this particular *cursus honorum*. Lewis furnished Head with the full details:

I have lately made a change of office, which is a promotion in point of salary, and also as to the importance of the duties. On these accounts I am bound to be pleased with the change. At the same time, I regret the Home Office, the duties of which suited me very well, and I do not feel that I have any particular aptitude for being the économe of the Government, and revising the items of treasury expenditure, which is the business of the Secretary of the Treasury. Tufnell[103] was tired of being the Parliamentary Secretary, and his health has not been good lately. His retirement made a vacancy in that office, which there was a difficulty in filling, until Hayter[104] was induced to take it. I was placed in Hayter's office, and Edward Bouverie[105] has succeeded me. One of the first fruits of this transfer is, that I have to serve on a commission for reporting on closing the country post-offices on Sunday, a subject which has stirred up the Sabbatarian mind of England, and has produced a wonderful quantity of petitioning and agitating. It is a question on which there are two irreconcilable parties, and whatever is done is sure to give mortal offence to one - possibly to both.[106]

But Lewis's promotion was overshadowed by the death of Peel. He fell from his horse on Saturday 29th and died three days later. Lewis gave Head a full evaluation of his character:

Peel's death has been a very sad event. He leaves a great blank in public life; his great experience, his extensive knowledge, his long official career, and his practised habits of debate and power of speech gave him a position in the House of Commons which nobody else filled. He had, it is true, lost his party, and he told for little in a division, but his voice had great weight in the country, and no speech of his was a matter of indifference even in the House. I cannot say that I prized his judgment very highly, nor do I think that as a *guide* in public affairs, when he had ceased to be an *administrator*, he was of great value. He did not see far before him; he was not ready in applying theory to practice; he did not foresee the coming storm. But, when it had come, there was no man who dealt with it so well as he did. For concocting, producing, explaining, and defending measures he had no equal, or anything like an equal. There was nothing *simile aut secundum*. When a thing was to be done, he did it better than anybody. The misfortune was, that he saw the right thing too late; and went on opposing it when men of less powerful minds saw clearly what was the proper course. Latterly, when he became more of a reformer, he was sometimes too bold.[107]

Throughout the summer and autumn Lewis was preoccupied with his *Treatise* and his office papers, the former getting more frequent mention in his Diary than the latter. Throughout August he was working on the chapter on 'Ideal models of government' which he finished at the end of the month[108] and he then immediately set about the chapter on 'The fallibility of political practice'. On October 2nd he noted in his Diary that he had:

> Finished the draft of the last chapter of my *Treatise*. The first two books are not yet begun. The four last are nearly complete.

The work was not substantially interrupted in the middle of the month when he came down to Herefordshire for the Agricultural Society's dinner, for Lewis took his office papers and his manuscripts with him. The by-election to replace Joseph Bailey, who had died, also took place. Herefordshire had three MPs and there was only one candidate for the vacancy left by Bailey's death:

> Booker was elected today. Bodenham tells me that the election was flat, a small attendance of gentlemen, no row or opposition. Arrived at Foxley to dinner. Slept there.[109]

Lewis had little enthusiasm for Booker, thinking him 'a flaming Protectionist from Glamorganshire, who will, I fear, give some trouble'.[110] At Foxley Sir Richard Price found Lewis an easy if not an entertaining guest, so when the dutiful Sir Richard attended Hereford fair day Lewis stayed behind to work on his *Treatise*. Next day it was to work on office papers as well as the *Treatise*,[111] but he did go with him to the cattle show and dined afterwards with the MPs for both shire and city of Hereford. He returned thanks when the health of the county members was proposed by the strongly protectionist farmers and used the opportunity to speak about Hereford's prospect of acquiring a railway. A railway, as Wegg Prosser was to point out, was 'a most important ingredient to agricultural success'[112] and by aiding and abetting its arrival in Herefordshire Lewis could relieve the protectionist hostility towards him. The *Hereford Times* reported:

> It was impossible to avoid the conviction forced upon them by the unfortunate circumstance of Herefordshire being almost

the only county in England in which there was no railway. It could hardly be said that they were themselves to blame in this matter, because there was an act obtained to make a railway from Hereford to Gloucester, which the Great Western Company undertook to construct. He was afraid that the agricultural interest was not the only interest which was suffering distress at the present time, as some of them might perhaps be aware, from experience, that the railway interest was not very prosperous. It was the want of prosperity of the railway interest, and particularly of the Great Western Company, which had prevented the making of the railway from Hereford to Gloucester. Some gentlemen, among others Mr Wallace Hall[113] and Mr Vaughan,[114] had taken a very laudable interest in the matter, and to whom the county must feel greatly indebted for the attempt they had made to come to some arrangement with the Great Western Company for the completion of the line from Gloucester to Hereford. He had himself been present at a meeting with the Great Western Company, at which an attempt was made to adopt measures for the completion of the line. At one time they were very sanguine that the line might be made, though their expectations were afterwards somewhat damped: he was, however, still in hopes that, by different companies and different interests combining, it might be possible at no very distant period to complete the line from Gloucester to Hereford ... Having made these remarks, he would only add that, if it should be in his power to assist in furthering the project by any negotiation with the Great Western or other Companies, his services would always be at the command of the county.[115]

The notion of a railway linking Hereford, Ross on Wye, and Gloucester was first mooted in 1844 when the route was surveyed. It was abandoned, however, in 1847 for lack of funds. On 5th November Lewis met 'with the Great Western Railway Directors on the subject of the railway from Gloster to Hereford'.[116] A month later he was back in Hereford at

> a meeting at the Shire Hall for promoting the proposed railway from Ross to Hereford, a full attendance of gentlemen. My father & Gilbert came. I proposed one of the resolutions. Brunel made a clear & able statement & the meeting went off well.[117]

Capital of £275,000 was proposed for the 22^{1}/$_{2}$ miles involved and Lewis told Head 'a large sum in shares has been subscribed, and it is nearly enough, but I have not yet heard whether it is quite enough'.[118] The necessary legislation was obtained in 1851, Lewis attending the Committee stage.[119] In October he

> Attended a meeting of the Directors of the Hereford & Ross Railway at the Green Dragon. Settled the agreement to be entered into with the Great Western.[120]

The line's construction, however, took several years because several deep cuttings were involved, four tunnels and four crossings of the Wye. The first five miles from Grange Court to Hopesbrook were completed in July 1853 and the line in 1855.

Lewis was also involved in the early attempts at establishing the Worcester and Hereford Railway, believing that railways had more to offer the farmers of his constituency than did Protection. The *Hereford Times* again:

> Since he had been their Member, he had done whatever lay within his limited means to provide their interests, and he had supported, to the extent of his power, the railway now in course of construction from Gloucester to Hereford, and had acted as a member of the direction. He also moved the second reading of the bill for the Worcester and Hereford Railway, the bill was unfortunately lost in the House of Lords, but which he under-stood was likely to be renewed in a future session. To works of this sort he confessed he looked with much more confidence for improving the condition of the agricultural class in this county, than to the phantom of Protection.[121]

The necessary legislation was not obtained until 1853, the House of Lords insisting that the company should remain truly independent with no subscriptions from the bigger companies like the Great Western. The line opened in 1860.

Back in London work on the *Treatise* continued, done, it seems, at the Treasury rather than Kent House:

> Attended each day at the office & continued writing my *Treatise.*[122]

Working at home was perhaps difficult: Kent House was opposite the site of the Crystal Palace, and Lewis explained to Head:

> There is a great interest and expectation about the effects of the Crystal Palace. It is not a popular subject at Knightsbridge, particularly at this moment, when we are overrun with the

workmen who stream along the road at meal-times as if a manufactory was breaking up. I have never been able to make out
precisely what good it is to do; but it is a 'grand idea,' it
'embodies the spirit of the age,' &c &c., and so I suppose it will
have some effect. It will certainly bring a great many people to
London, and increase the profits of hotel and lodging
keepers.[123]

Lewis's aunt, Lady Duff Gordon, went with her daughters to see
things for herself:

We went ... to see the building now erecting in Hyde Park for
the Exhibition of 1851. I never was more interested and
amused, than at seeing the work proceeding, in length it is 1846
feet, in width 408 feet, there will be 3,230 Iron Columns, 34
miles of Gutters, 202 miles Sash Bars, & 900,000 feet of glass.
The space for Exhibiting is almost 21 acres.[124]

Early in December Lewis *had* to work at home:

Had a return of spitting blood this morning. Staid at home &
wrote *Treatise*, also disposed of office papers.[125]

Two days at home and then it was back to the office and the
Treatise until Christmas, which was celebrated at Grove Mill and
allowed him a day's break: that spitting of blood concentrated his
mind and his Diaries show he was uncertain as to his expectation of
life:

Thursday 26th December to Thursday 2nd January 1851.
Disposed of office papers. Finished the First Book, which
completes the first draft of the entire work, with certain
portions, chiefly examples, left unfinished. I began it about
Whitsuntide 1849 & I expect to complete the revision of it in
another year, if I live so long.

Kent house was a hive of literary activity at this time. Theresa
Lewis was working on her *Lives of the Friends and Contemporaries of Lord
Chancellor Clarendon, illustrative of portraits in his Gallery*,[126] and Lewis
himself had sought relaxation from the affairs of the Treasury and his
Treatise in writing contributions for *Notes & Queries*.[127] One of these
dealt with the hippopatamus, interest in which had been aroused by
the arrival of a young animal in the Zoological Gardens in Regent's
Park. Lewis reviews the references to the hippopotamus in classical
literature:

The earliest mention of the hippopotamus is in Herodotus, who in ii.71 gives a detailed description of this inhabitant of the Nile.[128]

But Lewis thinks that none of the Greek writers appear to have seen a live hippopotamus, nor, unlike the tiger, was one ever seen in ancient Greece. On the other hand both the hippopotamus and crocodile made their appearance at Rome in the Imperial games. Then Lewis points out that whereas the Greek writers constantly call the animal ιπποποσαλο, the Latin *hippopotamus* according to the ordinary rule of Greek composition means, not a *river-horse*, but a *horse-river*. Lewis considers the word hippopotamus to have been a Roman corruption of the Greek substantive and adjective, and not a proper Greek word. He was also puzzled why an animal in shape and appearance resembling a gigantic hog should be called a horse.[129]

Lewis's interest in natural history made him a frequent visitor to Regent's Park. He was there, for example, one Saturday in June 1851, after a morning in the office:

Went in the afternoon to the zoological gardens to see the Urang Utang recently imported. It was originally brought from Borneo, but had been some time at Singapore. It is male, the female died on the passage. Its upper limbs are longer & stronger than the lower. It has 4 hands. Its natural movement is evidently climbing & it must live chiefly in trees. It advances more with the help of its fore than of its hind arms. It is manifestly a quadruped & not a biped. When led by a man, it can walk on its legs, or lower limbs, but holds a stick in its other forearm as a support. This mode of progression is however constrained, & unnatural to the animals. The prints of the Urang Utang which represent it in an erect form while in a state of nature must be unfaithful & fanciful.[130]

The Times described this four-year-old ape 'as by far the finest example which has yet been brought to Europe'.[131] Apes, however, were quadrupeds and humans were bipeds, and that seems to have been all that mattered in Cornewall Lewis's eyes. But then the publication of Darwin's *On the Origin of Species by means of Natural Selection* was still eight years away.

Lewis's second paper in *Notes & Queries* was in response to a query about the *Adventures of Gaudentio di Lucca* and their alleged authorship by Bishop Berkley.[132] In Lewis's opinion the claim that the

Adventures were a translation from the Italian was a mere fiction, nor was their any evidence to support the view that Bishop Berkley was the author:

> The work is evidently an English composition. It belongs to the class of *Voyages Imaginaires*, and its main object is to describe the institutions and manners of the Mezoranians, an Utopian community, supposed to exist in the centre of Africa.[133]

A more lengthy paper on the age of trees next diverted the attention of this scholarly part-time gentleman-politician. He reviews the evidence for the longevity of the baobab, cyprus, yew, lime, and oak, and then asks:

> Can any of your correspondents state what is the greatest number of rings which have been actually counted in any yew, or other tree, which has grown in the British isles, or elsewhere? It is only by actual enumeration that vegetable chronology can be satisfactorily determined: but if the rings in many trees were counted, some relation between the number of rings and the diameter of the trunk, for each species, might probably be laid down within certain limits. These rings, being annually deposited, form a natural chronicle of time, by which the age of a tree is determined with as much precision as the lapse of human events is determined by the contemporaneous registration of annalists.[134]

He concludes:

> Perhaps some of your correspondents may be able to point out authentic evidence respecting the true dates of ancient trees. A large tree is a subject of interest to the entire neighbourhood: it receives an individual name, like a river, a mountain, or a building; and by its permanence it affords a fixed point for a faithful local tradition to rest upon. On the other hand, the infidelity of oral tradition is well known; and the mere interest which attaches to a tree of unusual size is likely to give birth to a romantic legend, when its true history has been forgotten. The antiquary and the botanist may assist one another in determining the age of trees. By the authentic evidence of their duration, which the former is able to furnish, the latter may establish tests by which their longevity may be calculated.[135]

The Great Exhibition was opened by Queen Victoria on 1st May 1851, and, as a Minister of the Crown, Lewis was in attendance. He was converted and visited it again five times within the month. Before the end of May he was writing to Head:

> As your province seems now quiet, could you not come over this summer and see the Great Exhibition? It is a wonderful sight, quite unlike anything which ever before existed; from its gigantic dimensions, the multitude, variety, the completeness, and the individual excellence of the articles exhibited. It is a complete repertory of the useful arts for the whole world, exhibiting the best works of each country. Its success has been beyond all expectation, the opinion in its favour is unanimous, the *frondeurs* are silenced, and the receipts are immense.[136]

By September he was writing to Head:

> The Exhibition has been wonderfully successful. The foreigners have admired and been pleased. Numbers of French and a good many Germans came over. They stayed only a few days – and spent but little money – and saw as many sights as they could. All the authorities – the Commissioners, the Woods, the Government, and the Court – are in favour of removing the Crystal Palace when its work has been done. There was a sort of popular feeling in favour of keeping it, which found an expression in the House of Commons, but nobody has a purpose to suggest, and the money for purchasing and maintaining it is not forthcoming; so I expect to see it disappear at the fated time. There is really not an intelligible reason to be assigned in favour of its permanence.[137]

But retained it was, and when the Exhibition closed in October, having been visited by over six million people, it was rebuilt at Sydenham in south London, Lewis attended the ceremony of erecting the first column.[138] Within two years he had changed his mind, its commercial success having brought about the change of heart:

> Went with Theresa & Therese to the new Crystal Palace at Sydenham. Met my father and a large party. It is a grand & splendid work, admirably executed & with extraordinary spirit & enterprize considering that all the money has been furnished by a private company. Mr Phillips, who is in the service of the company, informed me that the entire expense wd be short of a million sterling, & that they had already let stalls to the amount of £25,000 a year.[139]

The Great Exhibition and discussions about the future of the Crystal Palace, visits to the Zoological Gardens and articles for *Notes & Queries* all robbed him of time on what mattered most. Even an August visit to Herefordshire for a Bow Meeting at Whitfield, which all the county attended, was a tiresome diversion. It was barely redeemed by the fact that when he visited the tent in which estate labourers were being given their dinner they proposed his health, and he was on the train back next day to London and the *Treatise*.[140] As usual Head was kept up to date over progress:

> For the present, whatever spare time I have is occupied with my political *Treatise*, which I expect to finish by the end of the year, so as to print it in the course of the spring and summer of 1852. It will consist of two volumes, and therefore will occupy some time in printing. It will go over the same ground as that treated in Mill's *Logic*,[141] but will not agree in all his views, and will be fuller and more detailed. Mill's *Logic* is, as you say, an admirable book. It has not, I think, been sufficiently praised or estimated at its worth. It is a superior book to his *Political Economy*.[142]

Using, as he told Head, all his *horae subsecivae*,[143] Lewis continued to work on his *Treatise* for the rest of 1851, confessing within the privacy of his Diary:

> During the Session, I have at often times, continued the revision & completion of my *Treatise* arranging the notes & filling up unfinished facts.[144]

He continued, with visits to the British Museum checking references, to work on the book, which he contemplated would be of some six hundred closely printed pages and in two volumes, throughout the summer and autumn. Then on a Monday morning in December, after going to the office from Kent House:

> I took with me the entire manuscript of my *Treatise* (which is complete, with the exception of a few notes & some passages in the last chapter) and left it at Parker's shop in West Strand, in order that he might make the arrangements for commencing the printing. I began it about Whitsuntide 1849 & have been continually at work upon it (so far as my other occupations wd allow) ever since.[145]

But even before the completion of the *Treatise* Lewis was planning his next work:

I have sketched plan of a work on Federal, National, Provincial & Municipal Govt. which I intend to begin shortly. I have also formed the plan of a work on the Credibility of Early Roman History, going over the same ground as Beaufort, & examining the methods of the recent German historians. My belief is that Niebuhr[146] is inconsistent, & that he assumes the possibility of determining more in the early Roman history than can be known.[147]

The opening of 1852 saw Lewis at Grove Mill making preliminary notes for his Roman history,[148] and on 6th January he received the first proofs of his *Treatise*. Three weeks later he noted in his Diary:

The printing of my book has advanced as far as p.192 of the first vol. In correcting the proofs I merely remove the printer's errors.[149]

At the same time, in collaboration with colleagues in the Treasury, the Board of Trade, and the Irish Poor Law Commission, he was writing a pamphlet 'on the Finances & Trade of the Country'.[150] Then in February Russell's administration fell; Lord Derby became Prime Minister, and formed a Conservative government. Lewis was out of office. He evacuated his room, cleared away his papers, wrote an address to his constituents justifying his free trade opinions, and announcing himself as a candidate at the next election.[151] He was at his office in the Treasury for the last time on Saturday 28th February and spent the first three working days of his new found leisure doing some running repairs on the last chapter of the *Treatise*.[152]

But for some time Lewis had been aware that his Herefordshire seat, which he had won without a contest, was becoming progressively less secure. He discussed the matter with Head:

My seat in Herefordshire is in a very tottering state; two new Protectionist candidates are announced, viz. Charles Hanbury, brother of Bateman and Mr King King, of Staunton. Wegg Prosser has announced his: intention of retiring at the next election. It is possible that the Protectionist feeling may be less strong at the dissolution than it is now; but a good deal will depend on this harvest.[153]

Moreover, the anxieties he felt about Booker had proved well founded and showed themselves in October 1851 at the Agricultural

Society dinner at Hereford. Lord Bateman was in the chair and amongst the company there was a 'strong & general expression of protectionist feeling'. Indeed, Lewis found it difficult to get much of a hearing and the chairman had to intervene on his behalf. As *The Times* reported:

> Mr Cornewall Lewis rose to speak. 'I regret it is not in my power to congratulate this company upon any very prosperous condition of agriculture.' (Derisive cheers and hisses). 'But I fear I cannot congratulate the company present, either as owners or as occupiers, of any very prosperous conditions of agriculture.' (Hisses and derisive cheers).
>
> 'I cannot forget, I say, that scarcely nine months have elapsed since Her Majesty in her speech to Parliament, expressed her sympathy with the agricultural interest, ('And that was all') - that the distressed owners and occupiers of the soil ...' ('What nonsense' and derisive cheers, which for some moments interrupted the hon. member) 'You may naturally ask what your representatives have done for you' ('Nothing', 'Absolutely nothing', and great interruption).
>
> At this point the Chairman rose & begged the company to give Mr Lewis a fair hearing who continued and ended his speech in somewhat quieter circumstances.[154]

Lewis continued at considerable length and statistical detail, provoking the cry 'Cut it short'. Booker was the next to speak, and was greeted with repeated bursts of deafening applause, but like Lewis he also taxed the patience of his audience with statistics on the numbers of oxen, cows, calves, sheep, lambs, and pigs imported in recent years which led him to the conclusion that

> Our great towns and marts of industry were supplied with meat from abroad instead of from own produce (Cheers).[155]

But, Booker continued:

> There is another question of deep importance, well worthy of a refined, a cultivated, and a philosophical mind, such as that of Mr Cornewall Lewis, which affected the state of the population.[156]

This was the far lower rate of increase in the population of exclusively agricultural counties like Herefordshire, in comparison with neighbouring counties with mixed economies:

> It would be a libel on the buxom, rosy-cheeked women of Herefordshire to say that at least they were not as good breeders ss their own cows, or that their qualifications were not superior to those of the half-starved creatures in the over-crowded alleys of the towns, called women, but who had none of the 'points' of a woman, either before or behind; and it would be a libel, too, on the broad-shouldered men of Herefordshire to say that they were not as sure foal-getters as the men of any other county, or even as Prince Albert himself. (Oh, Oh.)[157]

The explanation, in Booker's opinion, for the decline was emigration and the remedy lay in the restoration of protection. When the London newspapers came to report the occasion, both *The Times* and the *Chronicle* commented 'with severity on a coarse passage in Booker's speech'. Hearing of this, to keep his own plate clean, Lewis wrote to Russell to explain why 'he had not remonstrated against the language used'.[158] It was a necessary precaution, as a letter to *The Times* soon showed.

> I do not so much complain of the hon. Member's speech, because it is characteristic of the man, and is sure to meet with the condemnation it deserves from every right minded individual; but what I do complain of is that Mr GC Lewis, MP, who was present, did not instantly rise to complain of this most indecent attack upon the Royal Consort of Her Majesty, in whose pay he is, and whose most devoted servant he ought to consider himself.[159]

Protection, though obviously still an issue in Herefordshire, to Lewis's mind had been abandoned by its gentlemen and the intelligent, remaining a tenet of belief only amongst the hot-headed and short-sighted:

> The Protection cry has very much lost its *national* importance. If the Protectionists were to come in they would not venture to propose a restoration of the Corn Law, but would merely dabble a little with shiftings of taxation. As respects *particular* seats, however, the cry is still alive. It can be used with effect for local purposes, as in Herefordshire. The gentlemen for the most part see the inutility of attempting a reaction against the large towns and all the intelligence of the country; but the farmers are more hot-headed and short-sighted, and more easily duped by interested leaders.[160]

On 22nd February 1852, Lewis, the free trader, in expectation of a general election in the near future, wrote to his kinsman Richard Banks of Kington, a lawyer and banker who acted as his political agent:

> I must begin now to look about me with a view of ascertaining what support I am likely to receive in the county, & of making preparations for a contest.[161]

In his reply Banks wished him luck and assured him that, despite his position as a free trader, he was at least safe in the Kington neighbourhood.[162] There were those, however, amongst the gentry who thought that there was something improper in a contested election, and John Arkwright of Hampton Court wrote to Charles Hanbury that though he thought the latter was highly qualified to represent the county he was going to use his influence in favour of Booker and King *only*, in the hope that the disagreeable turmoil of a contested election may thereby be avoided.[163] Arkwright was a protectionist and so made no mention of Lewis, the free trade candidate.

Lewis set off from Kent House on 5th March to catch the morning train from Paddington for Gloucester, where he took the coach to Hereford, staying the night at Bodenham's. His brother Gilbert came over from Monnington on Wye and the three of them discussed Lewis's electioneering prospects. Gilbert reported that Lewis's recent address to the electorate 'though plain spoken on the subject of Protection, had been well received', but Bodenham was less certain; accounts were conflicting. After spending Saturday morning writing canvassing letters, Lewis went with Gilbert to Monnington, where James Davies, of Moor Court, joined them for dinner. Sunday, not withstanding Gilbert's clerical duties, saw more canvassing letters and another address being written. On Monday Lewis rode over to Garnstone to Daniel Peploe Peploe, who, though committed to Hanbury's cause, agreed to allow Lewis to canvass the Garnstone tenants. In the evening it was on to Moor Court for the night when he and James Davies were joined for dinner by his kinsmen Richard Banks and his son Richard William Banks. Tuesday, it being Market Day, they all went to Kington where Lewis felt he had an eminently successful canvass, with only one refusal:

> The shopkeepers are evidently free traders.[164]

Things went well, too, he thought, at Ledbury and Hereford, where he 'was dragged thro' the town by men, with flags, music, &c. and the popular feeling is decidedly in favour of free trade.'[165] Ross and Leominster, he thought, went equally well and at Bromyard the horses were again taken out of his carriage and he was dragged round the town by his supporters, with flags and music. It was the same, too, at Hay.

He also canvassed the villages, going in a gig up to Longtown in the Black Mountains. Making a speech at the inn, he found the village 'a striking & beautiful spot' and, with the antiquarian's eye, noted 'the well preserved remains of an old round tower'. Then it was back to Gloucester and 'thence by express train to London'. As he sat back in the cushions of his first class carriage he concluded, with some satisfaction, that:

> The general result of my canvass has been successful. The change of govt has been my great ally, which has nearly silenced the Protection cry. The farmers have practically discovered the dishonesty of their leaders, which in opposition would never have appeared.[166]

However, the Protectionist cry had not been silenced and a few days later Lewis was admitting to Banks: 'The Leominster district is where I fail most & I see no means at present by which a breach can be made in the enemy's line in that quarter.'[167] Booker had spoken of politics as a February to September activity,[168] and Lewis, though he had been a junior minister, saw them in the same light. It was now Holy Week, so Lewis forgot about electioneering and started on an article on Lord Derby's ministry which he had promised for the *Edinburgh Review*, laying it aside for Good Friday, but resuming work on it on Easter Eve and finishing it on Easter Day.[169] He then turned his attention to the *Treatise*:

> Tuesday, 13th April 1852. K[ent] H[ouse]. Sent the press the last chapter [c.27] of my *Treatise on Politics*, & began the preparation of the Index. The accounts I have received from Bodenham since I left Herefordshire, with respect to my election, are on the whole satisfactory.
>
> Wednesday 14th April to Saturday 17th April. Continued my Index, corrected the proofs of my article & returned it to the press.

> Saturday 17th April. Wrote canvassing letters.
>
> Wednesday 21st April. This is my birthday, I am 46 years old. Attended a meeting of the Senate of the University of London. Dined at Lansdowne House.
>
> Monday 26th April. Finished the Index to my *Treatise* & sent it with the last corrected proof to the press. I have thus completed this work, not withstanding the occupations of Parliament & of a busy office, & the printing of it, written 3 years from the time when I began is composition, viz Whitsunday 1849.
>
> Saturday 8th May. Returned to the press the title page, contents, &c of my *Treatise*. It is now ready for publication.

Lewis returned to Ross on 11th May for a conference with the local solicitors Hall, Minett, and Hooper.[170] They disapproved of his plan to canvass in the parishes, perhaps recognizing his limited skills in public relations, and recommended him to issue an election address instead:

> I accordingly wrote out an address, the heads of which I had previously settled with Bodenham, shewed it to Hall & Minett, & dispatched it to Hereford for publication. Slept at Barrett's Hotel.[171] My proposed canvass in the neighbourhood of Ross was discussed & the difficulties appeared so great that it was agreed to suspend it until I saw Bodenham.[172]

He was back in London on Friday where the gratifying news awaited him that the *Treatise* had been published the previous day.

Returning to Herefordshire at the end of May he stayed at Moor Court with James Davies and found that the north-western part of the county more receptive. *Things*, however, interested him more than *people*, so that when he called on John Clarke of Kinnersley, he says nothing about the meeting in his diary, but noted that Kinnersley castle, wherein the farmer-squire lived was a 'curious old house. The most modern part is Q[ueen] Elizabeth'.[173]

In this round of canvassing Presteign, Staunton on Arrow, Pembridge, Lyonshall, Sarnesfield all had their visits. Back at Kington, he canvassed the market, and when he addressed the voters 'at some length, several questions were put to me by different persons'.[174] Then it was over to the other side of the county to Ledbury, Much Marcle, Bosbury, and Woolhope. Travelling on horseback, often for eight or nine hours, even twelve hours on occasion, he met, he admits in his diary, with but 'indifferent success'. To make matters worse, the weather was bad, and he fell off his horse.

Besides protectionism, another local issue the importance of which Lewis tended to underestimate was that of Roman Catholicism. Anti-Roman Catholic sentiments, especially in south-west Herefordshire, were strong, and Lewis seems to have been less aware of them than others. According to his diary his nomination for election on 13th July 1852 was a very eirenic affair. He was staying at the deanery and drove out to Whitecross:

> where I got on horseback, & rode with a large cortege of my friends into the town. My party was as numerous as those of the 3 other candidates put together. Aftds at the Shirehall where the nomination of the candidates for the county took place. I was nominated first, then Booker, King, & Hanbury. The show of hands in my favour was much larger than that for any of the other candidates. I spoke for rather more than an hour, & was well listened to. There must have been nearly 1000 persons in the hall.[175]

The *Hereford Times* gave a less felicitous account of things. When Mr JF Vaughan of Courtfield, a well know member of this leading Herefordshire Roman Catholic family, and of whom Herbert Vaughan, who was to be created a cardinal in 1893, was then a young kinsman, rose to speak:

> he in vain endeavoured to address the meeting. Ev'ry attempt was met by groans and hisses, chiefly emanating from a section of the lower class of the Protectionists, and repeated cries of No Popery! Down with the Priests, etc.[176]

The High Sheriff intervened to defend Vaughan's right to speak: 'as an elector of the county, he has a right to do'. But the confusion continued, upon which Archdeacon Lane Freer rose and asked:

> Is this what you call your protestant liberality? Is this your love of fair play? I appeal to you for the sake of our credit and honour to give Mr Vaughan a hearing. Don't let it be said that you refused to hear a gentleman who wished only to ask a simple question, for no other reason, than because he was a Roman Catholic.[177]

Voting began on Friday 16th July and Lewis had in a printed letter not only reminded his supporters of the dates of the poll, but provided them with a list of coaches to take them from the railway stations to the polling stations, as well as a list of agents to be contacted for further information and assistance. Lewis himself stayed in Hereford at the deanery, but the news was not good:

> the poll was favourable to me in the Hereford district, but as the accounts of the other districts arrived, the numbers inclined against me, & at the end of the day I was in a minority of about 140. I consulted in the evening with Bodenham as to keeping open the poll for another day, & determined to do so, in order to test the feeling of the county, but without any hope of reversing this day's poll.[178]

Things went no better on Saturday and Lewis's minority increased to 194. He went to dinner with his brother at Monnington rectory, where his father and step-mother joined him. At least Frankland Lewis had no anxieties about the safety of his seat, though earlier on there had been rumblings against him in the Radnor boroughs:

> Certain parties in this select district which numbers 487 votes, being dissatisfied with the conduct of the sitting member, Sir Thomas Frankland Lewis, it has been determined to oppose his return at the next general election, and no less than five resident gentlemen have placed themselves at the disposal of the committee just self constituted. No real contest has occurred in these retired and ancient boroughs since 1780.[179]

On Sunday morning after church Lewis heard from James Davies that there had been riot at Ross, the polling booths had been smashed, and the polling books destroyed. A message from Bodenham confirmed this was so.[180]

Lewis left Monnington on Monday for Hereford and the declaration of the poll:

King	3167
Booker	3143
Hanbury	3030
Lewis	2836

He seems to have been little moved by the result. He made a long speech and discussed with the Sheriff as to what should happen over the lost Ross poll books. He stayed the night at the deanery and returned to London next day.[181] His aunt Lady Duff Gordon was much more upset:

We heard from L[ad]y Lewis & Alice [Duff Gordon] that George Lewis had lost his election: Hanbury, King, Booker elected for Herefordshire, three Protectionists! Very disgraceful for Herefordshire to have not returned one free Trader!! We were very sorry as we thought George secure.[182]

Back at Kent House he wrote to thank his electors and then:

began to write the Second chapter of an *Enquiry into the Credibility of the early Roman history*, for which I have collected notes since last autumn. I expect it to make a volume, & I hope to finish it in less than a year.[183]

In his diaries Lewis offered himself no explanation for his defeat, but his belief in free trade, sympathy for Roman Catholics, and lack of the common touch all contributed towards putting him at the bottom of the poll, which his brother Gilbert ascribed to the hostility of 'the smaller voters'.[184]

James Davies of Moor Court wrote to Lewis with his sympathy, whilst giving a sad insight into the conduct of elections in mid-19th-century Herefordshire:

I was sorry not to have a Glimpse of you after your defeat which was an Event I did not expect & which I am sure has grieved very many Persons who either wholly or partially voted for your opponents. I rejoice however to hear that you have borne the Disappointment manfully and it is no small Consolation to feel that you have got thr' the Struggle with a very high Degree of Credit in every respect. I must own I should have cared less than I do if we had been beaten by fair means, but the Threats, bullying, Intimidation, Promises and perhaps a little Bribery have unquestionably stolen from us a large number of votes. I have seen many Contests and never witnessed such Coercion, force, and Obstruction as did at the Kington Poll and that by persons called Gentleman and Clergyman, whose conduct most certainly was the Cause of what little Disturbance occurred there.

Parson Blissett was most prominent on the 1st morning I saw him continually attacking every one of our Color, who was being quickly conducted to the Booth & struggling to get him out of our hands by main force, so that I felt under the disagreeable necessity of telling him pretty freely my opinion and in plain words, publicly, that he was a disgrace to the Church & the Magistracy. After all I calculate that the falling off in the

> Kington District was not much more than 5 pr Cent of the gross number of Promises, tho' we lost some few Plumpers[185] we expected who were compelled to split.
>
> I was never inclined for the Ballot until now, and I am now convinced that it is necessary to obtain that or some other improved mode of managing Elections.[186]

The 1832 Reform Act had given Wales five additional members, bringing the total up to thirty-two. One of these seats was occupied by the member for the county of Radnor, and another by the member for the Radnorshire boroughs to which Presteign was added to Cefn Llys, Knucklas, Painscastle, Radnor, and Rhaeadr. In the counties the male forty-shilling free holder was joined by male tenants who paid an annual rent of £50 or more, and the borough franchise was reformed by granting the vote to men who held real estate worth at least £10 a year.

In Wales one adult male in five had the vote. But since the £50 tenant was wholly dependent upon the goodwill of his landlord, and voting was done in public, the landowners virtually controlled Welsh parliamentary representation. In August 1852 Nassau Senior came to stay at Harpton and he tells how one afternoon:

> We set out in a great cavalcade, Sir Frankland, Miss Gordon, Miss Lister, George Lewis, Lady Theresa, and I, to ride to Water-break-its-neck, and thence over the lofty downs forming a part of the high naked country called Radnor Forest. Our progress through New Radnor was impeded by voters and canvassers who had to be greeted and thanked.[187]

Moreover, the opportunity to vote was infrequent because contested elections were considered to be unnecessary disruptions of rural order. Frankland Lewis was first elected in 1828 as the member for Radnorshire, and was unopposed. It was the same in 1830. In 1847 and 1852 he was elected unopposed for the Radnorshire boroughs. It was the same, too, for Cornewall Lewis in 1855 when he succeeded his father as the member for the Radnorshire boroughs, and again in 1855 and 1859. Indeed Cornewall Lewis never won a contested election.

He set out his thoughts to FL Bodenham, the Hereford lawyer who had acted as his agent in his Hereford contests. He acknowledges that the extension of the franchise would be to the Liberals' advantage and accepts the existence of 'the politics of the vote purchaser'.

The eventual introduction of the secret ballot was, however, inevitable, perhaps even welcome to Lewis after his own experiences in 1852 when he lost his Herefordshire seat, though the secret vote was no guarantee against intimidation.

> There can, I think, be no doubt that a £10 franchise in the counties would be favourable to the Liberal interest. It is equally clear that a reduction of the borough franchise must have a democratic tendency. It would *certainly* in the large towns strengthen the Radical interest. In the towns of moderate size, and in boroughs such as Radnor, it would strengthen the Liberal interest generally. Where the small voters were venal, the politics of the purchaser would determine their votes, but I cannot think that *unpurchased* they would often be found on the Tory side. A new Reform Bill, lowering the borough franchise, followed by a general election, would probably give such an impulse to the question of the ballot as to carry it in the House of Commons. The House of Lords could not long resist. I cannot think, looking to the habits and feelings of this country on the subject of elections, that it would be possible to carry a Ballot Bill with a clause for fining or imprisoning a voter who exhibited his vote. The change would be so complete that one can hardly conceive such a provision acquiesced in. Now, if the concealment is optional and not *compulsory*, I am disposed to think that the Ballot would have little effect. There are in every constituency a large number of independent voters who care for nobody, who have political opinions, and who wish to proclaim them. All these would continue, if permitted, to vote openly. There are also a large number of persons, not so independent, and with little or no regard for politics, but who wish to please or serve somebody by their vote, and to place him under a sort of obligation. These of course consider it a great hardship to be debarred from voting openly. If these two classes are added together, I think you will in most constituencies leave only an inconsiderable minority. These persons might wish to find safety in concealment; but would concealment avail them? Would not those who had the means of intimidating or annoying them treat concealment as evidence of guilt, and proceed to extremities unless they were satisfied that the voter voted according to their wish? If this was the way in which the system worked, an optional Ballot would leave matters pretty much as they are ...

A new Reform Bill would increase the cry for Ballot in two ways. In the first place, it would increase the number of borough members pledged to radical measures. In the next place, it would strengthen the argument for the ballot by adding to the number of poor and dependent voters.[188]

Chapter Four:
Editing *The Edinburgh Review*

Lewis's 1852 Herefordshire election expenses were nearly £6,800 which he had to pay off by borrowing from his wife's marriage settlement. The chief expense was at Ross, which exceeded those at Hereford, Kington, and Peterchurch put together, and where the hotel bill alone was £700:

> My expense is about equal to the amount of my savings during the time I held the office of Poor Law Commissioner.[1]

Within a fortnight, however, Lewis was being sounded out about his interest in an unexpected Parliamentary vacancy at Peterborough. This was due to the sudden death of the Hon Richard Watson,[2] a relative of Charles William Wentworth-Fitzwilliam, the third Earl Fitzwilliam, who regarded the two Peterborough seats as being in his gift, though this claim was not unchallenged.

The Liberals had won all of the four elections at Peterborough between 1832 and 1847, and all the winners were either Fitzwilliam's blood relatives, aristocratic Liberals, or members of the Liberal gentry recommended by Fitzwilliam, who before succeeding to his father's title in 1833 was known as Viscount Milton. The Viscount was conspicuous for his support for such Liberal causes as the 1832 Reform Bill:

> When wise Lord Milton fiercely screamed
> 'No taxes till the Bill is law',
> To all the Whigs Lord Milton seemed
> The noblest Lord they ever saw.[3]

In August 1852 Sir George Grey, the former Home Secretary, who had lost his seat for North Northumberland, was the first choice of the Liberals, with Lewis as their back-up:

> Friday 6th August 1852. K[ent]H[ouse]. Received today a letter from Ld Fitzwilliam informing me that the vacant seat at Peterborough had been offered to Sir G Grey, but that it is not certain he will accept it, & if he declines, he will offer it to me. I wrote to thank Ld Fitzwilliam for the offer, & to accept it in case Sir GG shd refuse. Called on Sir Jas Graham & had a long conversation with him.[4]

But Grey wanted 'freedom for a time from the demands of the House of Commons', and declined the honour of standing for Peterborough.[5] Two other candidates were also considered: Ralph Bernal and Edward Horsman, both of whom, like Lewis, had lost their seats in July.[6]

Meanwhile Lewis continued with his Roman history and called again on Sir James Graham to discuss matters further[7] before going down with the family to Harpton, where a letter followed him from Fitzwilliam.

> On Friday I received a letter fiom Ld Fitzwilliam directed to me in London informing me that Sir G Grey had declined to stand for Peterborough & asking me to come to him at Wentworth. I wrote saying that I wd go to him on Monday.[8]

Leaving Harpton early in the morning and travelling by train from Ludlow, by way of Shrewsbury, Stafford, Lichfield, and Derby, Lewis arrived at Wentworth Woodhouse in the late evening.[9] This handsome 18th-century mansion, with a frontage of 600 feet, has the longest front of any English country house, and John Carr's architecture[10] seems to have interested Lewis more than his own political future. He was particularly impressed by an inscription in the mausoleum, which Pevsner considered to be 'an outstandingly fine and noble structure'.[11]

> Saw the Mausoleum, with Bushe's inscription. The word *realise*, which has been objected to as an Americanism, occurs in it. Ld Fitzwilliam explained to me the state of things at Peterborough, & gave me some letters for the chief persons.[12]

Lewis left Wentworth in the afternoon by 'Direct Northern train' for Peterborough where he was met by JD Simpson, Fitzwilliam's electoral agent and who considered his arrival premature. Though Lewis had been invited to stand by Fitzwilliam, and though it was, no doubt, no more than a formality, the local Liberal Committee had not yet officially invited his candidature. Lewis took the next train to London and Simpson called the Committee into session and Lewis was unanimously selected as the official candidate. Their letter of invitation arrived at Kent House by the early post next morning.

> Wednesday, 18th August 1852. K[ent] H[ouse]. Sent a letter by the early post in answer to an invitation from a Committee of Electors at Peterborough to become a candidate & fixed Friday to attend a public meeting.

> Thursday, 19th August. Left Kent House by an evening [train] for Peterborough, arrived at the Angel Inn about 8 o'clock & attended a meeting of my supporters belonging to L[or]d Fitzwilliam's party. Slept there.

Lewis, however, was either unaware of the political situation at Peterborough, or was insufficient of a democrat to think it worthy of his attention. It was enough for him that he had been asked to stand by Lord Fitzwilliam and the fact that there was a strong Liberal element in the city which thought it should be involved in the choice of candidate was irrelevant. Consequently, he was in for a surprise when he attended the meeting of Liberal voters.

> Friday, 20th August. Angel Inn, Peterborough. Attended a meeting of Electors & spoke at length, in order to explain my political opinions. I was listened to patiently & attentively, but in consequence of a schism between the Whig party supported by L[or]d Fitzwilliam, & the radicals, the latter proposed & carried a resolution hostile to me. After the meeting, I issued an address, declaring myself a candidate. Called on Mr Strong,[13] & left him a letter given me by L[or]d F[itzwillia]m.

> Saturday 21st August. Peterborough. Canvassed a part of the town, & called on the Bishop[14] & Dean.[15] There is in today's *Times* an imperfect & inaccurate report of yesterday's proceedings at the meeting.[16]

The meeting took place at the Corn Exchange and did not go well. According to *The Times* he was hissed at and insulted by sarcastic comments from the audience throughout.[17] This differs from Lewis's version of things in his diary, and the local paper, the *Mercury Standard*, agreeing with Lewis's account, reported that he was listened to with perfect attentiveness. All the same all the reports agree that when, at the end of the meeting, a vote was taken, Lewis lost, and a resolution declaring that he was not entitled to the support of the Liberal electors of Peterborough was adopted by a large majority.[18]

Lewis sought solace on Sunday by attending Evensong at the cathedral, before resuming next day his canvass of the city and the surrounding hamlets, accompanied by Simpson and other prominent Liberals. Simpson assured Fitzwilliam that Lewis's canvass had been extremely successful and that he had gained at least 17 votes.[19] But by Wednesday the experience of the last six days was causing Lewis to have second thoughts about pursuing the contest. Using its expense as his excuse he wrote to Fitzwilliam:

> Wednesday, 25th August. Canvassed the rest of Peterborough. Wrote an address, thanking the voters, after my canvass. Also wrote a letter to L[or]d Fitzwilliam, which I gave to Mr Simpson, informing him of my difficulty in meeting the probable expenses of a contest, & offering to withdraw. Left Peterboro' by the 2 o'clock train, & slept at Shrewsbury.[20]

From Shrewsbury he caught the morning train for Ludlow, using the newly-opened Shrewsbury and Hereford Railway which had been opened as far as Ludlow since April. He arrived at Harpton in time for dinner, but rail travel did not agree with him, and on Friday he was:

> In bed for part of the day from a headache produced by the shaking of a rough railway Carriage.[21]

Reports of Lewis's poor Peterborough reception reached Esther Crummer at Howey Hall and she expressed her concern to nephew RW Banks:

> Mr George Lewis's being a candidate for Peterborough it appears from the Papers that he has had a cool reception but I hope he will succeed.[22]

Staying at Moor Court the following weekend with James Davies, Mrs Crummer's brother, Lewis heard from Fitzwilliam:

> objecting in a very decided manner to my withdrawing at Peterborough. He acknowledges that he led me to expect that the expenses of a contest wd not exceed £4 or 500, whereas they are estimated by Mr Simpson to be at £2000, & he offers to save me harmless for everything beyond the promised sum. As Ld F puts the offer on the ground that my withdrawal wd endanger the seat, I have accepted it.[23]

After brief visits to the Kington Flower Show, Garnstone, and Bishopstone, Lewis was in Hereford by the end of the week for a meeting of the Diocesan Board of Education,[24] where he moved a vote of thanks to Dr Renn Hampden, the bishop, for whom he had little time. This, however, did not prevent him from dining and sleeping at the Palace that night. Then after a weekend with the Clives at Whitfield, he returned to London,[25] having given Peterborough little further thought. Instead he:

> Began writing an article on the late Elections & Free Trade for the *Ed[inburgh] Review*.[26]

Lewis seems to have been unperturbed by the news he received a few days later that the Independent Liberals of Peterborough had found a candidate more to their taste in the person of George Hammond Whalley, who had stood unsuccessfully for the Montgomery boroughs in July.[27] Work on the article for the *Edinburgh Review* continued for another week or more whilst Whalley began to consolidate his position amongst the Peterborough electorate:

> Thursday 16th September 1852. Mr Whalley had a meeting at Peterborough, which was attended almost exclusively by radicals. They passed a vote in his favour.

The article was finished the next day and Lewis's brother-in-law, the Earl of Clarendon, read it without enthusiasm. More exciting, perhaps, was the news that Whalley had announced his intention of canvassing Peterborough and in an interview with Fitzwilliam's solicitor unsuccessfully sought his lordship's support for his candidature. Whalley countered with the proposal that both he and Lewis should retire from the contest:

> This proposal was rejected, & the interview ended. It is doubtful whether he will ever get so far as a canvass.[28]

Unimpressed, Lewis resumed work on chapter three of his Roman history. This was soon interrupted, however, by the arrival of the proofs of his article for the *Edinburgh Review* and the news that:

> Mr Whalley had canvassed Peterboro, & is supported by a large portion of the Tory party.[29]

Perhaps more welcome were the letters from Lord John Russell and Sir James Graham approving of the article in the *Edinburgh Review*. Work on the Roman history continued and when on 12th October he heard from Peterborough that 'Mr Whalley definitively announces himself a candidate' Lewis's response seems to have been to apply himself to his Roman history with renewed energy:

> Continued my Roman history. Finished the chapter on the Public sources of the early history. Began the following chapter.

Lewis had little time for Whalley, dismissing him as:

> a very low fellow as an opponent, who is ready to do or say anything to please anybody, or to gain any advantage. Luckily, he has very little money, and the respectable Tories are afraid of him.[30]

The Times agreed that he had no declared political principles, though felt he made up for this deficiency with the enthusiasm of his campaign, his slogan being 'Let's make the town free' which had considerable appeal to those who resented Fitzwilliam's hold over Peterborough. The apathy of Lewis and his supporters was seen as being due to their reliance upon the hopelessness of any successful opposition to Fitzwilliam's influence.[31]

All the same, by early November Lewis was taking Whalley's opposition seriously, interrupting his history to go up to London from Watford to meet Nelson Wilkinson, one of Fitzwilliam's political agents.

> Went up on Tuesday the 2nd to London, & met Mr Wilkinson.
> Heard account of my prospects at Peterboro.

Apparently encouraged by Wilkinson's news to continue in his electoral inactivity, Lewis returned to his Roman history, interrupting the work to go up to town to call on Fitzwilliam and his father. Even the funeral of the Duke of Wellington on 17th November did not distract him, though Theresa and the two girls went up to London to see it. Then on the 24th he went from Kent House to consult his friend Richard Dawes, the Dean of Hereford, apparently 'about Whalley'.[32] Next day he left London on the 5 o'clock train for Peterborough to begin some serious canvassing which took him, accompanied by some local worthies, to the cathedral close and some of the neighbouring streets. 'The accounts', said he, 'of my prospects here are good', which was just as well, because his electioneering technique was poor indeed:

> Mr Lewis did not pay court to the electors. He did not canvass many who only required to be asked for their vote. One elector stated publicly that Mr Lewis had behaved as if the favour were to be conferred on the electors instead of on himself.[33]

Lewis's friend, William Hayter, MP for Wells, moved the writ in the Commons for the election on the evening of Friday 26th

November, but floods prevented its arrival in time at Peterborough for its declaration on Saturday, so this had to be deferred until Monday. Lewis passed a wet Sunday writing letters, before continuing with his canvassing on Monday. By Wednesday there was a feeling of excitement in the town and it was reported that:

> Such is the agitation which prevails in the town that some fears are entertained of a breach of the peace, against which, however, precautions have been taken.[34]

One potential cause for a breach of the peace was the body of 300 men, armed with staves, which Lewis's committee had hired. Their apparent purpose was to protect his supporters from 606 non-electors who had signed an address urging the electors to defend the rights of the town by polling for Whalley. Admittedly, these non-electors were later described as 'the very scurf of the neighbourhood'. The constable, however, who supervised the distribution of the staves was a member of Lewis's committee, which rewarded the protection men with refreshment tickets. It was also rumoured that several Fitzwilliam public houses offered supporters free hospitality.

Another cause of the excitement was Whalley's publicly avowed claim that he had been offered a sum of money if he would withdraw from the contest, which implicated the banker and former MP for Hereford, Ralph Biddulph, as well as Lewis's father. A public meeting was arranged for Thursday evening at the Corn Exchange, at which Whalley promised to prove his statement and Lewis to refute it in the most unequivocal manner. The meeting, it was reported, is:

> looked forward to with great anxiety, and is expected to be of a very stormy character.[35]

Lewis countered these accusations with a strongly worded circular, unmentioned in his diary:

> I distinctly repeat, in the most solemn and deliberate manner, that neither my father nor myself, nor any person authorized by him or me, or acting on his or my behalf, or with his or my knowledge or consent, either on Friday last or at any other time, offered any sum of money to Mr Whalley, or made any other offer or proposition to him whatever. I never authorized Mr Biddulph to make any offer of money or otherwise, or any proposition whatever, to Mr Whalley, in connexion with this election. I further declare in the most positive manner, upon the authority of letters since received from my father, that

although Mr Biddulph conveyed to him a proposition from Mr Whalley for a comparison of the Peterborough canvassing lists, my father declined to see Mr Whalley or to receive any proposition relative to the Peterborough election from him, and that he did not authorize or request Mr Biddulph, or any other person, to make any offer of money or any other proposition whatever to Mr Whalley.[36]

Then, detached from events as ever, Lewis spent Thursday morning riding from:

Milton with Lord Fitzwilliam, in order to call on Mr Strong, & ask him to nominate me. We found him at home & he acceded to the request. Aft[erwar]ds I returned to Peterboro.[37]

His account of the meeting is rather more aseptic than that in *The Times*:

in the evening I attended a public meeting, in order to refute Mr Whalley's charge ag[ains]t me that I had offered to buy off his opposition. The meeting was disorderly, but I succeeded in refuting the charge & the meeting was brought to a proper termination, chiefly by the firmness & good management of Mr Percival.[38]

What Lewis thought to be a 'proper termination' was seen by *The Times* as a 'satisfactory Compromise', in which Whalley 'was exculpated from the idea of having made a false charge, and, on the other hand, it was admitted that Mr Lewis was exonerated from the supposition of having any cognizance or connexion with such an offer.' Both men shook hands.[39]

The symbolic cordiality, however, of the handshake was soon forgotten and Whalley, who spoke for about two hours next morning at the nomination, was 'very abusive' of both Lewis and Fitzwilliam. Lewis himself spoke for an hour and then visited some electors in the knowledge that his best informed supporters were very confident of his success[40] But Saturday, the day of the poll, showed this confidence was quite misplaced:

This day the poll took place, & it ended unfavourably to me, with the following numbers.
Whalley   233
Lewis   218
The result was produced by a junction between the Radicals & Conservatives with the object of defeating the candidate

> supported by Ld Fitzwilliam. When the poll was over, I went to
> Milton, where I dined & slept. It was expected that the more
> respectable Conservatives wd not support a radical candidate,
> but this expectation proved to be delusive, nothing cd exceed
> the confidence of my supporters up to the last. They were in a
> complete fool's paradise.[41]

A triumphant Whalley was chaired through the streets of
Peterborough and a large key was displayed to symbolize the
unlocking of the borough from Fitzwilliam control. For his part, the
outraged Fitzwilliam threatened to sell his hounds, to turn out his
tenants in Peterborough's Bridge Street and elsewhere, and to remove
his custom and benevolent influence from those who did not vote for
his candidate.[42] This was a significant threat since just over 50% of the
Peterborough electorate lived under a roof owned by Fitzwilliam.

Lewis left Peterborough after the weekend on a Monday morning
train and was back at Grove Mill by 6 pm. There he was cheered to see
that the latest number of the *Economist* contained an article on his
'work on Politics, probably written by WR Greg'.[43] The condolences
also awaited him of his friend Sir James Graham who suggested
lessons to be learned from his defeat:

> The Whig aristocracy will, I hope, be convinced at last, that their
> hold on these small country towns is very precarious; and that
> their declining interests in these rotten communities ought not
> to stand in the way of sound Reforms affecting the Constituent
> Body.[44]

Sir Frankland Lewis shared his regrets over this sudden decline
in his son's political career with his cousin Lady Duff Gordon:

> He lamented very much for George being out of Parliament, &
> felt I thought great disappointment at this moment of Political
> changes at George not making a part in the Government which
> being out of Parliament prevents.[45]

TR Bromund made a detailed analysis of the 1852 Peterborough
by-election.[46] The result was as much a rejection of the Fitzwilliam
family's influence in Peterborough's affairs as it was of Lewis, who had
no local connections. There was a measure, too, of self-infliction in
Lewis's defeat: he did not try very hard to win the seat. His absence
from Peterborough for three months can hardly have helped him. He
disliked campaigning, tended to be long-winded and pedantic, and
the voters never warmed to him. His unsympathetic attitude both to

High Churchmen and to Nonconformist resentment of Church Rate also lost him support.

Whalley's campaign was far better organized and he himself was far more energetic and enthusiastic than Lewis. Moreover, by avoiding any serious discussion of political principles and by focussing solely on the issue of independence for the borough, Whalley commended himself to many at Lewis's expense. At the same time, the residents of Peterborough began to entertain expectations of steadily increasing political power since the enfranchisement of the £10 voters in 1832. The increasing population of the borough also helped to diminish the impact of Fitzwilliam's paternalism, and the arrival of the railway in 1845, by giving improved local access to national movements, further assisted this process.

A little over a week after his defeat at Peterborough Lewis was offered a post far more congenial to his talents than electioneering:

> Monday 13th December 1852. Mr Longman[47] offered me the editorship of the *Edinburgh Review* rendered vacant by the death of Empson[48] which had taken place on the previous Saturday. The salary of editor is £1000 a year, independent of the articles, which he may write. I promised to give him an answer in a few days.[49]

Lewis accepted Longman's offer and started work immediately: 'a number left unfinished by Empson is on the anvil, which must be published by the 8th of January'. This occupied all his time, not withstanding the intervention of Christmas, and he was determined the first issue of the *Review* should contain an article of his:

> Wednesday 22nd December 1852. Made arrangements for the forthcoming No. of the *Ed Rev.*

> Thursday 23rd December. Wrote out the plan of a political article for the next *Ed Rev.*

> Friday 24th December to Friday 31st December. Kent House. Employed all this week in writing an article on the fall of Ld Derby's govt.

Lady Duff Gordon thoroughly approved of her nephew's change of occupation:

> George Lewis is become Editor of the *Edinburgh Review* ... and much more suited to his habits than political life![50]

But Lewis himself had not completely abandoned his political ambitions as he soon confessed to Edmund Head:

> About three weeks ago poor Empson died, and Longman asked me to be his successor. There is a good deal of work to be done, but it is unaccompanied with the drawback of attendance at an office; and, situated as I was, I thought it wisest to accept. I shall try, if I can, to get a seat in Parliament; but if I was in Parliament and had an offer of office, I should refuse it, as the work of an office is incompatible with my present employment. Empson left the January number in an incomplete state, and I have been working very hard for the last fortnight in completing the arrangements for bringing it out. I am in hopes that you will be inclined to give me some help, any article on an American subject would be acceptable.[51]

On New Year's Day 1853 Lewis had the satisfaction of noting in his diary that 'in today's *Notes & Queries* there is an article of mine on the etymology of the word pearl', in which he noted that there is not a simple answer since the word occurs in all modern languages, both Romance and Teutonic. After some discussion he concluded that the proper Latin name for a pearl was *unio* rather than *margarita*, which was derived from the Greek; the common word for an onion, growing in a single bulb, was transferred to the pearl; and that the ancient meaning of *unio* is still preserved in the French *ognon*. Philemon Holland, who published his translation of Pliny in 1634, used the word pearl indifferently as the equivalent both of *margarita* and *unio*.[52] But of greater interest to the present discussion is the probability that this article, appearing as it did in print on 1st January 1853, was actually written the previous December whilst Lewis was electioneering at Peterborough. He seems to have preferred onions to electors.

Work recommenced on the Roman history, discontinued whilst he was electioneering at Peterborough: chapter seven was completed and chapter eight begun,[53] and the *Edinburgh Review* kept him both busy and contented, although there was the problem of Mr Bowen, a Brasenose don, who called at Kent House to complain that he had been unfairly attacked in a recent prematurely published article in the *Edinburgh Review* on 'Jervis's *History of the island of Corfu and the Ionian islands*'[54] by Lord Seaton.[55]

George Ferguson Bowen, a fellow and tutor at Brasenose, appointed Rector of the University of Corfu in 1847, had established for himself something of a reputation as an expert in Greek history and affairs.[56] In his article Seaton had alleged that Bowen was unfit to be Rector because of his extravagant garulity and involvement in Ionian politics.[57] Bowen visited Lewis on 17th January when the volume containing the article was not due for publication for another two days, but unfortunately:

> The distribution of copies had gone so far, that the number cannot be recalled or altered.[58]

Bowen threatened an action against Longman as the publisher of the article and Lewis wrote to Seaton as a matter of urgency.[59] Seaton replied that he had no objection to any correspondence Bowen might have with Lewis being published, and that his allusions to the Rector were inserted into the *Review* article because of what he, Seaton, considered to be Bowen's malevolent attacks upon him.[60] In further correspondence Seaton admitted that if Bowen did bring an action, the defence would have proof that he was indeed disobedient, garrulous, and absurd.[61]

It is not surprising that Lewis found much of his time occupied with the *Review*, though work still continued on the Roman history, and time was found to write an article on rabbits for *Notes & Queries*.[62] As was often the case, the piece for *Notes & Queries* was written in response to an earlier request for information. This time it was on the meaning and etymology of Conyngers or Connigries,[63] upon which 'AW of Kilburn' asked 'would any reader of *N & Q* kindly enlighten me on the subject?' Lewis was only too ready to oblige, despite his preoccupation with the next number of the *Edinburgh Review.*

> At Kent House. Much occupied with preparations for the April number of the Review. Some offers of articles, & some articles rejected, the revision of those accepted likewise occupies much time. Several proposals for articles on the Defences of the Country & on the Irish RC Church, all of which I have declined, thinking that the subjects can not be advantageously treated. Also proposals on Indian questions. I have likewise continued my work on Roman history.[64]

A welcome interruption came in the middle of February: university reform was in the air. In 1850 commissions were set up to inquire into Oxford and Cambridge, though neither were well received, and their work was obstructed. Lewis, however, favoured reform and welcomed the opportunity to assist in bringing it about:

> Received today a visit from Mr Lake,[65] Senior Proctor of Oxford, who, in concert with Dr Gaisford,[66] asked me to be one of the Examiners for the Ireland University Scholarship.[67] Understanding that this offer was connected with a wish on the part of some persons to improve the system of education at Oxford, I accepted the offer.[68]

It involved a week's work in March:

> Monday 14th March 1853. Left Kent House in the morning for Oxford. Arrived at Dr Jeune's[69] at Pembroke. Visited Edwin Palmer, one of my colleagues in the Scholarship examination, at Balliol. Settled with him the numerical values of the papers. Dined at Dr Jeune's. Read one set of papers after Dinner, Latin Prose Composition. None very good or very bad.

> Tuesday 15th March. Oxford. Read two sets of papers. Translation from Latin Prose, & into Greek Prose. Strange mistakes in both, but much knowledge of the languages displayed. Dined with Mr Conington[70] at University. Agreeable & intelligent conversation. Saw my other colleague, the Revd RC Powles.

> Wednesday 16th March. Oxford examination continued. Dined at Dr Jeune's with a large party.

> Thursday 17th March. Oxford. Examination continued. Dined at Dr Jeune's again a large party, several heads of houses.

> Friday 18th March. Oxford. I & my two colleagues met at Balliol after breakfast to compare notes. We had read 8 papers out of nine. We did not agree as to the candidates who had the largest number of marks, but we agreed as to the five best, though we placed them in different orders. We then went over the entire papers of these 5, reading all the compositions loud, & discussing the mistakes of the others & fixed a value for each paper in concert. The result was that the person who was highest according to my original reckoning came out the winner, with the full approbation of my colleagues. He proved, on opening the mottoes, to be Butler of University.[71] He is the son of the Dean of Peterborough, & a Rugby man. We also named Blomfield, Newman[72] & Robinson of Balliol, & Winstanley of University, as having distinguished themselves. Dined at Dr Jeune's.

> Saturday 19th March. Left Oxford by the morning train. Returned to Kent House.[73]

Lewis's account for Head of this Oxford excursion suggests he did not particularly enjoy it, it was inconvenient and even academically things were not what they were:

> The only interruption to the monotony of my life has been a visit to Oxford, where I went, in order to examine for the Ireland University Scholarship. I was asked to accept, and thought it right to go, although it cost me a good deal of trouble, and came at an inconvenient moment. I was disappointed, on the whole, by the exhibition made; some of the mistakes made even by the best men were amazing, and there was no great talent displayed by any one. Butler, a scholar of University, son of the Dean of Peterborough, a Rugby man, was the successful candidate. All the best men belonged to Balliol or University, and their eminence proves the success of the system of open scholarships, which must gradually spread to all the Colleges. Christ Church and Brasenose have lost all their distinction as places of learning, and Oriel is not very eminent.[74]

Another diversion was an invitation to stand for Taunton where a petition had been raised to unseat the successful candidate, Arthur Mills, on the grounds of bribery. Similar counter accusations were made against Sir Thomas Colebrooke whom Mills had unseated at the election. Anticipating that the outcome would be the unseating of Mills and the failure of Colebrooke to take his place, a Mr William Beadon of Otterhead near Honiton, a supporter of Colebrooke, invited Lewis to represent Taunton. Lewis, perhaps realising by now that contested elections were not his strength, and despite Beadon's assurances of success, declined.[75] The election committee eventually found both Mills and Colebrooke guilty of bribery through their respective agents and Mills was unseated.

So it was back to the *Edinburgh Review*. He supervised its production to the last detail, not only strengthening and editorially improving the articles and correcting and revising the proofs, but also calling on its printers in the City to give his directions personally. Then at last its successful publication was celebrated by dining at Longman's.[76] As usual, he tells all to his friend Edmund Head:

> I find that my *Review* work compels me to write so many letters of a quasi-official sort, that I have been remiss about all others. I have to keep a sort of office, without any clerks. There will be

some good articles in the next number of the *Review*, but it will be chiefly political, not literary. There is great difficulty in finding persons who can write well on literary and general subjects. Besides, my acquaintance lies chiefly among politicians. There is to be a good review of Alison's recent trashy History,[77] and also an estimate of Disraeli's political career; an amusing article moreover on the 'Welsh Clergy', by Conybeare, a son of the Dean of Llandaff now vicar of Axminster.[78] There will also be articles on 'Education' and the 'Income-Tax'. I shall be glad to know what you think of the number, as it is the first number really edited by me. If you wish, I can send you a copy.[79]

But the reception of Lewis's first *Review*, published in April, was not entirely favourable, the article by Abraham Hayward on Disraeli in particular giving offence. Hayward began life as a Tory, but on the split in the party in 1846 became a Peelite and free trader. His article in the *Edinburgh Review* was the first public expression of his dislike of Disraeli and, as usual, Lady Duff Gordon supported her nephew's decision to publish it so early in his editorial career:

I read an article by Hayward on d'Israeli in the *Edinburgh Review*. Severe but true, entirely condemning him upon his own words & books, and completely showing him up! People consider it ill-judged of George Lewis to have placed so bitter an article in his first *Edin Rev*. I don't feel it so! It is not vulgarly violent, but truth from his own life.[80]

The publication of the *Review* was followed by ten days confined to the house with influenza, interrupted with news of the Parliamentary history of Herefordshire and Peterborough, both constituencies being subject to petitions. The Herefordshire petition was withdrawn, but its Peterborough counterpart persisted. Early in May Fitzwilliam approached Lewis suggesting he should contribute towards the cost of the petition. He declined. The hearing itself lasted from 28th May to 7th June and resulted in Whalley being unseated on the ground that he had been guilty of treating.[81] He had held a tea-party for the wives of the voters, and had rented numerous sub-committee rooms from publicans, most of whom had voted for him, and had, no doubt, supplied persuasive refreshment to visitors at his expense. Lewis, however, decided not to stand again for Peterborough,[82] and Fitzwilliam's candidate this time was Thomson Hankey, a city merchant and one time governor of the Bank of England. But there was a successful petition against him as well, and another by-election called, for which Fitzwilliam turned once again to Lewis:

> Called on Ld Fitzwilliam who asked me if I wished to stand for Peterboro', but I declined on the ground that I shd be beat by a renewed coalition of the Tory & radical parties against me. Wrote on Roman history.[83]

The by-election took place in the summer of 1853, and Whalley was victorious. It was now Fitzwilliam's turn to petition and in July Lewis was examined on 'what had passed between [him] & Ld Fitzwilliam with reference to it'.[84] The petition was unsuccessful and Whalley sat for Peterborough until his death in 1878.

By the end of April Lewis had completed the tenth chapter of his Roman history and seemed little deflated by receiving the first volume of Dr Albert Schwegler's[85] work on the same subject, 'very ably written'. It had, nevertheless, to a considerable extent anticipated what he himself had been writing since August 1852.[86] Work was interspersed with articles for the *Edinburgh Review* from which in May he allowed himself an evening's respite by attending his elder stepdaughter's coming out.

> Wednesday 11th May 1853. K[ent]H[ouse]. Wrote *Review* ... In the evening, at a ball at the Foreign Office, at which Therese came out.

Another volume of the *Edinburgh Review* was published in July and to Lewis's relief he could write in his diary:

> I hear that the new number of the *Edinburgh* is considered a good one.[87]

A steady supply of trifles for *Notes & Queries* gave Lewis his relaxation. January's *Rabbits* were followed by a rather more substantial two part review of Thomas Markby's edition of Francis Bacon's *The Essays or Counsels, civil and moral, with a Table of the Colours of Good and Evil.*

> Mr Markby has recently published his promised edition of Bacon's *Essays*; and he has in this, as in his edition of the *Advancement of Learning*,[88] successfully traced most of the passages alluded to by Lord Bacon. The following notes relate to a few points which still deserve attention.[89]

On occasion even Lewis has to admit that his resources are not totally equal to the task he has undertaken:

> Mr Markby is at a loss to trace this quotation. I am unable to assist him.[90]

A third paper set out to elucidate the origin of the word namby-pamby.[91] In it he he concluded that Namby-pamby belongs to a tolerably numerous class of words in our language, all formed on the same rhyming principle. They are all familiar and some of them childish; which last circumstance probably suggested to Pope the invention of the word namby-pamby, in order to designate the infantile style which Ambrose Philips had introduced. He then appends a list of thirty words of similar form:

> Intended merely to illustrate the principle upon which this class of words are formed, and does not aim at completeness. Some of your correspondents will doubtless, if they are disposed, be able to supply other examples of the same mode of formation.

It was the Lewises's custom to leave London for August and the greater part of September, and for he and his family to make their way to Harpton, calling for a few days on friends and relations on their route. At Harpton his father and step-mother were there to greet them and they were joined a few days later by brother Gilbert and his wife Jane.[92] Other house-guests were the Hon Edward Turner Boyd Twistleton[93] and his sister, whom Lewis found 'intelligent and agreeable'.[94] Before his recent marriage to an American lady he had 'established himself and his excellent library in chambers in the Albany' where Lewis was unable to 'make out that he is doing anything'.[95]

At Harpton, Lewis, without being positively anti-social, found time to work on his Roman history, as well as to join the party riding on horseback round the Radnor Forest. Horsemanship, however, was not one his strengths, and a few weeks later he was to write in his diary:

> Fell from my horse in leaping over a ditch in a field without attention.[96]

It was whilst he was at Harpton that Lewis 'received a letter from C Wood',[97] offering him the government of Bombay, at £12,500 for five years.[98] Lewis replied next day:

> Acknowledging the importance of the offer, but expressing a doubt whether I should accept. The final answer is promised in a few days.[99]

The Harpton party was now joined by the Freers,[100] Berkeley Stanhopes,[101] and the Dews,[102] thereby becoming rather clerical.

There was more riding on the hills, then after nearly a week's thought and Roman history, Lewis wrote to Wood to refuse the offer of Bombay.[103] He later explained his decision to Edmund Head:

> I have had lately the offer of the Government of Bombay, which was made me in a flattering manner by Charles Wood. It was, however, impossible for my wife to leave Mrs Villiers, and there was a difficulty about taking Alice;[104] so that I decided at once, on domestic grounds, to refuse. I was not personally much tempted by the offer, notwithstanding the large amount of the salary. India is an interesting field, especially at the present moment; but it would have cut short a great many threads which I have begun to spin. I therefore remain constant to the *Edinburgh Review*, and am just about bringing out another number.[105]

Lewis was not unqualified for the post. He had spent time in 1848 at the Board of Control and was concerned there with Indian affairs, but there was one reason for his refusal he did not mention in his explanation to Head:

> I confess it seems to me that no man who is not in debt, or has not a large family, is justified in going out to a colony.[106]

With the claims of the government of Bombay behind him Lewis was able to give his attention to a more local institution, committed to keeping its members out of debt and to the relief of the needs of their large families, namely the Kington Society of Gentlemen, Mechanics, and Others:

> Friday 26th August 1853. Harpton. Attended a meeting of the Friendly Society at Kington & was in the chair, about 200 persons present.

Established in 1792, the Society held its meetings in Kington at the King's Head.[107] Besides its monthly meetings, there was an annual dinner during the town's wakes week in August. After a service in the parish church, members of the Society processed down the hill to the King's Head and dined together.[108] Lewis was very dutiful in these matters and was repaid by the support of the local electorate in 1847. It was the same in 1852 when he was abandoned elsewhere.

The Lewises returned to London in September by way of Worcester and Birmingham. They stayed at Worcester with the Cradocks on College Green.[109] At Birmingham they

> Saw Mr Chance's glass works, which he shewed us. He employs
> at these & some Chemical works about 2000 hands whose wages
> amount to about £2000 a week, or above £100,000 a year. Aftwds
> to Gillott's steel pen factory, which makes above 150 millions of
> steel pens in a year.

They went to church on Sunday at Birmingham parish church,
now St Philip's cathedral, and saw Mr Grantham Yorke, the incum-
bent, at his house.[110] Before leaving by rail on Monday from
Hardwick's Curzon Street terminus, Mr Yorke showed them Charles
Barry's King Edward's School, then in New Street, the School of
Design, and the new 'aloof and awe-inspiring' Town Hall.[111]

Installed again at Kent House, Lewis was able 'to perform the
obstetrical services for the October number of the *Review*'.[112] It was
safely delivered on 10th October and then, Roman history laid aside,
work immediately commenced on the next pregnancy, as it were:

> Monday 10th October 1853. Arrived at Kent House. Received
> the new no. of the *Edinburgh.*
>
> Tuesday 11th October. KH. Began an article of Fox's *Memoirs*[113]
> & the Buckingham papers for the *Edinburgh.*
>
> Wednesday 12th October. KH. Continued the article.
>
> Thursday 13th October. KH. Wrote on Fox &c. Dined at Ld
> Campbell's[114] met Macaulay.[115]
>
> Friday 14th October. KH. Wrote on Fox. Distributed the
> cheques of the new number to contributors.

The dinner at Lord Campbell's, who had been Lord Chief Justice
since 1850, would surely have been an interesting affair. Campbell was
not an enthusiastic golfer, at least for a Scot, but thought it, nevertheless, 'superior to the English cricket, which is too violent and gives no
opportunity for conversation'.[116] The quality, however, of Campbell's
conversation was doubted by some as much as that of Macaulay, and
in 1846 Lord Bougham and Vaux, one of the founders of the
Edinburgh Review, quipped

> Edinburgh is now celebrated for having given us the two
> greatest bores that have ever yet been known in London, for
> Jack Campbell in the House of Lords is just what Tom Macaulay
> is in private society.[117]

Lewis, too, was no great conversationalist.

As an editor Lewis was whole-hearted and ruthless, though one can understand his complaint that

> Prolixity is the bête noire of an editor. Every separate contributor has some special interest for wishing to write at length on his own subject.[118]

He would completely revise and change the style of an article if he felt so inclined and do so with little consultation with its author.[119] He was also happy to use the *Review* as a medium for publishing articles of his own which had been written on something of an impulse. The Roman history, or whatever major work he had in hand, would be totally abandoned, and all his energies applied to the article to get it finished for the next *Review* number. An example of this is the energy with which he set about writing his paper on Fox's *Memoirs* which occupied him, to the exclusion of all else, in the autumn of 1853, almost daily from 11th October to 7th November. Once done, with but a day's respite, he resumed work on the Roman history:

> Wednesday 9th November 1853. Kent House. Resumed my work on Roman history. Began eleventh chapter, on the period of the expulsion of the kings to the Burning of the City.

There were also visits to the British Museum library, where work was about to begin on Smirke's great circular reading room, to check facts, and proofs to correct of the next volume of the *Edinburgh Review*. But Lewis the scholar was also Lewis the antiquarian, and though he never became an FSA, he always was ready to acquire antiquarian detail. Thus, in December 1853 he fully recorded a visit to Kent House by Dr Symons, the Vicar of St Martins, Hereford.[120]

> I had a visit from Dr Symons of Hereford who told me that he was with the army at Corunna as a chaplain, at the time of the battle. He was with General Moore at his death, which took place in the afternoon about 4 o'clock, he died on a mattress on the floor in his own quarters. In the night the body was removed, for the sake of security, to the citadel. It was buried in the morning, about 8 o'clock, by daylight (& not by torchlight, as stated in Wolfe's ode),[121] the body was not in a coffin, but wrapped in a cloak. Few soldiers attended it, as most of the army were exhausted. Dr Symons helped to carry the body to the grave. He read the funeral service over it. The grave was on a bastion, without any stone. Dr Symons visited the place a few years afterwards. The body had then been removed, & there was a plain stone sarcophagus over it.[122]

Why the detail in his diary? Perhaps another piece for *Notes &* *Queries* was gestating. He seems to have found time, too, to help Lord John Russell on his *Memorials and Letters of Fox*,[123] and from Boxing Day to the end of the year he was engaged at Grove Mill revising 'the ms. of Fox's letters to Lord Holland per Ld John Russell, in order to add notes as to the facts alluded to'.[124] The publication of the first volume of this trilogy earlier in the year had sent Lewis off to check its facts at the State Papers Office:

> Visited the State Papers Office, in order to ascertain whether there was any correspondence relative to the double negocia- tion at Paris in 1782 referred to in Ld J Russell's recent memoirs of Fox. Found a long series of papers.[125]

Politics, however, had not entirely slipped from his mind, though pressing invitations 'to come forward as a candidate for South Staffordshire in place of Lord Lewisham'[126] were declined. Back in May, Lord Palmerston, then Home Secretary, had invited Lewis to serve on a commission with Henry Labouchere, whose long standing role as one of the two members for Taunton was not in dispute the previous February, and Sir John Patteson, to enquire into the consti- tution of the city of London. Lewis accepted even though 'the office was of course gratuitous'.[127] The commission did not begin its work for six months, but then, after dining at the Guildhall and at the Deanery of St Paul's with Henry Hart Milman,[128] no doubt to hear the City's own thoughts on the reform of its government its activity was intense. Meeting at 10 Downing Street, its sessions took place two or three times a week from late October into the new year. Lewis sent Head an account of its activities:

> My time during the last month has been principally occupied with an enquiry into the affairs of the City of London, of which there have been long reports in the *Times* and other papers. The subject has excited more interest than I expected; we found ourselves compelled to admit the reporters, and as the newspa- pers have plenty of space during the recess, they have been glad to fill it up with evidence on a subject which concerns so many persons. It is evident to me that the City have continued their old system just a little too long, that public opinion among the great body of the community has got ahead of them, and that when the exposure has arrived they find themselves with scarcely a friend out of their own ranks. They are like Louis Philippe when the day of adversity and trial is come: they have

nothing to look back upon but a long course of selfish and sordid conduct, and there are no acts which enlist any public sympathy in their favour.[129]

Had Lewis waited a fortnight or so before writing to Head, he could have given him some political gossip with which to warm the chill of the Canadian winter. As it was, it got no further than Lewis's diary. In December, over the dinner table, the Clarendons, related to Lewis by marriage through Therese Lewis, discussed the recent resignation of Palmerston as Home Secretary. He was uncomfortable with Lord Aberdeen's recent appointment as Prime Minister. Those dining at Kent House heard that:

> The Queen received the intelligence with much satisfaction, remarking that he was more dangerous in the govt than out of it.[130]

Lewis himself thought that Palmerston was 'no loss to the govt', for disliking the business of the Home Office, he had neglected it.[131] Lord Aberdeen apparently thought otherwise, and, made him Home Secretary. But according to Lewis, the day before Christmas eve, the conduct of politics fell from the hands of hands of the politicians in to those of the politicians' wives. When Lady Clarendon called on Lady Palmerston 'to express regret at Ld Palmerston's resignation', Lady Palmerston in response 'threw out a hint that the evil may not [be] irremediable, & intimated that Palmerston was willing to reconsider the question'. In consequence of this afternoon chatter in the drawing room Lewis was able to record in his diary that 'a negociation has been opened with Ld Aberdeen and the govt for arranging some compromise upon the Reform Bill, which will enable Palmerston to resume his office'.[132] Meanwhile Aberdeen had offered the Home Office to Sir George Grey, who was 'believed to be willing, but not desirous to accept'.

The year 1854 opened with Lewis in a mood of self congratulation:

> Sunday 1st January 1854. The Grove. Since the beginning of last year I have familiarized myself with the management of the *Edinburgh Review* and have found several new connexions. The last [Oct] number was very successful, chiefly on account of Conybeare's article on Church Parties.

Back in December, Lewis's view on Conybeare's article was slightly different:

> He [ie Conybeare] is a very clever writer, and his article has
> made a great sensation in the ecclesiastical world. The extremes
> of all parties dislike it.[133]

Nor would it have been well received in Wales. Neither Lewis nor
Conybeare seem to have appreciated that it was pastorally more
important for the clergy of the established Church in Wales to be able
speak Welsh, the language of the people, than to have a precise
mastery of English grammar. Connop Thirwall, bishop of St Davids
1840–74, whom Conybeare commends, appreciated this. He learned
Welsh and expected the same of his clergy. Lewis had no doubt heard
through his kinsman James Davies of Moorcourt how Thirlwall in
1852 had been anxious to induct a new incumbent for the
Breconshire parish of Bronllys, where James Davies had an estate,
capable of taking services in Welsh.[134]

In his diary the *Edinburgh Review* and his Roman history take
precedence over the threat of war. Thus on January 4th he notes that
he resumed his 'chapter on Roman history - progress slow', though on
the same day when he wrote to Head mention of the *Review* is brief
and delayed and it is the Crimea which occupies most of his attention:

> Everything in the East looks warlike: and if our fleet does not
> come into conflict with the Russian fleet, it will be a miracle. My
> expectation is, that before long England and France will be at
> war with Russia; as long as war lasts all measures of internal
> improvement must slumber.[135]

Enthusiasm, too, for Roman history was beginning to slumber
and Lewis complained to Head:

> I am writing regularly on the Roman history and have just
> finished Coriolanus. It is slow, tiresome work, and I shall not
> complete it till the end of the year.[136]

In February the Foreign Secretary, the Earl of Clarendon, Lewis's
brother-in-law, offered him the Permanent Under Secretaryship of the
Foreign Office, which he declined, 'as not being political'.[137] By this
he meant that the office lacked political power, rather than it would
have been politically unwise to lay himself open to the charge of nepotism. A little later he also declined an invitation to examine again for
the Ireland Scholarship at Oxford,[138] but accepted one to dine with
Lord Fitzwilliam, when surely the political fortunes of Peterborough
was one topic of conversation.[139] Perhaps the Crimea was another, for
as he told Edmund Head:

> The war still hangs fire in an extraordinary manner; but as a messenger was sent to St Petersburg last week with an ultimatum, the uncertainty must soon be dissipated. Our Government have no hope of peace; but the Emperor will fight with tremendous odds against him, and one does not see where his hope of success lies. What is singular in this matter is, that the French Government are not eager for war and the French people do not take it up warmly. They like fighting for plunder or territory, not for the balance of power, however much they may talk of glory.[140]

In the spring of 1854 Lewis reread Niebuhr and this rekindled his enthusiasm for Roman history:

> Continued Roman history. I am more & more impressed with the arbitrary method of Niebuhr, the wildness of his hypotheses, the extent to which he has rationalized and rewritten the history in the first half century of the Republic.[141]

The charismatic German historian Barthold Georg Niebuhr was one of the architects of Prussian independence from Napoleon. He was Prussian ambassador in Rome 1816–23, and professor of Roman history at Bonn until 1831. His three-volume *History of Rome* critically examined original sources and was translated into English by Connop Thirlwall and Julius Hare. His biography was published in 1852.[142] Lewis had a fluent command of German and was fascinated by the detailed scholarship of the Germans and their practice of 'the art of doubting rightly and believing rightly'. Lewis no doubt took Niebuhr in his stride, but the Oxford scholar Mark Pattison,[143] though using a translation, found the going far harder:

> one was expected at that time to know something of Niebuhr's views: I set out to discover these for myself, not in an epitome - there were such things - but by reading for myself the two volumes of Thirlwall's translation. A ploughed field was nothing to this. It was a quagmire, a Serbonic gulf, in which I was swallowed up.[144]

Lewis, however, worked his way steadily through the quagmire, though it took him several months:

> My own life has been lately of the most jog-trot order. I have been working steadily at my Roman history, and been following Niebuhr through all his wonderful perversions and distortions of the ancient writers. I have finished as much as occupies the

first seven books of Livy, and have only to go through the three remaining ones. I have never moved from town.[145]

Though modern scholars have seen the finished result as reflecting the dominance of Niebuhr,[146] Lewis himself did not entirely see it in the same light. He thought he had made the course of early Roman history intelligible, whereas Niebuhr 'was so capricious and inconsistent as to make everything unintelligible':[147]

> My criticism is purely negative. I set up nothing of my own. One of my objects is to show that Niebuhr's reconstructive theories are untenable, as well as the accounts which he sets aside.[148]

Work on Niebuhr was lightened by a family visit to the Crystal Palace on its new Sydenham site. Paxton's immense glasshouse enjoyed Lewis's whole-hearted approval now it was no longer opposite Kent House and had become a financial success.

The ghost of Niebuhr went too and part of its attraction for Lewis was the fact it was to house the largest and most complete collection of classical casts in the world.[149] In June Russell invited Lewis to join the government's executive commission responsible for implementing the reform of Oxford University.

> The Oxford Bill has been much debated in the House of Commons, and the Government expect to carry it. I received only yesterday a note from Lord John Russell, saying that two members are to be added to the five Commissioners already named in the Bill, and asking me to be one of them. I have consented, although the office is unpaid, and will probably be troublesome, difficult and unpopular. The duties do not appear to begin until Michaelmas 1855.[150]

It was, no doubt, very irking for Lewis, unpaid for his services to the Commission, that its two Secretaries enjoyed stipends of £800 per annum, £300 more than the best paid Oxford professor.

When Society left London in August, instead of going down to Harpton, Lewis with his wife and her two daughters set out for Germany. The decision to go to Germany was significant and must be linked with Lewis's interest in university reform and his appointment to Russell's Oxford commission. There were those at the university who feared that the impetus given to historical criticism by Niebuhr would lead to unorthodoxy and Pusey, whose high churchmanship was particularly obnoxious to Lewis, regarded Benjamin Jowett,

Regius Professor of Greek at Oxford and Canon Stanley of Canterbury who later became Professor of Ecclesiastical History at Oxford and Dean of Westminster, as suspect simply because they had visited Germany.[151] Both men were much respected by Lewis.

The Lewises spent ten days at Bonn where Niebuhr had held the chair of history. Here Lewis called upon Professor Christian Brandis, a colleague of Niebuhr, and 'obtained from him a full account of the university of Bonn'.[152] He also found time to write an article for the *Edinburgh Review* on 'Parliamentary Opposition';[153] a article like this would only take Lewis 'a large part of two days'.[154] The main attraction of Bonn, however, was a series of long conversations with 'M de Toqueville, with whom I have been in the highest degree pleased'.[155] This pleasure was soon to be over shadowed when Alice Lister, one of Lewis's two step-daughters, became seriously ill and it was not until they arrived back in London in early September that Scarlet Fever was diagnosed. Even at the end of the month Lady Duff Gordon was writing of having had

> A wretched account of both Theresa and Alice Lister from poor Theresa who seems to be quite at her wits end from watching and nursing.[156]

It took Lewis four days to deal with the 'large number of letters, proof sheets, & mss.' awaiting his return to England, and he then began sending chapters of the Roman history to the printers. The work was interrupted by an invitation to call on James Wilson, the founder of the *Economist* and Financial Secretary to the Treasury in Aberdeen's ministry. Wilson offered him, with the consent of Lord Aberdeen, the office of Commissioner of Land Revenue. The salary of £1200 was £200 pa more than he received as editor of the *Review*, and his reasons for declining it are interesting: 'it was incompatible with parliament & with the management of the *Edinburgh Review*'.[157] But it was not any seat in parliament that Lewis sought. He had declined that year to contest Wolverhampton and Taunton, either of which may well have been his without great effort in terms of electioneering. And he was about to do the same to Marylebone. When it became vacant in November by the death of Lord Dudley Stuart[158] Lewis was approached by three delegations seeking his candidature. All were unsuccessful, though he gives no reason in his Diary.[159]

Lewis's diaries, especially in their omissions, give frequent insights to their writer's interests. The battle of Alma took place on

14th September. A month later, when she was at Harpton Court, Lady Duff Gordon wrote in her diary that

> The newspapers [were] filled with painful and gallant details of our brave soldiers at the battle of the Alma.[160]

Lewis, on the other hand, at Kent House in the centre of things, makes no mention of the Alma in *his* diary:

> Alice is going on favourably - occupied with revising my Roman history & correcting proofs & some *Review* business.[161]

Writing later to Edmund Head he does mention 'the delusive success of the battle of the Alma' and then gives 'the rash and ill-calculated' expedition to Sebastopol some attention,[162] but even so there is an unreality in his comments. The important thing is to pronounce Sebastopol correctly:

> Everybody is now waiting for the news of the landing of the Sebastopol expedition (a word, you must know, which, according to the Russian pronunciation, has the accent on the penult, like homœopathy, the unmeaning letter being accented), I hear that the strength of the defending forces is imperfectly known; but if France and England make the attempt, they must go on fighting until it is successful.[163]

The siege of Sebastopol begun on 17th October and Lewis now tells Head:

> If you have a Thucydides or Grote's *History of Greece* you will find in Nicias's dispatch from Syracuse a curious parallel to the present state of things at Sebastopol, where he says that the Athenians, who came as besiegers, have become the besieged. It is to be hoped that the parallel will end here. At all events, Lord Raglan will not sacrifice his army to an eclipse of the moon.[164]

But in the privacy of his diary Lewis admitted that:

> Affairs are taking a very serious turn at Sebastopol. It is clear to me that the expedition ought never to have been risked.[165]

Balaclava on 26th September and the ill fated charge of the Light Brigade get no mention but of the battle of Inkerman, on 5th November, Head is told:

> saved the Allies from desperate danger. If it had not been for the extraordinary bravery of the Guards, the Russians would

have succeeded in occupying the heights, and in that case the whole army might have been destroyed.[166]

By the end of the year Lewis's anxiety about Sebastopol had escaped from his diary to his correspondence:

> What is to be the result of this ill-advised expedition to Sebastopol, it is difficult to conjecture. Our army is in a position in which it can neither advance nor recede. It can neither take the town nor re-embark ... It seems to me that the entire expedition is a mistake, and that, whatever the event may be, it must cost us infinitely greater sacrifices than the utmost success can compensate.[167]

Lewis though had little time to spare for the Crimea; the publication of his Roman history had reached a crucial stage. Revision of its text and the correction of its proofs occupied him throughout October and November and into December when, on the 20th the entry in his diary sounds almost like a sigh of relief:

> Completed the last chapter of my work on Roman history. Nothing now remains to be done but the final revision of the two last chapters, & an Index. *Review* work.

Christmas Day was spent at Kent House and the Lord's nativity duly observed with '*Review* work &c.'.

Back at Kent House after some time at Watford, Lewis dined with the lexicographer Dr William Smith who had collaborated in 1842 with Leonhard Schmitz in translating the third volume of Niebuhr's *History of Rome*. Smith made little impression upon him, but he met there Whitwell Elwin, the new editor of the *Quarterly Review*, whom he found 'a pleasing, sensible, and fair minded man'.[168] Work soon after begun on an article on an article on 'Modern English History' which was intended to be a review of Russell's latest volume of Fox's *Memoirs*, was interrupted by meetings of the Oxford Commission. It met in London and with a full attendance began work on the statutes of Pembroke College:

> The feeling of the Commission is decidedly in favour of maintaining the clerical preponderance of the university, with the exception of the Dean of Wells.[169]

The established daily routine, however, of proof correcting and writing was suddenly interrupted on Tuesday 23rd January by the arrival of the morning mail:

> Received by the post a letter from Lady Lewis, informing me
> that my father, then at Harpton, had been indisposed since the
> evening of the pervious Saturday, & that medical assistance had
> been called in, but not conveying any idea of danger, or even
> anxiety. About two hours afterwards received a telegraphic
> message, which my brother sent that morning from Harpton,
> conveying the sad intelligence that my poor father's illness had
> terminated fatally on Monday afternoon, & requesting me to
> come without delay to Harpton.[170]

Catching the one o'clock Gloucester express from Paddington,
and then on by another train to Hopebrook, Lewis arrived at Ross
before nightfall and stayed the night at Barrett's Hotel. The line to
Hereford was not to open for another six months and Lewis had to
catch the 8 o'clock mail coach next morning, travelling on in a fly
from Hereford to Kington and Harpton.

> Arrived there about 3 o'clock, & found Lady Lewis, Gilbert &
> Jane, & my aunt Miss Cornewall.[171] Heard the details of my poor
> father's death.

Lewis gives an objective account of the funeral in his diary:

> Today the funeral of my poor father took place at Old Radnor
> Church. The mourners were Lord Hereford,[172] Mr V
> Cornewall,[173] Capt Devereux,[174] Sir Alex Gordon,[175] Mr Davies
> of Moorcourt,[176] my brother & myself. Mr Mogridge,[177] the cler-
> gyman of Old Radnor, Mr Turner[178] of New Radnor, & the two
> medical men who attended my father likewise were present.
> Lady Lewis & Jane were with Gilbert & myself in the first
> mourning coach. The day was extremely cold, & snow fell, with
> a piercing east wind, during which time that the procession
> lasted. Nevertheless the concourse of persons was great, & the
> attendance in church numerous, marking the esteem & respect
> in which my poor father was held by the neighbourhood. He
> had been in possession of the Harpton estate for above 50 years.
> His marriage with my mother took place in 1805. He was buried
> in a brick grave in the centre of the chancel under the commu-
> nion table, in a spot recently selected by himself. The family
> vault was not opened.[179]

Lady Duff Gordon, however, tells how deeply Lewis 'felt his loss
& how stunned he was with the suddenness of the blow'.[180] But his
diary tells more of his father's medical condition than of his own
emotions:

It appears from conversations I had with Dr James[181] & Mr Bennett,[182] the two medical men who attended my father in his last illness, that they consider him to have died of angina pectoris supervening upon spasm of the intestines. The latter afterwards called the cause of death *syncope angonosa.*[183]

The funeral took place on Tuesday 30th January 1855, and two days later, on Thursday 1st February Lewis laid grief aside and with systematic application, which he never showed at Peterborough, he set about securing the Radnor boroughs as the means whereby he would re-enter Parliament.

Today I opened an address, offering myself as a candidate for the representation of the Radnorshire boroughs, in my father's place.[184]

To the Electors of the Borough of Radnor and of the other contributory Boroughs. In seeking to merit the confidence which you bestowed, with good reason, on my much lamented and honored father, I feel very sensibly my inferiority to him in the qualifications which would enable me to discharge my duties to you with efficiency. If, however, I venture now to offer myself to your consideration as a candidate for your suffrages, I take this step with the conviction that, though the value of my services would be less, I should not yield to him in zeal for your local interests, and in a desire to promote the welfare of the Boroughs.

My political principles, which have always connected me with the liberal party, with the party attached to political freedom and political improvement, remain unchanged. The present however, is not a moment of strong political feeling, or of active party dissension; the thoughts of all are centred in the war, which this country, with the powerful assistance of France, is now waging against Russia. Upon this question I will only say that, without expressing any opinion upon the wisdom of the expedition to the Crimea, and upon the propriety of the decision of Lord Aberdeen's government to advance from a defensive to an aggressive policy against Russia, I should be prepared, in the event of my becoming your representative, to give my vote in favour of such measures as would support our heroic army, in its exposed and trying position, and would tend, by honorable means, to bring about a peace which would secure the permanent interests of England in the East of Europe.[185]

The Act of Union of 1536 had given Radnorshire two Members of Parliament, one for the county and one for the boroughs, which in

1855 were Presteign, New Radnor, Knighton, Knucklas, Cefnllys, and Rhaeadr. Thus, in comparison with Peterborough the constituency was far flung, and it was a hard winter. But undeterred, having written to his constituents the day after he decided to stand, on the next day, he set off in his carriage with Richard Banks, of Kington, his agent, for Knighton where he 'canvassed the town with good success'. That was Saturday; on Sunday he went to church at New Radnor and then on Monday resumed his canvassing. At Presteign he again met 'with good success', calling afterwards on Col Richard Price of Norton Manor, MP for the County 1799–1847, and on Sir Harford Brydges, Bart, of Boultibrooke. On Tuesday, despite the snow, Lewis and Banks went in the carriage to Penybont where they took post horses and carried on to Rhaeadr in the western extreme of the county. Here they 'canvassed the town with Mr Lewis Lloyd,[186] Mr Oliver,[187] & others [and] had an excellent reception'. On his way back to Harpton Lewis called on 'Mr Severn[189] at Penybont Hall & found him at home' which bearing in mind the weather was not surprising. On Wednesday Richard Price and Sir Harford Brydges returned Lewis visits earlier in the week. Then, on Thursday, after almost a week of solid canvassing in which the snow even held up the mail:

> My brother, Mr Davies & Mr Banks came to breakfast, attended at the town hall, Radnor, where I was proposed by Mr Lewis Lloyd & seconded by Edwards of Hindwell.[189] No other candidate was proposed, & I returned thanks.[190]

The voters were rewarded by Lewis with a lengthy acceptance speech reported, to Lewis's satisfaction, in the *Hereford Times* 'almost verbatim as it was delivered'. He also considered the paper's account of the accompanying proceedings to be 'quite accurate'. He stated his well-known position as a free trader:

> British agriculture stands upon a rock. It needs no protection from fiscal regulations. The energy, the enterprise, the skill, and the vast resources of the British farmer places him in a position which renders him proof against all foreign competition.[191]

The Crimean War was, of course, still a preoccupying concern, and there were those who wanted the prestige of the Army to be enhanced at the expense of the Navy. But not Lewis:

> I must tell you frankly that I am not prepared to support an entire change in the military system of England ... The navy has

ever been the right arm of England, and the popular service of the country.[192]

Such sentiments commanded sympathy in Radnorshire, where though it was the most inland of the Welsh counties, its oaks were still sought after for ship-building.

Before returning to London and Parliament Lewis looked into his late father's finances and discovered he had 'left scarcely any money'. The new baronet was still going to be preoccupied with his financial position:

> Collected & arranged bills. Had a conversation with Charles Price[193] about the rental & management of my father's property. He puts the rental at £4000 a year, & the estate expenses at £1000. There is a lease of Old Radnor tithes, which produce about £1000 a year, with an annual rent, & a fine of about £1500 once in 7 years. My father has left no assets in money & simple contract debts to the amount of about £1000. The mortgage & bond debts appear to be £18000 or £20000.[194]

Lewis and his wife set out for London on Monday 12th February, staying overnight in Hereford with the Bodenhams and calling on the Dean, Richard Dawes. He dined with his cousin Velters Cornewall, not yet racked with insanity. Arriving at Kent House on Tuesday he took to his bed with a cough which became worse before it got better, though this did not prevent him from writing letters and working on the *Edinburgh Review*. Nor did it prevent him on the following Monday, 19th February 1855 from taking his seat in the House of Commons, four weeks to the day after the death of his father and whose parliamentary seat he now occupied.[195] And it was, as he told his friend WR Greg in response to the latter's letter of congratulation:

> accomplished without difficulty, as no candidate appeared against me in the field, and I had not even to make preparations for a contest. My desire for office at present is scarcely above freezing point.[196]

Chapter Five:
Back in Parliament

Sir George Cornewall Lewis took his seat as the member for the Radnor Boroughs on 19th February 1855, but it was meetings of the Oxford Commission and the revision of proofs that occupied him rather than parliamentary business. Perhaps because the Bishop of Ripon[1] & Lord Ellesmere[2] were not present he found the 'discussion rather desultory'. The commissioners who were present worked on the revision of the statutes of Exeter College and Lewis considered Sir John Coleridge[3] and Sir John Awdry,[4] both judges, 'very reasonable', whereas the Dean of Wells[5] was 'cautious & small minded, though conscientious'.[6] Then, at the end of the week, he received a letter, which he claimed to be unwelcome 'in the highest degree'.

> I received a letter from Clarendon informing me that the cabinet had that afternoon decided that the office of Chancellor of the Exchequer should be offered to me. This communication was unwelcome to me in the highest degree. I did not wish for office, but I saw at once this was an offer which I could not refuse without great difficulty. After dinner I received a note from Lord Palmerston, asking me to call upon him at 11 o'clock the following morning.[7]

Aberdeen's ministry had fallen over public dissatisfaction over its administration of the Crimean War, and after Derby and Russell had failed to form ministries, the Queen turned to Palmerston, who was prepared to accept the commission of inquiry into the conduct of the war, which Aberdeen had refused. Gladstone,[8] Graham,[9] and Herbert,[10] however, all disagreed over there being a commission and resigned.

Edward Cardwell[11] and Thomas Baring[12] having both declined invitations to take over from Gladstone as Chancellor of the Exchequer, Lewis's return to the Commons was for Palmerston providential.

> I called on Ld Palmerston according to appointment. He made me the offer of the office of Chancellor of the Exchequer. I said I felt strongly the duty of every person who could render service, to assist the govt in the present emergency, but I distrusted my own ability & accepting. He entered in a very friendly way into my feelings, but gave a decided opinion in favour of acceptance. From him I went to Clarendon, who advised me to lose no time in seeing Gladstone. I took this advice, & called on Gladstone in Downing Street. I found him at home, & having told him what had passed, I consulted him about accepting, & enquired what assistance he wd give me. Nothing could be kinder, more friendly or more handsome than his conduct. He promised me the fullest communication of information, & of his views respecting the budget, & said he would act as if he was the head of another department of the govt. This interview decided me to accept & I accordingly called on Ld Palmerston just before dinner time & gave in my acceptance.[13]

Gladstone's account of the interview with Lewis is remarkably consistent with that of Lewis himself:

> On Sunday, Sir George Lewis called on me and said my office had been offered to him. This was after being refused by Cardwell and Baring. He asked my advice as to accepting it. This I told him I could not give. He asked if I would assist him with information in case of his accepting. I answered that he might command me precisely as if instead of resigning I had only removed to another department. I then went over some of the matters needful to be made known. On Tuesday he came again, acquainted me with his acceptance, and told me he had been mainly influenced by my promise.[14]

Why did Lewis accept the office Chancellor of the Exchequer? What had made him deny his earlier protestation of constancy to the *Edinburgh Review*, which he now hastened to abandon?[15] Why was he now prepared to serve under Palmerston, the same man of whom he had once said:

> Heard Palmerston make a very indiscreet speech upon the alteration of some names on a committee. It struck me that he wd not be fit to lead the House.[16]

Lewis had told Palmerston that he was moved to take office by a sense of duty, but he gave Head a somewhat different explanation. Had he refused he might have laid himself open to the charge of cowardice:

I was to follow Gladstone, whose ability had dazzled the world; and to produce a War Budget, with large additional taxation, in a few weeks. All these circumstances put together inspired me with the strongest disinclination to accept the offer. I felt, however, that in the peculiar position of the Government, the office having been already refused by Cardwell and F Baring, refusal was scarcely honourable, and would be attributed to cowardice; and I therefore most reluctantly made up my mind to accept. I remembered the Pope, put in hell by Dante, '*Che fece per viltade il gran rifiuto*' [Who through cowardice made the Great Refusal].[17]

Lewis's appointment was not well received by the London press:

The office that has been filled by a Disraeli and a Gladstone, the most popular and peculiarly gifted members of the House of Commons, will not be distinguished by one who has never displayed any of those qualities which a Chancellor of the Exchequer eminently needs. Cold, formal, repelling, by no means remarkable as a speaker, and possessing an extraordinary notion of his own fitness for any and every department, this gentleman, who is just suited for a commissionership, or a head clerkship in one of the public boards, is thrust into an office of the greatest magnitude, and a position of the most striking prominence, without training for the one, or the popular qualities for the other. In spite of the general and growing feeling against mere aristocratic influence, the present appointment is mainly owing to the family connection between the new Minister of Finance and other members of the Whig Cabinet; for besides being in some way connected with Lord John Russell, he is the brother-in-law of the Earl of Clarendon. I may add that Sir George has been for the last two years the editor of the *Edinburgh Review*, the great organ of the Whigs.[18]

His own family was equally surprised, and Lady Duff Gordon exclaiming when she heard the news; 'the electric telegraph announced George Lewis as Chancellor of the Exchequer. I don't believe it for he can't speak in the House!'[19] By all accounts Lewis was a poor public speaker and he was aware of this, but he did not think it an important disqualification, as he told his friend Greg:

You must remember that one of the first qualifications of a minister is to obtain public confidence; and no amount of brilliancy in speaking will supply this capital defect. Fox, and Burke, and Sheridan are remarkable proofs of this truth. It is not neces-

151

sary to have a great orator at the head of each department, as you may see by looking at the list of the Cabinet in Pitt's long administration, which lasted seventeen years, against an amount of talent which, as it was at its commencement, has never since been equalled.[20]

Nor did he think family connections and aristocratic influence, condemned by the *Standard,* things to be avoided in politics. Lady Duff Gordon spoke of him as her favourite nephew and he showed his affection for her by appointing her eldest son, Sir Alexander Gordon, as his private secretary.[21]

George Lewis [now Chancellor of the Exchequer] has appointed Alex his private secretary. I trust that he may fill the situation well & diligently! This is kindly done by George and as Alex has been 26 years a Clerk in the Treasury, and is in the Revenue Office, he must know his worth.[22]

Events now moved swiftly. Lewis's acceptance of office meant that according to custom, the Parliamentary seat he had held but a fortnight was now vacant and he would have to stand for re-election. He wrote to the ailing James Davies of Moorcourt and to Richard Banks to set matters in motion locally, though he felt he was too busy himself to come down to New Radnor and pay his constituents the courtesy due to them:

Every hour is at this moment of value to me. I shd wish, if it were possible, to be spared the necessity of travelling down for the election, but I will make the journey & shew myself, if it be thought advisable. Upon this subject, I shd be very thankful for your advice.[23]

Richard Banks's advice was tactful but firm:

I think that it will be safer that you should appear upon the hustings on Monday. A large majority of your constituents would I am sure reasonably dispense with your personal attendance, yet there are some who are very likely to turn your absence to an evil account to your prejudice ... If you can not possibly attend perhaps you had better delay the announcement to the latest moment.[24]

The anxiety of both Banks and Davies on Lewis's behalf was not unjustified. There had been rumours, unfounded in the event, at the earlier election that Robert Baskerville Mynors of nearby Evancoed was going to be a rival candidate.[25] This was sufficient to move James

Davies to go up to London to see the still hesitant Lewis, and to convince him that he should come down for the election:

> Having seen Mr Davies today, & had some conversation about appearing at my election, I have decided that the safest course will be for me to be present.[26]

Richard Banks, however, still thought it prudent to write to the proprietor of the *Hereford Times* that though the election for the Radnorshire boroughs was going take place on Monday 5th March at 11 am, it was still 'uncertain whether Sir GC Lewis will be able to attend on account of the pressing duties of his office'.[27]

The weather still looked a better reason for Lewis's absence. Lady Duff Gordon received from Gilbert Lewis at Monnington:

> A wonderful account of the cold and of the ice & the snow in Herefordshire. In February the river Wye was entirely frozen over, sufficiently strong to bear horses & carts to pass it.[28]

And when the thaw set in on 1st March there were floods and Hay bridge was washed away. But in London Lewis was sworn in as a Privy Councillor at Buckingham Palace and at the end of the week he did indeed leave for Harpton, calling on the dean and the Bodenhams as he passed through Hereford. He found his step-mother, Lady Lewis, at Harpton on her own. Perhaps it was a sign of Lewis's own uncertainty about the election, which made him on his way home after Sunday morning church call on Sir William Cockburn[29] of Downton and port wine fame. There were fences to be mended here, for Cockburn did not share Lewis's politics nor was he a guest at the Harpton table. But Lewis need not have worried, for on Monday morning, when he went over to New Radnor 'for his election', he was, in answer to the Town Bailiff's question, the only candidate. To his gratification, 'the feeling of the people' being 'very favourable' they were rewarded for their loyalty with a speech and a present of coal for the poor. After a celebratory luncheon at Harpton, Lewis left by fly and mail coach for Gloucester for the night. Next morning he:

> Left Gloster by an early train, arrived in London about $1/2$ past 11. To the rooms of the Chancellor of the Exchequer in Downing Street ... Had several interviews. To the House, & took my seat.[30]

It had all been very easy and brought about by no more than a weekend of hard travelling. But there was the usual price to pay, and by the end of the week he had been 'at home all day, with a cough'.

But the inconvenience of a cough did not stop work being resumed on the Roman history:

> Completed title page, contents, addenda, &c of my work on Roman history, for the printer. The remaining sheets of the 2nd volume have been corrected since my return to London.[31]

The history was published on 7th April 1855 and Lewis was very satisfied with the sales it achieved, three hundred copies in two months. He was, however, disappointed by the fact that, though it had been noticed in some of the newspapers, it had 'not hitherto been reviewed by any competent judge'.[32] Indeed, he had to wait until September when reviews appeared, first in the *Leader*, and then in October in the *Examiner* and the *National Review*. Goldwin Smith's[33] 'excellent critique of the book' in the *Leader* particularly pleased him. Lewis himself had no doubt about the merit of the work in comparison with its rivals. One morning in December in the carriage on his way from Kent House to his Downing Street office he 'looked over' Dean Liddell's Roman history, recently published.[34] The appointment of the reforming Liddell to the deanery of Christ Church earlier that year had pleased him, but the history, in his opinion, was a poor thing:

> The early part is nothing but a *réchauffé* of Niebuhr, without originality. It had been printed before the publication of my *Inquiry*, as he states in his preface.[35]

All the same Liddell's history, especially in its later abridged form, enjoyed 'a permanent circulation'. Other reviews trickled into the press, their arrival, or prospective arrival, faithfully recorded by Lewis:

> There is to be an article on my book on Rome, by Bunbury,[36] in the new number of the *Quarterly*. I am told that it is a qualified defence of Niebuhr. It is remarkable that Niebuhr has not yet found a champion, although more than a year has elapsed since my work was published.[37]

Bunbury's review gave Lewis little pleasure and was dismissed as 'a poor performance ... a mere expression of dissent, with scarcely any attempt at reasoning'.[38] But he had the consolation that the book was to be translated into German, and though his translator seemed 'stronger in medieval than in classical antiquities', a new edition would at least give him an opportunity for additions and corrections.[39]

He shared the opinion that a prophet is not without honour, except in his own country:

> I have gladly accepted this offer, which is highly gratifying to me, as it will give publicity to my work in a country where the largest number of competent judges on the subject exists.[40]

Lewis was now immersed in public life and the squire of Harpton was attending royal levees and dining at Buckingham Palace. The Queen perhaps found him easier than his predecessor Gladstone:

> At the levee, dined at the Palace. The Queen spoke to me after dinner, & had a conversation of some length about my appointment.[41]

Lewis himself felt uncomfortable as the successor to Gladstone 'whose ability dazzled the world', all the more so because he had to produce a war budget in a few weeks. All thoughts of spending Easter at Harpton were abandoned:

> There are ... all the preparations to be made for the impending Budget, and measures to be taken for providing sufficient sums to meet the enormous extraordinary expenditure which the war in the Crimea is causing. Gladstone has been very friendly to me, and has given me all the assistance in his power ... I had intended to go down to Harpton at Easter, but this will now be impossible.[42]

Lewis's less conscientious ministerial colleagues seem to have left him alone in town so that when he went to the Mansion House for a dinner in honour of the Duke of Cambridge, recently returned as a general from the Crimea, Lewis found himself the only minister present. Consequently it was he who 'returned thanks for the health of Her Majesty's Ministers, & gave the health of the Lady Mayors'.[43] This we know from his diary, but what we are not told is that he arrived at the banquet well after the company had been seated and begun their meal. There were those who felt it little wonder that Sebastopol was not going well:

> 'Too late!' 'too late!' for ever 'too late!'
> Still our unfortunate Minister's fate.
> It was not till the weather began to cool
> That they thought of attacking Sebastopol:
> It was not till they'd wind, and snow, and rain
> That they thought of mounting a winter campaign;

It was not till most of the soldiers froze
That they thought of sending out winter clothes;
It was not till by loud complaints pursued
They found means to convey them daily food:
It was not till the wounded had strew'd the ground
That the surgeons of enough of hospitals found:
It was not till thousands by sickness died
Were adequate comforts and drugs supplied.

In all things alike, it is ever their fate,
In great or small - they must be 'too late':
Where they appear, it is mournfully true,
That this destiny sticks to the Cabinet crew.
E'en if one is engaged to a City feast,
Invited to be the Chief Magistrate's guest,
He omits preparation to be in his place
Till the rest are all seated, and finished the grace;
Then, hurriedly dressing, he flies to the group,
'Too late' for the fish, and 'too late' for the soup.
I would say, if I were the Lord Mayor Moon.[44]
We cannot get rid of such rulers 'too soon'.[45]

A fortnight later Lewis presented his first budget to the House: 'I made the financial statement. I did not feel in good health, & I was not satisfied with my speech'.[46] He later elaborated on this brief statement in his diary in a letter to Head:

My Budget was an alarming task, on account of the magnitude of the sum to be raised. The additional taxes were, however, assented to without resistance by the House, who feared a larger addition to the Income Tax, and thought that if they objected to my proposition taxes which they disliked still more would be substituted. I had great anxiety and difficulty about the loan, for (luckily) it had been so long since the system of war loans had ceased that the official traditions were lost, and I could scarcely find anybody to give me any information on the subject who had himself had any personal knowledge or experience. There are few persons now in office who were public servants in prominent positions during the late war. However, I contrived to avoid all pitfalls, and the loan was negotiated upon terms favourable to the public and sufficiently advantageous to the contractors. The money market was in a state favourable to such an operation; for at present there is an abundance of money, but a want of profitable investment for the purposes of trade. No wild speculations are in fashion, so that there is a run upon

Government securities. The funds are high and Exchequer bills at a good premium, although the rate of interest upon them has been lately reduced a little.[47]

Lady Duff Gordon who, it will be recollected, was quick to express her sentiments on the unsuitability of her nephew for the office of Chancellor of the Exchequer, was reassured by her son Alexander Duff Gordon, Lewis's private secretary:

Alex writes very cheerfully and happily about George Lewis, and thinks that his straight forward guiless probity tells, & satisfies, and pleases people.[48]

It would be interesting to know whether Lewis's 'straight forward guiless probity' commended him in the social round of City life which he records without comment, as when on a single evening he:

Dined at the Trinity House, where Prince Albert as master presided. I proposed the health of the Governor of the Bank. Went afterwards for a short time to a party at Sir Rod Murchison's.[49]

The debate in the House on decimal currency occupied his interest rather more than Murchison's party the night before:

Debate on Decimal Currency on Mr Brown's motion.[50] I spoke at some length in opposition to the motion … but an introductory declaration in favour of a decimal coinage was carried agst the govt.[51]

The trimmings of public office were not entirely distasteful and Lewis seems to have derived some pleasure from having his official photograph taken for the Queen by Mayall's of Regent Street,[52] or attending 'the Court of Exchequer, in my gold robe, for the roll of sheriffs'.[53] But his health derived little benefit and such entries became more common in his diary as:

Passed all day in bed with a violent attack of sickness with a violent headache, which lasted for more than 24 hours.[54]

Later in the year he was consulting once again the ageing Mr GJ Guthrie, disturbing him on a Sunday, though the complaint was a week old:

Today I consulted Mr Guthrie about an opaque spot in my right eye which appeared suddenly while I was walking a week ago. He says it is caused by the rupture of a small vessel in the retina or immediately behind it, that it is owing to overwork of brain & eyes. He prescribes abstinence from reading & writing and puts me under a course of mercury with the view of increasing vascular action & causing absorption.[55]

He saw Guthrie several times who held out little hope that Lewis would regain what sight he had lost.[56] Lady Duff Gordon was very worried by his appearance and Lewis was worried by his having lost some government papers he had been working on during the journey up to town from Harpton:

> George Lewis dined with us looking very ill. He has something the matter with his eye and Guthrie has ordered him to take calom[el] until salivation is produced! I was quite unhappy at seeing him so very low and uncomfortable. He is also worried in having lost a Despatch Box on the Rail Road coming up.[57]

Lewis was now able to travel all the way to Hereford from Paddington by a Great Western express, an event he recorded in his diary when first done on 22nd August 1855. The purpose of the journey was to attend the funeral of one of Lewis's cousins, Lord Hereford, of Tregoed, above Hay. He was forty-six and it was only in the previous January that he had been one of the mourners at the funeral of Sir Thomas Frankland Lewis. Funerals and the causes of death interested Lewis more than parties:

> Friday 24th August 1855. Monnington. Went with Gilbert in his carriage to the Hay in order to join the procession of Lord Hereford's funeral. Walker Devereux accompanied the body from London which it left in the morning. The mourners were the young Ld Hereford, Walter Devereux, Bradshaw,[58] Mr Fairfax, brother in law of Ld H, Mr Hunter, a relation of Lady H, Velters Cornewall, Gilbert & myself. The funeral took place at Glasbury church, in the family vault. Lister Venables[59] read the service. The coffin was covered with crimson velvet & much ornamented. The cause of his death was pleurisy, with great effusion of water in one lung, & cancerous state of the spleen. After the funeral which took place at about 6 o'clock pm, Gilbert and I returned to Monnington. Theresa arrived from London to dinner.

The Lewises remained at Harpton for the autumn, with occasional sorties up to London for Cabinet meetings. The Chancellor of the Exchequer was now the country squire walking on the Radnorshire hills and attending local flower shows. And whilst parson

Gilbert was shooting grouse, Lewis was sorting out their father's affairs.

> Sunday 26th August. Harpton. Church at New Radnor. Walked under Smatcher [hill].

> Wednesday 29th August. Harpton Gilbert came to shoot grouse. Attended in the morning at Presteign for the flower show. Lunched at Mrs Evans[60] & addressed the assembly afterwards in the open air. Occupied during the last few days in examining my father's papers. I have destroyed many & arranged the rest.

> Thursday 30th August. Harpton. Gilbert shot on the Vron Hill, killed 10 grouse.

> Friday 31st August. Harpton. Gilbert shot at Black Yat & killed about 12 birds, including two black game.

But with Gilbert back in his parish, Lewis resumed work on an article on Fox's *Memoirs* for the *Edinburgh Review*, which he had left off in February. There was a tea party for the school children of New Radnor given by Mr Turner, the new rector, to attend with Therese and the girls, and a Bow Meeting at Moreton Court where he 'proposed some healths at the dinner'. There were too the usual headaches.

But the shadow of the Crimea hung heavily even over Smatcher:

> The general feeling of the country is decidedly warlike. They are not deterred by the pecuniary sacrifices which the war requires, by the burdens which it imposes, or by the small amount of national interest which it involves. They consider the campaign in the Crimea as a duel with Russia, and they will not recede until we have made our utmost exertions to take the place.[61]

Lewis however could see little purpose to a war which abstracted forty millions a year from the national income, and burned it in gunpowder at the Crimea.[62] Then on Tuesday 11th September came the news that Sebastopol had been taken four days earlier:

> This is a great event, as it relieves the mind of the country from the state of painful suspense & uncertainty in which it has been kept for nearly a year by the precarious position of our army before Sebastopol … *Ed Review*, official business. In the afternoon drove to Eywood, & attended a flower show. The Kington bells were ringing for the good news.[63]

The autumn saw a good deal of entertaining at Harpton; Lewis and his wife establishing the house as their country home. Sir Frankland Lewis's widow made her home in London and visitors to Harpton began to notice changes. These, at least for Lady Duff Gordon, though she does not describe them, were not for the better:

> It was for me a painful effort to visit Harpton all changed! & I could not understand it without its poor lost master Sir Frankland … Ly Lewis has been kindness itself to us when here. But she never formed any part of the place in my mind. I know much more about it and all its early ways than she ever could do.[64]

Typically Lewis was not there to welcome his aunt and cousins on their arrival: he was at yet another Agricultural Society Dinner.

> Attended a meeting of the Agricultural Society at Knighton as President. I took the chair at dinner, & gave the toasts. Had a good reception.[65]

According to Lady Duff Gordon, whose grasp of accuracy was admittedly uncertain, the meeting was at Knighton and not Presteign as she believed, Lewis had made ten speeches, a very large number, even for Lewis. She was on more certain ground, however, when at the end of her week's stay at Harpton, she wrote of her 'old favourite nephew George, he was as kind and as demonstrative as it is his nature to be'.[66]

In some measure Lewis enjoyed the sycophancy of the local community and the patronage it bestowed upon him through the Corporation of New Radnor. A charter of incorporation was granted to the borough in 1562 by Elizabeth I, and it enjoyed the right to have its own recorder, coroner, receiver, sergeant at mace, and to be governed by a corporation of twenty-five Capital Burgesses. The Lewises of Harpton were consistently pre-eminent in its affairs, but by the time the town ceased to be a borough in 1886, it had lost all pretensions to municipal dignity. The Charity Commissioner who came to direct the disposal of the borough's assets remarked he did not believe there was another such borough in the country.[67] Lewis, however, attended the Corporation's dinners dutifully and took its business seriously:

> Attended a meeting of the Radnor Corporation, & proposed officers for the annual election. Afterwards dined at the Bailiff's dinner, & presided. Robert Mynors [of Evanjob] dined & proposed my health in a complimentary speech.[68]

There were important appointments to be made, too, and here again Lewis was not afraid to draw upon the talent of his neighbours:

> Wrote to Lord Palmerston to propose Pressly as Deputy Chairman of the Inland Revenue Board, & Sir J Walsham [of Knill Court] as the new Commissioner.[69]

House guests at Harpton that Autumn also included, besides 'Aunt Gordon', such scholarly friends as Nassau Senior and George Grote, as well as the local gentry and clergy. They rode on the Radnor Forest and Hergest Ridge, taking in the splendour of the views, and dining together at Harpton in the evening.[70]

There were reciprocal visits to Staunton Park and Eywood where Lewis sat down to dinner with an epitome of Herefordshire society:

> Met Lady Emily Foley & Lord Wm Graham, Pemberton Leigh, & Berkeley Stanhope, Miss Bickersteth, handsome, but odd & unattractive.[71]

Eywood was built in the early 18th century as a country seat for the earls of Oxford and Mortimer, and though Victorian taste thought its park abounded in scenes of woodland beauty, the house itself was dismissed as being without either the grace of proportion or the charm of colour.[72] In 1855 it was the home of Lady Langdale who, as Jane Elizabeth Harley, eldest daughter of the 5th Earl of Oxford, had married Henry Bickersteth, who was then the family physician. But renouncing medicine for law, he eventually became Master of the Rolls and was ennobled as Lord Langdale. He died in 1851. Lady Foley of Stoke Edith Park, was Emily, the much-fabled fourth daughter of James, the third Duke of Montrose. She, too, was a widow, her husband Edward Thomas Foley, MP, having died in 1846. Lord Graham was her brother, and at that time MP for Grantham, which he represented as a Tory.[73] The Revd Berkeley Stanhope was the third son of Sir Edwyn Stanhope, Bart, of Home Lacy, and married a daughter of John Arkwright of Hampton Court near Leominster. A Fellow of All Souls, he was for many years the rector of Byford, and his pastoral energies were rewarded by James Atlay, Bishop of Hereford, by making him archdeacon of Hereford. He was a frequent visitor to Harpton. Thomas Pemberton Leigh 1793–1867, a former colleague of Lord Langdale, was ennobled in 1858 as Lord Kingdown, and the handsome but odd and unattractive Miss Bickersteth was a kinswoman of Lord Langdale. Knowing Lewis's distaste for small talk, one wonders what were the themes of dinner time conversation. Perhaps mention was made of Lewis's visits, short and brief, up to town 'on receiving unfavourable news of the money market'.

Five days after the Eywood dinner Lewis made one of these journeys up to town for a cabinet and a meeting with Baron James Rothschild, of Paris, and head of the French branch of this distinguished family of bankers. Rothschild had seen Palmerston the day before, and had 'come to England to induce the Bank of England to lend two millions of bullion'. Interviews followed between Lewis and the Governor and Deputy Governor of the Bank of England before his return to Harpton.[74] Next day he was out riding on the Radnorshire hills with his wife and George Grote. A fortnight later he was able to write in his Diary at Downing Street that the 'state of the money market is a little better' and that he had dined with Grote. He gave Henry Reeve, his successor in the *Edinburgh Review*, and, according to Lady Duff Gordon, 'now grown a perfect Falstaff in size',[75] a fuller account and explanation of events:

> I acted on your friendly hint, and accelerated my journey to London by a week. I had previously intended to come up on Saturday next. As it was, however, it turned out luckily, for [Rothschild] is come over on a sort of mission from the Bank of France; and I had an opportunity of conferring with him while he is in London. The drain of bullion upon the Bank of England has been greater and more rapid than I anticipated. It has been caused mainly by the remittances for the war, and the action of the Bank of France, to which some other accessory causes have been added. The Bank has not behaved imprudently, nor has the Government done anything which can be complained of. The balances in the Exchequer are large, and the payments have been made without pressing on the resources of the Bank. There has not been over-trading, and stocks are low. In order to act upon the exchanges, the Bank must resort to measures of a stringent kind for contracting a trade which is not otherwise than wholesome. This will produce distress, but the policy is inevitable. The high price of corn will also affect the revenue by diminishing the consumption of tea, sugar, spirits, beer, and other similar articles. I fear, therefore, that if the war is to be prolonged for any considerable time, we must look to carrying it on under less favourable financial conditions than those which have hitherto existed. The revenue and trade of the country are in a sound state. The difficulty

arises solely from the drain of bullion, and from the measures to which the Bank is driven in order to counteract it.[76]

Christmas in 1855 was spent at Grove Mill and, according to his Diary, Lewis kept the Lord's nativity by carefully reading the third volume of Macaulay's *History of England* which had just been published. But even in the season of good will Lewis could see clearly faults in the work:

> The style seems to me too diffuse: the history of a long period cannot be written on the scale which he has adopted. There is too much minute effect, & amplification of subordinate details, which means the general result distracts the attention.[77]

Lewis read Macaulay until New Year's Eve, finding it 'very able but too prolix' but in writing to Head he had to admit that, despite its faults, it had had 'a prodigious success'.[78] He himself continued work on his *Dialogue on the Best form of Government* and found time, too, at his Downing Street office to reel off for the Oxford University Press 'a Latin explanation of some nursery rhymes, intended to ridicule the method of interpreting the inscriptions in ancient Italian languages'.[79]

The financial success of the Great Exhibition, which made a profit of £186,000, enabled its Commissioners, encouraged by the Prince Consort, to purchase land at Kensington Gore whereon the prince hoped to see established a great institution for the 'dissemination of a knowledge of science and art among all classes'. There was a good deal of opposition to the scheme and Lewis, who was now a Commissioner, was amongst those from whom the prince sought both support and advice. So after Sunday morning church we find him going by invitation from Kent House to Buckingham Palace:

> I called by appointment at Buckingham palace & had an audience of the Prince. He explained to me at length what had passed respecting the ground at Kensington Gore, purchased by the nation, & the Exhibition Commissioners, & stated his views as to its application.[80]

A couple of days later Lewis went to South Kensington with Sir William Cubitt, the civil engineer, 'and inspected the large iron building in progress'.[81] This was the temporary building of the Museum of Science and Art, which on account of the mode of its construction, iron clad with corrugated iron, was dubbed by George Godwin, the editor of *The Builder*, as the 'Brompton Boilers'.

There was another meeting of the Commissioners of 1851 in April:

> The prince in the chair. Ld Derby, Disraeli, Gladstone & about 30 others present. A long report was criticised & agreed to. Much discussion & the meeting lasted 4 hours. Aftds at Downing St & at a cabinet.[82]

Lewis was a conscientious Commissioner, regularly visiting the Kensington site and noting its national purpose in his diary with something approaching approval:

> I visited the buildings connected with the Science & Art Department at Kensington Gore. It is the centre of a school of art, with affiliated establishments in the country, on a large scale.[83]

Queen Victoria maintained that 'her own darling', as she put it, had the very highest esteem, regard, and respect for Lewis,[84] and this seems to be so. The Prince Consort sought his opinion in depth not only on the development of South Kensington, but also on the future of the National Portrait Gallery.[85] Its foundation in 1856 was largely due to the endeavours of Philip Henry Stanhope, 5th Earl Stanhope, with the support of Macaulay and Carlyle. In February 1856 Stanhope made a third, and this time successful, attempt to get passed a motion to establish 'a gallery of original portraits, such portraits to consist as far as possible of those persons who are most honourably commemorated in British history as warriors or as statesman, or in arts, in literature or in science'. The project enjoyed the support of both the Queen and the Prince Consort. Three months after the debate, the Commons voted a sum of £2,000 towards the establishment of a 'British Historical Portrait Gallery'. At the end of June Lord Elcho[86] introduced a motion for a Commission to be set up to enquire into the site of the Gallery. Lewis, without giving a reason in his diary, was against the motion, which nevertheless was carried against the government by a small majority.[87] The following Sunday Lewis dined at the Palace and Prince Albert discussed the matter with him, but his opinions made less impression upon him than the attractiveness of the Princess Royal:

> Dined at the palace. The Prince spoke to me about the National Gallery commission. I sat next to the Princess Royal at dinner, her manner peculiarly kind, & attractive. She is very like her mother in appearance & manner.[88]

The Gallery was formally established in December 1856, and amongst its founder Trustees were Stanhope as Chairman, Macaulay, Disraeli and Lord Ellesmere. Its temporary premises at 29 Great George Street, Westminster, were opened in January 1859. Lewis did not attend.

The opening of the Congress of Paris in 1856, at which England was represented by Lewis's kinsman Lord Clarendon, saw the formal conclusion of the Crimean War and Lewis spent the summer and autumn of that year quietly at Harpton:

> undisturbed by red boxes full of unpleasant despatches about foreign affairs; and my chief occupation has been to correspond with the Governor of the Bank about the state of affairs in the City during the late depression, and with divers authorities[89] on the subject of the currency about the renewal of the Bank Act of 1844. The political state of the country is now tranquil to the point of stagnation. The only thing that keeps us at all alive is the disputes got up by the Foreign Office.[90]

There was also 'correspondence relating to taxation, currency, joint stock banks, &c',[91] and a visit at the end of September from Sir Alexander Spearman,[92] with his wife and daughter, provoked 'much conversation … on banking and finance'.[93]

Lewis seems to have enjoyed the round of agricultural society and corporation dinners, which despite their modest character he often chose to use for significant statements. The American Civil War had replaced the Crimea as the focus of interest in foreign affairs, and Lewis's views were influenced by his understanding of classical history and the institution of slavery in the ancient world:

> I see no solution for the political differences of the United States, but the separation of the Slave and Free States into distinct political communities. If I was a citizen of a Northern State, I should wish it. I should equally wish it if I was a citizen of a Southern State. In the Northern States the English race would remain unimpaired. But I cannot help suspecting that it degenerates under a warmer sun, and that a community formed of Anglo-Saxon masters within the tropics and negro slaves would degenerate. I see no reason why the pure English breed should not be kept up in the Northern Provinces and the Northern States. It may also be kept up in Australia, which has a climate suited to our race, and has fortunately been kept untainted by the curse of coloured slavery.[94]

So it was that at a dinner in Hereford of the Herefordshire Agricultural Society in October 1856, where, in his own judgement, he 'was sufficiently well received' he first alluded to his loss of the seat the previous year and then to the Civil War. As regards the former he concluded that:

> The seat which I lost might now be recovered for the Liberal party, if there was a good candidate, but the difficulty is to find one.[95]

He then turned his attention to the American war:

> If I was a Southerner, and if I wished to preserve slavery at all risks, I should certainly be for a separation. Some extracts from Southern papers, which were lately copied in the *Times*, expressed in plain and naked language the doctrine of the ancient politicians, that every community of free citizens must rest upon slavery, and that the working classes ought to be slaves without reference to the colour of the skin. I think they are imprudent in holding this language. The real strength of their case and the real practical difficulty lies in the physical and mental inferiority of the negro race, and in the unfitness of the whites for field labour under the tropics. If it was a simple slavery like that of the ancient Romans - a white slave class in a temperate climate - a practical solution might be found.[96]

Before going to that dinner with the Hereford Agricultural Society and discoursing on world events, Lewis concerned himself with local matters and attended a meeting of the directors of the Hereford and Gloucester Railway. The railway opened in 1855 and was much used by Lewis for going up to London. He also saw it as a means of improving the postal service with Hereford and beyond, a service he made great use of, and was always attending to its improvement. Lord Bateman[97] was also present, representing the Great Western Railway, and it was agreed that 'on going to London' he should 'communicate with Mr Rowland Hill[98] & Mr Saunders'.[99] The reliability of the railway may have been another matter for Mr Saunders' attention:

> Left London by the morning train, but was delayed between Gloster & Ross by the fracture of a part of the engine, & did not arrive at Hereford till near 8 o'clock. In consequence slept at the Green Dragon.[100]

Another local matter concerned Lewis that autumn, namely the County and Borough Police Act of 1856, whereby counties which lacked a county police force were to establish one. In October 1856 Lewis took the oath at Presteign as a magistrate for Radnorshire and joined his fellow magistrates in their county meeting. Their main business was a preliminary discussion on implementing the Police Act. It was so protracted that Lewis had to dine and stay the night with Richard Green Price at Norton Manor and they returned to Presteign next day for the adjourned magistrates' meeting. There they

> Settled the outlines of the plan & appointed a deputation to confer with the Herefordshire magistrates on the subject.[101]

Ten days later he was back at Presteign:

> Attended a meeting of the Committee of Magistrates at Presteign, to consider the subject of Police. Settled the outlines of the plan & appointed a deputation to confer with the Herefordshire magistrates on the subject.[102]

The Radnorshire deputation consisted of Lewis, Sir John Walsh of Knill, and the Revd Richard Lister Venables of Llysdinam. On a Saturday morning in early November they set off by the *Arrow* to meet their counterparts in the Herefordshire committee of magistrates 'to make arrangements respecting the election of a chief constable for the two counties'. The preliminary steps were agreed to, but when Lewis tried to persuade the committee to include Breconshire and Monmouthshire in their arrangements he made no headway:

> The exclusive county feeling was insuperably strong on this head. Even with regard to Radnorshire there was no great willingness.[103]

Lewis seemed unaware that the counties of Radnor and Monmouth were in Wales and Herefordshire was not. He was not alone in this, and some of the Radnorshire bench shared his insensitivity to the growing awareness of nationality in 19th-century Wales. Lister Venables in particular would have been more than happy to have seen Wyeside parishes in the southern part of the county incorporated into the diocese of Hereford, like Presteign, and Old and New Radnor, at the expense of the diocese of St Davids. Captain James Drummond Telfer, RA, took up his appointment on 3rd February as Chief Constable of Radnorshire and Herefordshire Constabulary, though the Radnorshire Constabulary was a separate unit under the control of the Court of Quarter Sessions for Radnorshire.[104]

Another local matter for Lewis's attention was the future of John Beddoes School in Presteign. He was a trustee and it was in an advanced state of moral and physical decay. In 1847 the Welsh Education Commission described it as grossly inefficient, the boys ignorant, the master incompetent, the trustees negligent. The head-master from 1854, the Reverend Charles Blackburn, BA, was little better than his immediate predecessors, and the school itself was described in 1856 as 'almost unfit for a stable or cowhouse'.[105]

At the end of August 1856 Lewis rode over from Harpton to attend a lengthy meeting of his fellow trustees:

> a meeting of Trustees of Beddoes charity, Sir Harford Bridges, Mr Ormerod, Mr R Price, Mr Stephens, & others.[106] Mr Stephens read a draft of a proposed scheme, the discussion of which occupied about five hours.[107]

He was back again at Presteign the following Wednesday when the trustees continued their discussion.[108] Lewis's fellow trustees, however, were not always so diligent and when he rode over to one of their meetings in September 1860 he found 'there was not sufficient attendance to make a quorum'. But he put his time to good purpose and 'inspected the new building erected for the school, which is completed'.[109] This new school building was largely the result of a bequest from Edward Lee James, a prominent Presteign lawyer and property owner, but it improved matters little. Consequently it could still be reported in 1870 that 'the management of the school's affairs has been conducted with great remissness for a long time'.[110]

Horseback journeys to meetings were a particular hazard for Lewis who was not much of a horseman and his diaries often refer to mishaps:

> Rode, fell from my horse in remounting in consequence of the horse giving a sudden turn. I fell on my hand, but was not seriously hurt.[111]

Shooting, too, seems not to have been amongst his rural pleasures and it was his parson brother, Gilbert, who came over to Harpton from Monnington to shoot on the Vron hill or at Black Yat, Lewis being content with recording the size of the bag: 'Gilbert ... killed 10 grouse'; 'Gilbert shot ... & killed about 12 birds, including two black game'.[112] Friends came to shoot as well, making August in this respect a busy month:

Monday 11th August 1856. Harpton. Tomkyn Dew & Capt Stanhope[113] came.

Tuesday 12th August 1856. Harpton. Dew & Stanhope shot on Black Yat & killed 7 brace of grouse.

Tuesday 26th August 1856. Harpton. Capt Dan Webb[114] came to shoot. He killed 7 birds.

Wednesday 27th August 1856. Harpton, Webb shot.

There was constant to and fro-ing, and Harpton was seldom empty during the late summer. Thus on the same day that 'the Scudamores, Webb, & Gilbert went away, also Miss Cornewall', the Lewises went over the Radnor Forest to Penybont Hall, where they 'found Mr & Mrs Severn, son & two daughters … and dined and slept'. Two days after their return, 'Clarendon's three daughters & Governess arrived'.[115] The servants' hall at Harpton had as varied a list of visitors as the dining room itself, and one of those who shared the table with the Clarendons' governess was Richard Gibbs. He worked for the Geological Survey 1841–72 and was accompanying Murchison, who was making a surprize visit to Harpton after many years' absence. Though Government geologists no longer wore uniform and were allowed instead to don top hat and frock coat, the change of dress seems not to have achieved the change of status it was intended to bring about. Gibbs was not at the dinner held at Harpton in Murchison's honour on the day of their arrival in Radnorshire. The other guest was Peter Rickards Mynors of Evanjob, one of the local gentry who subscribed in 1839 to the publication of Murchison's *Silurian System*.[116]

Murchison wanted to re-examine the local geology and the fossils RW Banks had found on Bradnor hill and on the Monday after his arrival at Harpton he and Lewis, with Gibbs following at a respectful distance, rode over to Kington where Banks joined them. Banks later related events:

> Sir Roderick visited the Bradnor quarries with Sir Cornewall Lewis and myself. He found a *Pteraspis* in the upper beds; and Gibbs, his collector, carried away, among other specimens, a swimming foot, with the fringe-like pincer, of *Pterygotus gigas*.[117]

Then they rode on to Knill 'to trace the succession of the beds'. The day's riding ended on Old Radnor hill, 'which certainly consists of indurated Caradoc sandstone'. Next day Lewis and Murchison were back on their horses:

Rode with Murchison by Evanjob hill & the Cold Oak to Presteign & back by the road. Examined the old quarries by Corton, & saw the situations of the strata in that district, which are confused & thrown together, but are clearly shown at different points.[118]

On Wednesday 'Murchison went away' and the King of Siluria seems not to have appeared again in person in the vicinity of Harpton.

There were acts, too, of filial piety to be undertaken, such as writing an epitaph for his father's memorial in Old Radnor church and hanging his father's portrait in the dining room at Harpton. It was a copy of the original painted by the fashionable portrait painter Henry Wyndham Phillips, which hangs in the Shire Hall at Presteign. It was the gift of his step-mother, Lady Therese Lewis, but not generally thought to be a good likeness, Lewis's cousin Alice Duff Gordon dismissing it as 'red faced and vulgar looking'.[119] And the one thread of continuity in all this diverse activity was Lewis's revision of his Roman history.

Early in November Lewis returned to London 'for Cabinets and other November occupations' in the hope of returning to Harpton for Christmas.[120] At the party at Harpton on the Friday before Christmas there were in number 'in all about 100' and a 'Christmas tree in the dining room'.[121] The Christmas tree seems to have been an innovation that year for Harpton, though it had been a feature at Windsor since at least 1847.[122] Lewis's brother Gilbert from Monnington, his cousins Velters, Fanny and Henrietta Cornewall from Moccas, Lady Jane Walsh and her daughters from Knill, and the Miss Kings from Staunton Park were all at Harpton, but the evening was no more than a brief festive interlude for Lewis, and next day until the 23rd it was back again to official business and the revision of his Roman history.

It was a white Christmas with a further fall of four inches over night and 'the thermometer very low' and Lewis returned to his 'official business: revision of Roman history' until, a thaw having set in, he and Lady Lewis went to stay at Staunton Park for Mrs King King's New Year's Eve ball. Even so, time had to be redeemed and he rode in the afternoon with Mr King King to see railway works in progress near Pembridge. On New Year's day 1857 the Lewises returned to Harpton.[123]

More snow kept Lewis from the first cabinet meeting of 1857 and the revision of his Roman history took its place, interrupted by visit to Garnstone for a few days to attend a ball at Sarnesfield. Back at

Harpton an abscess in the jaw made him a poor host for the visit of Nassau Senior and Mrs George Grote and after their departure, inflammation of the eye prevented him from going up to London for another cabinet meeting. But the news 'that the army & navy estimates, as prepared amount to 24 millions'[124] saw to it that he *was* in London for the next meeting of the cabinet. The peace was proving more expensive than the war. Gladstone, when he was Chancellor, had tried to meet its cost by using income tax, his 'engine of gigantic power'. The tax, however, was extremely unpopular and Lewis wanted to reduce it.

Lewis estimated the war had cost £77,588,711 and in preparing his third budget in 1857 he met a deficit of over £8m, by raising a loan:

> I stated with some fullness, & without reserve my objections for the proposed increase of the army & navy estimates from 16 millions, the amount before the peace, to 24 millions. After a long discussion, it was agreed that the estimates should be revised … I drew up a memorandum recommending a reduction of the estimates to 20 millions, and sent it to Ld Palmerston, who goes to Windsor tomorrow to discuss the estimates with the Queen & Prince & Duke of Cambridge.[125]

Lewis's fullness and lack of reserve was effective and at the next cabinet meeting the Army and Navy estimates 'were reduced from their original amounts by about 3 millions'.[126] Next day Lewis and his wife travelled down to Windsor. The guests included both Russian and French diplomats:

> Our apartments were in the Lancaster Tower. We found Persigny,[127] Chreptovich[128] & Madm Chreptovich, the Russian minister & wife, Clarendons, Ld Aberdeen,[129] Ld & Lady Delawarr.[130] In the evening, acting in a temporary theatre, a translation of Michel Perrin, & a vulgar English piece.[131]

Before leaving Windsor:

> The Prince sent for me & I had a long conversation with him about the Army & Navy estimates, the National Gallery Commission, and the provision to be made for the Princess Royal and the royal children.[132]

Lewis was preoccupied now, not with the revision of his Roman history, but with the preparation of his budget. Lady Duff Gordon recorded how on a Sunday afternoon early in February he called upon her at Hertford Street:

> Lady Lewis called here, then George Lewis whom I had not seen for ages! He talked of his Income Tax &c &c. His *simplicitè de caractere*, joined to his known intelligence & knowledge & great gentleness & smoothness & imperturbability makes him very agreeable to me and very unlike any one ever sees, and gives one more the impression of what an old Greek must have been.[133]

When Lewis came to announce his budget to the Commons on Friday 13th February, his statement took nearly three hours, but he thought 'the plan was well received'. Next day Lady Duff Gordon related her nephew's performance with her customary enthusiasm tinged with exaggeration.

> I [dined] at Ly Lewis's ... and I went to an enormous Assembly at Ly Palmerston's, the great thought of the whole day was George Lewis's speech of the night before, on the ways & means and his giving up the war 9d in the pound [as it is regularly called]. This reduction in the income tax caused a great sensation, & a great boon to all. I calculate that to me it will make a difference of £58 6s 8d pr annum in my income! The speech appeared to be well thought of. He spoke for $3^{1}/_{2}$ hours![134]

In Lewis's own account of things, the 'enormous Assembly' was given but a passing reference: 'in the evening at Lady Palmerston's', and it was what happened earlier in the day which mattered:

> I attended a meeting of the Commissioners of 1851. The prince presided. I had afterwards some conversation with him relative to the preparation of the plan of a provision for the royal children.[135]

By the weekend the soundness of Lewis's budget, at first well received, was being held in doubt by both Gladstone and Disraeli:

> Gladstone had calculated that there wd be a deficiency of five millions, & this supposed deficiency having been communicated to the Derbyites, they believed that there was a fatal flaw in the plan, & Disraeli came down with a notice of resolutions, by which he believed he could turn the govt out. They made no answer to my explanation, & reserved themselves till Friday.[136]

Friday brought forth a 'dull but temperate speech' from Disraeli to which Lewis thought he made an adequate reply. With Gladstone, however, it was different:

> He made a furious personal attack on me, charging me with deliberate misrepresentation of fact.[137]

Hereford in London was agog:

> We talked much of Mr Gladstone's speech & attack on George
> Lewis & his budget. George Clive[138] said it was 'beautiful to hear
> his [*ie* Gladstone's] oratorical powers. But his speech was power-
> less from wanting truth & decision'. His attack was tremendous
> on George Lewis, which has only damaged himself & probably
> done George much good.[139]

Lewis himself called that Sunday on Sir Charles Wood who since
1855 had been First Lord of the Admiralty in Palmerston's administration. Together they went through Gladstone's speech, and letters
followed from Lewis to Gladstone and the Speaker. It seemed that a
repetition of the confrontation with Ferrand of 1847 was imminent:

> I sent a letter to Gladstone stating that I shd at the meeting of
> the House ask for an explanation of a remark in his speech
> which I considered as reflecting on my personal honour. I wrote
> at the same time to the Speaker informing him what I had done.
> The Speaker wrote back to say that I could not even before the
> close of the debate, ask a question respecting words, of which
> no notice was taken at the time. I accordingly sent Gladstone a
> second note, enclosing a copy of the words to which I objected,
> & requesting him to give an explanation of them. This was the
> course indicated by the Speaker. Gladstone came to the House,
> but offered no explanation before the debate. Soon after the
> commencement of the debate, I received a letter from him,
> written in a friendly tone, & disavowing all offensive meaning. I
> accordingly asked Wilson[140] to go to him, to say that I was satis-
> fied, & did not wish for any public explanation. Ld J Russell
> made an able & impressive speech, exposing Gladstone, &
> supporting the budget, which had great weight with the House.
> The rest of the debate was insignificant.[141]

When Gladstone was Chancellor he felt that he had retained
income tax 'in a time of peace' purely 'for the purpose of introducing
great improvements into our financial system', with Parliament's understanding that it would then be got rid of. Thus Lewis's reduction of
income tax which had so pleased Lady Duff Gordon had equally
displeased Gladstone by its survival:

> Had I been capable for the sake of any temporary advantage of
> coming down to the House and proposing the financial arrange-
> ment of 1853 at the cost of future years I should have been the
> veriest charalatan and the basest swindler that ever stood at the
> table at this house.[142]

The sensitive Lewis thought that by implication Gladstone was slandering him. Meanwhile, Lady Duff Gordon, apparently unaware that her nephew and Gladstone had made peace, felt she should keep her own fences in order:

> I went to Mrs Gladstone's party, I was anxious to go to her that she might not think that her husband's Politics and wonderful attack on George Lewis's Budget and very unparliamentary language could alter my old regard and affection for her.[143]

In January, when Lewis had been prevented from leaving Harpton for a cabinet meeting, he had sent Palmerston a paper stating his objections to the proposed course of 'armed negotiation' against China and Japan. Britain wanted the Chinese market opened up and matters had come to a head with the Chinese authorities at Canton seizing what was claimed to have been a British ship, the *Arrow*. The memorandum impressed Palmerston but not sufficiently to dispose of the arguments in favour of armed negotiation. Lewis's views, however, were shared by Cobden,[144] who introduced a motion censuring the government's handling of affairs at Canton. 'The govt', recorded Lewis in his diary, was 'beat by a majority of 16'.[145]

> At a cabinet, where the question of resignation & dissolution was fully discussed & decided in favour of the latter. The approaching confinement of the Queen,[146] & the inexpediency of disturbing her with a change of ministers & household, was an element in the decision ... Ld Palmerston went to the Queen at Windsor with the decision of the cabinet.[147]

Lewis had little to fear from the hustings because it was unlikely that he would be opposed at New Radnor and he returned to Harpton to assist his colleagues in their contests, but not before he had been

> To the British Museum & with Panizzi[148] inspected the new reading room.[149]

Lewis did, perhaps for decency's sake, do two day's canvassing on his own behalf. At Presteign with Jonathan Green, the Knighton lawyer, kinsman, and partner of Richard Green (Price) of Norton Manor, and calling, too, on Sir Harford Brydges at Boultibrooke, he concluded that everything 'was quite smooth'.[150] Next day at Knighton he felt he had 'an excellent reception'. Complacency again prevailed on the following Saturday when he went over to New Radnor for nomination and election:

> I was proposed by Mr R Green & seconded by Mr Adcock
> Phillips. The attendance was good, & perfect unanimity seemed
> to prevail. My speech was well received.[151]

This was not always the case and he could be received with far less
deference in the House than he was accustomed to receive in New
Radnor town hall. Thus, when he

> opened the question of the allowance for the Princess Royal's
> marriage. The House was impatient & my statement was too
> long & detailed for their taste. It was ill received.[152]

Whilst down at Harpton Lewis also gave the youthful Sir Henry
Cotterell a day's support. He was standing as a Liberal for Herefordshire, and Bodenham, his agent, thought his prospects were good. Lewis
accompanied him on his canvass of Kington, 'which was eminently
successful',[153] and it was 'with great satisfaction' that he heard:

> The result of the Herefordshire poll. Cotterell has come in at
> the head of the poll by a large majority.[154]

In consequence the delighted Lewis called on the Bodenhams and
arranged a public dinner at Hereford to celebrate his protégé's election. He came down from London specially, returning next day by the
early train for a cabinet:

> presided at a large dinner in the Shire Hall, in celebration of
> the return of Cotterell & the city members. Near 300 persons
> present. The dinner went off well. Slept at Bodenhams.[155]

Perhaps the dinner was made all the more successful in Lewis's eyes by
Bodenham's news that Sir Henry Cotterell was going to pay all his own
election expenses.[156] Lewis had expenses enough of his own in the
discharge of his official duties, so that, for example in May 1857
Richard Banks bought on his behalf from Urwick & Wrighton, the
Cheapside Wine Merchants, a dozen Chateau Margaux at £25 0s 6d as
Lewis's contribution to Quarter Sessions claret at Presteign.[157]
There was a marked dichotomy between Lewis's public duties at
Harpton and Kent House. Whereas from Harpton he drove to
Kington to inspect the workhouse, from Kent House he attended 'the
opening of the great reading room at the British Museum'[158] or drove
down to Sydenham with Theresa and Alice to the Crystal Palace, 'a
splendid & interesting & wonderful sight', though in Lewis's opinion
too far from London to be successful as a popular attraction.[159] Six

weeks later Lewis himself was part of 'a splendid & interesting & wonderful sight' when he went up with Theresa and Therese to the Oxford Encaenia to receive the honorary degree of DCL, staying the previous night with the Principal of Brasenose, Theresa's kinsman, Edward Hartopp Cradock:

> Attended the Commemoration & received the honorary degree of Doctor of Civil Law. Dr Williams of New College officiated as Vice-Chancellor.[160] My reception by the undergraduates was good. The Latin poem on Sebastopol had much merit. The Newdigate exhibited considerable talent, but the old Popian cadence is now abandoned, & the versification a style of Shelley or Keats is imitated. Returned to London by an afternoon train.[161]

Lewis was barely back in London and his new doctor's robes back on their hanger when the news came of the Indian Mutiny and occupied several cabinet meetings. Lewis was not unduly disturbed:

> The disaffection seems confined to the Indian army of Upper India & not to extend to the population. It pervades the army widely & appears to be of a religious character.[162]

He was more interested in the fact that old friends were in town. De Toqueville breakfasted at Kent House and like Sir Edmund Head, on leave from Nova Scotia, also called several times. One reason Head was in England was to be sworn a Privy Councillor,[163] for which Lewis had used his influence to bring about, a fact he was not averse to Head knowing:

> My dear Head, There are not many things in the personal relations of official life from which I derive much satisfaction; but I had real pleasure in seeing you take your seat at the Council Board, and in thinking that I had been to some extent useful to you in the matter. No honour was ever better deserved; and I trust that you may find this proper recognition of your services strengthens your position in your Government.[164]

For one who disliked such pleasures, Lewis's social diary was remarkably full, so that, for example on the first Saturday in July, having attended a meeting of the committee of the Exhibition Commissioners at Buckingham Palace, and called in at his Downing Street office before a cabinet meeting next door, he went over to Berkley Square to dine with Lord Hatherton.[165] Then there was a visit from Edmund Head before an evening party at Lady Derby's in St James's Square.[166]

There were more meetings with de Toqueville and the Eton Dinner to preside over at Willis's Rooms, 'About 30 persons present. Dr Hawtrey & the Head Master'.[167] There is no mention, however, in Lewis's diaries of his wife's 'morning music' at Kent House of which Lady Duff Gordon thoroughly approved:

> I went to Theresa Lewis's Morning Music which was really very good. Miss Trehearne sang very well and a great deal single parts in Choral music and about 14 others, young & middle ages, and when all was over Miss Thellingson acted one thing, the Loss of Balaclava [Tennyson] and then the Widow's Son.[168]

The following Sunday Lady Lewis dined with Lady Duff Gordon and her daughter Alice and was anxious to discuss a matter in which Lewis had neither experience nor advice to offer, namely the matter of the prizes for the forthcoming Herefordshire Bow Meeting. Lady Lewis was Lady Paramount for the year, and the choice, if not the cost, of the prizes was a responsibility of her office. Alice Duff Gordon was a committed and successful archer and here was an opportunity to choose a prize she had every chance of winning. Thus, it was agreed that Alice Duff Gordon and Lady Lewis would go out early on Monday and Tuesday morning to buy prizes.[169] Lewis was at the House where the Divorce Bill was the main subject for debate and at Cabinets still discussing the Indian Mutiny:

> At the Cabinet. Indian affairs discussed. It appears to me, on reading the official papers, that the mutiny was really produced by undue severity in dealing with the religious scruples about cartridges.[170]

Lewis was later to tell his friend Head:

> I have been reading some letters from the wife of a Scotch officer in the native cavalry regiment which began the mutiny at Meerut. They confirm very strongly my belief, that, although there was much smouldering discontent, there was no precon-cert, and that the outbreak was caused by mismanagement and want of judgement in the English commanders.[171]

Whilst Lady Lewis 'went into the country' to preside over the Bow Meeting at Clungunford, Lewis went with his step-mother to the theatre, an activity much more to his taste. They saw Madame Adelaide Ristori, at the height of her dramatic powers and fully recovered from her recent accident in a Neapolitan theatre in which she was severely burnt and cut, in Schiller's *sturm und drang* 'Maria Stuart'.

'She is a splendid actress' wrote Lewis in his diary.[172] A week later after attending the House and a Cabinet he went to Kensington to dine with the Postmaster General, the Duke of Argyll. It was a small and exclusive gathering at which the Indian Mutiny was the principal topic of conversation. Lewis was joined by:

> Lord Lansdowne, Ld Granville, Macaulay, Labouchere, C Greville & Sir J Melville, Director to the E[ast] I[ndia] Company. Much conversation on Indian affairs. The news which had arrived today was considered on the whole not unfavourable.[173]

From Easter Lewis had also been working on a preface for the German edition of his Roman History being prepared by Professor Liebrecht of Liege, and whilst it was supposed to be chiefly an answer to the parallel work of Philipp August Boeckh, it gave him the opportunity to launch another broadside against the academic ghost of Niebuhr.[174] This was fired in *Notes & Queries*, on 2nd May 1857, in the form of an article on 'Niebuhr on the Legend of Tarpeia'.

Niebuhr maintained that the story of Tarpeia's treachery, whereby she betrayed Rome to the Sabines, only to find that her promised reward was to become the instrument of her death, was a still a popular legend in the early 19th century because it had been preserved by oral tradition. Indeed Niebuhr had been informed in Rome by some local girls that Tarpeia still sat at the heart of the Capitoline Hill, covered with gold and jewels, and bound by a spell. She had, however, in the course of history, only been actually seen once, and that was by the mother of one of the girls. Thus 'genuine oral tradition has kept the story of Tarpeia for five and twenty hundred years in the mouth of the common people, who for many centuries have been strangers to the names of Clodia and Cornelia'. Lewis disagreed:

> The experience of all countries contradicts the supposition that a genuine oral tradition, respecting any matter of fact, can be preserved for a period of time at all approaching that indicated in this passage; namely, 2500 years, composed of 700 years before, and 1800 years after, the Christian era. The narrative of Niebuhr is circumstantial; but considering the liability to mistake or deceit in the case of a stranger imperfectly acquainted with the habits of the common people, it is to be regretted that he did not record the names of his informants, and particularly of the person who was supposed to have seen the enchanted Tarpeia.

In November 1856 Lewis had sought the assistance of a certain Dr Pantaleoni, 'an accomplished Roman physician' to verify Niebuhr's story. But in this the learned doctor failed:

> With respect to the popular legend described by Niebuhr, I have made all possible inquiries through people living is that quarter of the town, and by their profession and character conversant with the lower orders; but I have not succeeded in discovering any trace of it, and it is certain that I could not have failed in verifying it if it at all deserved the name of *popular*.

Both Lewis and Pantaleoni agreed that if Niebuhr's legend had any genuine popular existence, the probability was that it was derived from a medieval origin, 'and was borrowed from some northern story similar to those of enchanted persons sitting under ground which are collected in Grimm's *Deutsche Mythologie*, c. 25 of the first, or c. 32, of the second edition'.

Three weeks later, again in *Notes & Queries*, Lewis's friend Edward Twistleton took up the attack on Niebuhr:

> The credit demanded far a supposed faculty of historical divination in Niebuhr, in regard events of which there were no contemporaneous written accounts, is perhaps more than can be reasonably conceded to any one. But at any rate it will probably be admitted, that the claim to such a faculty can only, with any plausibility, be advanced in favour of an intellect which has always shown, when it has been tested by facts, that it has not been duped by imagination into forming illusive conclusions and judgements.[175]

Twistleton argued that Niebuhr's intellect was not of this calibre:

> In 1792 the Abbé Soulavie published a spurious work of his own, called *Mémoires de la Minorité de Louis XV*, as a production of the celebrated Massillon.

Niebuhr not only failed to see through the imposition, but in a letter to Count Adam Moltké, dated 16th January 1809, he praised it in the following terms:

> Massillon's *Petit Caréme*, the sublimity and splendor of which you know ... induced me to read his *Mémoires de la Minorité de Louis XV* a book which, in my opinion, is not only the best historical book in the French literature, but is not inferior to any in any other modern language, and may be compared to the ancients.

Despite appearances to the contrary, there was no collusion between Lewis and Twistleton, and in the autumn Lewis wrote to Twistleton, having read his attack on Niebuhr, enclosing a copy of his own article:

> I enclose a number of *Notes & Queries*, in which you will find an article illustrative of your exposure of Niebuhr's wonderful delusion respecting the historical forgery of Soulavie.[176]

It is difficult, however, in retrospect to see why it was so important to both Lewis and Twistleton to discredit Niebuhr. He had died in 1831, some twenty-six years ago, so he was hardly much of a danger to either men. Ironically, though, Lewis himself was in the process of bringing his own academic reputation into danger.

In 1844 Minoides Menas, a Macedonian Greek, with a reputation for learning, had found in the convent of St Laura on Mt Athos a 10th-century manuscript of Babrius which was lost in the Middle Ages. Published in several continental editions, it was then given to

> English scholars under the masterly editorship of Sir George Cornewall Lewis. From the appearance of this edition may be dated the restitution to Babrius of the literary honour so long usurped throughout the literature of Europe by Æsop.[177]

Lewis's edition was published, with notes, for 5s 6d in 1846. Then eleven years later, in June 1857, Minoides Menas informed Lewis that he had discovered another Babrius manuscript which he lent to Lewis for transcription, a Sunday's labour.[178] It was, no doubt with Lewis's approval as a Trustee, that in 1857 the British Museum purchased both manuscripts from Menas. Then 'to the eternal disgrace of English scholarship'[179] the second manuscript was edited by Lewis, the fruit, according to his diaries, of twelve day's sporadic work, interspersed with attendance at the House and visits to the British Museum, 'referring to books'.[180] Its publication[181] in 1859 was soon followed by an English verse translation by the Revd James Davies, né Banks, of Moorcourt,[182] a kinsman of Lewis, and to whom he dedicated it. At 6s, postage 4d, 'cloth bound and elegantly printed', it was well received, and was reviewed by the *Hereford Times* with loyal enthusiasm:

> The points of difference and the more obscure allusions in the text are ably elucidated by Mr Davies, who has performed his work throughout in a scholarly manner. His verse is easy, his diction simple, terse, and clear, and he has produced a fable-book which is admirably adapted to take the place of the imper-

fect collections of Æsopian wisdom which have hitherto held the first place in our juvenile libraries.

But it was not long before the second collection of the fables was pronounced by scholars to be an apocryphal concoction, the work of Minoides Menas. The exposure was led by John Conington, Professor of Latin Language at Oxford with a paper in the *Rheinisches Museum* of 1861, which was subsequently expanded into an article for the *Edinburgh Review.*

But to return to the autumn of 1857. Arriving at Harpton in early September Lewis opined that the alterations proceeding at the west end of the house promised to be a great improvement.[183] They were probably the work of Nicholson, the Hereford architect, and were in a grand baronial style which neither harmonised with Nash's Georgian frontage to the main house, nor did it have any uniformity in its choice of stone with the main building. Ironically it has survived whereas Nash's elegance was demolished in 1956. The work did not interrupt the usual autumnal round of house guests, nor did the refurbished stables do anything towards enhancing Lewis's weak horsemanship. Lady Lewis was still in office as Lady Paramount for the Herefordshire Bow Meeting and Alice Duff Gordon back to test her prowess stayed at Harpton where she did other things besides practising her archery. Of these she sent her mother a regular account:

> I heard from Alice with an account of a 16 miles ride to Abereddow [*sic*], Terese, George Villiers and Theresa & Villiers's nieces & two Governesses & Alice Lister in the carriage. She was charmed with the scenery, on the banks of the Wye & the confluence of the Rivers Wye & Eddow [*sic*]. Returning home, George's horse fell flat down with him [he was stunned & his nose was bruised but not really hurt] and afterwards Theresa's horse [*Radnor*] fell with her. She also fortunately escaped unhurt.[184]

Grand extensions, however tasteless, are proportionately expensive and the private resources of the Chancellor of the Exchequer were, at least by his standards, modest. Some rationalization of the Harpton estates, contemplated by Sir Frankland Lewis before his death, was now a matter of some urgency. Lewis wrote to his brother Gilbert:

> I hear that Downton estate is in the market, & that the price will be about £27,000. C[harles] Price [the bailiff] tells me that my father [he died 22nd January 1855] had intended to buy it, by selling Pilleth, with the addition of some money of Lady Lewis's.

How do you feel about the sum under my marriage settlement? With that money & with Pilleth, then purchase might probably be effected. There is a danger of John Whittaker[185] selling his estate near St Weonard's, & buying it, & perhaps Sir J Walsh might buy it, & enlarge the house & reside.[186] Edwards of Hindwell had bid about £26,000 for a cousin of his.[187] The sum bargained on by Lockburn was £23,000. I am not very eager about the matter, but it certainly is an object, if it cd be accomplished.[188]

The Downton estate was in the hands of another Lewis family, of no connection with that of Harpton, and there was a long standing rivalry between them. Cornewall Lewis's ancestor 'Old Burgess Lewis' who had defeated Lord Harley for the Radnor Boroughs seat in 1715, was himself defeated by the 'Stranger to Radnorshire', a certain Edward Lewis of Putney, in the election for the same seat in 1761. Whereupon Edward Lewis, with a degree of political provocation, bought Downton House barely a mile from Harpton Court.[189]

In 1805 Frankland Lewis was approached by Percival Lewis of Downton, 1757–1821, with a view to the former's buying the estate:

I have sent you a Particular as well as the annual value of my estates in Radnorshire intended to be sold, with the exception of Downton mansion house. The annual value of the estates has been ascertained by Mr Wainwright of Hereford, and the tithes by Mr Harris of Leominster:

The two Downton farms	£429
Brookside farm	209
The two Knowl farms	112
Jack Green	44
Luthers & Catherine Pughs	129
Forth & Newgate farms	120
Pant Jenkin farm	21
Badland & Hangingheld	158
Lower Badland farm	12
The Duke's Arms	13
Swan House Inn	4
Tennis House	6
Sundries in New Radnor	3
	£1260
Land tax redeemed	£24
Tithes: Llanfihange Nant Melan	133
Nantmel	251
Glascombe	255
	£639
Grand Total	£1923

Neither Timber or Tolls of Knighton or several small detailed estates are set out in this Particular.

I am. Dear Sir, Yours most faithfully,

Perc'l Lewis.[190]

But Frankland Lewis did not proceed further with this business except in 1809 to buy the small farm of Pant Jenkin in the adjoining parish of Llanfihangel Nant Melan for £57.[191]

In October 1821, on the death of Percival Lewis, an advertisement appeared in the *Hereford Journal* offering Downton House for rent:

> To be let and entered on immediately and for a term of years the mansion House of Downton with offices, coach house, fish pond, well stocked with fish, and meadow land of the richest quality in the midst of which which the house is desirably situated and protected by ornamental plantations, containing upward of 28 acres. Within 1 mile of New Radnor where a Daily Post arrives, and 5 miles of Kington. an excellent market town to which there is a good turnpike road and from whence a regular communication by coach to all parts of the Kingdom.[192]

The same newspaper carried another advertisement telling of the forthcoming auction of all Downton's

> household furniture and effects, billiard table with cues and maces, pictures, small cellar of wines, dairy and brewing utensils. The whole may be viewed two days previous to the sale & catalogues may be had at the Hotel. Hereford and the principal inns in Kington, Leominster, Hay, Presteigne, Knighton and Ludlow.

Downton was leased to a member of the Cockburn family, which despite its Scottish origins, had established links with Radnorshire,[193] and Cockburns continued to live at Downton until the 1870s. In 1858 however, the opportunity arose for Lewis to acquire the Downton estate when Percival Cray Lewis and his surviving sister, Augusta Ann Lewis, decided upon its sale.

To help the completion of the purchase Lewis proposed to sell Pilleth Court in north-east Radnorshire. Built *c.*1600 of brick and stone, it was, according to Jonathan Williams, 'the residence of the respectable family of Price of this parish',[194] and related to the Prices of prestigious Monaughty. Its local status in the 17th century is reflected in the fact that according to the Radnorshire Hearth Tax Return of 1670 it was assessed as having seven hearths.[195]

There was a connection between Pilleth Court and Harpton as early as 1665[196] involving Margaret Pryce of Pilleth, widow, with property which later became part of the Harpton estate.[197] In 1805 the property figures in the marriage settlement of Thomas Frankland Lewis on his marriage to Harriett Cornewall, Lewis's mother,[198] by which time it had presumably been in the Lewises' hand for some time. Under the Lewises, however, Pilleth Court went into decline and when the Cambrian Archaeological Association inspected the house in 1847 and though it was then only occupied by a farmer, it was thought to be 'interesting'.[199] A year later this remark stimulated the Association's correspondent *Viator* to make

> a point of passing by that secluded spot in a later border-journey. The hall, now the kitchen, in the ancient mansion there, I found had been recently despoiled of its Dais and pillars, and transformed so as to suit the taste of its beautifiers.[200]

Lewis was familiar with the property[201] but its architectural merit escaped his interest, another example of how, despite his ancestry, anything Welsh was unable to engage his attention. On the other hand, however, its financial potential interested him greatly and in February 1858 the house and the 697 acres of farm land attached to it was sold to Richard Green Price for £14,300.[202]

In May 1857 Percival Cray Lewis and his sister Augusta wanted £26,000 for the Downton estate, which Bodenham advised Lewis to purchase. Its acquisition, in his opinion, being of much importance to the Harpton estate, was capable of bearing an increased rent. But after the sale of Pilleth there was shortfall which would have to be met, with the agreement of the trustees, by a loan of £11,000 from Lady Lewis's marriage settlement.[203] But the sale of Pilleth, as has been seen, tarried, and in December 1857 Percival and Augusta Lewis were asking Cornewall Lewis for £20,000 of the purchase money and Bodenham was warning him that another purchaser was waiting in the wings. However, after much negotiation and with the financial help of Gilbert Lewis, the purchase of Downton was at last completed eleven months later in November 1858.[204]

Chapter Six:
Party Politics

1857 ended painfully for Lewis with two days of 'severe toothache'. Relief at Harpton was not near at hand, for Mr Levason, the Hereford dentist, only came to Kington to hold his surgery in Milner's Hotel four times a year. But Lewis was well enough to go to Daniel Peploe Peploe's well attended ball at Garnstone, staying the night there and returning to Harpton for the New Year. He made his customary attendance at the January Quarter Sessions, driving over to Presteign with Sir John Walsh of Knill, to discuss increasing the size of the police force 'to meet the requisitions of the Government.' Four additional constables were appointed in 1857, but HM Inspector of Constabulary was dissatisfied:

> I am still of the opinion that another Superintendent is required, as it is perfectly impossible for the present Superintendent to supervise the constables of the whole county in an efficient manner.[1]

The Quarter Sessions, strengthened no doubt by the advice of Lewis as a former Under Home Secretary, sanctioned the appointment of a second superintendent at a salary of £80 pa, with a horse allowance of £40 pa. The county now had a police force of two superintendents, two sergeants, and eleven constables,[2] and Lewis returned to Harpton to write papers on Indian Finance.

The Lewises left Harpton for Kent House in the second week of January and when the toothache returned next week he was able to visit a dentist. The affairs of the British Museum, of which he was a trustee, were to engage Lewis for the first half of the year with more than monthly meetings.[3] Sir Robert Smirke's building, despite the completion of the circular reading room in 1857 to the designs of his brother Sydney Smirke, was inadequate for the needs of its growing collections:

> I attended a meeting of the Trustees of the British Museum, who discussed the question of making an addition to the Museum, or of detaching a portion of its collections ... The Trustees resolved to recommend the purchase of ground at the north end of the Museum.[4]

Gladstone, Disraeli, Lord John Russell, Macaulay, the Speaker of the Commons, and the Duke of Somerset[5] were amongst Lewis's fellow trustees, and the matters discussed at their meetings were not always directly related to the well-being of the museum. The India Bill and the Oude dispatch both figured in their 1858 conversations. The Bill transferred the territories and properties of the East India Company to the Crown and set up a Principal Secretary of State and a Council for the government of India, whilst giving the Governor General the title of Viceroy. Certainly both Lewis and Macaulay were knowledgeable on Indian affairs and in 1847 whilst at the Board of Control Lewis had studied Indian history in depth, and Macaulay produced a draft Indian penal code in 1837 which was introduced in 1860. The Oude dispatch originated from Lord Ellenborough, President of the Board of Control, and rebuked Lord Canning, Governor General of India for his handling of the affairs of Oude in the Indian Mutiny.

The provincial splendours of the Peploe Peploe ball at Garnstone with its 240 guests a month earlier must have paled with those of the marriage of the Princess Royal on 25th January. Lewis was at both:

> At the marriage of the Princess Royal. I was in the Chapel Royal & saw the procession pass. The appearance of the dresses was splendid, & all the arrangements excellent. Prince Frederick William[6] spoke his words in a firm loud voice. The Princess Royal[7] was inaudible. The service was fully read by the Archbishop of Canterbury.[8] The exhortation was well delivered by the Bishop of London.[9] The Queen seemed much agitated, & the Princess Royal overcome.[10]

But the shadows cast by the repercussions of the Orsini plot meant that the Chancellor of the Exchequer could not linger at the Princess Royal's nuptials. Lewis had business at his Downing Street office to attend to and then a Cabinet meeting, for the Italian revolutionary Count Orsini had nearly succeeded in assassinating Napoleon III in a plot hatched in London and implemented with bombs from Birmingham:

when the Attorney General & Sir R Mayne, Chief Commissioner of Police attended, and it was agreed to arrest upon suspicion a man named Bernard suspected of complicity with Rubio and Orsini, two of the Italians concerned with the late attempt on the life of Louis Napoleon.[11]

Then 'in the evening' he was 'at a large concert at the Palace'.

Two days later there was another ball, this time at the French Ambassador's. Lewis never mentions whether or not he was accompanied on these occasions by Lady Lewis, or whether he danced. But he put his time to good advantage:

> In the evening at a Ball at the French Ambassador's. Had a long conversation with Lord Stratford, who seems in good health.[12]

Stratford Canning, 1st Viscount Stafford de Redcliffe, 1786–1880, was the long-serving and influential British ambassador to Turkey, so the conversation was unlikely to have been limited to the state of the viscount's health.

On 12th February 1858 Lewis made what some considered to be one of his most successful speeches in the House of Commons. It was in support of the first reading of Palmerston's bill for the better government of India. Its success was probably due to the fact, that contrary to his custom, it was spontaneous and extempore:

> I spoke later in the evening, in answer to Baring.[13] I expected Vernon Smith[14] to follow Baring, I had not prepared myself to speak, but being well acquainted with the subject, I was able to trace the history of the Company without preparation.[15]

Next day he was gratified to find that the speech 'had given satisfaction', and so, pleased with it, he had it published.[16] But a few days later, however, Palmerston's government was defeated on account of its handling of the Orsini plot. Lewis was in favour of the government's immediate resignation and in a long conversation with Palmerston told him so.[17] Next day Lewis dined, surely not by coincidence, at the Palace. His opinion on the political situation was sought by both Victoria and Albert:

> had a long conversation with the Queen & the Prince about the resignation of the ministry. They … were aware of the declining energy & increasing unfitness of Ld Palmerston.[18]

The government's resignation followed and Lewis went to his Downing Street desk for the last time on Thursday 25th February:

> At Downing Street for the last time, occupied all day in clearing
> away papers & parting with the persons in the Treasury &c. I leave
> the finances of the country in a perfectly good state, but there will
> be a considerable deficiency to provide against in next year.

When he had his final audience with the Queen to deliver up his
seal of office she expressed her regret at his resignation. When,
however, he informed her that he was handing over the finances of
the country in a good state to his successor, 'from a remark which the
Prince made upon this', he suspected that 'Lord Derby had been
giving her a different & a false impression'.[19]

Lord Derby became Prime Minister in Palmerston's place and
Disraeli, who succeeded Lewis as Chancellor of the Exchequer, wrote
asking him for an interview. Lewis in response called on him next day.
Lady Lewis was now wintering at Rome with Lady Duff Gordon and
her daughters, and complaining there 'much of the cold'[20] so Lewis
had to face the political cold on his own. Friends, however, offered
their condolences, and Edward Twistleton, for example, wrote to him:

> I was very sorry to hear that you individually ceased to be in the
> cabinet. It must be a great satisfaction, however, to have been
> Chancellor of the Exchequer for three years in difficult times
> with credit and honour.[21]

It was a period of recriminations and disharmony which Lewis
observed with some satisfaction, thinking it would hasten the Liberal
return to government:

> Every day brings new disclosures, and we shall soon be fully
> informed as to the intentions of these apostles of resistance to
> democratic aggression, and these organs of the great
> Conservative party. If they go on as they promise, we can do
> nothing better than support them. Their reckoning will be with
> the gentlemen at their backs.[22]

The Liberals, however, had their own dissension and Lewis was
well aware of the acute rivalry between Lord John Russell and
Palmerston. A year earlier he had noted in his diary that Russell:

> wishes to set up for himself as leader of the Liberal party in
> opposition; he is extremely jealous of Palmerston.[23]

Lewis was now the principal intermediary between the two men.[24]
He well appreciated the situation, and at Harpton, back in August
1852, in discussing Russell with his friend Nassau Senior, had acknowledged that

No one would think of forming a Whig Cabinet and leaving out of it a man of his wide views and resolute character, and of his experience and skill as a leader and debater. Then all the principal members of the party are connected with him by blood, or alliance, or friendship. I agree with my father that Lord John and Palmerston are indispensable, and as neither would serve under the other, we must look for a third man as Premier.[25]

The third man in the opinion of both Lewises, father and son, was the third Marquess of Lansdowne, the Liberals' elder statesman. Russell himself, long ago, had lamented that the pure gold of Lansdowne's integrity was not 'mixed with a little more alloy of ambition and self-love'. But in 1858, now 76, crippled with gout, having declined a dukedom the previous year, he was well beyond what little ambition he had ever had, and was ready for retirement. So, without a third man, Lewis had to admit in July 1858, after five months in opposition, that the disunion was as great as it ever was and that real rivalry remained between Russell and Palmerston.[26]

Though out of office, Lewis, of course, still had responsibilities as the member for the Radnor boroughs, and as such attended the House and contributed to its debates. Thus, in March 1858, his interest in Irish affairs going back to his appointment in 1833 as an assistant-commissioner to inquire into the condition of the Irish poor, he spoke on Aberdeen's bill for the abolition of the office of Lord Lieutenant of Ireland and its replacement with a secretary of state. He was in favour of change, but not yet. Whilst the office was a relic of a provincial or colonial system of government, he was

> averse to the substitution of a new secretary of State for Ireland. We must look to abolition when Ireland can be governed without special & local organisation.[27]

Some thought he was splitting hairs, and he was not helped by his weak delivery, so that when he seemed to be concluding his speech, several members jumped up wanting to speak themselves, but Lewis had not finished, and resumed. The result was 'great hilarity'.[28]

At the end of session, in late July, Lewis brought in to the debate his experience as the previous Chancellor the Exchequer to criticize Disraeli's policies in the same office:

> Sir G Cornewall Lewis enters with criticisms of the finance of the Ministry. His object was to shew that, instead of a surplus, there would be a deficit, for that Disraeli has taken into account

as assets the balances in the Exchequer - thus indirectly increasing his means. Disraeli replied & seemed to prove that all is well & that we shall have a larger surplus than he had estimated - to such an extent that he expected to pay off one million of debt.[29]

In the midst of his delicate intra-party negotiations, and normal parliamentary activities, Lewis still found time to write a series of pieces both for the *Edinburgh Review* and *Notes & Queries*. He read widely and quickly in preparation, reading for example, one Sunday:

> after church ... Dr Vincent's *Book on the Navigation of the Ancients in the Eastern Seas*, an excellent & not sufficiently esteemed treatise.[30]

He wrote, too, with equal speed:

> Wednesday 3rd March. I began an article for the *Ed Rev.* in continuation of that on Addington[31] in the last number.

> Friday 12th March. I began a political article on the changing administration for the April number of the *Edinburgh Review*.

> Sunday 21st March. Revised my article, & sent it, with the exception of the conclusion, to the Editor of the *Edinburgh Review*.

> Monday 22nd March. Wrote the conclusion of my article & sent it to Reeve.[32]

> Thursday 25th March. Received the proof of my political article.

> Sunday 28th March. At church. In the afternoon, called on Reeve & began with him the revision of my political article for the *Ed Rev.*

The first of the *Notes & Queries* articles appeared in July 1858, five pages of double columns on 'The Amber Trade of Antiquity':[33]

> The Greeks were for centuries acquainted both with tin and amber, probably through the intermediation of the Phœnicians, without obtaining any certain knowledge of the places from which they came. Their incurious ignorance, however, was not confined to the two articles in question: it extends likewise to ivory.[34]

His conclusions were not undisputed and a correspondent to *Notes and Queries*, observed that Lewis in saying that 'there is no mention of amber in the Old Testament' had made an oversight, 'for the word occurs twice at least'.[35] A fortnight later Andrew Steinmetz[36] took the matter further:

> Sir GC Lewis says 'there is no mention of Amber in the Old
> Testament'. The word occurs thrice in Ezekiel, i.4.and 27, and
> viii.2. The phrase is similar in the three instances, 'as the colour
> of amber'. The subject is not devoid of interest, and I have
> bestowed some little trouble in turning it over.[37]

At this stage the editor, with some impatience, intervened in support
of Lewis:

> It is obvious from Sir GC Lewis's Note referring to the mention
> of amber in Ezekiel, that his remark applies, not to the word,
> but to the substance.[38]

There followed a note, in two parts because of its length, 'On the
supposed Circumnavigation of Africa in Antiquity':[39]

> On the whole, we may safely assent to the position ... that 'a
> bare assertion of the performance of any voyage, without conse-
> quences attendant or connected, without collateral or contem-
> porary testimony, is too slight a foundation to support any
> superstructure of importance'; and we may conclude that the
> circumnavigation of Africa in the time of Neco [early 7th
> century BC] is too imperfectly attested, and too improbable in
> itself, to be regarded as a historical fact.[40]

The publication in 1858 of Liebreckt's German translation of
Lewis's *Enquiry into the Credibility of the Early Roman History* made his
work the subject several reviews, such as the one which appeared in
May 1858 in the *North British Review*, LVI on 'Philosophy and History:
Niebuhr and Sir GC Lewis'.[41] Characteristically however, though he
thought Liebreckt 'on the whole' had done his work well, he still
managed to find 'a few oversights'.[42] Even so, the sales of the German
translation were better than those of the original.

But Lewis was not the only out of office politician to turn to his
pen. In early May Lewis reported to Edmund Head, with a measure of
sarcasm that:

> Gladstone has lately published a marvellous book on Homer, in
> three thick volumes. There is a volume on the mythology, in
> which he traces a large part of the Greek mythology to tradi-
> tions from the patriarchs, to whom he moreover assumes that
> Christianity was in some way revealed by anticipation. Hence he
> finds the doctrine of the Trinity in Homer, and holds that
> Latona is compounded of Eve and the Virgin Mary. It seems to
> me a *réchauffée* of old Jacob Bryant.[43]

The Lewises went to Harpton for Easter, arriving at Kington by train on Maundy Thursday to find hat it had snowed that morning. It snowed all day on Good Friday and Lewis 'staid at home with a cough'. It continued stormy and cold all the following week, giving him a welcome opportunity to get on with his work for the *Edinburgh Review*. The week ended with a good rent day, bringing in £1,451, and the following Monday they all returned to London by train.[44]

Back in town, days of toothache, which kept him at home, but did not stop him writing, alternated with meetings of the Senate of London University. All the same, when he came to write his customary birthday review of his health on 21st April he felt able to note:

> This day I am 52. Hitherto I have not found my bodily health fail, except that my breathing is shorter upon slight exertion than it used to be.

In May he launched on a new theme for the *Edinburgh Review*, gathering material for an article on Celts and Germans, and visiting the library of the Athenaeum to consult its periodical literature. The House did not sit on Derby day and the Celts and Germans benefited from his undivided attention, but by the end of the month another project was forming in the mind of this compulsive writer:

> I have moreover begun to read through my notes on the Posthumous Psychology of the Ancients in order to see how they can best be put in a form suited for publication. They are sufficient to form an entire volume.[45]

With Parliament in recess Lewis and his family went as usual to Harpton for the summer and autumn. They were back at Harpton on the 5th August, a Thursday, and no sooner was the unpacking done, (it took all day Friday) than Lewis was at his desk, tinkering with the current article for the *Edinburgh Review*, working out the plan for 'a Treatise of Federal, National, Provincial, & Municipal govt.', producing a fair copy of an article for *Notes & Queries*, and completing some 'former articles on ambiguous prophecies'.[46]

His rhythm of activity was undisturbed by visitors, so that despite the arrival of Charles Villiers, Velters Cornewall, and 'young Walsham', Lewis continued with the scheme of his Treatise whilst they entertained themselves shooting at Gladestry,[47] though he joined the general party for a drive to Eywood. When his aunt Lady Duff Gordon and her two daughters arrived at Harpton on their annual tour of

Herefordshire and the Welsh border, he gave her a review to read of one of his latest essays on the 'Administrations of Great Britain from 1783 to 1830', which he contributed to the *Edinburgh Review*.[48] She also 'looked over George's learned book *Inquiry into Roman History*, whilst George, Therese, Alices twain, took a long ride'.[49]

Lewis was probably as equally unrewarding as a guest as he was as a host. When the family went over to stay at Staunton on Arrow with the King Kings, he seems to have remained in his bedroom where he:

> Translated a passage from a German program on the impossibility of voyages of Phoenician traders to the Baltic, for *Notes & Queries*.[50]

But when the Lewises went to the Eywood Bow Meeting, he was prevailed upon to leave his books and manuscripts at home. He was not much of an archer, but before leaving Eywood for Harpton, he had gleaned some gossip from Lady Langdale which occupied an uncharacteristically large entry in his diary:

> Lady Langdale told me yesterday that her mother Lady Oxford believed that Lady Douglas had been mystified by the Princess of Wales about the birth of Wm Austin & she gave me a curious anecdote of the reason of Lady Oxford for this belief. When Lady Oxford was at Naples Madame Murat[51] told her that she had been assured by the Princess that Austin was her son. Lady Oxford asked if she had carried her confidence one step further, & mentioned who was the father. Madame Murat replied in the affirmative, & said that it was Prince Louis of Prussia. Lady Oxford laughed at this, told Madame Murat that the whole story was a hoax, & that Prince Louis was not in England at a time which rendered his paternity possible. Miss Cornewall, who has been staying here, had heard (from the old Lord Malmesbury?) a story that the Princess Caroline, when unmarried, had appeared at a Court ball with a pillow tied round her person, so as to create the appearance of pregnancy, that her mother & others were much disturbed at this, but that she contrived after a time to untie the pillow, & to drop it, so as to show her natural shape.[52]

A month or so later an anecdote on a not dissimilar theme came Lewis's way when he was dining with the magistrates at the Quarter Sessions:

> Dined with the magistrates, 18 present. Col Wortham, Superintendent of Roads, was present. He was at St Helena when Napoleon died, & heard from the physician who examined his body that his testicles were so small that they had a difficulty in understanding how he could have had children. Yet he certainly had natural children, as well as the King of Rome, as to whose genuiness no suspicions ever existed.[53]

The dinner time conversation at Harpton was at a far more serious level:

> Mr James Davies & Mr Mark Pattison dined here. Had much conversation with the latter on literary subjects.[54]

Mr Davies was, of course, Lewis's kinsman the Revd James Davies of Moorcourt with whom he was to collaborate with the ill-starred edition of the *Fables of Babrius*. Mr Pattison was the Revd Mark Pattison, Fellow of Lincoln College, where Davies had been an undergraduate. In 1850 he was one of Davies's sixteen referees when the latter was seeking a headmastership. He was soon to be the author of a paper on 'Tendencies of Religious Thought in England 1688–1750' in *Essays and Reviews*, published in 1860. His was the least controversial contribution to a book which caused a furore, going into thirteen editions in five years. Over four hundred books, pamphlets, and articles were written in reply to it, and it was condemned by the bishops. Two of the authors were found guilty of heresy, but Pattison survived, however, unscathed, and became Rector of Lincoln College in 1861. It is perhaps surprising that Lewis and Pattison only spoke, albeit at length, on *literary* subjects, for theologically, with their mutual respect for German scientific literary criticism, which the Essayists applied to theology, they had much in common.

After Mark Pattison there came Lord John Russell and two of his daughters. Russell read an article of Lewis's which was about to appear in the *Edinburgh Review*. He gave Lewis some criticisms, but 'none of great moment' and the weather being fair he and Lewis rode 'with a large party round the Forest, a fine day & we saw the distant view to great advantage'.[55]

Public duties, however, took precedence over writing and scholarly talk, and despite the incessant rain, Lewis drove over to Boultibroke for a horticultural show on the 18th August and to Knighton the next day for the opening of the new railway from Craven Arms:

> Drove to Knighton & back, attended the opening of the railway from the Craven Arms to Knighton. Lady Jane Walsh cut the first turf, in a pretty valley beyond the town. Between 3 & 400 sat down to a cold dinner at 2 o'clock in a large tent. Many speeches delivered, generally good. Mr Windsor Clive[56] presided. I gave the toast of the Landowners on the Line.[57]

The day made heavy demands on the county constabulary, enlarged on Lewis's advice earlier in the year, which it was entirely able to meet. Some of its officers deemed to have joined in the celebrations with excessive enthusiasm. Consequently one was fined £1 for being absent from duty and being found drunk in an outhouse, and another was fined £2 for being absent from duty. He was found drunk in bed at 12 minutes to 2 on the morning after.[58]

Lewis undertook a brief tour around Rhaeadr of the western extremity of his parliamentary constituency, dining and staying the night at Nantgwyllt with Thomas Lewis Lloyd, and riding with him over to Cwmelan on the other side of the Elan valley, the home of Lady Otway.[59] On his way back to Harpton he called on Thomas Prickard, at Dderw. He found the country thereabouts, yet to be flooded by Birmingham Corporation for its reservoirs, 'very picturesque', a characteristically restrained turn of phrase in contrast to Jonathan Williams's description of the same landscape:

> The Vale of the Elan, fertile by Nature, rich by culture, and abounding in objects of grand, picturesque and magnificent to Cwmelan and Nantgwyllt.[60]

He sat on the New Radnor bench, with two local clerics, Mr Turner, the Vicar of New Radnor, and Mr Moggridge, the Vicar of Old Radnor, and convicted three local publicans of serving their customers with false measures. And in the same week he presided over the annual dinner of the Kington Odd Fellows and 'gave the toasts'.[61] Later there were meetings to attend at Presteign of the Trustees of Beddoes Charity at which dire decisions had to be made to salvage the future of the school:

> We decided to close the school & dismiss the schoolmaster from 1st January next in order to accumulate a fund for building a new schoolhouse.[62]

The matter of John Beddoes School having been laid to rest, there was then an appointment to be made of a county surveyor. First the short list had to be drawn up:

> I rode to Presteign to attend a meeting of magistrates appointed to examine the applications for the office of County Road Surveyor, with a salary of £130 a year. There were 42 applicants, out of whom we selected the six best.[63]

A week later it was back to Presteign, Col Wortham, the Superintendent of Roads, himself in attendance from London. Only five of the six short-listed accepted the invitation to be interviewed:

> I went with Lister Venables to Presteign, & attended a meeting of the County Roads Board. Col Wortham was present. Out of five candidates we selected a Mr Wood, the Surveyor of the Halifax Highways.[64]

The 1858 November Rent Day brought with it the additional satisfaction of being the first time that he received rent from the newly acquired Downton estate. There are few references to the working of the Harpton estate in the Lewis diaries, probably because he took little direct part in its management, but he did that month on one occasion, after working on his Politics Treatise, help Charles Toogood, one of the gardeners, to mark oaks for thinning in the Frostal plantation. It put Lewis into an unusually nostalgic frame of mind:

> Occupied with my Politics Treatise. I marked oaks in the Frostal plantation with Toogood. This plantation was made by my father about the time of my birth, or a little later, I remember the trees quite young. He told me that it was made upon a ploughed field. It has undergone some subsequent additions, the trees are of different ages.[65]

Throughout the summer Parliamentary reform had been a matter for discussion by Liberals and Tories alike and Lewis used the quiet and peace of Harpton to consider his own attitude to the issue. The Radnorshire weather concentrated his mind:

> St Martin has played us a trick this year. Instead of summer, he has sent us cutting cold winds from the north-east.[66]

Lewis liked to use the annual dinners of the local agricultural societies to air his political theory, hoping thereby to redeem what he would otherwise think to be misspent time. Thus when he attended and presided at the dinner of the Knighton Agricultural Society in early October, despite the presence of Sir John Walsh, MP, who represented the Tory interest, he could not refrain from making 'some remarks on reform'.[67] Nor was he dissatisfied with the result, noting in his diary:

> The remarks on Reform which I made at Knighton are noticed at many Conservative meetings.[68]

But at Harpton, if the truth were to be said, Lewis was just as interested in classical history as he was in parliamentary reform. The Italian distribution of vultures, eagles, and date palms interested him just as much as the implications of the secret ballot. Henry Reeve, his successor as editor of the *Edinburgh Review*, had challenged some of Lewis's statements in his *Enquiry into the Credibility of the Early Roman History*. As a result Lewis has to admit to Reeve that he was in error over the eagles. Such an admission was rare indeed:

> In vol. i. pp. 390–407 I have shown that the occurrence of vultures in large flights in the plains of Italy is inconsistent with natural history. Even in the Alps and high grounds which the vulture alone frequents it is a solitary bird. I see that in p.516 I have mentioned eagles, which I ought not to have included, but I believe that my statements about the vulture are correct. The vulture is stated to be still found in the mountains of southern Italy, and Brydone says that it is found in Ætna.[69]

Lewis returned to the matter of the vulture in 1859[70] and seems to have somewhat changed his opinions. He concludes, after a review of the relevant classical references, both Latin and Greek, that:

> It may be concluded as tolerably certain that the vulture was as rare a visitant of the plains of Italy in ancient as it is in modern times. The ancients were not always precise in distinguishing species in natural history: thus they confounded the cat and the weasel, two species which seem to us very different; and it is probable that they may have sometimes confounded the eagle or other large carnivorous bird with the vulture.

It was all the fault, in Lewis's view, of Artemidorus of Ephesus, 140–180 AD, who mentioned what he believed to have been an the ancient Italian custom of not killing vultures and that it was impious to hurt them:

> It is probable that for Ισακψ in Artemidorus, we should read Ιρπαμψ or Ιβγθψ. Even at the present day the vulture occurs frequently in Spain.

Lewis was more defensive about the date palms where Reeve's knowledge seems to have outrun his:

> My statement respecting the date-palm is taken from Rothman's curious tract on *Ancient Climate*, which is quoted in the note to vol. i., p.515. I afterwards found a similar statement in Tournon's book on Rome. I knew that there were one or two palms at Rome in warm situations, but had no idea that there were as many as you mention. There are (or were) two or three scrubby ones at Nice, but none at Pisa.[71]

On the matter of the eruptions of Mt Ætna Lewis was on stronger ground. He was geologically informed, a Fellow, though lapsed, of the Geological Society, and on personal terms with Lyell and Murchison:

> I forgot to answer your question about the antiquity of eruptions at Ætna. Lyell treats the subject at length in his *Principles of Geology*,[72] and states that the volcanic character of the mountain ascends to thousands of years anterior to any historical period. He arrives at this conclusion upon geological data.[73]

Besides his pieces for *Notes & Queries* Lewis had a pair of articles in hand for the *Edinburgh Review*. Familiar as modern scholars are with lengthy waiting times between submitting an article for publication and its eventual appearance in print, it is with some envy that one reads how Lewis could submit a paper in November and seriously expect its publication in the following January. One was on 'The History and Prospects of Parliamentary Reform' which he believed 'would be read with interest while the question is pending'.[74]

However, before November was out, a more immediate political issue than parliamentary reform faced Lewis. On 24th November Lewis heard of the sudden death from apolexy of Thomas William Booker, one of the three MPs for Herefordshire:

> Lord Wm Graham, brother of Lady Emily Foley, is brought forward by the Conservatives as his successor, & will probably be returned without contest.[75]

But the Liberals of Herefordshire wanted a contest and wanted Lewis to be their candidate:

> I received this morning a letter from Archer Clive, lamenting the want of a Liberal candidate for Herefordshire, to stand against the nominee of Lady Emily Foley, & proposing to me to start from the post, & to try to win the county without a canvass.

> In this event Velters Cornewall & himself would propose & second me without notice. I have declined this offer without hesitation. My engagements with my present constituents are such as to prevent me from contemplating the sudden desertion of them which this step wd imply. There is no great public principle at stake upon an election contest now. The present ministers are conservatives only in name: they are prepared to sacrifice any principle for another month of office.[76]

Another unstated reason, mentioned earlier, for rejecting the invitation may have been the realization that hitherto Lewis had always found contested elections difficult to win; loyalty to his constituents in the Radnor boroughs would be rewarded with a safe uncontested seat at the next General Election. Anyhow, the same post brought Lewis what he considered to be a much more attractive proposition:

> I have likewise received a latter from Dr Liddell, the Dean of Ch[rist] Ch[urch] offering to propose me for election as an Honorary Student of the College. I have accepted this offer.[77]

The course of Lewis's *Edinburgh Review* article on 'The History and Prospects of Parliamentary Reform' did not run as smoothly as he had hoped. Nineteenth-century contributors to learned journals were not troubled by peer review, but Reeve, the *Edinburgh*'s editor, did discuss its contents with Lewis's brother-in-law the Earl of Clarendon.

> I received a letter from Reeve, saying that he had been at the Grove, & had talked at length with Clarendon about the coming Reform bill. C[larendon] had mentioned to him the views in my letter. They both agreed that the *Ed Rev* ought to have an art. on Reform in the January number, & that I shd be the best person to write it. I received a letter from Clarendon to the same effect.[78]

A slightly ill at ease Lewis replied to Reeve, for work on the article was in fact already well advanced:

> I wrote in consequence to say that I was willing to undertake it, provided Reeve approved of my views as to the character of the art. which I stated to him.[79]

Reeve accepted Lewis's proposals, who now wrote to Lord John Russell for his approval, for the matter of reform was politically warm, if not actually hot:

> I wrote in consequence at length to Ld John, in order to ascertain his opinion how far it wd be desirable to enter into the details of a measure in the *Ed Rev.*[80]

Russell's reply expressed his regret that Lewis was writing an article at this time on reform at all:

> In consequence I wrote him an explanatory letter & enquired if he thought that a historical sketch with general remarks on the present position of the question, but without any plan, wd be open to objection. I also wrote to Reeve to suspend my engagement.[81]

Russell's response was to 'renew his objections', though he thought there was some usefulness in a purely historical review. Lewis informed Reeve that he would, after all, prepare an article for his consideration, but this was not a new article, and he simply 'resumed the composition which had been interrupted'.[82] Work on it continued to Christmas Eve, but stopped on the 25th December, it being Christmas Day, and Lewis went to church at New Radnor. On the 27th life was back to normal:

> I revised the MS of my Reform article & sent it to the printer.[83]

Lewis did not return to Kent House until the third week of January and until then writing and local business occupied him. The condition of the local roads particularly engaged his attention. He and King King of Staunton on Arrow rode to inspect the road from New Radnor to Kington at the Old Radnor lime kilns where the coming and going of cart loads of lime rutted the road heavily. Lewis attended the meeting of the County Roads Board at Presteign, and with Miles of Dunfield prepared a report on the rating of the borough of Radnor. There was a further meeting, too, of the trustees of John Beddoes Charity to discuss building the new Presteign school.[84]

Soon after returning to London he heard of his election by the town council as Chief Steward of the City and Borough of Hereford:

> I have accepted the office, which is honorary.[85]

He dined at the Fishmongerers' Company and returned his thanks on his health being drunk, and attended discussions at the House on the style of building for the new Foreign Office. The debate was whether the new building should be Victorian Gothic or 16th-century Italian Renaissance, and the decision was political, the Tories favouring romantic gothic and the Liberals, under Palmerston, disdaining anything smacking of Tractarianism. The Renaissance eventually won the day. He also:

> Attended a meeting of the Exhibition Commissioners at the House of Lords, the prince in the chair. A long discussion on a proposal of the Society of Arts for another great exhibition in 1861. A cautious answer was sent, asking for information.[86]

There were meetings of the Trustees of the British Museum and of the Senate of the University of London to attend.[87] There were social occasions, too. An evening with Sir Roderick Murchison, a weekend at Warfield Park, near Bracknell, with Sir John Walsh, where he noted with sorrow that the

> library was a good one when formed by his father about the beginning of the century, but has not been kept up.[88]

There seemed also to be plenty of time for contributions to the *Edinburgh Review*, and his review of Charles Ross's recent three volume edition of the correspondence of Lord Cornwallis, Governor General of India and Lord Lieutenant of Ireland, apparently occupied him throughout February.[89] But work also continued on the political treatise, and *Edinburgh Review* essays were in hand on extradition, and foreign jurisdiction. In March there appeared the first of Lewis's 1859 series of notes for *Notes & Queries*.[90] His subject was the confusion surrounding Tartessus and Gades amongst the ancients. This he clarified:

> The accounts handed down by the Greek and Roman writers are unanimous in representing Gadeira, or Gades,[91] as an ancient foundation of the Phœnicians of Tyre. Its peculiar position, an island or peninsula, easy of defence and convenient for trade, lying at the mouth of the Mediterranean, communicating with a fertile and metalliferous region, and washed by a sea abounding in fish, marked it out as an advantageous spot for a commercial station.

However, such ancient writers as Arrian, Pliny, and Cicero confused Gades with Tartessus, a region of southern Spain, round the middle and lower Baetus,[92] but to the north of Gades. It was probably the Biblical Tarshish. The point of Lewis's note on the subject was to illustrate that whilst the Greeks extended their navigation and trade, at a comparatively early period, as far as the mouth of the Guadalavir and the country adjoining that river, here their commercial enterprise stopped. As Polybius in the 2nd century BC noted, the Straits of Gibraltar were rarely passed by the dwellers upon the Mediterranean, owing to their want of intercourse with the nations at the extremities of Europe and Africa, and their ignorance of the external sea. There was a certain topicality to this paper because later in the year the cabinet, with Lewis present, discussed at length the possibility of 'a telegraphic cable to Gibraltar'.[93]

Against this background of sustained literary scholarship Lewis was also engaged in intense political activity, in which he was the go-between whereby the still estranged Palmerston and Lord John Russell communicated with each other. Parliamentary Reform was now the principal domestic political issue. The Liberals were still in opposition and were uncertain as to the intentions of the Conservative Derby administration. In the second half of January Lewis discussed things with his brother-in-law:

> I saw Clarendon, who has been at Windsor Castle. The plan of
> the govt Reform Bill has not yet been submitted to the Queen.[94]

A week or so later Lewis called on Lord John Russell and 'had a conversation with him on public affairs', then it was it was an afternoon visit to Palmerston.[95] A few days later Lewis dined with Palmerston:

> About 30 present, chiefly members who held office in the late
> govt. Ld Palmerston read us before dinner the Queen's Speech
> of which Lord Derby had sent him a copy ... It states the atten-
> tion of Parliament will be called to the question of Reform. Ld
> Palmerston looks as well as last year. He is now in his 75th year.[96]

In the Commons Disraeli announced that the government's Reform Bill would be proposed in time for the Second Reading to be taken before Easter.[97] Another round of political dinner parties ensued:

> Dined at the Club. Ld Aberdeen & Ld Lansdowne, both much
> aged ... Dined at the Palace, conversed at some length both
> with the Queen & the Prince, with the former on the Reform
> Bill, & with the latter on foreign politics.[98]

After church on Sunday 'several persons called' and speculation on the Reform Bill was the theme of their conversation:

> Lord John considers the Reform Bill is a party measure of which
> the effect will be to increase the Tory power, & is disposed to

vote against the second reading. Conversation with many members on the Reform Bill. The impression on our side is unfavourable to it. Nobody thinks it will pass as proposed, but opinions are divided as to the policy of opposing the second reading. There was a meeting of the Conservative Party today at Ld Derby's. He announced to them his intention of maintaining his Bill as proposed, & dissolving if the clause disfranchising freeholders in boroughs is rejected.[99]

Derby's bill extended the vote to £10 householders to both the counties and the boroughs. It introduced a lodger franchise of £20 per year, and insisted that forty-shilling freeholders living in a borough must vote in that borough and not in adjacent county, as previously allowed. Over this provision Derby was unprepared to compromise. The bill also included what John Bright denounced as its 'fancy franchises'. These would have extended the vote to members of certain professions, government pensioners, university graduates, and those with deposits of at least £60 in savings banks. Seventy small boroughs were to loose their seats, 18 of these going to the large boroughs and 52 to the counties.

Russell called at Kent House, expressed his views, and asked Lewis to inform Palmerston of them:

Ld J Russell called upon me & said that in consequence of a parliamentary dinner at his house on the preceding day, he had decided to call a meeting of the Liberal Party at the Thatched House Tavern, on the 14th in order to state to them whether he shd or shd not oppose the Second reading of the Govt Reform bill. He requested me to inform Ld Palmerston & to state that he had not yet made up his mind as to his vote. I afterwards called on Ld Palmerston & had with him a long conversation on the subject. The result was that he expressed a disposition rather to vote against the second reading than for it & that he thought it necessary to agree with Ld John about a plan before he said anything about attending a meeting. After some discussion he agreed to a £8 rental franchise for boroughs & £15 for counties. I afterwards went back to Ld John, & informed him of what had passed, with which he seemed satisfied. He thought it impossible to propose a higher franchise than £10 for counties, & he proposed a disfranchisement of about 30 seats.[100]

At the same time Lewis had his parliamentary duties: he was chairman for the committee stages of the Mersey Dock and the Merchant Shipping bills.[101] In readiness for the second reading of the

Reform Bill, Disraeli had persuaded his Conservative colleagues to accept a reduction of the county franchise from £50 to the borough figure of £10, together with the creation of special franchises which would give votes to what was termed the 'upper working class', and a redistribution of fifteen seats in favour of large unrepresented towns. On the other hand, the forty-shilling freeholders in boroughs were to be deprived of their dual vote in the county constituencies. On the other side of the House, Palmerston and Lord John Russell managed to bring themselves to join on a motion to lower the borough qualification. The debate occupied several days at the end of March and towards its conclusion Disraeli, in Lewis's opinion:

> made an effective speech, in good taste as to avoiding personal imputations, in a tone resembling a funeral oration on the govt. Upon a division in an extraordinarily full House, there appeared a majority of 39 for the opposition.[102]

In consequence the government advised a dissolution of Parliament. Lewis records with a delphic touch that he spoke 'in a debate relative to the grounds of the Dissolution', before going on to dine with the Marquis of Lansdowne at Lansdowne House in Berkeley Square, and afterwards to a Mayfair party at Lady Palmerston's. It needs little imagination to guess what was discussed at both gatherings.

A General Election held little anxiety for Lewis, for it was unlikely that his Radnor seat would be contested. So there was time at his disposal, whilst others canvassed their constituencies, for some more work on the Political Treatise. His birthday on 21st April prompted the observation:

> Today I have reached the age of 53. Except that my breath is somewhat shorter than it used to be, I do not as yet feel the effects of age.[103]

Lewis celebrated the day by calling on his aunt, Lady Duff Gordon at Hertford Street. She was delighted:

> George Lewis [called] who sat some time & was very pleasant, very unlike other people. He always seems to take all things en grand, & so smoothly![104]

The Lewises returned to Harpton for Easter, and on Easter Monday Lewis himself canvassed Presteign with Jonathan Green, the Knighton lawyer. On Wednesday he went to Kington and attended Mr Humphrey Mildmay, the Liberal candidate for Herefordshire on his canvass. He comes in without a contest.[105]

And on Thursday he drove over to Knighton and canvassed the town with Richard Green. Friday it rained, and Lewis stayed at home and 'wrote and read'. On Saturday he noted:

> Attended my election at Radnor. I was proposed by Mr Prickard of Rhayader & seconded by Mr Banks of Knighton. Afterwards I made a speech of thanks and stated my views of politics. By the afternoon train I went to Hereford and slept at Bodenhams.[106]

He called on the bishop and the dean and dined with Mr Mildmay, but the overall election news, received at Hereford by the electric telegraph, was not good:

> The accounts of the borough elections show that the gains of the govt are considerable.

The unopposed candidates for Herefordshire were two Conservatives, King King and Lord William Graham, with Mildmay representing the Liberals. Lewis went to the Shire Hall on Monday for their formal nomination and election and heard what he considered to be 'a good speech' from Mildmay, before returning to Harpton on the afternoon train.[107] On Thursday, having been over, the day before, to Presteign where at another meeting of the Beddoes Trustees 'we agreed to take steps for rebuilding the school', Lewis returned to London and the new Parliament.

Derby remained in office: but though the Conservatives had strengthened their position by thirty more seats, they were still short, by eleven, of an overall majority. Once again Lewis assumed his role as the go between as Palmerston and Lord John Russell planned their strategy for Derby's downfall. Lewis and Palmerston both attended the Queen's concert on Friday 13th May, and, as neither was particularly musical, they discussed politics. Palmerston, who was about to go Brocket Hall, Lady Palmerston's Hertfordshire estate:

> spoke of the advisability of communicating with Ld John, & asked me to be the bearer of a message, as he returned to Brocket on the following day. Ld P. thought that the opposition ought to bring forward an anti-ministerial vote on the meeting of Parliament. He disapproved of a resolution censuring the disso-lution, or condemning the foreign policy of the govt. or pledging the House to an immediate Reform Bill, & he preferred a direct

vote of want of confidence. He requested me to ascertain Ld
John's views on this point, & if he concurred, he [Ld P] suggested
that steps shd be taken for ascertaining the views of other leading
men on the opposition side of the question.[108]

Lewis went off on his errand to Pembroke Lodge in Richmond
Park on Sunday after church. Lord John Russell

concurred with Ld P's view, & undertook to make some communications to ascertain opinions. He suggested a form of resolution, & names of mover & seconder.[109]

Arrangements were made for Palmerston and Russell to meet
face to face at last:

It seems that Ld John has proposed to Ld Palmerston to call
upon him & that he [Ld P] did come to Pembroke Lodge. The
latter was to go there on Friday for an interview.[110]

That was on Friday 20th May; on Sunday afternoon Lewis was
back at Pembroke Lodge where Lord John Russell assured him that
amongst 'the leading men on our side' a vote of no confidence was
the preferred way forward. The strategy now had to be settled and on
Wednesday Lewis went down by train with Lord and Lady John Russell
to Wilton House, near Salisbury, the country seat of Sidney Herbert.
On Thursday decisions were made:

Had a long conversation on the intended anti-ministerial vote
with Sidney Herbert & Ld John. We discussed the different
contingencies in the event of the resignation of the govt. & told
him we thought the best arrangement was that Ld Palmerston
shd be First Minister & that he shd lead the House of
Commons.[111]

Lewis returned to London on Friday with Russell and resumed
work on his *Essay on Foreign Jurisdiction*. Sunday had become the day
for negotiation, but this Sunday he was unwell and stayed at home and
'wrote some essay.' So it was Monday before Lewis went over to see
Palmerston:

I called on Ld Palmerston who told me he had authorized Ld
Granville to inform Ld J Russell that he was willing to abide by
the Queen's decision, & to serve under him, if the Q[ueen]
employed Ld JR to form a ministry. I talked to Ld P at length
about a meeting of the party, & of the communication to be

made to it. I also told him I thought he ought to be Prime Minister, but to allow Ld John to lead the Commons.[112]

The new House of Commons first met next day, Tuesday 31st May, and Lewis prepared himself for the new session by continuing with his *Essay on Foreign Jurisdiction*. On Wednesday it was Palmerston's turn to call a council of war, from which Russell was absent:

> I attended a meeting at Ld Palmerston's, Clarendon,[113] Granville,[114] D of Argyll,[115] C Wood,[116] & Sir G Grey,[117] we decided in favour of an amendment on the address, & of a meeting of the party on Monday next.[118]

Next day Lewis called on Russell at 31 Chesham Place, and:

> had a long conversation with him for the purpose of satisfying him of the importance of promising such a cooperation with Palmerston in the formation of a liberal govt. as will remove the difficulties of the party. He entertains a resentful feeling of the manner in which he left Ld Palmerston's govt in 1855, but seemed to entirely forget that he has since had his revenge. He promised to consider what I said, but wd give no answer until he had seen Bright.[119] He promised to attend the meeting.[120]

Lewis then went on to Belgrave Square to see Sir Charles Wood.

> Had a long conversation with him, chiefly with the view of convincing him that the only possible form of a liberal govt, which wd offer any prospect of stability, wd be to make Ld Palm Prime Minister in the House of Lords, with Lord John leader of the House of Commons.[121]

It was now Wood's turn to be the mediator. First, he called on Sir James Graham, who shared the same opinion as Lewis and Wood, and then he went on to Palmerston 'and communicated to him these opinions'.

> Graham thinks that Ld P & Ld JR should agree to serve each under the other, whichever may be Prime Minister, but that whichever is Prime Minister should go into the House of Lords. Ld P refused to agree to these terms.[122]

Later in that day Palmerston had to face an interview with Lord John Russell at Pembroke Lodge at which the latter undertook, at least, as Lewis cautiously noted, 'according to Palmerston's account of events', to attend the forthcoming meeting of the party and 'to state there that he would cooperate with the other leaders in the formation of a liberal government'.[123]

Lewis recovered from his reconciling exertions with two whole days working on his *Essay on Foreign Jurisdiction*.[124] He did a little more work on the essay on Monday morning before he

> Attended a meeting of the Liberal party at Willis's rooms, 272 members present. Ld Palmerston & Ld J Russell addressed the meeting for the purpose of recommending a vote of no confidence on the address, & of declaring that they were prepared to cooperate in a formation of a govt.[125]

The Trelawney Diaries have a less aseptic account of this meeting to mark the reunion of the Liberal party:

> The general tone & feeling of the meeting were very good. Bright was remarkably discreet & moderate. Lord John & Palmerston rivaled each other in expressing disinterestedness & readiness to co-operate. The entente cordiale seemed perfect, till Roebuck[126] threw his shell into the party, that shell being well charged with the elements of disunion. The gist of his speech was this: he disbelieved in the possibility of a cordial combination of the various sections of the Liberal party &, in particular, he doubted whether the 2 rival Lords would long co-operate in the same Cabinet. He, also, thought that it was not good policy to turn out the existing government without some approach to certainty of securing better men.
>
> I noted that, when Roebuck was making his onslaught, Lords Palmerston & John Russell were very skilful in their mode of dissembling their annoyance. Palmerston leant forward with a sort of smile of half astonished curiosity as much as to say, What can Roebuck mean? P. affected the air of 'un homme incompris', good natured but puzzled. Then he used his hand as if deaf so as to leave it uncertain whether the worst hits reached him. Lord John bore his share with good temper. I observed that at one passage he drew a deep sigh. Roebuck had several interruptions, but no cheers of approval.[127]

The truth of the matter is that it is difficult to know which took priority in Lewis's order of things: whether it was the unity of the Liberal party or his *Essay on Foreign Jurisdiction*. He called on his way back to Kent House 'on Waddington & Merivale[128] in order to obtain information for my *Essay*' and worked on it next day before gong to the House for the Queen's speech and vote of no confidence:

> Vote of no confidence moved by Lord Hartington[129], witty & in good taste. Disraeli spoke second, ingeniously & with much sarcasm. Palmerston concluded the night. Debate adjourned till Thursday.[130]

On Wednesday, Thursday, and Friday Lewis was working on the *Essay*, though on Friday he attended and spoke on the last day of the adjourned debate on the Queen's speech:

> I spoke between 8 & 9, but the House was impatient, & I cut short my speech & did not execute what I intended. We divided at 2 o'clock and had a majority of 13 against the govt in the fullest House ever known.[131]

Lord Derby resigned and the way lay open for the Liberals. Next day, Saturday, Lewis completed his *Essay*, 'with the exception of a few passages to be filled in' and was visited by Lord Granville whom the Queen had commissioned to form a government. Granville had already seen Palmerston who had agreed to serve under him as leader of the House of Commons.

> He then went to Ld John Russell, who declined to join unless he was Prime Minister or leader of the H[ouse] of C[ommons].[132]

Herbert, Gladstone, and Grey had all let it be known that they would serve under Granville, but Lewis

> expressed to him an opinion that it was most important to secure the cooperation of Ld J[ohn] R[ussell] & he went away.[133]

He had already seen Clarendon who advised him to abandon the attempt. So much for the public displays of Liberal unity of the previous Monday at Willis's Rooms. Sunday being Lewis's day for mediation, he went to see Granville to discuss the progress of his attempt to form a government. The latest development, he discovered, was that the radical Thomas Milner Gibson[134] had refused to join Granville unless Russell was a member of the government. In Lewis's opinion 'mediating was hopeless, & that it seemed best for Granville to resign his commission'.[135]

He found that Palmerston, Grey, and Wood all shared this opinion when he went by invitation that afternoon to Palmerston's. Palmerston, however, was not minded to take Lewis's advice:

It was agreed that Granville's commission wd probably fail, & that the Queen wd send for Ld Palmerston. We discussed what wd happen upon this contingency. I urged Ld P to go to the House of Lords & leave the lead of the House of Commons with the Presidency of the Council to Ld JR. This he positively declined to do.[136]

Events then moved swiftly. Granville abandoned his attempts and Palmerston was sent for. On Monday morning Lewis received a note from Palmerston:

I received a note from Ld Palmerston informing me that Ld J[ohn] R[ussell] took the Foreign Office, & asking me to be Chancellor of the Exchequer. I afterwards went to his house by appointment ... My name was put down for Ch of Exch, but I stated that I did not wish to make any claim to it, in case Gladstone decided to have it ... In the evening I received the proofs of the two first sheets of my pamphlet on Foreign Jurisdiction, which I corrected.[137]

Lewis was correct in thinking Gladstone would want to be Chancellor of the Exchequer and on Tuesday he had a note from Palmerston offering him the Home Office instead.[138] The composition of Palmerston's Liberal cabinet reassured high Conservative opinion, containing as it did three dukes, and a brother of a fourth, five peers or sons of peers, three baronets of ancient standing and landed property, of whom Lewis was one, and only three men without titles.[139]

For Lewis there still seemed an uncertainty as to his priorities:

Saturday 18th June 1859. Corrected the remaining proofs of my pamphlet. Went to Windsor castle by a special train, & attended a council of the new ministry, at which I was sworn in as a Secretary of state, & received from the Queen the seals of the Home Department. After the Council I returned to London.

Monday 20th June 1859. I went to the Home Office & had an interview with my predecessor.[140] Afterwards at the first cabinet of the new ministry. No business of importance transacted.

Wednesday 22nd June 1859. At the office. Queen's concert.

Chapter 7:
Home Secretary

Lewis's first duty in June 1859 as Home Secretary was to attend the palace in order to present the new Bishop of Bangor to do his homage to the Queen.[1] He then had to go down to Harpton for re-election, his seat having become vacant on his appointment as Home Secretary. It was, of course, little more than a formality:

> Monday 27th June 1859. I attended at the town hall at Radnor for my re-election. I was proposed by Mr Cecil Parsons,[2] & seconded by Mr Richard Green.[3] I returned thanks in a speech of some length. In the afternoon I went to Kington & travelled by the 4 o'clock to Oxford. Went to the house of the principal of Brasenose & slept there.

The Oxford election was afar more spirited affair. Gladstone had been a member for the University since 1847, and though he was returned unopposed in May 1859 there was some opposition to him in the University in the June election following his appointment as Chancellor of the Exchequer. There were those who thought that by joining Palmerston's Liberal administration he was being a turn-coat, amongst these was Lord Chandos[4] who contested the seat as a Tory. In these circumstances Lewis thought it appropriate to break his journey up to London at Oxford:

> I attended at Convocation, and gave my vote for Gladstone against Lord Chandos. Gladstone was about 30 ahead, and the election apparently going in his favour. I left Oxford by the 2 o'clock train for London. On my arrival I went to the office.[5]

He need not have bothered for Chandos only polled 859 votes against the 1,050 for Gladstone. Lewis's Harpton circle however did not share his Gladstonian sympathies. His kinsman and literary collaborator, the Revd James Davies, and Elizabeth Davies, the Aunt Betsy of the Banks family, did not give Gladstone their support. In the 1853 contest, when fierce opposition was led by Gladstone's fellow High Churchman, Archdeacon Denison, James Davies, though no High Churchman himself, cast his vote with the opposition. Aunt Betsy reported this from Aberystwyth where she was nursing Marianna Banks, one of Lewis's many cousins:

> Pray do not rob yourself of any more black puddings, they are too good, the blanc mange Marianna does not touch, so please send no more. It rejoiced me much to find James had not gone to vote for Gladstone, I hope and trust he will be turned out.[6]

Despite his churchmanship Gladstone enjoyed the nonconformist vote and nonconformity was particularly odious to James Davies and Aunt Betsy, who complained when the misdemeanours of the Vicar of Kington became something of a public scandal:

> Who can go to church to hear such a man and I expect no redress from the Church's court, I suppose we must go to chapel, despite ourselves.[7]

Lewis did not particularly enjoy the Home Office:

> I have found the Home Office excessively troublesome, rather than laborious. My entire time has been occupied by an uninterrupted succession of petty business, each subject, however, having a certain importance, and requiring attention and accuracy, in order to avoid scrapes. The session will probably end about the fifteenth [of August], and then I go to Harpton to give a bow meeting at the end of the month.[8]

He would have preferred to have been the Chancellor of the Exchequer again and Trelawny noted how once in Gladstone's absence 'Cornewall Lewis almost took his colleague's business into his own hands'.[9]

The 'uninterrupted succession of petty business', which so irritated Lewis, included a lengthy meeting of the Ecclesiastical Commission to discuss improving the stipends of some of the deans. It was followed next day by a meeting with a deputation of Roman Catholics on the provision of chaplains for prisons and workhouses,[10] with the Queen's ball separating the two events. Perhaps a summons to Osborne came into the same category, for it attracted little attention in his diary apart from the fact that he had 'walked around the grounds' and that he travelled back to London with Prince Alfred whom he found to be 'a merry good humoured quick unaffected boy'.[11] He was back, though, at Osborne within a few days:

> With other ministers, to attend a council, at which the Queen's speech was agreed to. When the ministers returned, I remained at Osborne, in order to accompany the Queen to the Channel Islands. At 6 pm we went on board the *Victoria & Albert*. We anchored in Alum Bay. The *Emerald* a frigate, the *Fairy* and the *Osborne*, two steamers, escorted the Queen.[12]

Again the politics of the visit made little impact upon him and what was noteworthy for him was the fact that

> The use of the French language has diminished rapidly in Jersey & Guernsey since the increased communication with England consequent on steam navigation. The handbills & inscriptions are now almost exclusively in English.[13]

On the royal party's return to Osborne he did not linger: arriving there at 10 am he was his way to London by mid day. But this time domestic affairs barely engaged his attention, even the forthcoming marriage of one of his step-daughters:

> The marriage of Therese with Mr Harcourt was settled yesterday.[14]

It made more impact upon his aunt Lady Duff Gordon:

> Sunday 21st August 1859. Yesterday morning I received a letter from Theresa Lewis, announcing her daughter Therese Lister's marriage to Mr Wm Vernon Harcourt, a clever young lawyer well known as the writer in the *Saturday Review*, a grandson of the old Archbishop of York, no fault but want of money!

Back at Harpton, with the 'Office business sent down', the Bow Meeting which he had earlier mentioned to Edmund Head as forthcoming received rather more attention:

> Bow meeting at Harpton. Lady Langdale was Lady Paramount. Good attendance, & splendid weather. Everything went off well.[15]

Lady Duff Gordon, who was staying at Moccas, agreed, even if her daughter Alice, Lewis's cousin, ended the day prizeless:

> A glorious day if possible finer than any we have had, all the
> Party but Georgy & me, went to the B[ow] Meeting at Harpton.
> They came back at two in the morning, all had gone off very
> well [no prize gained by Alice or by anyone I cared for], the
> Garden in great beauty, all went off very well.[16]

The real focus of Lewis's attention, however, was neither the Bow
Meeting nor his step-daughter's betrothal. It was the troublesome and
laborious matter of Dr Thomas Smethurst who was found guilty of the
murder of Isabella Bankes whom he had previously bigamously
married and who was to be hanged in ten days time.

> Many communications respecting the case of Smethurst, tried
> by CB Pollock, & sentenced to death.[17]

In 1828 Dr Thomas Smethurst, then still a minor, married, at St
Mark's church, Kennington, Mary Durham, a woman twenty-seven
years his senior. Then, thirty years later, in December 1858 at a church
in Battersea, he married bigamously Isabella Bankes, a forty-three-
year-old spinster of modest private means and who had done well
from her late brother's will whereby she secured a life interest in
£5,000. Before this second marriage, the first Mrs Smethurst, now
seventy-four, acquiesced in their all living together as a *menage à trois*
in a Bayswater boarding house. This continued until the landlady
objected and then Isabella moved to Richmond where she was joined
by Dr Smethurst, who continued to pay the first Mrs Smethurst's rent.

At the end of March 1859 Isabella Bankes became ill and the
local doctors were consulted. She failed to respond to their treatment,
however, and died on the 3rd May from what they believed to be
poisoning. A post-mortem examination showed that she was in the
early stages of pregnancy. Smethurst was charged with murder and
after a trial lasting five days, the jury only took thirty minutes to decide
he was guilty. The judge congratulated them on the soundness of their
conclusion and arrangements were made for Smethurst's execution
on Tuesday 6th September at Horsemonger Lane Gaol.

The case excited much interest and doubts were soon raised as to
the justice of the verdict:

> As a general rule, where the verdict is unanimous and without a
> recommendation either from the jury or the judge, who consti-
> tute the proper legal tribunal, it is not customary for the Crown
> to interpose unless some new evidence in favour of the prisoner
> is produced. But this case is almost unprecedented in the annals

of the administration of justice. For in this case it is not merely a question of who committed the crime of poisoning. The doubt, to which so many high medical authorities participate, is whether there was any actual poisoning at all. An immense number of medical men from all parts of the country have come forward with cases of dysentry accompanying pregnancy, precisely similar to the symptoms of Miss Bankes. When it is also taken into account that no arsenic or other 'irritant poison' was found in the body, it is evident that it would not be satisfactory to carry out the extreme penalty of the law, from which there could be no appeal or redress.[18]

Lewis returned to London and spent four days examining and discussing the transcripts, reports, and correspondence relating to the case. Finally, he called on Robert Ferguson, MD, a physician and much-respected specialist in gynaecology.[19] The balance of informed medical opinion was that Isabella Bankes *could* have died of natural causes, and that afternoon, Friday 2nd September, Lewis signed a respite for Smethurst during the Queen's pleasure and sent it to the High Sheriff. An editorial in *The Times* approved:

It will, we think, be with a feeling of relief that the public will learn of the respite of Dr Smethurst, who, if the law had been allowed to take its course, would have been executed on Tuesday next for the murder of Isabella Bankes.

Those who were clamorous against delay have little conception of the mass of documentary evidence to be perused, and the correspondence to be read, and the interviews to be granted, in order that no part of this most difficult subject should be left without most full and impartial scrutiny.

The Secretary of State could have come to no other decision than the one he did, after the most mature and calm consideration of all the circumstances. The great design of the punishments inflicted by the law is not vengeance, but prevention and example. The maxim of giving every prisoner on trial for his life the benefit of every reasonable doubt is as wise as it is humane, and it is as applicable to the Secretary of State in the last resort as it is to the jury who first try the case. There were so many people reasonably doubting the verdict in this case that an execution could neither be satisfactory nor just.

It is not true that the Chief Baron, as is alleged, expressed himself as not offering any opposition to the clemency of the Crown, although the learned judge was treated to some superfluous obloquy upon the statement that was put forth. Neither is it true that Sir George Lewis at any time gave occasion to the suspicion that he was indisposed to interfere with the sentence of the law. He came to no decision whatever until he had duly and gravely investigated the whole case. It was a most difficult one to decide. But we believe that the thinking part of the public will be unanimous in favour of the decision which has been deliberately adopted by the advisers of the Crown.[20]

Having spent the weekend preparing a memorandum on the case for the Queen and an accompanying letter, Lewis returned to Harpton. Smethurst received a royal pardon, but in a second trial, this time for bigamy, he was sentenced to a year's imprisonment. He was released from the Wandsworth House of Correction in November 1860 'considerably reduced in bulk'.[21]

Despite his preoccupation with the Smethurst case, Lewis found time to attend cabinet meetings and to catch up with gossip:

Dined at Sydney Herbert's with some of the Cabinet. Granville and C[harles] Wood told me what had taken place at Osborne. Matters were near a rupture between the Q & Ld P & Ld JR.[22]

Perhaps it was as a relaxation that Lewis now wrote a piece on 'The Lion in Italy' for *Notes & Queries*, which appeared in September 1859.[23] He starts by noting how in *Julius Caesar* Shakspeare causes Casca to relate to Cicero that:

Against the Capitol I met a lion
Who glared upon me and went surly by,
Without annoying me.

He then points out that later Cassius also alludes to the prodigy of a lion in the Capitol, whereas Calphurnia saw a whelping lioness. However, the prodigies of the lion in the Capitol, and of the lioness whelping in the streets of Rome, do not occur in any ancient writer and were introduced by Shakspeare himself. Their introduction proves him to have overlooked the fact that the lion was never a native of Italy. Lewis then goes on to discuss the occurrence of the lion in northern Greece and of the leopard and tiger in Asia Minor.

Then with undeniable pleasure Lewis concludes his piece by pointing out that Dr Clarke,[24] whose *Travels in Greece, Egypt, and the Holy Land* were published in 1817, forty-two years ago, so the point had little topical interest in 1859, was mistaken in believing he had seen the footprints of a tiger in the snow on Mt Gargarus in the Troad. Dr Clarke's guides were apparently mistaken:

> The tiger is not a native of any country west of the Indus, and the footsteps seen by Dr Clarke were certainly not those of a tiger.

But why did a busy man like Lewis think it worth while to take the time to put Dr Clarke right thirty-seven years after the latter's death? Scholars are concerned with seeking out the truth, but in Lewis's case the search was often seasoned with a *soupçon* of malice. Dr Edward Clarke, the traveller and antiquary, ended his days as the Librarian of the University of Cambridge, and did what he did long before the advent of steamships, railways, and the electric telegraph. The wonder of Clarke is not what he did, but that he was able to do it at all. It was the same with John Narrien, a stone mason's son, who became FRS in 1840, a distinction Lewis never achieved, and Professor of Mathematics at Sandhurst. His *Historical Account of the Origin and Progress of Astronomy*, was published in 1833, and in 1894 was still described as a 'a work of considerable merit and research'.[25] In 1850 readers of *Notes & Queries* were advised:

> If an English reader wants to know Ptolemy's astronomical methods and hypotheses, nothing will suit him better than Narrien's *History of Astronomy*.[26]

Narrien's 'useful and honourable career' at Sandhurst, 'terminated with his resignation, on the failure of his eyesight, in 1858',[27] but in 1861, a year after Narrien's death, Lewis thought it appropriate to give his readers a catalogue of the mistranslations in Narrien's *History of Astronomy*,[28] telling them that:

> Mr Narrien's acquaintance with the Greek language must have been of the most limited description, though his book is principally a history of the Greek astronomy.

At the end of September 1859 Lewis went to Balmoral. It was a laborious journey, but he had the companionship of Lord John Russell for part of the way:

> Left London by the morning train of the N Western & travelled to Carlisle & Stirling to Perth, in company with Ld J Russell, who got out at Stirling. Slept at the George Inn Perth where I arrived at about 1 o'clock.[29]

Then on by road from Perth to Balmoral by way of Blairgowrie, Spittle of Glenshee, and Braemar, arriving for dinner. It was a rainy day and Lewis complained he 'saw little of the country'. He was at

Balmoral for a week but says nothing in his diary about the castle, which had only been completed three years before and its tartan décor was still strikingly fresh.

The Queen bought the Balmoral estate in 1848 but the house was too small and between 1853 and 1856 Prince Albert, who had already tried his hand at domestic architecture at Osborne on the Isle of Wight, now turned his attention to Balmoral under the watchful eye of the Aberdeen architect William Smith. The whole was built in local granite in Scottish baronial style and dominated by a massive, almost detached turret-crowned tower. The Queen spent part of every spring and autumn there and the informality to the Balmoral routine surprized some of its visitors. Lewis found his fellow guests were the Prince of Wales, Sir George Grey[30] and Lord Charles Fitzroy, with Lady Churchill as a lady in waiting, and Miss Cathcart as maid of honour,[31] but had little to say about them.

Much of Lewis's time at Balmoral, the weather having improved, was spent riding in the woods with Lady Churchill, Miss Cathcart, and Sir George Grey. There was, too, a drive to 'Mar Lodge, deer shooting lodge of Ld Fife',[32] walking over to Abergeldie where Lord and Lady John Russell were staying, and an evening ball.[33] More substantial fare came on Sunday when Lewis went to Crathie parish church. Built in 1804 and overlooking the old kirkyard which contained the remains of the original 14th-century church, this was a far more austere building than its successor of 1895:

> At the kirk. Dr Lee[34] performed the service. He preached a powerful sermon, after service he called on me, and gave me a long explanation about the patronage of the Scotch kirk, which is exercised by the Home Secretary. The prince came to my room & I had a long conversation with him.[35]

There was consolation, too, in the fact that whilst he was at Balmoral *Notes & Queries* published his piece on 'The Ancient Names of the Cat', a subject he had already touched upon in defending his *Enquiry into the Credibility of the Early Roman History* against its critics. He argued that the ancients did not distinguish accurately between the cat and the weasel, and sometimes used their names indiscriminately. As in Greek, so in Latin the names for cat, *feles*, and weasel, *mustela*, are used without distinction. The word *catus* denotes an animal kept for the destruction of moles, so was probably of the weasel tribe and not a cat. *Catulus* appears to be a diminutive form of *canis*. The word *feles* is lost in the Romance languages which use the derivative of *catus*. It is the same with modern Celtic and Teutonic languages.[36]

It was back to the saddle, however, never Lewis's favourite pasttime, on Monday, riding with Sir Charles Phipps[37] to Invercauld, Mr Farquarson's[38] for a 'picnic in the woods to a large party'. There was more more riding with Sir Charles on Tuesday, for which perhaps Lewis thought he received his due reward when later that day the Queen gave him a set of lithographs of the royal family. Next day he left Balmoral for Aberdeen and the two-day journey back to Harpton[39] where Home Office business awaited him and a meeting of the Beddoes Charity trustees at Presteign. This was lightened by a visit from his old friend Edward Twistleton, generating 'much conversation on speculative subjects' and the will on Lewis's part to play the truant and miss three cabinet meetings.

Lewis did, however, send Palmerston a brief account from Harpton of his visit to Balmoral:

> Nothing material passed during the week that I staid at Balmoral. The Queen is wonderfully devoted to an outdoor life, & to excursions to hills & lochs & moors. She cares little for weather, & stays out from 11 or 12 o'clock till dinner time. Her strength and endurance are quite marvellous. The seclusion of Balmoral, & the consequent liberty which she enjoys, are highly agreeable to her. The Prince takes great pleasure in deer shooting, & seems almost engrossed with it. He shoots no grouse.[40]

He was in London before the end of the month for a cabinet meeting, a meeting of the Privy Council at Windsor, for which in the absence of Granville he acted as president, and an audience with the Queen. He remained in London for the marriage of his stepdaughter:

> Saturday 5th November 1859. The marriage of Thérèse to William Harcourt took place at All Saints Church, Knightsbridge. I gave away the bride. The ceremony was performed by bride's uncle.[41]

Whatever the splendour of the occasion it was modest in comparison with the Lord Mayor's banquet which Lewis attended a few days later, though his account was no less economical than that of his stepdaughter's wedding:

> At the Lord Mayor's dinner. I answered to the toast of HM ministers, in the absence of Ld Palmerston at Windsor.[42]

According to *The Times* Lewis was one of a thousand guests and 'the hall was fitted up for the occasion with all the splendour that marks this time-honoured festival'. But he 'was very indistinctly heard from the incessant hubbub going on in the hall' and the paper could only report what Lewis 'was understood to speak'. Having explained that he was replying to this particular toast because in the absence of the Prime Minister and Foreign Secretary the task had devolved upon him 'in accordance with the rules of official precedence' he spoke at some length before protesting that:

> It will not be expected that I should detain a company composed of many persons who are not politicians with length-ened remarks upon the measures which Her Majesty's Government may contemplate in the existing state of the country. I need only say that their time has not been wasted or their attention diverted from the discharge of their public duties; that early in the ensuing session they will be prepared to redeem the pledge they formerly entered into to submit to the consideration of the Legislature a measure for the amendment of the representation of the people. [Cheers].[43]

There then followed a thorough review of foreign policy which concluded in terms worthy of Palmerston himself:

> Whenever public danger does arise Her Majesty's Government will feel it their duty to take every necessary step for the protec-tion of our shores; and in doing so they feel confident that they can at all times rely on the spirit of a great, a generous, and a mighty people. [Cheers].[44]

Electoral Reform was indeed engaging Cabinet attention and Lewis interspersed meetings of the Cabinet Committee dealing with the issue with episodes of writing papers on 'Killing no Murder', on the *bonasus*,[45] the Greek name which he preferred for the bison, for *Notes & Queries*, written in a day, and a visit to Windsor Castle. He was joined at Windsor by the Duke and Duchess of Manchester.[46] William Drogo Montagu, the 7th Duke of Manchester was married to the Countess Louise Frederice Auguste von Alten of Hanover, and no doubt her presence at Windsor was welcome to Prince Albert. Other guests were the Duke of Newcastle, Secretary of State for the Colonies, and Lord Derby, Prime Minister in the previous administration, and his wife. On the first night Lewis had to endure after dinner theatricals. He went back to London next morning for a cabinet meeting and a session at the Home Office before returning to Windsor for dinner and

> conversation with Prince & Princess Fred Will of Prussia & with the Queen & Prince.[47]

What really interested him, however, at this time were two new projects which he had in mind. On the first Sunday in November he wrote in his diary:

> I have lately been studying works on astronomy, both ancient & modern, with a view of writing on the early Roman calendar.[48]

The book occupied him until the summer of 1861 when it materialised as *An Historical Survey of the Astronomy of the Ancients*.

The second project was to edit a *Dictionary of the Physical Sciences in Antiquity* with the lexicographer William Smith.[49] At the invitation of his old friend George Grote he went down to Surrey for a weekend to Barrow Green near Oxted where Grote now lived. He met there Smith and Robert Lowe who 'vied with Gladstone in aptness of classical quotation'.[50] The scheme came to nothing and he returned to London with a heavy cold.

The year ended with the loss of two friends and this led Lewis to some rare expressions of emotion:

> I heard to day of the death of John Austin, which took place on Saturday last at Weybridge. Of all the men whom I have known in the course of my life, he is the one who turned great abilities to the least account, either for his own benefit or for that of the public. He might have written a great work on the philosophy of law, which he had profoundly meditated & which he understood better than any person with whom I ever conversed.[51]

Then, having spent Christmas at Grove Mill, he returned to London on 27th December to work at the Home Office. A couple of days later he left the Office to dine with William Smith who told him that Macaulay had died quietly the previous day, sitting in his library in an easy chair. Lewis was moved to write to Sir Henry Holland, physician in ordinary to the Queen and a kinsman by marriage of Macaulay, to suggest that the burial of poor Macaulay shd take place in Westminster abbey.[52]

Lewis's wish was fulfilled and Macaulay was buried in Westminster Abbey on 9th January 1860 in the Poet's Corner, at the foot of Addison's statue. Lewis was a pall-bearer.

1860 started at Kent House with a review of the previous year:

> During the past year I have written some articles in *Ed Rev*, several long contributions to *Notes & Queries*, a pamphlet on Foreign Jurisdiction, & I have published an edition of the Second Part of the *Fables of Babrius*. The Home Office, which I have had since June, occupies much time with its correspondence, or with the details of the criminal cases. The attendances on the Cabinet, for foreign affairs, & the preparation of the Reform Bill, have been frequent, & there was little interruption even during the summer & autumn.[53]

It was foreign affairs and the preparation of the Reform Bill which took Lewis to Windsor Castle for a few days. The French ambassador, the Duc de Persigny and the Foreign Secretary, Lord John Russell, were fellow guests. A play on the first evening and an exposition next day by Prince Albert of 'the very curious' royal collection of miniatures preceded the real business of the occasion:

> After dinner I had some conversation with the Prince about the Reform Bill and explained our views.[54]

Illness kept Lewis for half of February from both the House and his desk. When he spoke in the House 'he prosed and seemed half asleep'.[55] In his diary he described his complaint as 'neuralgia in the head' and though he made occasional visits to both office and House he always found the exertion greater than he could bear.[56] Later he wrote to Sir Edmund Head, putting it all down to bad drains at the Home Office:

> I am afraid that I have allowed long time to elapse without writing to you, and without thanking you for your last letter. The interval has been lengthened by a troublesome attack of neuralgia in the head, from which I have suffered much since the beginning of February and from which I am only just now recovered. My doctor thought it was produced by malaria, owing to the neglected state of the drainage at the Home

Office. It was accompanied with great depression, and for a time I could do very little work.[57]

Malaria at this time was believed to be caused by 'bad air'. Then followed 'an obstinate attack of influenza'[58] lasting ten days, but he was recovered for Russell's introduction of the Reform Bill on March 1st:

> The Reform Bill has, on the whole, been well received. The measure was carefully prepared, and it is studiously moderate with respect to disfranchisement and the distribution of the liberated seats. It makes a large addition to the existing constituency both in counties and boroughs. It is not expected that the Conservatives will make any fight on the second reading.[59]

Recovery of health also allowed Lewis to resume working on an article for the *Edinburgh Review* on George Rose, the Whig politician and friend of Pitt,[60] and to attend the marriage of Amy Villiers, the eldest daughter of the Bishop of Carlisle, and a niece of Lady Lewis. Henry Montagu Villiers was soon to be translated from Carlisle to Durham where his twelve-month episcopate gave him time enough to present his new son-in-law, the Revd Edward Cheese, MA, in Orders but three years, to the living of Haughton le Skerne, with a stipend of £1,300 pa, of which his lordship was the patron, and to appoint him as his chaplain. A devout churchman, such appointments did not disturb Lewis's devotion.[61] The parishioners and the press thought otherwise.

The churchwardens of three adjoining Darlington parishes petitioned the Bishop of Durham. The population of the parish of Haughton le Skerne was 1,000, whereas that of the three adjacent parishes was 15,000, and likely to increase considerably due to the railway works being established at Darlington. The emoluments of these three parishes were £225, £200, and £175 pa, and the churchwardens thought that the pastoral needs of the area justified the creation of a new parish from part of the territory of their parishes and part of that of Haughton le Skerne. This would, of course, also involve a redistribution of endowments. Villiers received the petition at Auckland Castle graciously, but went on to say:

> I am sorry to say, I cannot comply with the wishes of the requisionists. I have already given the living of Haughton le Skerne to a gentleman whose talent, piety, and pastoral activity will soon convince the parishioners that their interests have been attended to.[62]

One reason the bishop rejected the petition was that its implementation would involve the diminution of the patronage of the Duke of Cleveland in whose gift lay Darlington parish church. Other correspondence revealed that two local landowners had offered land for a church and school, were the scheme to have been carried through, and an anonymous Cambridge clergyman asserted that from his personal knowledge Villiers's episcopal predecessor had resisted the redistribution of the endowments of Haughton le Skerne, when the new dioceses of Manchester and Ripon were being formed to serve the pastoral needs of industrial north, on the grounds that:

> If deprived of them, the Bishop of Durham would have no means of adequately providing for and remunerating such clergymen as had distinguished themselves by long and useful service in the large northern towns.[63]

Clericus Cantabrigiensis maintained that this was well known in the Durham diocese and that it could not be assumed that Villiers alone was unaware of this arrangement:

> Under these circumstances the appointment of Mr Cheese is a breach of episcopal trust as serious and deplorable as it is possible to conceive.[64]

Ecclesiastical affairs were within the sphere of interest of the Home Secretary and Lewis's handling of the riots at St George's in the East are described elsewhere in this book. Was he silent about Haughton le Skerne out of embarrassment arising from family connections with the episode or was he indifferent to this aspect of the Church's ministry? Lewis's fellow Liberal, Sir John Trelawny, the tireless advocate of the reform of Church rates, saw the implication of the Haughton le Skerrne episode quite clearly:

> The Nepotism of the model evangelical Bishop of Durham in giving Houghton le Skrene (some £1,360 a year) to Mr Cheese, his son-in-law, in spite of the wishes of the inhabitants in the vicinity to make better provision for an increasing population, has come most appropriately. If the Church fall, it will not be from adversaries without but from folly within.[65]

But to return to 1860, when Lewis was engaged in a study of Old Testament chronology. Darwin's controversial *Origin of Species* was published in 1859, followed by the equally controversial *Essays and Reviews*, the work of a collection Anglican academics, in 1860. Lewis makes no mention of either book, though *Essays and Reviews* were discussed in the House, Convocation, and the press. Their publication, however, and the simultaneous emergence of Lewis's interest in the Old Testament seems unlikely to have been coincidental. Two of the contributors to *Essays and Reviews,* Mark Pattison and Benjamin Jowett, were personally known to Lewis[66] who was familiar with the new German scholarship. He wrote at length about Biblical chronology to his friend Edward Twistleton and offered to lend him books on the subject.[67] But in the House Lewis discoursed on a lighter subject, namely, Lord Haddo's motion to refuse money to art schools in which undraped females were used as models. As Trelawny put it in his Diary:

> The House was not quite as decorous as it might have been. Palmerston made fun. What were to be the limits of permissible nudity? Crinolines too, & the present 'voluminous' fashions came under his notice. Even Cornewall Lewis contrived to raise mirth, when he began by saying with great solemnity that he spoke without 'practical' acquaintance in these matters.[68]

In June Palmerston withdrew the 'carefully prepared and studiously moderate' Reform Bill to the preparation of which Lewis had contributed considerably. He had little enthusiasm for reform and the bill seemed likely to fail. The usually sober minded Lewis, for some unknown reason, was in festive mood:

> The House was rather a full one. Palmerston looked rather glum & nervous. He seemed to mutter & frequently moved his limbs. Gladstone was busy on papers - Charles Wood & Cornewall Lewis were interchanging chuckles, in evident delight.[69]

But this was all rather out of character. He was back in his more usual form when it came to the Committee stage of the Census Bill. Its 1851 predecessor, prepared when Lewis was an Under Secretary at the Home Office, had included questions on religious attendance. Lewis was now Home Secretary and proposed the insertion of similar questions on the religious profession of all the members of a household, with the difference that this time answers were obligatory. This was successfully resisted:

> There was rather a smart debate. Sir Cornewall Lewis made a learned-foolish speech, in which he contrived to offend dissenters very bitterly & not altogether please Churchmen. Lewis is a sort of gauche doctrinaire - he is full of knowledge,

but cannot steer clear of damaging words & topics. His illustrations either provoke a smile or make the persons angry whom he desires to conciliate. It was evidently his game to get his government out of a false position - gracefully &, with kindly & considerate words. He, on the contrary, laboured to prove the course right which Ministers had adopted at first - &, in doing so, he lost the good effect of timely concession by offensive insinuations & comparisons.[70]

Ten days later Lewis was to tell his friend Edmund Head that:

This had been the most fatiguing session I remember since I have been in Parliament; but the work has been done by no means proportioned to the fatigue. I heard the other day a story of some county magistrates who insisted that the convicts on the treadmill in the county prison should be made to believe that they were grinding air, when they were, in fact grinding corn. There is no necessity to practise any such delusion upon us: we are quite aware that we have been grinding air.[71]

Lewis's interest in astronomy, first shown in November 1859, now grew in momentum. As part of his preliminary reading he read the French astronomer Jean Baptiste Joseph Delambre's *Histoire de astronomie ancienne*, published in 1817, and over Christmas, spent that year at the Grove, got to grips with Boeckh's *Manetho*[72] in German, and the first volume of the translation of Bunsen's *Egypt*.[73] Astronomy, like geology, was a study deemed worthy of the attention of 19th-century gentlemen and on St David's day 1860 Lewis visited the astronomer Sir James South at his Kensington home,[74] and from his private observatory saw Venus, Jupiter, and Saturn, noting that the belt of Jupiter was 'extremely faint', and that the ring of Saturn was 'a most remarkable and striking object'. Then on a Sunday in May after church he went to Greenwich and 'visited Mr Airy, the Astronomer Royal, at the Observatory'.[75] By the end of the month he was able to write in his diary:

I began to write a *Historical Survey of the Astronomy of the Ancients*, for which I have been lately collecting materials. I began reading for it at the end of last year, my attention having been directed to the subject by the statements respecting the decimestrial year.[76]

The decimestrial year was divided into ten rather than twelve months and was used by the early Romans. Lewis now entered into an outburst of daily activity. His interest was now so totally focussed on astronomy that he wrote in his diary on 23rd of June when there was a

> General holiday on account of the review of the volunteers. I wrote on astronomy, & went in the afternoon for a short time to the office.[77]

Thus wrote a future Secretary of State for War. The review took place in Hyde Park, which was opposite Kent House, and *The Times* wrote of it, with the Italian struggle for unification and the aspirations of Prussia in mind, to say nothing of uneasiness over the ambitions of Emperor Napoleon III, that:

> Saturday the 23rd of June, of this stormy and threatening 1860, will henceforth be a memorable and remembered date in the military annals of the nation. The reddest of red letters cannot give it more than due prominence in the calendar of national events; it is the day that saw the culminating point of the revival of the military spirit of the British people.[78]

And so Lewis continued to write even when his diary was full of other engagements:

> Saturday 30th June 1860. Wrote astronomy in the morning, then at a Council at Buckingham Palace. Afterwards at a Cabinet at Ld John Russell's house.

In October he was in Oxford for an academic meeting, for which he stayed with his wife's kinsman, Dr Cradock, the Principal of Brasenose College. In the evening he dined with Dr Liddell, Dean of Christ Church; Dr Jeune, the Vice-Chancellor; Dr Scott, the Master of Balliol, and Benjamin Jowett, Regius Professor of Greek. But before meeting such an august company of Oxford academics, there was something else to be done:

> Before dinner I walked with Dr Cradock, & called at the Observatory, but the observer was out.[79]

So he went instead to inspect the University's new natural science museum, which, though it enjoyed Ruskin's whole hearted approval, he found it to be no more than 'a well constructed building'.

Six months later he was able at last to write:

> I have finished 7 chapters of my work on Ancient astronomy. All that remains to be done is, the revision, & the completion of a few unfinished parts, & a final chapter on the navigation of the Phoenicians.[80]

By the beginning of August the manuscript was in the hands of his London printer who shared his sense of urgency so that the proofs arrived at Harpton on a Sunday:

> Sunday 18th August 1861. Harpton. At New Radnor church. I have received the first sheet of my volume on the history of astronomy, the ms of which I sent to the press before I left London.

Life at Harpton during the parliamentary recess left Lewis no time for country pursuits and, as usual, house-guests saw little of him:

> Monday 19th August to Sunday 8th September 1861. At Harpton. Office papers each day. Corrected proofs of my astronomy. Completed the passage on hieroglyphics.

> Friday 13th September to Friday 4th October 1861. At Harpton. Office papers every day, also corrected some sheets of my astronomy. Read the *Purgatorio* of Dante. Wrote a paper on the Roman book trade.

> Saturday 5th October to Monday 14th October 1861. At Harpton. Continued my article on Colonial Expenditure. Corrected the proofs of my work on astronomy.

The book was published in January 1862 and within six weeks arrangements were in hand for its translation into German, but Lewis makes no mention as to the manner of its reception. He does mention, however, a visit he made in February to the British Museum, on his way home from Euston station, to consult William Vaux on the interpretation of cuneiform inscriptions.[81] Perhaps he felt some of his conclusions needed reinforcement. The critic of *Blackwood's Edinburgh Magazine*, however, thought Lewis and Gladstone were birds of a feather:

> Chancellors of the Exchequer burrow in these fields of ancient lore, as diligently as if they expected to find something there to stop a deficit. Mr Gladstone must have bestowed at least as much pains upon Homer as upon his budget; and Sir Cornewall Lewis will perhaps live as a scholar when forgotten as a politician. The facts of Roman history, the fables of Babrius, the astronomy of the Egyptians, are in his eyes as important as the bills of the current session.[82]

In May, after a day spent between the office and the House, Lewis went in the evening to a meeting of the Society of Antiquaries at which his astronomy was discussed. Lewis had cast doubt on the traditional view that ancient Egyptian could be partially interpreted from Coptic which was held to be in some measure its continuation. Reginald Stuart Poole, of the Department of Antiquities of the British Museum opened the debate, Lewis replied and the distinguished Egyptologist Charles Wycliffe Goodwin answered him:

> Mr Poole of the British Museum made a speech, in support of the received method of interpreting Egyptian hieroglyphics, and in answer to the arguments in my vol. on ancient astronomy, I answered him, & Mr Goodwin answered me.[83]

Bruised but undefeated, Lewis resolved to put his 'speech on hieroglyphics in writing, & to communicate it to the Society for insertion in their printed Transactions'.[84] At Harpton he also used the forthcoming German translation of the *Astronomy* as an opportunity for a few running repairs and wrote what he called 'an ironical essay on the application of the Egyptological method to modern history'.[85] It was published anonymously in November 1862.[86]

By now Lewis's reputation as a historian of astronomy was well established: he was dining at the Freemason's tavern with the Club of the Astronomical Society, and having his health proposed by the Astronomer Royal.[87] Not unmindful of his debt to Airy, Lewis attempted to acknowledge and repay it, and informed Palmerston:

> It has occurred to me that there is an honour which wd be worthily bestowed, and which wd be well received by the scientific world, I mean that of knighthood for the Astronomer Royal, Mr Airy. He has now filled that post for many years. His mathematical qualifications are of the highest order, his merits as an observer have been recognized by all Europe, & he has distinguished himself by his readiness to assist the numerous persons who apply to him for information and advice.
>
> I would propose that he shd simply be knighted, a ceremony which the Queen, I presume, wd, now perform in some indirect manner. Sir Wm Herschel, who had the great telescope at Slough, was knighted by George the Third, indeed, I believe, he was made a baronet. If you should approve of this proposal, I should be quite ready to apply to the Queen for her consent.[88]

Lewis's proposal was unsuccessful and Airy had to wait until 1872 for his knighthood. Lewis's usually prodigious biographical knowledge let him down on this occasion: Sir William Herschel, FRS, Court

Astronomer to George III, was knighted by that king in 1816 and it was Herschel's son, John Frederick William Herschel, who was made a baronet in 1838.

Not all of Lewis's conclusions, as might be expected, can stand the passage of time. For example, in its review of the book, *Blackwood's Edinburgh Magazine* noted that:

> Sir Cornewall Lewis, who, after a really critical and scholarlike examination, declares there is no evidence for any building in Egypt - no, not the Pyramids - anterior to Solomon's temple, BC 1012.[89]

More recent scholarship, whilst more or less agreeing with his dating for Solomon's Temple by placing his reign over Israel *c*.962–922 BC, date the pyramids to the period 2700–2500 BC.[90]

The Parliamentary Session of 1860 was prorogued on 28th August. Trelawny thought 'it has been a Parliament of Magpies thus far' and that it would be 'a difficult task to prove the Session not abortive'.[91] Lewis's aunt, however, Lady Duff Gordon, was happy to read in her newspaper praise at least for her nephew:

> The Newspaper gave us the death of the Session of Parliament … It does not spare Mr Gladstone & his financial arrangements, praises George Lewis & wishes he was Chancellor of the Exchequer, saying that after Mr Gladstone he 'would relieve the dazzled House, like a quiet Green after a blaze of Scarlet![92]

Official papers now made their way daily to Harpton and managed not to become confused with those on astronomy. Lewis found time to ride over to Presteign for a meeting of the trustees of the John Beddoes Charity, only to discover once again 'there was not sufficient attendance to make a quorum', so he inspected the new school building instead, now complete.[93] A week or so later his sense of commitment to local matters caused him leave his astronomy, official papers, and the revision he had in hand of a French translation of pamphlet on Foreign Jurisdiction, to dine at the Bailiff's Feast at New Radnor. The Bailiff for the year was the Revd William Prosser Williams, Vicar of Llanfihangel Nant Mellan since 1831, and who was to remain so for forthy-three years, until his death in 1874.[94] There being no parsonage at Llanfihangel, Williams lived at New Radnor, where the Lewises looked upon him with a certain amount of theological suspicion, scenting a slight whiff of Tractarianism about him. This showed itself when he offered an 'image of a lamb' for the new church at New Radnor. The offer was refused for fear that it might lead to a figure of the Virgin Mary being installed, to whom the church had been dedicated since its foundation in the twelfth century.[95]

For much of October Lewis had Harpton to himself, Lady Lewis being called away for Thérèse's confinement, 'which passed away happily'. At the end of the month he returned to London for a meeting of the trustees of the British Museum, the Lord Mayor's banquet, and a round of cabinets, all, as has already been seen, against a background of astronomy. Even when summoned to Windsor Castle, he managed to get in a morning's astronomy beforehand.[96]

New Year's Day 1861 at Kent House saw Lewis writing on astronomy before going to the Home Office where he reviewed his physical condition:

> My health & bodily strength have not undergone any material change in this year, I was for a time much weakened by the illness which I had in March.[97]

Nevertheless, coughs kept him in the house and when it came to his birthday on 21st April, giving rise to another medical self-review, he had to admit that though his health had not been materially impaired in the last year, there had been 'several indications of weakness in the bronchial tubes'. As if to prove the point, next day he was 'at home all day, unwell'.[98]

Perhaps it was a combination of his preoccupation with astronomy and declining health which made some people think that, at least as a parliamentarian, he was not what he was. It seemed that parliamentary office was teaching him a new, less precise, morality. Thus, in February 1861 Lewis, as Home Secretary, was asked about an instance at Rochdale in which a judge of the county court had disqualified a witness on account of her lack of religious belief in life after death.[99] In his reply Lewis gave the impression that he found Mrs Maden, the lady concerned, 'a litigious and ill conditioned woman wrangling with her own mother about a piano', whilst implying that Trelawny, his questioner, had his facts wrong. Publicly, out of courtesy to the Home Secretary, Trelawny accepted Lewis's version, but privately he saw things very differently:

> I always thought him gauche & heavy - but, at least, an honest doctrinaire. But he appears to have been an apt scholar of the ways of office, one of which is to get rid of difficulties by the *suppressio veri* or its distortion (as most convenient).[100]

The case went to appeal and the opinion of the county court judge was unanimously upheld.[101]

In March 1861 when a motion for the introduction of the £10 county franchise was being debated, Trelawny, a back-bencher and self-described 'Liberal radical' noted for his consistently courteous parliamentary manners, wrote in his diary:

> The conduct of Ministers, who came into office by carrying a resolution that a minor proposal or two in Disraeli's Reform Bill was open to objection & then remain content to shelve the subject, would seriously injure men either not wealthy or not connected with the aristocracy. C[ornewall] Lewis signally disgraced himself - in a jesuitical, tortuous, inconclusive speech. He spoke agt. Locke King's measure[102] - & then astounded the House by 'However he meant to vote for it!' Well might Osborne[103] denounce the general insincerity of Parliament.[104]

Lewis's own account of things was very bland and gives the impression he played no part in them:

> Wednesday, March 13th 1861. At the House. Locke King's motion on the County franchise negatived on division. Then at a Cabinet & at the office.

Later that day Trelawny's own bill was discussed. It provided for an affirmation as an alternative to the swearing of an oath to tell the truth in legal proceedings. Again, Trelawny found himself doubting Lewis's political integrity:

> ... Hardy[105], Malins, & C[ornewall] Lewis opposed me. Malins is a lawyer of ingrained prejudices. Narrow by nature, his profession has made him narrower still.[106] Hardy is clever & wordy. Too clever one would think for the speech he made. But Lewis earned the palm for superior merit in the practice of the art of sinking. He well knows the law & the facts - he is profoundly read in philosophy & jurisprudence - & I have no shadow of doubt agrees entirely with me - yet, he opposed me - & that in a speech of the jesuitical kind of his later manner. Well, the future must decide between us. I would rather be thought to sin with Hobbes & Bentham than be right in the estimation of Hardy & Malins even with Lewis for their backer.[107]

For Lewis the real business of the day was the fact that he dined at the Palace and that the Queen wanted the assistance of her Home Secretary:

> The Queen asked me to ascertain if she could confer the title of Royal upon Prince Louis of Hesse who is about to marry the Princess Alice, and is only 'Grand Ducal Highness'.

A few days later Trelawny came to write on occasion of Lewis's 'injurious support', and when it came to the former's motion on County Rates, he claimed that:

> Lewis made a speech which was opposed in spirit to all but the very naked principle of my measure & yet expressed his intention to vote for the 2d. reading. As Osborne said it was in effect the same speech he made on Locke King's Bill, substituting 'nevertheless' for 'however'. This alluded to certain tricks of Lewis in using particular words repeatedly in the same speech. For instance, he says 'Well' at the beginning of each new argument.[108]

All in all, Trelawny thought Lewis had not come up to expectation, and this was illustrated in the unsuccessful third reading of Trelawny's bill for the abolition of Church rates:

> As usual of late, Cornewall Lewis made one of his undecided speeches stating that he shd. vote with me & yet throwing discouragement on my bill. Lewis is not rising in the estimation of the House - he is gauche; &, if honest, contrives to appear dishonest. This sounds harsh but, really, it is difficult to speak well of these temporising courses. Perhaps, weakness of character & timidity may be the more charitable explanation of some of his proceedings.[109]

The truth of the matter was that Lewis was becoming weary and frustrated with grinding Parliamentary air and he was not averse to the possibility of working in a different aether. He worked at the Parliamentary mill as much out of duty as of ambition, but there was a consideration which should, in his opinion, override these two factors. Lewis's health was declining, and though, when writing later to Mrs Austin on this topic, he thought his health had improved, he assured her that:

> if I thought that it was materially affected by my present mode of life, I should not hesitate in giving it up; it would cost me

nothing, as far as my own tastes and inclinations are concerned, but rather the reverse.[110]

He was not going to make the mistake of his friend Herbert:

> Poor Sidney Herbert died of the Bright disease. He was not sufficiently frightened about himself in time, and went on with his office when should have devoted himself exclusively to his health.[111]

Herbert's mistake, however, was to effect Lewis profoundly. In early July 1861 he wrote to his brother Gilbert:

> It seems that Sidney Herbert's state of health is such as to render it impossible for him to retain his office, and that another arrangement for filling it will certainly become necessary. Lord Palmerston's wish is, that I should change to the War Department. He thinks that it is necessary that there should be a commoner at the head of this office, and he is unable to prevail on any other person in the House of Commons to accept it. The proposal is in the highest degree distasteful to me, but I do not well see how I can refuse to acquiesce in the transfer. In the event of the change taking place, Sir George Grey would return to the Home Office. I know scarcely anything of the details of military administration, and I should have to learn my business from the first elements.[112]

This last observation was true, but Lewis was at least very knowledgeable about military history. In 1858 he discussed with his friend Henry Reeve the recently published account of the battle of Waterloo by Jean Baptiste Adolphe Charras, *Histoire de la campagne de 1815. Waterloo*, published in Brussells in 1857:[113]

> I think Charras hypercritical and unwilling to give Napoleon credit for what he accomplished. Charras evidently wishes to throw the blame of defeat from the French army on their generals and to deny the Superiority of the English troops, which he never admits. There is a passage from a letter of the Duke of Wellington to Lady Mornington, his mother, quoted in Scott's 'Visit to Paris in 1815'.[114] The Duke said that 'Bonaparte did his duty - that he fought the battle with infinite skill, perseverance, and bravery: and this' (he added) 'I do not state from any motive of claiming merit to myself; for the victory is to be ascribed to the superior physical force and constancy of British soldiers'. I cannot help thinking that this is the true explanation - that the two generals were evenly matched, and that the

English troops fought better than the French. Charras's theory is that the troops were equal, but that the English were better commanded than the French.[115]

A week later Lewis was writing again to Reeve about Napoleon. Once Lewis had taken hold of a subject he was always reluctant to let it go until he had explored it fully to his satisfaction:

Napoleon lost the battle of Waterloo; and it is possible that some other management might have succeeded better. He may have made some errors; but would Ney, or Soult, or any other of his generals have made so few? I have often heard my father quote a remark of the Duke of Wellington, that if he had had his Peninsular regiments at Waterloo, the battle would not have lasted till two o'clock. I think he said this to my father, or in his presence. I confess it seems to me, on the whole, that Napoleon fought the Waterloo campaign with extraordinary skill. It was a desperate game, and he was forced to play his last card. France was, in truth, sick of him, and the Allies were determined to bring him down. Delay would only have made his position worse. As to the Peninsular war, it certainly operated to a certain extent as a diversion and a drain - but the question is to what extent? The view which I have taken accords very much with that entertained by Lord Aberdeen, whose letters I will show you, together with those of my other correspondents, if you like to read them.[116]

Lewis's lack of enthusiasm for moving to the War Department was shared by the Queen who hoped 'that the arrangement would only be temporary', an idea Palmerston thought absurd.[117] Friends urged him not to make the move:

I am much advised by different friends to refuse the War department, for which they consider me unsuited, they doubt my success, & believe that the appointment will be ill received by the public.[118]

Sydney Smith confessed he could 'fancy no fish more out of water than Lewis amongst Armstrong guns and General Officers'.[119] But in the end Lewis, friends, and the Queen acquiesced and on the 25th July Lewis went by special train to Osborne for an audience with the Queen to surrender his seals of office as Home Secretary and to receive those of Secretary of State to the War Department. His first day at his new office revealed his cloud had a silver lining:

> At the War Office. Transacted the business, which seems less in amount than it is supposed to be.[120]

More time, then, for astronomy and other enthusiasms,[121] as he told Edmund Head:

> I have not written to you since my change of office, which, as you may suppose, was not of my seeking. The reports which were current as to the very laborious nature of its duties, turn out, as I partly suspected, to be quite fabulous. What it may be during war, I know not; probably its duties are then harassing and anxious, but during peace its duties appear to be less than those of the Home Office, so far as mere correspondence is concerned, and during the session, the parliamentary attendance is much lighter.[122]

Parliament was prorogued on the 6th August but before the Lewises could set out for Harpton they received the news of the serious illness of the Bishop of Durham, Theresa Lewis's brother, Henry Villiers. Theresa went to Auckland astle and Lewis remained at Kent House where three days later he heard by telegram of the bishop's death. He attended the funeral a week later, staying only overnight, and travelling by rail to Knighton, by way of Manchester, Crewe, and Shrewsbury where he took a train to Knighton by way of the newly opened Craven Arms line. The journey to Harpton was completed by fly.[123] He travelled alone, Theresa 'very much cast down' according to Lady Duff Gordon, remaining at Bishop's Auckland for the comfort of her sister-in-law.

The inconvenience of these frequent railway journeys commended to Lewis the advantages of the line being extended from Kington into Radnorshire, with a station at New Radnor, or even Harpton itself. This led him to find time to ride into Kington for a public meeting to discuss the matter.[124] However, despite its advantages for Lewis, the line was not completed until 1875, but Lewis's younger and more agile brother Gilbert was known to travel to Kington and back from Harpton on the footplate of the contractor's engine whilst the work was in progress.

At the time of the Kington meeting Harpton Court was unusually full of other potential passengers. Thus, when Lady Duff Gordon and her daughter Alice arrived, from the Archer Clives at Whitfield, on her annual tour of inspection on 'a very misty mild day ... in the train to Kington, and on to Harpton' she found:

George & Theresa & Alice Lister all well & Dr & Mrs Craddock
with them. Mr & Mrs Green Price & two clericals dined, the air
at Harpton felt much lighter and pleasanter than at Whitfield.
George very well & agreeable. Alas for my deafness, I feel it sadly
here where all are pleasant.[125]

Alice Lister was Theresa Lewis's niece, and Mrs Craddock, the
wife of the principal of Brasenose College, was Theresa's sister. One
wonders who the 'two clericals' were who dined at Harpton again next
day and contributed to the pleasure of the occasion. One afternoon
they all drove, Lewis included, to Water Break its Neck 'and there',
with the exception of Lady Duff Gordon, whose size made it something of an engineering feat to have got her in in the first place, 'all
got out of the carriages and walked about'. And that was not all, for
next day, Lewis dragged himself from his books and papers to walk
with his cousin Georgiana Duff Gordon and to lead her pony. Later in
the week George Venables, 'an agreeable and clever man' whose
conversation, in Lady Duff Gordon's opinion, though she could hear
nothing of it, 'suited George [Lewis]', with Mr King King of Staunton
on Arrow, joined the party.[126]

George Stovin Venables, MA, QC, was the brother of the Revd
Richard Lister Venables of Llysdinam, and built the new parish
church of Newbridge on Wye entirely at his own expense. At
Cambridge, he won the Chancellor's medal for English verse in 1831,
and was a member of that exclusive literary society, the 'Cambridge
Apostles'. Here he knew Tennyson, JF Stephen, FD Maurice, the
Lushingtons, and other men of some distinction. His own literary
output was considerable: contributing articles to the *Saturday Review*,
the *Foreign Quarterly Review*, and the *Spectator*. For a number of years he
composed the financial survey of the calendar year for *The Times*.

He was not, however, always to enjoy enthusiastic approval from
the Lewises. In 1881 he very unfavourably reviewed a novel, *Two Pretty
Girls*, by Mary Anna Lewis, Lewis's niece:

Ladies who write novels are for the most part, like other ladies,
familiar with only one kind of social experience. Some of them
blunder strangely in their representation of the manners and
customs of the classes which belong to so-called society. Miss
Lewis is evidently not less dependent on vague conjecture when
she describes a needy professional home in a country town, or
the gorgeous establishment of a rich London stock broker. If
she had the opportunity of consulting competent authorities

she would learn that the middle class, whether rich or poor, is not necessarily quarrelsome and rude at home, or offensively sycophantic in its intercourse with the outer world ... Exclusiveness is perhaps unavoidable in the present state of society; but there is no reason why the inmates of a privileged circle should cultivate animosity and contempt for their less fortunate neighbours. The mistrust, which has in different parts of the world identified savages and frontier tribes with demons, seems still to survive among separated classes. The vicious outcasts from aristocratic society in the *Two Pretty Girls* are scarcely more true to nature than the tyrannical earls and profligate baronets who are said to adorn the pages of plebeian fiction.

Both Mary Lewis and her sister Elinor were close friends of Agnes Minna Venables, Stovin's sister-in-law, and they were not pleased by the review. George Stovin Venables, however, was quite unmoved, and his review seems to have done little harm to sales, for a second edition was published in 1882 by the prestigious London publishers, Routlege & Sons. Happily, cordial relations were eventually restored between Harpton and Llysdinam.[127]

At the same time as George Stovin Venables was visiting Harpton and so suiting Lewis with his conversation, Lord and Lady Stanley of Alderley also came to stay. Edward John Stanley, second Baron Stanley of Alderley, was made Postmaster General by Palmerston in 1860. It was his wife, however, Henrietta Maria Stanley, who no doubt attracted most interest and attention. Accustomed to express herself with 'uncompromising frankness', she enjoyed the friendship of FD Maurice and Benjamin Jowett. An ardent Liberal, she promoted women's education, and was to be associated with the foundation of Girton College, Cambridge and the Girl's Public Day School Trust, as well as a having a concern for making medical education available to women.

Lady Duff Gordon tells how, when Stanley and Lewis had to go up to London for a Cabinet meeting, Henrietta Stanley and Theresa Lewis went again to Water Break its Neck. She did not accompany them so, unfortunately, her diary tells nothing about their conversation.[128] The visit of the Stanleys, perhaps coincidentally, saw old habits reassert themselves with Lewis and he began an article for the *Edinburgh Review*, appropriately for one in charge of the War Department, on 'Colonial Military expenditure'. The stream of 'clericals' noted by Lady Duff Gordon continued to her satisfaction with the Revd Henry Thomas Whateley, MA, coming to dine. He was the new vicar of Kington, having been offered the living by his uncle, the Bishop of Worcester. Lady Duff Gordon thought he was 'intelligent and agreeable' and noted that he had mountaineering in Switzerland amongst his portfolio of accomplishments.[129]

The Cabinet meeting only kept Lewis in London for a few days, and by the end of the week he back at Harpton, but its visitors had all gone, and ten days later there was snow on the surrounding hills, though the dahlias somehow survived. They were to succumb to a frost a few days later.[130] This drove him back to the warmth of Kent House.

A month later, kept at home himself with a cough, Lewis was to hear from Sir Charles Phipps of the Queen's household that the Prince Consort was ill with what was described as gastric fever. 'At present though the malady is grave, the symptoms are favorable'. But by the end of the week the prognosis was far more serious: 'this evening the Prince's malady took an unfavorable turn, and he was supposed to be sinking but he rallied during the night'. Next day the Duke of Cambridge called and informed Lewis that 'the Prince's state was nearly hopeless'. He died late that evening.[131]

Lewis shared the bulletins of the Prince's illness with Lady Duff Gordon, going round to her King Street home with the latest news:

> Saturday, 14th December 1861. Later George Lewis called here & his account, the last, at 6 o'clock was very hopeless 'unconscious & the extremities cold.' He has no hope. He talked of his great value, his excellent & high qualities. His good sense & his perfection in his Domestic Life as Husband & Father, a great & terrible loss he will be to the Queen & all England.

In his own diary Lewis recorded the Prince's deteriorating condition:

> It seems that the Prince became much worse on Friday night, & it was thought he was sinking. The remedies revived him, & he lived through another day, but he seems scarcely to have recovered his consciousness, for he did not recognize the Prince of Wales who came in the early morning of Saturday.[132]

Lewis tells how Lord Granville,[133] Lord President of the Council, when he went down to Windsor to the see the Queen, found she had 'borne the shock with wonderful fortitude' and 'wished everything to be brought to her, by which she meant, not to any other member of the Royal family'. Whilst preparations were made for the funeral at Windsor she moved to Osborne 'and bore the journey well'. The irrevocable loss of the Prince was brought home to Lewis when, within a week of Albert's death, he attended a meeting of the Council to remove all reference to the Prince's name from the liturgy of the Book of Common Prayer.[134] Lewis was quick to share his thoughts with his friend Henry Reeve:

> The Prince's death is a terrible calamity; and it will be so regarded by the public, though they do not know the extent of their loss. It will entirely alter the Queen's existence: he cannot be replaced. I am quite unable to estimate the probable consequences of this most disastrous event.[135]

The funeral was on Monday 23rd December 1861:

> I attended the funeral of the Prince Consort at Windsor. I went down in a special train in the morning, & we assembled in a large room near St George's chapel, called Wolsey's chapel. There we put on our scarves & hatbands, & afterwards went into St George's chapel, where we sat until the procession arrived. The Prince of Wales, Prince Arthur, & the Duke of Saxe Gotha were the chief mourners. The ceremony was solemn & impressive, after the funeral we had some luncheon in the castle, & returned to London.

Next day, Christmas Eve, Lewis was at War Office before going down to the Grove at Watford, where he 'began a *Dialogue on the Best Form of Govt*. The plan of it was composed more than 30 years ago, when I was in Italy'.[136]

Chapter 8:
Lewis the Churchman

Lewis was a son of the Church of England and his family had a strong clerical tradition which began in the early 18th century with the Revd Dr Hugh Lewis, second son of Lewis's great grandfather, Thomas Lewis. Educated at Christ Church, Oxford, Hugh Lewis took holy orders and became Chaplain to George II, when Prince of Wales, and continued in this situation after the prince's accession to the throne. He was appointed a Canon of Windsor and was buried in wool at Windsor in May 1742.

Another, less closely related, member of the family to hold a Windsor canonry, en route for higher things, was Ffolliot Herbert Walker Cornewall. His family was rooted in Shropshire and Herefordshire,[1] and, educated at St John's College, Cambridge, he became chaplain to the House of Commons in 1780, the year his brother Frederick entered the House as member for Ludlow. The canonry at Windsor came in 1784, and the deanery of Canterbury followed in 1793. He was consecrated Bishop of Bristol in 1797 and translated first to Hereford in 1803, and then to Worcester in 1808.

The branch of the Cornewalls from which Lewis was descended through his mother, lived in Herefordshire at Moccas Court. Lewis's cousin, George Henry Cornewall was a clerical baronet. After Rugby and Trinity College, Cambridge,[2] he took Orders, and having served a curacy in Cheshire, he was inducted to the family living of Moccas in 1868. Living in Moccas Court, he engaged the services of an asistant curate who lived in the rectory[3] whilst he himself was involved in the affairs of the county as a magistrate and Deputy Lieutenant.

Lewis also acquired clerical relatives by his own marriage. The most distinguished of these was his brother-in-law, Henry Montagu

Villiers, successively Bishop of Carlisle, 1856–60, and then Bishop of Durham, 1860–6.[4] He is remembered as

> A kindly man of simple piety. The worst that could be said that he presented his son-in-law to a wealthy living.[5]

A clergyman of the evangelical school, he made his reputation as vicar of Bloomsbury.

Another episcopal influence, though no relation of his, was Thomas Musgrave, Bishop of Hereford before being translated as Archbishop of York[6] in 1847. Like Villiers, he was an evangelical, and shared Lewis's liberal politics. At Hereford he was both efficient and generous, reviving the office of rural dean and donating, for example, to the new organ at Kington parish church.[7] He was diligent, too in visiting the remoter parts of his diocese, coming to New Radnor in 1845 to consecrate the new parish church, an event recorded in the *Illustrated London News*:

> The day will be long remembered by the inhabitants of New Radnor as a scene of high gratification. The ceremony was performed by the Lord Bishop of the diocese, assisted by the Very Revd the Dean, (the Rector), and Clergy. The service was interspersed with some devotional and impressive compositions of church music, by the members of the Hereford Cathedral choir and the organist; the Bishop kindly preached a sermon on the occasion, and there was a large collection made towards the cost of the building at the church doors. The hospitable mansions of Downton and Harpton were thrown open to visitors; and it was a day of great festivity throughout the borough of Radnor.[8]

After Musgrave's translation to York in 1847, Lewis was a frequent caller and dinner guest at the archbishop's town house.

Relations with Renn Dickson Hampden,[9] Musgrave's successor at Hereford, were less cordial. Lord John Russell, as Prime Minister, recommended Dr Hampden for nomination by the Queen, but some doubted Hampden's orthodoxy and thirteen of the bishops presented an address of remonstrance to the prime minister. On the other hand, fifteen Oxford heads of houses sent Hampden an address expressing their satisfaction with his religious belief, and their confidence in his integrity. At Hereford his liberal views were thought heretical and there was considerable local opposition to his appointment which was thought to have been unnecessarily provocative.

In December 1847 Lewis confided to his brother, Gilbert, that despite this opposition, Hampden would probably be installed as Bishop of Hereford, and the government, of which he was a supporter in the Commons, would thereby offend a large part of the Church. The choice of Hampden for the see of Hereford, in his opinion, was in itself a great political error, apart from all questions of theology.[10] In this sentiment he was echoing what *The Times* had said a few weeks earlier:

> There is no party whatever, at least none worth taking into account, to whom the new appointment to the See of Hereford can possibly be agreeable. It is not a question Between High Church and Low Church, or between the Church and the Dissenters. Lord John Russell may depend upon it that in appointing Dr Hampden he has committed a political blunder.[11]

The Hampdens seemed to have lived quietly in the palace with, according to the Census returns of 1851 and 1861, a small staff, which included, for the needs of Mrs Hampden, a Swiss lady's maid. It was perhaps, too, for Mrs Hampden that the palace drawing room was enlarged by amalgamating it with the adjoining library, 'a finely proportioned dome being made in the centre of the ceiling to correct its comparative want of height'. This formed 'a spacious appartment with half a dozen windows opening into the Palace gardens'.[12]

It is no surprise that the bishop was away confirming on one occasion when Lewis called, for he is remembered as a dutiful and conscientious bishop who administered his diocese 'as an exemplary prelate'[13] for twenty years to its great benefit. But Lewis thought otherwise and in March 1850 wrote to his brother Gilbert that the diocese was as if struck by paralysis since Hampden became its bishop.[14] He was, it seems, in Lewis's opinion, like his preaching, 'dull and ineffective'.[15]

Lewis may have once suspected the bishop of not writing his own lectures, but we find them eventually exchanging letters on academic matters and there was, for example, in 1862 an exchange between them of works on ancient philosophy and astronomy, shared interests.[16] The Bishop published that year his *Fathers of Greek Philosophy* and Lewis his *Historical Survey of the Astronomy of the Ancients,* and his *Suggestions for the Application of the Egyptological Method to Modern History; illustrated by examples.*

Hampden had given the 1833 Bampton Lectures on 'The Scholastic Philosophy considered in its relations to Christian Theology.' High Churchmen at Oxford considered them unorthodox because Hampden argued that the authority of scriptures was of greater weight than the authority of the Church. Consequently, when Lord Melbourne offered him the Regius Professorship of Divinity at Oxford there was some resistance to his appointment within the university and Hampden offered to withdraw his acceptance. Melbourne, however, refused to allow this, declaring that:

> For the sake of the principles of toleration and free inquiry we consider ourselves bound to persevere in your appointment.[17]

Lewis had not yet read the lectures six years later when his friend and correspondent, Edmund Head, drew his attention to them. The fact he had not yet read them did not prevent Lewis from feeling there was no smoke without fire or from suspecting that Hampden himself lacked the wit to see the implications of some of his statements:

> Your account of Hampden's book makes me curious to read it. I always suspected that it was more heterodox than Senior[18] and others were willing to admit: for the Oxford people do not in general make a great stir about nothing. It is very probable that Hampden did not himself see the consequences of his own arguments.[19]

Hampden's arrival at Hereford, surrounded as it was by controversy, moved Lewis to read the lectures and in November 1848 he wrote to Head not unfavourably of the experience:

> I have read lately Hampden's Bampton Lectures, which, in point of ability and knowledge of the subject, seems to me the first theological work which has been produced for a long time in this country. Parts of it are obscure in point of conception. His metaphysics and logic are not in fact very profound; but his account of the origin of some of the doctrines, particularly the Trinitarian and Eucharistic, are admirable. It is a book quite worth reading. But as to the question of orthodoxy, I confess I cannot defend him. He has been unskilfully and dishonestly attacked, and has been charged with opinions which are not in his book. He cannot be convicted of heresy on any one doctrine, it cannot be proved, for example, that he is a Socinian. But his argument goes distinctly and fully to the rejection of every

system of dogmatic theology, above all, to the rejection of every creed involving the use of scholastic phraseology, such as the Nicene and Athanasian creeds. As these creeds are recognised in our articles as well as liturgy, I do not see how his orthodoxy can be maintained unless he abandons part of his book.[20]

Perhaps Lewis's opinions on Hampden were modified by the hostility the Bishop suffered from his dean, the Very Revd John Merewether whose opposition to the Bishop was only equalled by that to him as dean from Lewis.

Merewether enjoyed the patronage of William IV and was presented to the living of New Radnor in 1828 which he seldom visited during the twenty-two years he was its incumbent. In 1832 he became dean of Hereford and in 1836 the Herefordshire vicarage of Madley also became his. In readiness for the preferment he deemed his due, he took his BD and DD in 1832, and was elected an FSA in 1836, for he was by now an established clerical antiquary. Intellectually Merewether was worthy of Lewis's respect and his antiquarian interests stood him in good stead in 1840 when Philip Hardwick, the architect planning alterations to the bishop's palace, but better known as the architect of the Euston Station Arch, warned the dean that the east end of the Lady Chapel was in immediate danger of collapse.

Merewether brought in Lewis Nockalls Cottingham, an architect who specialised in the gothic idiom and under his direction the dilapidated east end of the Lady Chapel was re-constructed without and renovated within. Further investigation disclosed danger from the central tower which had to be under-pinned, stone vaults removed, and piers and adjoining arches rebuilt. Screens were demolished and Norman arches with a triforium above were revealed, so too was a series of episcopal tombs and effigies. The work was still in hand when Cottingham died in 1847.

Merewether played an active part in the restoration. He donated £500 towards its cost, and communicated to the journal *Archæologia* accounts of the discoveries which were made whilst the work went on. In 1843 he published a *Statement on the Condition and Circumstances of the Cathedral Church of Hereford*, with notes on the effigies and illustrations of the cathedral's structural condition. He also found time to conduct an archaeological excavation in Wiltshire on Silbury Hill which was published posthumously in 1851 as the *Diary of a Dean: being an Account of the Examination of Silbury Hill and of various Barrows and other Earthworks on the Downs of North Wilts.* The very competent technical drawings are all his.

The size and condition of the rectory at New Radnor did not encourage residence, though in the early days one of the dean's sons seems to have done duty in the parish.[21] In 1829 and 1830 the Revd Francis Merewether signs the registers as his kinsman's curate.[22] A Cambridge LLB, he was inducted in 1833 to the Herefordshire living of Clehonger at £626 pa. The patron of the living was the Bishop of Hereford, then Dr Edward Grey, brother of Earl Grey, the Prime Minister, and whose Whig sympathies he shared,

> though of late he was much and strenuously opposed to those measures of theirs which have for their object the destruction of the established church and the revered institutions of the country. He was considered to be a very sound divine and an excellent Greek scholar, perhaps the best in the country.[23]

In 1840 Francis Merewether was also presented to the living of Woolhope, adjacent to Clehonger. The patrons were the Dean, his kinsman, and Chapter of Hereford. He was still there in 1881 and it was during his incumbency that in 1851 the Woolhope Naturalists' Field Club was founded, the pre-eminent antiquarian society of the Marches. He was active, too, in the Herefordshire Bow Meeting.

John Merewether himself made occasional appearances at New Radnor,[24] but the dean's relations with his New Radnor parishioners were less than successful. When he described them as 'smockfrocks, hobnails, and insolent' one of the local gentry, Major JA Whittaker, of Newcastle Court, was under the impression that he was included in the dean's remarks and compelled him to come over to New Radnor and publicly sign a letter of apology.[25] It has to be said, however, that Major Whittaker was as much a thorn in the flesh of the Lewis family as he was in that of the dean.

Merewether had his own episcopal ambitions which were fed by the promise of their fulfilment made by the dying William IV in 1837. But he was several times passed over. 'Politically suitable, since he organised the Tory party at Hereford elections, [he] reminded Peel of the royal promise and said that a bishopric would be most congenial to his feelings'.[26] But Peel did not feel bound by the late king's intentions, and Melbourne, Russell, and Palmerston did not share Merewether's politics.

But it was more than sour grapes that caused him strenuously to resist the appointment of Renn Dickson Hampden to the see of Hereford. Unknown to each other both men had been rivals in 1840 for the bishopric of St Davids.[27] Happily for the Welsh Church neither were successful and Connop Thirwall was consecrated to preside over the affairs of the diocese of St Davids which he did with distinction for thirty-four years.

On the 21st December 1847 Merewether set out his objections at length in a memorial to the Queen which he also published in *The Times*. Lewis thought in so doing he was 'doing his best to prolong the agitation'.[28] Two days later, on 23rd December, again at great length, Merewether, as the Dean of Hereford, wrote to Lord John Russell to inform him that when the Cathedral Chapter gathered at the end of the month formally to elect Hampden as their bishop, he would vote against the motion. The Prime Minister's reply was brief and to the point:

> Sir, I have had the honour to receive your letter of the 23rd instant, in which you intimate to me your intention of violating the law.[29]

The election took place at Hereford on the 28th of December and Merewether did indeed break the law: he and Canon Huntingford, one of the cathedral's four residentiary canons, voted against Hampden's election and the Dean went on to refuse to affix the Chapter's seal to the document recording the bishop's formal election, and wrote a letter of justification to *The Times* on New Year's Day 1848.

These events caused Lewis confess to his brother:

> The Dean of Hereford has suddenly become a hero, a capacity in which I did not expect to meet him. *The Times* of to-day, by the pen of Mr Mozley, nearly deifies him. I cannot understand what should have driven him to such extremities. We shall all be anxious to hear what were the proceedings of to-day. Julius Hare has written a pro-Hampden pamphlet, which the *Chronicle* praises …[30]

The Times continued in its support of Merewether, and it was now that Lewis at last decided to read Hampden's Bampton lectures. In his opinion, neither Dean nor Bishop had come out the affair with much credit and the integrity and sincerity of both men was a matter of dispute and he wrote to his friend, Head, accordingly:

> *The Times* failed altogether in making a hero out of Merewether.
> I do not know whether you saw the articles in the *Chronicle*
> against him. They were remarkably pungent, and there was no
> answering them; so *The Times* let their man drop. The affair, I
> hear, is not yet over; but it is clear that, bishops and deans in
> these degenerate days have no taste for martyrdom, and dislike
> flying in the face of power. The Government will prevail; but the
> victory will be dearly bought, and will cost much too high a
> price. I have sent for Hampden's: *Lectures,* and am going to
> follow Wilberforce's example, and read them.[31]

Hampden was consecrated on 26th March 1848, but Merewether
continued in his opposition and on 23rd May 1848 Cornewall Lewis
recorded in his diary:

> Early at the House. Then went to a dinner of the Herefordshire
> Society at the Freemasons Tavern. Returned thanks for my
> health as County member, about 50 persons dined. The Dean of
> Hereford introduced the subject of his quarrel with the Bishop
> against the feeling of the company. He met with no sympathy.
> Aftds returned to the House, where Fergus O'Connor and
> Cobden attacked one another about Reform in Parliament.

Hampden, however, did not have to endure the hostility of his
dean for long, for Merewether died prematurely two years later in
1850, at the age of fifty-two. Despite the aspersions cast upon him by
Lewis, by anyone else's standards he was a distinguished clergyman.
Lewis, however, on hearing the news of Merewether's death, was
moved to write to Head:

> the Dean of Hereford, much to the relief of New Radnor, has
> lately died.[32]

The excitement caused in 1847 by Dr Hampden's appointment
to Hereford and his antipathy to John Merewether seem to have
eclipsed interest on Lewis's part in the Gorham case. Gorham was an
evangelical clergymen who, on account of what he deemed to be his
doctrinally unsound views on baptism, the Bishop of Exeter refused
to institute to a living in his diocese to which he had been presented
by the Lord Chancellor. The matter dragged through the ecclesiastical courts and judgement was eventually given in favour of Gorham.
This outcome caused great offence to High Churchman and aroused
a storm of controvesy. Many clergymen seceded to Rome, including

Henry Manning, the future cardinal, and Robert Wilberforce, brother of the Bishop of Oxford. Though the controversy went on for two and a half years, Lewis made but one passing reference to it in his diaries. This is perhaps made all the more surprising by Lewis's friendship with Lady Langdale. Widowed in 1851, Jane Elizabeth Harley was the eldest child of Edward, fifth Earl of Oxford and Mortimer, and had married Henry Bickersteth who was enobled as Lord Langdale in 1836 and as Master of the Rolls presided over the Gorham judgement.

———————

When Sir Thomas Frankland Lewis died in January 1855, George Cornewall Lewis, as his eldest son, erected a monument to his father's memory in Old Radnor parish church and composed its inscription:

> In religion he was a firm adherent of the Protestant faith, according to the tenets of the Church of England. In all the relations of private life he was blameless. He was an attached husband and an affectionate father.

Lewis himself never defined his understanding of the nature of the Protestant faith, a term which appears nowhere in any of the various editions of the Book of Common Prayer, though when in 1625 Charles I affirmed his allegiance to the Protestant Religion it implied opposition to both Roman Catholicism and Puritanism. For Lewis, father and son, it was largely a matter of opposition to Tractarianism and the Puseyites, elements within, rather than without, the Church of England. Centred at first upon the University of Oxford, the Tractarians were committed to the restoration and defence of what they believed to be the catholic doctrine and traditions imbedded in the Prayer Book and Thirty-nine Articles of Religion of the established church.

The Lewis hostility to Tractarianism showed itself in the design and building of the new parish church at New Radnor, 1841–45. Thus, when the Revd WP Williams, the rector of the adjacent parish of Llanfihangel Nant Mellan and who lived in New Radnor, offered to present 'the image of a lamb' to the new church, its acceptance was opposed by Frankland Lewis for fear that it might eventually lead to the church being decorated with a figure of the Virgin Mary, to whom the church had been dedicated since its foundation in the 12th century.[33] At the same time Frankland Lewis wanted a lectern of the 'usual construction' to be substituted for the proposed revolving double sided lectern, 'as a Tractarian could use it to face an imaginary deity.' He also disagreed with the suggested position of the font.[34] The overall design of the church showed a robust disdain of the standards set by the Ecclesiological Society and its very small apse-ended chancel precluded any liturgical extravagance in ritual or ceremony should a future incumbent develop such High Church tendencies.

Such designs had a vogue in the diocese of Hereford and enjoyed the Lewises' approval. So in September 1849 when Cornewall Lewis and his wife were staying with the Prices at Foxley, they joined in helping to raise money for a new parish church in Hereford:

> Friday 7th September 1849 At Foxley. Went to bazaar at Hereford for St Martin's church. Theresa & Lady Price had neighbouring stalls.

> Saturday 8th September. At Foxley. Went to bazaar which was concluded today.

The history of St Martin's, on the Ross road, goes back to the Middle Ages, the present building, however, was designed in 1845 by RW Jearrad who was active in the Cheltenham area as a builder of hotels as much as churches. Like New Radnor parish church, St Martin's has lancet windows and a thin tower, though the latter also has a small broached spire. Nicholson and Sons altered the chancel in 1894, otherwise the similarities may have been even more striking.

It has to be remembered, of course, that it was in 1841, when plans were first mooted for a new parish church at New Radnor, that John Henry Newman, Vicar of the University Church at Oxford, and, at that time, a leading Tractarian, published Tract XC, in which he argued that the doctrine contained within the Thirty-nine Articles was compatible with Roman Catholic doctrine. In 1845 he became a Roman Catholic.

Whilst Sir Thomas Frankland Lewis was concerning himself with securing a new parish church free of Tractarian influence, his son was travelling in Germany, where he encountered an upsurge of nationalism amongst German Roman Catholics. It was a movement which in his opinion enjoyed an integrity which the Tractarians and Puseyites lacked:

> They are just the reverse of our Puseyites, who are Catholics calling themselves members of a Protestant Church; these people are Protestants, calling themselves members of a Catholic Church. They differ moreover from the Puseyites in two other respects; one, that many of their priests have sacrificed their emoluments when they changed their opinion, the other, that the converts are chiefly among the middle class, merchants, tradesmen, &c.[35]

Lewis's anti-Tractarian views were shared locally by his Kington kinsman the Revd James Davies, né Banks, who in 1851 was seeking the headmastership of Ludlow Grammar School. The school's Trustees were anxious not to appoint a Tractarian and it had been the same in 1850 when he sought unsuccessfully the headship of the Crypt School in Gloucester. Banks attempted to allay any suspicions about his churchmanship by attending a meeting in Gloucester in November 1850 which the archdeacon had providentially convened in protest against the restoration that year of the Roman Catholic hierarchy in Britain by Pope Pius IX:

> I am going to Gloucester on Friday to a meeting summoned by the archdeacon to devise measures against the Pope's encroachment; which meeting I take it is a very providential opportunity of shewing people that one is a bona fide Church of England man, & not a Romanist in disguise. I certainly did not hesitate a moment, but made up my mind to go to Glos. the moment I had the circular.[36]

But when it came to Ludlow it seems that Banks had not done enough to reassure the Trustees about his orthodoxy, and having complained in November 1851 to his brother Richard that 'the Ludlow story seems interminable' went on to say that he has heard that the 'Trustees were anxious to get a man who was no Puseyite' and that he had merely said 'he belonged to no party' which, in the opinion of the Trustees 'all those who have gone to Rome had said at one time or another.' Banks was indignant, for his family was well known in south Shropshire and his 'father could assure any of the Ludlow people that I was as firm as a rock in the Church of England'.[37]

There was much talk of 'Papal Aggression', a term coined by the Prime Minister, Lord John Russell, in a letter to the Bishop of Durham which was published in *The Times* on the 7th November 1850. In it Russell, normally tolerant in matters of religion, referred to the 'late aggression of the Pope upon our Protestantism' as being 'insolent and insidious'. Lewis, writing to Head about the letter, thought that

> there were some unfortunate expressions in it, not necessary for his purpose, which offended the Catholics.[38]

All the same,

> the creation of dioceses in the ambitious manner in which it was done, was, however, a very wanton atttack on the Protestant feeling of the country, which was quite contented to slumber if it had not been roused by the Pope. No doubt the Pope and his advisers had been misled, by the Puseyite conversions, into supposing that all England was ready to go to Rome. By this time they have probably discovered their error.[39]

Indeed, Russell justified Hampden's appointment to Hereford on the grounds that:

> The appointment was calculated 'to strengthen the Protestant character of our Church so seriously threatened of late by many defections to the Church of Rome'.[40]

Lewis agreed with Russell that the real danger, however, was not so much the assertion of Roman Catholic claims, as Anglican clergymen who practised and advocated Roman doctrines and practices:

> I do not expect that this row will alter the relation between Cathlolics and Protestants in this country; the storm will blow over, and both parties will be as they were. But it will bring the Puseyites to their bearings; it will be an *instantia crucis* to them which will compel them to choose one road or the other. The extreme left will become Roman, the middle and the extreme right will gradually drop the 'ritualism' and the other distinctive attributes of Puseyism, and relapse into old-fashioned High Church opinions, such as used to be held at Oxford thirty years ago.
>
> It is expected that the Government will bring in a Bill prohibiting the Roman Catholic bishops from assuming territorial names of sees. If this is done, it will be a very innocent piece of legislation, but it will probably produce an infinite quantity of *deraisonnement*, and bad theological politics.[41]

The Ecclesiastical Titles Act of 1851 *did* forbid the assumption of territorial titles by Roman Catholic bishops. Lewis thought it a waste of parliamentary time, and a wrangle over trifles, reiterating his conviction that the real cause of anxiety were Dr Pusey and the Oxford Movement. There was more Roman Catholic resentment of the Act in Ireland than in England, and Paul Cullen,[42] the Roman Catholic Archbishop of Armagh, presided over a mass meeting of Irish Roman Catholics in Dublin to protest against the Act. He took the chair, using the title of Archbishop of Armagh, which Lewis thought was near to breaking the law:

> The Anti-Papal Bill consumed the chief part of the session; as a measure of legislation, it is wholly unimportant. The whole dispute seems to me *nuga caprina*. Neither the assumption of the territorial title, nor the prohibition to assume it, is of the slightest practical moment. The English bishops, for the present, submit to the law. The Irish bishops, against whom it was not directed, are beginning to make a bluster; but I expect that it will be a *fuoco di pagli*. Paul Cullen's acceptance of the chair at the Dublin meeting, when he was moved into it as Archbishop of Armagh, was very close to a public assumption of the title. The signatures in the newspapers prove nothing. The titles may have been added by a printer's devil. The real cause of the Catholic revival in this country is not political; it is due exclusively to the Oxford School. They, and their adherents, have made converts among the clergy and upper classes in *England*, upon theological grounds. In Ireland, where the political influences are more felt, there have been no conversions to Catholicism.[43]

No prosecutions ever resulted from the Ecclesiastical Titles Act which was repealed in 1871 by Gladstone who had opposed it in the first place. Anti-papal meetings, however, were held in Herefordshire, as elsewhere, but unlike the Revd James Davies, Lewis did not attend them: to his mind the whole business had got out of proportion:

> There has since been a county meeting on the Papal Aggression, which I did not attend. The amount of nonsense which has been talked on this subject has been very large.[44]

Nonsense it may have been, but it was eventually to be a factor in Lewis losing his Herefordshire parliamentary seat. When he was electioneering at Hereford in 1847 one of the relieving officers of the Hereford Poor Law Union refused his vote because Lewis, to his mind, was too tolerant to the Roman Catholics.[45] Lewis was unopposed and so the sentiments of the electorate had little on his election. But in

1852 he was accused of being a Roman Catholic and FL Bodenham his agent thought the consequences of this misapprehension could be serious. 'The Monmouthshire freeholders are a very difficult lot' Bodenham informed him, and had a horror of Roman Catholicism. A local clergyman had spread this misinformation to the small freeholders of Foothog, near Llanthony, and this had given his opponents the confidence that his chance of representing the county again was entirely gone.[46] Bodenham also sent him a list those to whom Lewis should write letters of denial that he was a Catholic.[47]

Interestingly Bodenham himself had Roman Catholic connections. Charles Bodenham of Rotherwas was married to a wife of Polish descent and when Cornewall Lewis's cousin, Caroline Duff Gordon stayed there in September 1866 she relates how:

> We breakfasted late as the family had their prayers in the RC Chapel from 9 30 onwards before Breakfast. Alice & my maid Louise went to the Protestant Church at Dynedale $1^1/_2$ miles off in hard rain. The RC Bishop Brown and Mr Wegg Prosser dined.[48]

The RC Bishop Brown was the Right Reverend Thomas Joseph Brown, OSB, who was bishop of the Roman Catholic diocese of Newport and Menevia from its inception in 1850, as one of the fruits of the so-called papal aggression of that year, until 1880. He was a distinguished theologian and controversialist. Mr Wegg Prosser was an Anglican convert to Roman Catholicism and by whose generosity Belmont Abbey near Hereford was largely built. Its foundation stone was laid in 1854 and both church and its attendant monastic buildings were completed in 1858.[49]

Anti-Roman Catholic sentiments, especially in south-west Herefordshire, were strong, but Lewis seems to have been unaware of them. According to his diary his nomination for election in July 1852 was a very eirenic affair,[50] though the *Hereford Times* gave a less felicitous account of things.[51]

Lewis was silent about all this, though it must have contributed to his appearance, six days later on July 19th, at the bottom of the poll which his brother Gilbert ascribed to the hostility of 'the smaller voters'.[52]

By March 1853 Lewis was identifying ultratractarians within the Church of England.

> The chief point which the most ultratractarians now contend for is *confession*, but the bulk of the party are merely very high-churchmen. They are against Rome and its distinctive tenets, but wish to have a powerful hierarchy, with extensive powers and exalted position of bishop and priest, great funds at their disposal, mute acquiescence on the part of the laity, and so forth; but no union with Rome.[53]

In 1856 *Archaeologia Cambrensis* announced that the church at Old Radnor was undergoing thorough reparation and restoration. The medieval screen was the main victim of this all too thorough restoration and it reflects Lewis's dread of Tractarianism and Popery which caused it to lose all its painted colour and gilding and 'the representation of saints and religious persons placed in ranges, compartments, or niches', which the Radnorshire historian Jonathan Williams described after visiting the church half a century earlier. The illustration of the screen in 1858 volume of *Archaeologia Cambrensis* shows how thoroughly the paint and gilt had been pickled off during the restoration.

In a way that this should have happened under the aegis of Cornewall Lewis is surprising, for he was a considerable antiquarian. In 1851 whilst he was at the Treasury he found time to ask through the columns of *Notes & Queries*:

> Does the custom of dressing the churches at Christmas with holly and other evergreens, prevail in any country besides England?[54]

He was familiar with the custom locally and at adjacent Kington the parish clerk was paid 2s 6d on Christmas Eve to dress the church with evergreens[55] and at Harpton in 1856 the custom was adopted of having a Christmas tree in the dining room.[56]

Besides the colouring of the screen, there were other losses, too, at Old Radnor and since *Archaeologia Cambrensis* noted with approval that at nearby Presteign 'all the abominations of pews, galleries, and other disfigurements of a tasteless and irreligious age have been removed, and the sacred edifice now presents a most gratifying appearance' it seems that it was at this stage that Old Radnor lost its three decker pulpit and box pews, 'abominations and disfigurements' whose passing is nowadays much regretted.

Perhaps Lewis's anxiety in 1856 that Tractarianism could yet emerge at Old Radnor had some foundation, for only a year later, in 1857, it was revealed in the pages of the *Hereford Times* that an ultra-tractarian was serving the remotenesses of Presteign as an assistant curate and that sacramental confession had arrived in Radnorshire. An outraged correspondent inquired:

> Sir, I shall feel greatly obliged if you can inform me how long auricular confession has been a doctrine of the Church of England? as I always thought it was confined exclusively to the Greek and Roman churches, until its introduction into this parish by one of our curates; and as this doctrine in connexion with the establishment may be as new to many of your readers as it is to me, I will just state that gentleman's mode of procedure in a case that came under my own observation on Saturday, the 24th instant.
>
> A poor but respectable widow, residing in this town, being ill, the revd gentleman visited her for the purpose (as she and her friends thought) of imparting spiritual consolation and instruction; but judge of her surprise, when, after making some inquiries respecting her temporal affairs, and politely asking her daughter to leave the room, he began to urge upon her the absolute and indispensable necessity of auricular confession in obtaining salvation. The bare idea of confessing her sins to a worm of earth like herself was so opposed to her unsophisticated notions of our holy religion, that she became almost speechless with astonishment.[57]

The Revd Oliver Ormerod, MA, was rector of Presteign from 1841 to 1880, and obtained a license to be non-resident in 1847. During his frequent and prolonged absences the needs of the parish were served by a succession of assistant curates of varying churchmanship. Omerod himself was a confirmed eccentric, and Kilvert tells how, when it came to the collection of alms in the service, he used to place his pocket knife on the offertory plate, saying he had no change.

The eccentricities of Mr Omerod were rather outshone by those of another local clergyman, the Revd Dr Edward Thompson, Vicar of Kington 1850–1860. His parish adjoined that of Old Radnor, but his name nowhere appears in the Lewis diaries which cover the period of his incumbency. In May 1854 he caused the bells of Kington parish church to be rung for two days, at his own expense, it was rumoured, a 'victory having been achieved over the great Mr Davies, Banks, and

Co' who had unsuccessfully opposed the Leominster and Kington Railway Bill. The lawyers and bankers James Davies and Richard Banks were, it will be recollected, Lewis's kinsmen as well as his political agents. Lewis, for his part, was a great patron of the railways in Herefordshire.

It was Dr Thompson's custom to keep firearms in his bedroom, but in 1854 a petition was signed by thirteen of the town's leading parishioners, including James Davies and Richard Banks. Their complaint was that Dr Thompson, married with an adult son, had been harbouring in the vicarage bedroom not only firearms, but also a certain Mrs Harriett Sophia Augustienne Maria Binches, apparently a notoriously lewd and unchaste woman with whom he had committed adultery and admitted to holy communion. Hampden, as bishop, was asked to investigate the matter. It all dragged on at length and Thompson survived.

In March 1854 the vicar issued a statement in which he hoped 'all angry feeling and ill-will towards him would be subdued and that all may strive together in the true spirit of love and humility, not regarding the vehicle in which the truth is conveyed but Him from whom it emanates.' Perhaps his statement met with some success for he remained vicar until 1860 and it was in his time that the large vicarage was built which served the incumbents of the parish until 1965 when it was replaced by the present bijou. He lived in his new vicarage in some style so that when he died in 1860, his effects included '100 dozen of selected fine and rare old wines'.[58]

When, in June 1859, Lewis became Home Secretary, he became responsible for law and order. It was not long before he was officially involved in what must have been for him a very disagreeable matter: the riots at St George's-in-the-East. This London parish

> had a population of 30,000, a church to hold 2,000, dunes of empty pews and fifty or sixty faithful worshippers. It was the land of docks and sailors, of dining-saloons and filthy bars, of public houses offering squads of harlots. The 733 houses within four streets of the church included 154 brothels.[59]

Since 1842 it had, in the person of the Revd Bryan King, a clergyman of moderate Tractarian sympathies. For fourteen years King ministered to his little congregation and led their worship in the way his conscience bade him. He was, though, opposed at every turn of the way by hostile churchwardens elected by an equally hostile vestry which resented the imposition of Church rates even more than than the incumbent's gentle ritualism. In 1856 he was joined by the Revd Charles Lowder, a rather more robust ritualist, who had recently founded the Society of the Holy Cross to strengthen the spiritual life of the Church, defend its faith, and to provide missionaries to work in a parish context. He was previously a curate at St Barnabas, Pimlico, a daughter church of St Paul's Knightsbridge, eschewed for its church-manship by Lewis but favoured by Lord John Russell, his parliamentary leader.

Lowden's activities may well have been the subject of Lewis's dinner table talk even before the latter became Home Secretary. For not only had Lowden worked at Knightsbridge in a neighbouring parish before going to London's East End, but also once there, he established a refuge for the redemption of prostitutes in the country at Sutton in Surrey, some twelve miles from London and adjoined on its western boundaries by the parish of Cheam where both George and Gilbert Lewis were frequent visitors at the home there of Sir Edmund Antrobus, Gilbert's father-in-law.[60]

> A month before Lewis's appointment as Home Secretary, at St George's-in-the-East a hostile parish elected an evangelical clergyman, the Revd Hugh Allen, to a lectureship which was attached to the church, and neither the incumbent nor the Bishop of London had the necessary legal authority to veto his appointment. An avowed opponent of what he deemed to be popery, almost daily reports began to appear in *The Times* of violent scenes in the parish and in its parish church. Sunday afternoons at St. George's were the zoo and horror and coconut-shy of London. The best days witnessed pew doors banging or feet scraping or hissing or coughing or syncopated responses. The worst days witnessed gleeful rows of boys shooting with peas from the gallery, fireworks, flaming speeches from tub-orators during service, bleating as of goats, spitting on choirboys, a pair of hounds howling gin-silly round the nave, cushions hurled at the altar, orange-peel and butter, kicking or hustling of clergy. One of the altar carpets was crammed into a stove and pew number 16 in the south aisle was used as privy.[61]

All this was in protest against the incumbent and his curate's ritualism, and was orchestrated by the evangelical parish lecturer,

Allen. The churchwardens, one a Methodist, the other a publican, were disinclined to obey the bishop's direction that they should keep order and in November 1859 fifty uniformed police were brought in to act on their behalf. This they did for six weeks until Lewis had them withdrawn, fifty-one rate payers having petitioned him against their presence.

On 30th January 1860 Lewis was questioned in the House about what was happening at St George's-in-the-East:

> G Cornewall Lewis very gauche in his reply - even for him. Police are to be stationed outside the Church to arrest persons who shall intend to make a disturbance (great laughter). It will not be easy even for detective officers to divine intentions.[62]

And nor was it, and the disturbances at St George's on the following Sunday were as unseemly as ever. Further questions to the Home Secretary ensued, and Lewis assured the House that it was not his intention to make any alteration to the arrangements at St George's. There would be a body of police outside, but none inside the walls of the church.[63] That was on Monday, and it was not in Cornewall Lewis's nature to deceive, so during the week it must have been that he had second thoughts which led him to a new strategy which involved an element of surprise. Not even the churchwardens were taken into his confidence:

> As soon as the church doors were thrown open on Sunday morning a body of policemen, headed by Mr Superintendent Howie, marched into the church and stood in twelves, in four rows, namely, twelve on the north and twelve on the south side of the nave, twelve in the south aisle and twelve in the north. Two others took guard of the altar. On previous occasions these gentlemen occupied pews, and bore the character of worshippers, although their knowledge of church observances was, to use the words of Lord John Russell (borrowed from Thucydides) 'conspicuous by its absence'. On Sunday morning they were policemen and nothing else. They stood on duty and had nothing to do with the service. Their instructions were evidently imperative, for although the whole of them stood with their faces to the altar, they all turned right about face whenever an unlucky fellow coughed, or whenever a pew door was shut to with unnecessary violence ...
>
> Prior to the evening service an immense mass of persons assembled in Cannon Street, and it was with great difficulty that

the police could keep them back. When the procession of priests and choristers entered the church there was a good deal of coughing and hissing, but the presence of the police prevented any violent outbreak ... The service was constantly interrupted by coughing and whistling but there was nothing like the disturbance of the previous Sunday evening ...

As soon as the preacher entered the pulpit, in his surplice, there was much stamping of feet and coughing, but he took no notice of it ... The rev. gentleman delivered his sermon with tremendous energy, and was successful in obtaining a pretty fair hearing. As soon as he had finished his sermon the police commenced clearing the church, an operation which they accomplished without much difficulty.[64]

Getting nowhere, Lewis decided upon a change of strategy and withdrew the Sunday morning police presence at St George's:

Sir G Lewis, having reconsidered his determination in reference to the presence of police in the parish church of St George in the east, there was not the disturbance on Sunday last which previous Sundays have witnessed ... The morning service ... was the most pacific which St George's has witnessed for a long time past ...[65]

Lewis himself spent that weekend housebound with neuralgia, and it was not until Friday he was able to go the Commons, and even then for only a couple of hours, finding the exertion greater than he could bear. By the following Wednesday he was able

to attend the morning sitting of the house & found that the exertion was not too great, also at the office for a short time.[66]

St George's-in-the-East had taken its toll and it cannot have been without misgivings that he sent fifty policemen into a Tractarian church to preserve order for a liturgy with which he had little sympathy. Sunday service at New Radnor and Watford may have been short on sophistication, light on pulpit eloquence, but it had the seemliness and orderliness which he sought in his worship Sunday by Sunday.

———————

It was perhaps Lewis's preoccupation with the outrages at St George's-in-the-East which caused an event of far greater theological importance to have escaped Lewis's notice. For some years Biblical scholars specialising in textual criticism had been disputing the traditional views of the authorship of the Pentateuch and Epistles as well as the dating of the gospels. The German University of Tubingen was the continental centre of this work but it was closely followed by scholars in England. In 1860 seven Oxford scholars of liberal outlook published their views in *Essays and Reviews*. Six of the writers were clergymen, one was a head of an Oxford college, two were professors, and one was a headmaster.

In five years *Essays and Reviews* went into thirteen editions, and over four hundred books, pamphlets, and articles were written in reply to it. It was condemned by the bishops in 1861, two of its authors were found guilty of heresy by the Court of Arches in 1862, though acquitted on appeal of the Judicial Committee of the Privy Council in 1864. 10,906 Anglican clergy in England and Wales and Ireland signed a declaration affirming all that it questioned, just under half of the Anglican clergy of those provinces. But nowhere in Lewis's diaries or his correspondence is there any mention of this controversy which, bearing in mind his concern over the Tractarians and papal aggression, is surprising.

One of the Essayists was Benjamin Jowett, 1817–93, who had been elected Regius Professor of Greek at Oxford in 1855, and was to become the Master of Balliol College in 1870. In his essay he urged his readers to '*interpret the Scripture like any other book*'. Though he went on to say 'there are many respects in which Scripture is unlike any other book; these will appear in the results of such an interpretation',[67] there were many who were offended by this sentiment. Jowett was an ordained clergyman of the Church of England, and as such had on several occasions publicly assented to its thirty-nine articles of religion, article VI of which speaks of 'the canonical books of the Old and New Testament, of whose authority was never any doubt in the Church.' Likewise at the making of deacons, the ordinand is asked the question 'Do you infeignedly believe all the Canonical Scriptures of the Old and New Testament?' To which question the required response is: 'I do believe them'. Just as Lewis had argued that the Tractarians should either abandon their well endowed livings or what he considered to be their Roman doctines and practices, there were those who now sought the same logic from those Essayists who were in orders. But Lewis was not amongst them.

Essays and Reviews was published in February 1860 and the intense heat generated by its debate was to take years to cool. But on 17th October 1860 Lewis went up to Oxford:

> Wednesday 17th October. Left Worcester by a Morning train, &
> went to Oxford. Dined & slept at Dr Cradock's, Principal of
> Brasenose. Met at dinner, Dr Liddell, Dean of Ch. Ch. Dr Jeune,
> the Vice-Chancellor, Dr Scott, Head of Balliol, & Mr Jowett,
> Regius Professor of Greek.[68]

It was indeed a distinguished dinner party. Dr Edward Hartopp
Cradock was a longstanding friend of the family.[69] Henry George
Liddell was dean of Christ Church 1851–91. Robert Scott was Master
of Balliol 1854–70, and Dean Ireland's Professor of Exegesis 1861–70.
He was dean of Rochester from 1870 until his death in 1893, but is
remembered most for his lengthy collaboration with Liddell in
producing their Greek-English Lexicon which 'opened a new epoch
in Greek scholarship' and went through eight editions between 1843
and 1897. Francis Jeune was Vice-Chancellor of the University
1858–62 and Master of Pembroke College 1843–64, when Palmerston
nominated him to the deanery of Lincoln. His stay was there was short
and he became bishop of Peterborough later in the same year. He was
an evangelical and university reformer. But whatever the themes of
their dinner time conversation, *Essays and Reviews* was not amongst
them, and Jowett's presence excited no comment in Lewis's diary.

Another contributor to *Essays and Reviews*, though not at the
Brasenose dinner party, was Mark Pattison. His contribution on
'Tendencies of Religious Thought in England 1688–1750' has since
been judged as being 'learned, temperate, and impartial'. Little fault
was found with his article, 'except the fact that it had appeared in
company with the others'.[70] Pattison was fellow of Lincoln College,
when James Banks had been a scholar, and he called upon him in
1851, as one of sixteen referees to support his aspirations to school
headships. It is of interest to us that the Reverend James Banks,
kinsman, friend, and literary collaborator of Lewis, should have used
one of the contributors to this controversial volume to support his
claims to be 'a good Church of England man.'

In February 1861 the Archbishop of Canterbury and twenty-five
bishops wrote to the Revd HB Wilson,[71] another of the contributors to
Essays and Reviews, 'expressing the pain it has given them that any clergymen of our church should have published such opinions'.
Hampden of Hereford was one of the twenty-five bishops who added
their signatures.

Unruffled by *Essays and Reviews*, Cornewall Lewis received with
equal *sang-froid* the more radical views, this time propagated by a

bishop, of John William Colenso. The diocese of Natal was founded in South Africa in 1853, and Colenso, a well-known Cambridge mathematician, was enthroned as its first bishop. He was to be a diligent and successful missionary bishop. Mastering the Zulu language, he published both a grammar and a Zulu-English dictionary. He also found time to publish a *Commentary on Romans* and an *Introduction to the Pentateuch and the Book of Joshua*. In the preface to this second book, he says that the initial motive for writing it came from a Zulu, helping him to translate the Old Testament, asking him whether the story of the Flood was true.

This challenge and his mathematical calculations, measurements, and statistics forced Colenso to the conclusion that many statements in the early books of the Old Testament were not historically accurate: 'The Bible itself is not God's word' he wrote, 'but assuredly God's word will be heard in the Bible ... The ordinary knowledge of Christ was nothing more than that of any educated Jew of his age'. This combination of moral and mathematical misgivings was censured by the English bishops who urged him to resign. When he refused, Robert Gray, the Archbishop of Cape Town, tried him for heresy, found him guilty, deposed him and appointed a new Bishop of Natal. In Lewis's circle, this caused RW Bank's mother-in-law, the evangelical Mrs Hartland of Charlton Kings, to write to her daughter Mrs Emily Banks with some satisfaction: 'So Colenso is deposed. I hope this will be confirmed'.[72] Emily's sister, who was married to an absentee clergyman, shared their mother's sentiments.[73]

No doubt to Mrs Hartland's disappointment, Colenso refused to accept the Archbishop of Capetown's judgement and appealed to the Privy Council, which in 1866 found, on legal grounds, that the Tractarian Gray had not the authority to depose him. Thus justified, Colenso continued to regard himself, despite many hardships and the fact that the English missionary societies cut off his funds, as the rightful Bishop of Natal. He did so even after the appointment of his successor in 1869.

Banks on the other hand, went to hear Colenso on one of his English tours seeking funds and understanding, and found him an attractive man. It probably did not help domestic debate that both Thomas Huxley, with whom Banks enjoyed a measure of friendship, and Charles Darwin supported Colenso on being deprived of his see. An early friend and mentor of Colenso was FD Maurice, the Christian Socialist. He was to influence profoundly RW Banks's brother-in-law, the Reverend BH Alford, who lectured for many years at Maurice's Working Men's College.

More sympathy for Colenso came from Lewis himself who approved of the bishop's intellectual stance, finding that the bishop applied the same historical principles to the Old Testament as he did in his own writing on Roman and Greek history.[74] He did, however, express to his friend George Grote his belief that Colenso's work had been considerably softened before its actual publication.[75]

Then in 1863, the year in which Lewis died, came Joseph Ernest Renan's, 1823–1892, *Vie de Jesu*, which emphasised the humanity of Christ and regarded the miraculous elements in the gospel narrative as of little importance. We do not know how Lewis reacted, but it seems not to have disturbed his friend RW Banks, the churchwarden of Kington parish church, for he met Renan in 1889 in Brittany with the Cambrian Archaeological Association, and his photograph is in the Banks Archives.

On the 30th March 1851 an event occurred unique in our history. A record was made that Sunday of the number of people who attended every place of worship in England and Wales. The idea that it was possible to hold a religious census in conjunction with the normal census due that year originated with Lewis whilst he was an Under-Secretary at the Home Office 1848–50. The result is a vivid, though not necessarily accurate, picture of the state of religion in the middle of the last century. Many incumbents seized upon the fact that it was Mothering Sunday, the traditional day for servants to return home to see their families, to explain the poor size of their congregations. Others blamed the weather and one enterprising Herefordshire clergyman said his poor congregation was due to an influenza epidemic. Clergymen are rather like politicians; things are never their fault.

One thing was plain from the returns: a lot of people did not go to church or chapel on Sunday. It was also obvious that a great deal of church and chapel building was going on at this time, for it was generally believed that more places of worship were needed to accommodate the rising population and many of those which existed already needed to be rebuilt or replaced. It was also clear that as many people went to chapel as went to church. Likewise, the census revealed the inadequacy and inconvenience of the religious provision made by the established church.

The strength of nonconformity revealed by the census, the results of which were published in 1853, surprised Lewis and he felt that the bill of 1854 admitting nonconformists to bachelor's degrees at Oxford was a reaction to its findings:

> The Government has not prospered lately. The fate of the motion for admitting Dissenters to Oxford was singular; I have no doubt that the division was influenced by the knowledge of the fact disclosed by the religious census published in the winter, that the Dissenters are about half the population.[76]

Lewis was Home Secretary in 1860 when the cabinet was considering the census due in 1861. A religious inquiry was again contemplated, but there was strong nonconformist opposition:

> There is a great stir about a clause in the New Census Bill. It will, they say, compel everyone to state his religious opinions. Dissenters are furious. It is said that they are afraid lest their reputed relative strength in comparison to Churchmen suffer in Public estimation. But some philosophers object on another ground - viz, that to compel a man to state his real opinions in a country where some opinions are under a legal & social ban is calculated either to cause men to lie or to place them out of the protection of courts of justice & instances are adduced in proof. An oath of a person is not taken, he professes incredulity on certain points, such as belief in Hell. The subject is likely to rouse a very intense quarrel.[77]

In Trelawny's opinion the situation was aggravated by an inept speech from Lewis in which he:

> laboured to prove the course right which Ministers had adopted at first - &, in doing so, he lost the good effect of timely concession by offensive insinuations & comparisons.[78]

The timely concession, the good effect of which Lewis lost by clumsy words, was that the idea of the religious census was dropped. It was never successfully revived.

The 1851 religious census in exposing the strength of nonconformity renewed pressure for the abolition of the church rate to which nonconformists, as well as Anglicans had to contribute. Anglicans argued the justice of this on the grounds that the country's parish churches were national property, to the upkeep of which all should contribute. The Dissenters, on the other hand, whilst they were, on the whole, content for Churchmen to hold quiet possession of these buildings, believed they should do keep the fabric of these buildings in good repair at their own expense.[79]

At New Radnor in 1845 £500 towards the building of the new church was raised by a Church rate and one of those who objected was William Edwards of Hindwell, a tenant of Lewis, who signed the return for the religious census on behalf of the Quakers in 1851.[80] Lewis, however, considered the attitude of many nonconformists to be unreasonable:

> With regard to Church rates, I cannot but think that the course taken by the Dissenters, in insisting on their abolition and refusing all compromise, is unreasonable, but the question has been well agitated in the boroughs, and the pressure on Liberal members is great. The feeling on our side is extraordinarily strong.[81]

In January 1858 Palmerston's government, in which Lewis was Chancellor of the Exchequer, fell and Lord Derby formed a cabinet with Spencer Walpole as Home Secretary. In February 1859 he introduced a bill for the reform of the Church rate and Lewis described its reception in the House to his brother Gilbert:

> You will see a full account of Walpole's plan in today's *Times*, but you may perhaps like to have some particulars of the debate. Walpole's speech was much laboured & was delivered with an air of solemnity which bordered on the ludicrous. His quotation from Horace was appropriate & the House seemed to understand it. His plan was received with perfect coldness on our side of the House. His own party did not seem to relish it, but they cheered him when he sat down, & will all of them support it. The power to charge estates in perpetuity will be nugatory, or nearly so. The Bill, so far as its rent operation goes, consists of two parts. First, the power to dissenters to take their name off the rate, (borrowed from our plan). Secondly, the conversion of the rate into a landlord's rate. I have always been in favour of the first of these methods, & a few years ago it wd have settled the question, but Walpole & his friends then opposed it. I am afraid that it now comes too late. As to the second I see great difficulties as to a vestry composed exclusively of owners. In a parish owned by one landlord, he wd be the entire vestry, & cd, if he chose it, refuse the rate. I believe however that the rector & churchwardens are ex-officio members of the vestry. Walpole's explanation was feeble, & he did not seem to be

aware of the main objections to much of his scheme. I do not much expect that the bill will pass.[82]

Lewis was right. Within the week Walpole had resigned, though on a different matter, and his successor, Thomas Henry Sutton Sotheron-Estcourt, intimated his intention to withdraw the bill. In response to an invitation from the frustrated Liberation Society, Sir John Trelawny, the member for Tavistock, accepted the parliamentary leadership of the movement for the abolition of the Church rate and to this end introduced his own bill. It came up for its second reading in July 1859 and was carried by a majority of seventy: Lewis spoke in the debate and a few days later received a letter from the Lord Wensleydale of Ampthill Park, a retired judge, complaining that in his speech on the Church rate Lewis had not shown his usual accurate knowledge of the law. He was in error, perhaps with the experience of Old Radnor church in mind, in suggesting that parishioners were not bound to repair their parish church.[83]

The second reading of Trelawny's bill saw its majority dwindle to twenty-nine, and Trelawny complained:

> Our case has retrograded. Cornewall Lewis prosed. He seemed half asleep ... Disraeli made the best point - contending that my bill tends to breaking up the parochial system & substituting centralization ... [84]

The bill's third reading took place in June 1860 and Lewis, still Home Secretary, spoke this time more effectively in its favour:

> At the House. Third reading of the Church rates abolition Bill, on which I spoke. The numbers on the division were even, 274 for each side. The Speaker gave his vote with the noes, on the ground that both sides of the house agreed in thinking that the Bill was a settlement of the question & that the rejection of the bill would give an opportunity for a reconsideration of the subject.[85]

From this point, it has been said, the cause of abolition went downhill. There was another debate on the bill in May 1862 which Trelawny recorded in some detail, and in his eyes Lord Wensleydale had got it right, Lewis, for all his academic brilliance, did not, in this respect, understand the law:

> A defeat on Church Rates by one vote 287 to 286 ... Both parties strained every nerve. ... Cornewall Lewis proved that he did not

understand the law & he did not feel much heart in the cause in hand. He is in the habit of sneering at arguments of members who have motions & then voting for them. This he consistently did in my case; without effect, however, for his observations were hazy & inaccurate & rather told in a sense opposite to his intentions. Macdonough, an Irish lawyer, set him right in his law.[86]

Lewis himself, now an unenthusiastic Ministerial head of the War Department, covers the events of the day tersely:

Attended morning sitting of the House, & spoke on Church rates.[87]

The abolition of the church rate was eventually achieved by Gladstone in 1868.

In April 1853 Lewis complained to his brother Gilbert about the unfortunate condition of the Welsh Church, although the Welsh bishops, in his opinion, had lately been less drowsy than they used to be.[88] Indeed, it was Connop Thirwall, the eccentric, but far from drowsy, bishop of St Davids, who took exception to the behaviour of the Revd Gilbert Lewis. By some deft clerical acrobatics he was both Rector of Monnington on Wye and of Gladestry, despite their being not only different counties, but also in different dioceses.

Writing to Gilbert in 1860, Lewis informed him of one of the hazards of being able to recommend to the patrons of clerical livings suitable candidates:

I have recommended a Mr Benjamin Hill, a brother-in-law of Mr Bankes of Knighton, for the Chancellor's living of Norton. Sir Harford Brydges[89] wished to obtain it for a certain Jefferys Hills & he has in consequence threatened me with his severest displeasure. His notion of his own importance is quite pretentious. It is very difficult to give away livings without making numerous enemies.[90]

Lewis regarded the Revd William Jefferys Hills, MA as 'an untried man', whereas 'Mr Hill will be a great blessing to the locality'.

When Merewether, the Dean of Hereford, died in 1850 Lewis informed his friend Sir Edmund Head:

Many people wish Gilbert to become a candidate, but he prefers remaining as he is, and has no wish to be a Church dignitary.

> The Deanery of Hereford is not very tempting: £1,000 a year
> with a house in ruins, and the Cathedral to subscribe to.[91]

This was not quite accurate: Gilbert was very anxious to become canon of Worcester. But this letter tells us more about Lewis than about his brother. He had little time for the Puseyites and felt they should forfeit their stipends for their beliefs, but here we find him judging a senior office in the Church of England in purely material terms. There is, perhaps, little spirituality in Lewis. He had, too, a professional interest in deanery finance:

> Wednesday 29th June 1859. Kent House. I attended a meeting
> of the Ecclesiastical Commission, when the question of an addi-
> tion to the stipends of some of the Deans was debated at length.

The Hereford deanery went, not to Gilbert, but to Richard Dawes, MA, DD, a mathematician and educationist.[92] He enjoyed the Queen's approval and in 1856 she wanted to prefer him to the see of Carlisle, but Palmerston thought otherwise, insisting that all Crown church appointments were a prime ministerial prerogative:

> ... the queen ... fancies, poor woman, that she has peculiar
> prerogatives about [sic] the Church because she is its head.[93]

This at least must have given Lewis some satisfaction, for Palmerston's choice for Carlisle was Henry Montague Villiers, the evangelical rector of St George's Bloomsbury, and Cornewall Lewis's brother-in-law.[94] That year however did see Palmerston, at Cornewall Lewis's request, presenting Gilbert Lewis to the residentiary canonry at Worcester Cathedral which he so much desired.[95] Palmerston, for his part, felt that

> his chief means of giving employment are confined to the
> Church and even these means are very limited.[96]

1856 had been a bad year for Gilbert Lewis and in June, after a long illness his son, Lindsay, died. His wife, Jane, was also ill and had to go to Scarborough for some months for a cure. His aunt, Lady Caroline Duff Gordon, was very pleased about the canonry and thought it would do him good, though he already had two parishes to occupy his pastoral interests:

> Saturday 12th July. I heard what gave me great pleasure that
> Gilbert Lewis is to be the new canon of Worcester ... I am very
> glad as it will give him something new to do & to think about.

> Sunday 13th July. ... [Gilbert] is much bowed down with sorrow
> for the loss of his little boy Lindsay, and at Jane's protracted
> illness & being sent to Scarborough by Dr Packham for her
> health.[97]

Why was Gilbert so interested in the Worcester canonry? The
Lewises had no family livings. The patrons of Old Radnor were the
Dean and Chapter of Worcester and it was unlikely that Gilbert would
be presented to it because since 1834 it had been held by the Revd
Henry Fullelove Mogridge, MA, an exact contemporary of Gilbert,
and they graduated at Cambridge in the same year.[98] Anyhow, the
stipend of £200 a year and a mere three acres of glebe were not attractive, nor perhaps were the pastoral demands of a population of 1,349.

Mogridge remained at Old Radnor for thirty-two years and in the
1840s built himself a vicarage at his own expense, for which he had to
borrow £500. He seems, however, though he at least shared their politics,[99] not to have enjoyed the particular favour of either George or
Gilbert Lewis. In his account of their father's funeral in 1855 he is
mentioned by George simply in passing as 'Mr Mogridge, the clergyman of Old Radnor'. He was active in the repairs to the church in
1855–56, but Caroline Duff Gordon has little to say in his favour:

> I walked alone to Old Radnor Church & went into it. I have
> never been there since poor Sir Frankland was buried there,
> and George is going to put up a monument to his memory
> there. The church has been repaired since I have been & now
> the clergyman, Mr Mogridge does not chuse to do the Service
> there because 'he finds it cold'.[100]

The Lewises had more cordial relations with the Revd George
Richard Turner, MA, who became Rector of New Radnor in 1855. He
also enjoyed the approval of the Banks family. He was one of the six
sons of Sir George James Turner, DCL, FRS, and MP for Coventry
1847–51. In 1853 he became a Lord Justice of Appeal, remaining so
until he died in 1867. The rector had some distinguished relations as
well: his paternal uncle, William Turner was a diplomat and author
and a friend of Canning, and his great uncle, Joseph Turner, was in
succession tutor of William Pitt, Master of Pembroke College,
Cambridge, and Dean of Norwich.

Turner was popular with his parishioners and in February 1855
we find him writing to Lewis, congratulating him on his re-election as
the member for the Radnor boroughs and on his appointment as

Chancellor of the Exchequer. Lewis celebrated his re-election with a present of coal to the poor of New Radnor, which, on their behalf, the rector duly acknowledges. Then, later in the year, events took a different and somewhat surprising turn, and on Wednesday 31st October 1855 Lewis recorded in his diary:

> Harpton. Wrote some *Review.* In the evening just before dinner, came a letter from Lord Justice Turner who was staying with his son the clergyman at Radnor, proposing on behalf of his son to Therese. Theresa sent a civil refusal.

It is Lady Theresa Lewis who declines the offer of marriage on behalf of her daughter, Therese, since Therese was the child of Lady Lewis's first marriage. Lady Lewis obviously had no doubts about the matter and replied to Lord Justice Turner that night. This generated instant, but good natured, responses both from Lord Chief Justice Turner and his son:

> Thursday Nov 1. Harpton. Letters this morning from Lord Justice Turner & his son, taking Theresa's answer in good part.[101]

Four years later Therese married the distinguished lawyer and Liberal statesman Sir William George Granville Venables Vernon Harcourt, perhaps in the social stakes a far more distinguished matrimonial choice. Also, unlike Turner's father, a Conservative, he shared the same political sympathies as the Lewises. Mr Turner remained at New Radnor, and appears in the Duff Gordon Diaries as a frequent guest at Harpton until 1866, when he was presented to the living of Kelshall, near Royston, in Hertfordshire.[102]

But to return to Mr Mogridge, the Vicar of Old Radnor. Jonathan Williams, the Radnorshire historian, deplored the handling of the Old Radnor tithes and sympathised with the lot of its clergyman:

> The present lessee [of the tithes] is T Frankland Lewis, Esq, of Harpton Court, at a low rent, out of which is paid the salary of the vicar that is so small as to be insufficient to maintain him [ie the parson] in that degree of rank and estimation which he ought to hold in society. This custom, which is prevalent in many parts of Wales, tends to degrade the ministerial office, shake the stability of the church establishment, and open the door to schism and separation.[103]

Matters came to something of a head in 1846 when accusations were made at the Vestry Meeting against both the Dean and Chapter and the Lewis family to whom the tithes were still being leased. Major JA Whittaker of Newcastle Court,[104] demanded at the meeting that the Dean and Chapter should mend their ways and gradually restore the tithes to the use of the parish. He alleged that they and their lessess had between them made a profit of £32,000 during the thirty years up to 1841, but they had given 'not one farthing to the parish church which is in a state of great dilapidation'.[105]

Amongst the contributors from whom Lewis commissioned articles when he became editor of the *Edinburgh Review* in 1852 was the Revd William John Conybeare, whose paper on ecclesiastical factions enjoyed his particular approval.[106]

John Conybeare's father was dean of Llandaff and is gratefully remembered for restoring his sadly delapidated cathedral. Before that he had been vicar of Sully in Glamorgan. John, therefore had extensive first hand knowledge of the Church of England in Wales, but his judgement, in which Lewis had such confidence, on the Church in Wales was harsh:

> Even now, within sight of those cathedrals we associate with Copleston[107] and Thirlwall,[108] indigenous pastors are to be found who cannot speak English grammatically and who frequent the rural tavern in company with the neighbouring farmers.[109]

Lewis's gardening and bow-drawing, but largely absentee, brother was for him an example of the educated, respected, and disciplined clergy he desired to see dispensing the greatest possible good to the greatest possible number. There were, however, examples of the mountain clergy in his midst of whom, despite their pastoral devotion, he makes no mention. This is all the more remarkable because one of them, the Revd David Vaughan, occasionally served Gilbert as his curate at Gladestry.

David Vaughan was born at Nantmel, Radnorshire in 1819, a farmer's son. He was educated at Llanavan in Cardiganshire and entered St David's College in October 1845 as one of the thirty-six freshmen of that year.[110] A student of mature years, he was twenty-six and married. His wife was two years his senior and also came from Nantmel, and they had a son born in 1844. His background must have been reasonably prosperous, for besides having a wife and family to maintain, for all its intentions of being less expensive than Oxford and Cambridge, in 1848 it cost £50 a year to keep a student at

Lampeter. This was as much as David Vaughan earned in 1851 as Curate of Glascwm, and was prohibitive for many Welsh ordinands.

It is unlikely that David Vaughan received much encouragement for ordination from the vicar of Nantmel. Richard Venables was an absentee vicar who held the living with that of Llanyre in plurality with Clyro, as well as being Archdeacon of Carmarthen and a prebendary of Christ College, Brecon. From 1830 until his death in 1858 Venables lived mainly at Llysdinam Hall near Newbridge on Wye. Nor would there have been much encouragement from Richard Lister Venables, his son, who served as curate of Nantmel before succeeding his father at Clyro. It was there, in 1865, that Kilvert became his curate and Venables told his brother he was glad to have a university man, a great improvement on his predecessor. David Vaughan would not have been Venables's idea of the ideal curate.

Nevertheless, David Vaughan prospered at his studies of Lampeter and was elected Phillips scholar in June 1846. By the time he gained his certificate from the college in June 1849 he also had four children. He was made deacon by Connop Thirwall in December, 1849 in the chapel of the bishop's palace at Abergwili and served his title as curate of Glascwm where, according to the census of 1851, he was living in the vicarage with his wife, four children, and a servant. The newly ordained David Vaughan was thus sent to serve a parish which had an absentee vicar there, whilst being in only deacon's orders himself, and unable to celebrate Holy Communion for his parishioners. This state of affairs continued until 1851, when he returned to Abergwili to be ordained priest by Thirwall. He was then joined at Glascwm by a new vicar, the Revd Benjamin Marsden, whom Kilvert described as 'one of the last old-fashioned parsons' and who moved into the vicarage thereby displacing the Vaughan family.

Continuing as curate of Glascwm, David Vaughan made his new home in Newchurch from where Colva, one of the two outlying chapelries of Glascwm, was as accessible as it was from Glascwm. Newchurch at this time also had had an absent rector, the Revd JB Byers, for many years. Inducted in 1828, he had followed another absentee, none other than Richard Venables, vicar of Clyro, and who had been David Vaughan's absentee vicar at Nantmel. Venables's predecessor at Newchurch was also an absentee.

Thus Newchurch was looked after by a long succession of curates, some of whom were also absentees. In 1853, one of these was the Revd

JN Walsh, MA, headmaster of Lady Hawkins School, Kington, whom Gilbert Lewis was to use as his curate at Gladestry. Others were Benjamin Marsden, the new vicar of Glascwm; and David Vaughan.

The emphasis of Lewis's religious practice was not sacramental and there are no references to the eucharist in his diaries. There is though in his diary for 1859 a clue to his eucharistic standpoint. Good Friday that year, 22nd April, saw him at church at Ennismore Gardens. The following day he travelled, with his wife Theresa and step-daughter Therese, by the morning train from Paddington, arriving at Harpton in time for dinner. Easter Day, April 24th, was wet, he says, and he stayed at home. There is nothing about his going to church or reading prayers at home because he did *not* go to church, and there is nothing about his being unwell. Indeed next day, Easter Monday, he had energy enough to go to Presteign where he canvassed the town with Mr Jonathan Green, a local lawyer. But Lewis knew his Prayer Book and was familiar with the rubric: 'Every parishioner shall communicate at the least three times a year, of which Easter to be one'. Thus, the absence was intentional and its explanation lies in the likelihood that he made what he saw as his Easter communion on Good Friday at Ennismore Gardens. Mrs Esther Crummer of Howey Hall, sister of James Davies, one of Lewis's Kington friends, records in her diary for Good Friday that she went to church at Disserth and 'stay'd to the sacrament'. Nowadays Good Friday tends to be the one day of the year upon which holy communion is not celebrated, but some things were different in those pre-Tractarian days, and one can be quite certain there was not a trace of Puseyism at Ennismore Gardens whilst Lewis sat in one its numerous pews.

Chapter 9:
Sudden Death

The seasonal monotony of drawing up the Army and Navy estimates, a January chore for the Secretary of State for War, was relieved in 1862 for Lewis by the publication that month of his *An Historical Survey of the Astronomy of the Ancients*. It was received well and within six weeks arrangements were in hand for its translation into German. Reviewers were quick to point out that Lewis's approach to his subject was something of a new departure, 'written with a different object from that of any preceding historian'.[1] The astronomical histories, for example, of the great French astronomer and mathematician Jean Baptiste Joseph Delambre were the work of astronomers for astronomers, whereas Lewis was writing for a wider readership, since the history of astronomy:

> has numerous points of contact with the general history of mankind, and concerns questions which interest a wider class than professed astronomers, for whose benefit the existing histories have been mainly composed.[2]

Thus, it appeared to Lewis

> that an attempt might be advantageously made to treat the history of ancient astronomy, without exclusive reference to physical science, and without any pretension on his part to that proficient and comprehensive knowledge of modern mathematical astronomy which some of his predecessors in the treatment of this subject have possessed.[3]

One of the first reviews of the book appeared in the *Saturday Review*[4] and noted that in Lewis's eyes the new science of Egyptology[5] had a historical method of its own which hardly merited serious consideration. The German diplomatist and amateur theologian Christian Carl Josias Bunsen came in for Lewis's particular condemnation, and his judgement has been endorsed by modern critics who see his voluminous writings as having 'little enduring value'.[6] As a lawyer Lewis thought the Egyptologists disregarded all the rules of evidence and made unbounded demands upon their readers' credulity.[7]

But Lewis is too ready to tar uncritically scholars of very different stature with the same brush. That he should ridicule Bunsen is not surprising, his poor regard, however, for Carl Richard Lepsius shows less discernment. Nowadays Lepsius is remembered as the father of German Egyptology and is still regarded by some as doyen of Egyptologists. He surveyed the pyramids and in 1842–45 led the famous expedition to Egypt and Nubia sponsored by King Willhelm IV of Prussia, publishing his findings in twelve volumes, which still command respect.[8]

Lewis wanted the techniques of modern history applied to its ancient counterpart, whereas he saw the Egyptologist as one whose:

> imagination is captivated with the faculty of creating or annihilating dynasties by a magic stroke of his pen; he becomes, in the language of the ancient astrologers, a chronocrator.[9] He likewise appears to possess a sort of second sight, by which he is able to look back into the unknown past, and discern images invisible to ordinary eyes.[10]

In February seasonal ills and the Army and Navy estimates reasserted themselves and it was the bills of the current session, which in March took Lewis to Windsor:

> I went down to Windsor Castle, & had an interview with the Queen, & also with the Princess Royal, who was staying at Windsor. The Queen talked much about the Prince, & received me in his room. She looks thin, but does not seem out of health, though she thinks unfavourably of herself. She intends never to lay aside her mourning, never to partake in amusements, not to invite people to dinner &c. This I heard from the Princess Royal.[11]

Entries in Lewis's diary were becoming less detailed, and instead of being made day by day, often covered ten or more days.[12] News of published work seems to gratify him more than his politics:

> An article of mine on the Roman Book Trade under the Empire is published in *Fraser's Magazine* for April. It was written in the Autumn.[13]

His waning interest in politics, reflected in less detailed political entries in his diary, was also the subject of the entry on his birthday, 21st April:

> Today I am 56 years old. I am grown rather weaker & my breath is shorter. I feel the fatigues of office & parliamentary attendance, & should be glad to be relieved from both. I find, as I grow older, that my taste for study increases & my taste for business diminishes.

In this frame of mind, it is not too much of a surprise a few days later to find Lewis, who used to have so little time for the trivial, writing the epilogue for private theatricals at the Grove.[14] But cheer, admittedly of mixed quality, was at hand in the form of a review of the *Astronomy* in *The Times*. The anonymous reviewer admitted to a certain sensations of *déjà vu*. The memory of Lewis's two volume 1855 *Inquiry into the Credibility of the Early Roman History* was still fresh in the reviewer's mind:

> The historical survey of the progress of astronomical knowledge among the ancients which our industrious War Minister has given to the public bears the appearance of having grown out of the previous inquiry into the nature of Early History, a subject which has notoriously been a favorite with the translator of *Muller's Dorians*.[15] The connexion of the two is sufficiently obvious.[16]

There was no doubting Lewis's scholarship, but his style and presentation were a different matter:

> His book is a repertory of solid learning, and no less characterized by good sense than scholarship, but it must be confessed that it is heavy reading. His collections are extremely valuable, but they are rather poured out than worked up. The several chapters read like so many *pièces justiificatives* of opinions advanced elsewhere. In the sirloin placed before us the turnips and the oil-cake on which the ox was fatted remain recognizable, and this must needs dull the edge of any common appetite.[17]

All the same, the book was a welcome and an encouraging challenge to the long established German domination of classical scholarship.

> However, the sterling value of the book is such that if it find comparatively few readers, every one of these will probably be a purchaser; and the classical scholars of England, for whose good opinion the writer probably is more anxious than that of any other class, will feel pride in the performance of one of their own number unsurpassed by any analogous German publication during the last 20 years, and equalled by very few.[18]

Lewis was a Commissioner for the 1862 Great Exhibition which opened on May 1st. It was but a step from Kent House and Lewis was there:

> Attended the opening of the Great Exhibition at Kensington & walked in the procession with the other ministers.[19]

He went again on Derby day and it was the dress of those who attended rather than the quality of the exhibits that gained his comment:

> Day of the Derby, a holiday. I went to the Great Exhibition which was very full. There were scarcely any persons who were not well dressed.[20]

Good design was held to be a major consideration in arranging the exhibits and every important type and process of contemporary manufacture was on show, including the great chancel screen made for Hereford Cathedral awaiting installation. Nowadays it is seen as one of the monuments of High Victorian art, a masterpiece in the Gothic Revival style. It was designed by Sir George Gilbert Scott, and made by the Coventry metalworking firm of Francis Skidmore.[21] It was praised by the *Illustrated London News* as:

> the grandest most triumphant achievement of modern architectural art ... far the most important and most successful example of modern metalwork that has been executed.[22]

It is strange that Lewis made no mention of the screen in either his diaries or his letters, bearing in mind his connection with the city of Hereford and his friendship with the dean, Richard Dawes. Perhaps he shared the opinion of his aunt, Lady Duff Gordon, who was less enthusiastic than the *Illustrated London News* about it:

> Eastnor Castle. We went in very hard rain to see the cathedral, quite renovated since I last saw it, it is very beautiful now that all the stone work is cleared of the horrible whitewash, the new screen [that was exhibited in the Palace of Industry, the

Exhibition in 1862] is there, handsome & well done. But I don't think that it suits the Church, too much gilding about it.[23]

It is possible that Lewis's silence about this great talking point is connected with his disapproval of Tractarianism and his fear that high church principles may become rooted in the diocese of Hereford. His silence about its careful and imaginative medievalism was certainly unrelated to any lack of interest in history, and two days after his first visit to the Exhibition he was writing to Lord Stanhope, the historian and great advocate of a British National Portrait Gallery:

> I have written a letter to Lord Stanhope proposing a plan for a list of historical portraits in the United Kingdom, & have received his answer, approving of it.[24]

At the same time, another leading historian of the day was corresponding with Lewis. This was Edward Augustus Freeman, Fellow of Trinity College, Oxford. Twice overlooked for an Oxford chair, he was not elected there as Professor of Modern History until 1884. He could be very difficult, but 'though his temper was impatient, and he was apt to be rude to people who were distasteful to him, he was truly kind, generous-hearted, and loveable'.[25] Lewis was obviously not amongst those whom Freeman found distasteful and wrote to him:

> I hope I am not taking a liberty in thanking you for putting out your book on 'Ancient Astronomy', which I am reading with perfect delight. I cannot follow the astronomical part, but I cannot fancy a greater service to history than you have done, by upsetting all the Egyptian and Babylonian dreams which have filled people's heads for some years past.[26]

Lewis, though flattered, did not hasten to reply. Later, however, he did describe Freeman's *History of Federal Government,* as 'a work deserving the attentive perusal of all students of ancient history'.[27] Lewis's immediate attention was engaged by the fact that a meeting of the Society of Antiquaries was looming at which it was possible that the *Astronomy* would receive a less enthusiastic welcome. The meeting took place in the evening of 15th May, with the railway architect William Tite, a Vice-President of the Society and MP for Bath, in the Chair.[28] The principal speaker that evening was a distinguished Egyptologist, Reginald Stuart Poole, an Assistant in the Department of Antiquities in the British Museum since 1852, and his theme was the 'correctness of the method of interpreting hieroglyphics originated by Dr Young and developed by Champollion'. The physician and Egyptologist Thomas Young partially deciphered the Rosetta stone and Jean Francois Champollion was the French Egyptologist who in 1822 deciphered the system of Egyptian hieroglyphics with the aid of the Stone. Poole commenced his paper by calling attention to Lewis's attack on Egyptology in his *Historical Survey of the Astronomy of the Ancients*, arguing that he had not fully investigated the question.[29]

Lewis came to the meeting of the Society of Antiquaries, of which he was not a fellow, after a day in the office. Whilst he must have known what the subject was of the evening's lecture and that it would almost inevitably refer to the *Astronomy*, if no more than in passing, he was later to claim that his reply to Poole, given at the Chairman's invitation:

> was necessarily extemporary and unpremeditated: it followed immediately upon a discourse by Mr. Poole, containing a criticism of my treatment of the question of Egyptian Hieroglyphics in a volume lately published; it was in substance an answer to Mr Poole's arguments.[30]

His response was Lewis at his best: courteous but resolute:

> He began by stating that nothing could be more temperate or legitimate than Mr Poole's criticism on the remarks in which he had indulged in his work on the Astronomy of the Ancients. Those remarks he regretted the less as they had been the means of calling forth an exposition of so high a character from one of the champions of Egyptology, whose address he had listened to with so much interest. He saw nothing, however, in that address to modify the opinions he had put forward in his *Survey of the Astronomy of the Ancients*, respecting the current interpretation of Egyptian hieroglyphics. He had no wish to dogmatize on the subject. To invite discussion among the learned and to warn the public generally against a too credulous adhesion to the statements put forward by Egyptian scholars, were the only objects he had in view.[31]

Charles Wycliffe Goodwin replied to Lewis's impromptu speech. He was the only layman to contribute to the controversial *Essays and Reviews* of 1860, in which his 'plain-spoken essay' discussed the relationship between geology and the accounts of the creation in Genesis. An Egyptologist of great distinction, Goodwin's exchange with Lewis won a place in the *Dictionary of National Biography*:

In May 1862 at a meeting of the Society of Antiquaries, to which Goodwin sent several communications on those subjects, he replied to Sir George Cornewall Lewis' scepticism, expressed in person, as to the possibility of interpreting the ancient Egyptian by arguing that Coptic was in some degree a continuation of that language.

Lewis, however, was rather less gracious in his diary than he was in speech:

Mr Poole of the British Museum made a speech, in support of the received method of interpreting Egyptian hieroglyphics, & in answer to the arguments in my volume on ancient astronomy, & Mr Goodwin answered me. The attempts to support [the] system seemed to me feeble, & to add little or nothing new.[32]

The Society of Antiquaries, however, wanted to hear, or rather read, more and at its next meeting, with Lord Stanhope, the Society's president in the chair, a unanimous resolution was passed asking Lewis

that he would (if his leisure should allow) put in writing the valuable and interesting observations addressed by him to the Meeting of this Society on the 15th of May; and if he has the kindness to comply with that request, the Society would propose to themselves the gratification of making public, combined with the other selected papers in the *Archaeologia*, the communication afforded them.[33]

But Lewis declined the invitation on the grounds that his remarks were spontaneous and made in reply to the argument of another speaker.

In order to fit my remarks for publication in the *Archaeologia* it would be necessary to divest them of their controversial character, and to compose an essay, treating the question on affirmative grounds, independent of all reference to Mr Poole's address. It is possible that I may hereafter have time for such a treatment of the subject, but it would carry me beyond the limits contemplated in the Resolution of the Society.[34]

This reply is rather surprising because he had a pen of a ready writer and was not usually reluctant to go into print. Despite the prestige of the Society of Antiquaries, or perhaps because, as he said in his diary, their arguments were feeble and unoriginal, he considered them unworthy of his attention. This impression is supported by his reply to Freeman, written after the episode with the Antiquaries, in which he complains that no one has taken up his challenge:

> I am greatly pleased to find that a judge so competent as your-self approves of my chapter on ancient Egyptian and Assyrian history. It seemed to me that the Egyptologists and the Interpreters of cuneiform were taking undue liberties with the credulity of the public, and that it was high time for somebody to interfere. I wish that the task had been undertaken by some one who had more time to devote to the subject, and who had more knowledge of Oriental languages. But I have at least thrown down the gauntlet, and I am surprised that no one has hitherto taken it up, at least in print. I suppose they say that they are so insignificant as not to deserve notice.[35]

The often-acerbic Freeman was encouraging in his reply and was more than willing to help the *Astronomy* along with a sympathetic review.[36] The anonymous reviewer, however, in the *North British Review* was not unqualified in his praise, noting that Lewis's conclusions were usually rather than *always* sound:

> We have thus endeavoured, at a very humble distance to follow Sir George Lewis in his *Survey of the Astronomy and Chronology of the Ancients*, limiting ourselves to a brief and simple abstract of the more important or popular topics to which he calls our attention. Our readers must peruse the work itself to form an idea of the stores of learning it contains, the ingenious and profound criticisms which characterize it, and the sound conclusions at which its author usually arrives.[37]

What really mattered, though, in the opinion of the reviewer, was that in Lewis was one of the very few scholars and philosophers who had made their way into British politics.

> But, independently of the value of this work in its literary and scientific relations, it will be read with an additional interest as the production of one of the ablest and wisest of our modern statesmen. We have often had occasion to remark in these pages how rarely men of profound acquirements in literature and science have been called to discharge any public functions under government, either of a diplomatic or administrative nature; while in foreign countries, and under arbitrary govern-ments, the same class of men have been extensively employed. We have expressed our surprise that men of theoretical and

practical talent have not found their way into the House of Commons, where great questions of practical science and national interest are to be decided, and where wisdom without eloquence is one of the highest qualifications of a legislator.

Sir George Cornewall Lewis is one of the few examples of a public servant yoked in the harness of the State, and successfully pursuing the higher studies of literature, politics, and philosophy. The calm dignity and unswerving consistency with which he discharged the less responsible duties of official life, and the reputation he has acquired as a scholar and philosopher, have raised him to several of the highest positions in the Cabinet; and we have no doubt that, in the bright roll of public men, to whom Providence has committed the destinies of England, there will not be found a wiser and a safer pilot to conduct the vessel of the State through the perils which have for some time been looming in the horizon of our country.[38]

Whilst *An Historical Survey of the Astronomy of the Ancient* may seem a worthy diversion for the Secretary of State for War, it comes as something of a surprise to find him at the same time being equally energetic in an attempt to disprove the existence of centenarians. The subject had come up in the autumn of 1860 when Edward Twistelton was staying at Harpton. Twistleton, who seems not to have shared Lewis's opinion, in noting the conversation was careful to allow Lewis some ambiguity of expression:

> Sir GC Lewis told me at Harpton he did not think there was sufficient evidence to show that anyone had exceeded the age of one hundred and nine years. I did not understand him to deny the possibility of the fact; but to speak only of evidence for the fact.[39]

In May 1862 it was the subject of a correspondence between Lewis and Edward Twistleton, but Lewis's encyclopaedic memory recollected a paper on the subject nine years earlier in the *Quarterly Review*.[40]

> If I am not mistaken, there was an article on the Countess of Desmond in the *Quarterly Review* a year or two ago. There is likewise an account of old Parr by Hervey in Hervey's works,[41] as well as in the *Harleian Miscellany*. I believe that it may be stated generally that no instance exists of any member of a royal or noble family, whose birth was registered when it occurred, having attained the age of a hundred years.[42]

Interest in the Countess's alleged longevity had been revived in 1860 by the publication of the Ven Arthur Blenner-Hassett Rowan's *Olde Countesse of Desmonde, her identitie, her portraiture, her descente,*[43] and Richard Sainthill's two volume *Old Countess of Desmond, an Inquiry,* 1861–63.[44] The Countess of Desmond in question was sometimes stated to have died at the age of 140, and sometimes of 162 years and engaged the attention of the Victorian antiquary Revd William Dunn Macray.[45] It was his considered judgement that:

> On the whole, it may be concluded that the countess reached at least the age of 104, and that, until some further evidence, such as the date of her marriage, be forthcoming, it may further reasonably be conjectured that the addition of ten years would very probably be a nearer approximation to the truth.[46]

Old Parr was said to have reached the age of 152 years and 9 months, spanning the years 1483–1635, and was born at Winnington in the parish of Alberbury, thirteen miles west of Shrewsbury. In 1563, being then eighty years of age, he married his first wife Jane Taylor whom he buried in 1595. Ten years later he married Jane Adda, widow and in 1635 he came to the attention of Thomas Howard, second earl of Arundel, 'the most accomplished curiosity-hunter of his day', who determined to exhibit this 'piece of antiquity' at court. He sent him up to London by easy stages in a specially constructed litter. It was, however, all too much for him, and he died in November 1865 in Lord Arundel's town house. The physician William Harvey conducted an autopsy and noted the singularly healthy condition of his organs, ascribing his death mainly to the change of air. He was buried in the south transept of Westminster Abbey.[47] In the opinion of Thomas Seccombe:

> The exact age of Parr is attested by village gossip alone, and the statement that he was born in 1483 must be regarded as extremely improbable. Sir George Cornewall Lewis and WJ Thoms discredit the story of his antediluvian age as unsupported by a jot of trustworthy evidence.[48]

That the antiquary William John Thoms, FSA, shared Lewis's opinion is interesting and suggests it was not quite so idiosyncratic as might at first appear. Thoms, besides being for many years the secretary of the Camden Society, was first editor of *Notes & Queries*, to which Lewis was a frequent contributor.[49] His iconoclastic treatise on *Human Longevity, its Facts and its Fictions*, appeared in 1873, and raised a storm of dismayed protest by its forcible contention that the authentic cases in which human life had been prolonged to a hundred years and upwards were extremely rare. Although Thoms proved less sceptical than Sir George Cornewall Lewis, not even the histories of Jenkins, Parr, or the Countess of Desmond satisfied his tests of legal evidence.[50]

Lewis makes no mention of Henry Jenkins, who died in 1670, acclaimed as the 'modern Methuselah'. He claimed to have been born c.1501, but in the record of his burial in Bolton churchyard, he is described simply as 'a very aged and poore man'. His biographer in the *DNB* is of the opinion that 'belief in his marvellous age rests upon no better evidence than Jenkins's own contradictory statements'.[51]

In April 1862 Thoms published in *Notes & Queries*, an article from Lewis on the subject of centenarians. Despite his ministerial and academic commitments, Lewis had thought it an appropriate use of his time to research the subject in some depth:

> It may, I believe, be stated as a fact that (limiting ourselves to the time since the Christian era) no person of royal or noble rank mentioned in history, whose birth was recorded at the time of its occurrence, reached the age of 100 years. I am not aware that the modern peerage and baronetage books contain any such case, resting upon authentic evidence. I have been informed that no well-established case of a life exceeding 100 years has occurred in the experience of companies for the insurance of lives. These facts raise a presumption that human life under its existing conditions, is never prolonged beyond a hundred years.
>
> Nevertheless, the obituaries of modern newspapers contain from time to time, the deaths of persons who are alleged to have outlived this age. It may be conjectured that these statements of longevity are in general made on the authority of the individual's own memory. Now, there are many reasons why old persons should be mistaken about their age, if their memory is not corrected by written documents. Even with persons in easy circumstances, great age is a subject of curiosity, wonder, and solicitude; with persons in a humbler rank of life, it is a ground of sympathy, interest, and charity. It is therefore not unnatural that a person, whose real age exceeds ninety years and who has no contemporaries to check his statements, should, without intending to commit any deliberate deceit, represent his age as greater than the reality.
>
> The only conclusive proof of a person's age is a contemporary record of his birth, or the declaration of a person who

remembers its occurrence. If there are now persons living whose age exceeds 100 years, such evidence surely can be obtained, and its production would remove all doubt on the question.

The writer of these remarks has investigated several cases in which life was alleged to have lasted beyond 100 years, but it is difficult to obtain documentary evidence of the fact. The following case affords an illustration of the result of such researches. A pamphlet has recently been published at Oxford by Mr Tyerman, a medical practitioner of that city, entitled *Notices of the Life of John Pratt*, now in his 106th Year. In this pamphlet it is started that John Pratt is resident at Oxford and that the writer of it is personally acquainted with him. The account of John Pratt's birth and age given in it must rest on his own testimony. The account (p.4) is, that 'He was born at Grendon under Wood in Buckinghamshire, on the fifth day of March, 1756, and was the eldest of three children; that his father, who was a shoemaker, and a diligent man, died at the age of 75; that his mother completed her 105th year, and his great-grandmother her 111th.' Through the kindness of a friend, I have ascertained from the Revd M Marshall, the incumbent of Grendon-Underwood, in Buckinghamshire, that the parish register of the period (which is preserved) contains no entry of the baptism of John Pratt at or near the year 1766, although it contains various entries of baptisms, marriages, and burials of persons named Pratt from 1740 to 1783. The old man himself has no entry in a bible, or other documentary evidence in confirmation of his statement; and his account of his age appears to rest exclusively upon his own memory.

It is argued in favour of the belief in rare cases of excessive longevity that they would be in analogy with other ascertained peculiarities of human physiology. There have been men of extraordinary height; there have been minute dwarfs; there have been men of enormous fatness; there have also been men of extreme tenuity. Why then, it is asked, should there not be a few centenarians? This question may be answered by saying that such a duration of life does not seem, *a priori*, inconsistent with the laws of nature; but that the existence of very tall and very short, of very fat and very thin men, is proved by the indubitable evidence of eye-witnesses, whereas there is not on record, in published books, any conclusive proof of a life which has been prolonged beyond 100 years, under the existing conditions of our physical nature.

> I have, however, recently obtained the particulars of a life exceeding 100 years, which appear to be perfectly authentic, and to admit of no doubt. Mrs Esther Strike was buried in the parish of Cranburne St Peters, in the county of Berks on the 22nd of February, 1862; she was the daughter of George and Ann Jackman and she was privately baptized on June 3, and publicly baptized on June 26, 1764, in the parish of Winkfiefd, in the same county. She was therefore in her 103rd year. Certified extracts of the two registers proving these facts have been furnished to me through the kindness of the Revd C.J Elliott, Vicar of Winkfield.[52]

Not surprisingly Thoms endorsed Lewis's paper as 'valuable'. The state registration of all births, marriages, and deaths in England and Wales began in July 1837, though from 1801 a national census was taken every ten years, the accuracy of which before 1841 was often uncertain. Before 1801 the registers of baptisms and funerals kept at parish churches were the main sources of documentary evidence for longevity. Their entries were made by parish clerks, often of uncertain education in general and literacy in particular. Entries in family Bibles were frequently no more reliable. Consequently unsubstantiated traditions of longevity abounded and Lewis's article brought forth a good number of them in the pages of *Notes & Queries* and Thoms cautioned his readers to apply Lewis's standards of scholarship to their researches:

> We hope that, in future, correspondents who send us instances of longevity will follow Sir George's example, and first ascertain that there exists some evidence that the parties were really of the age stated. Ed. *N&Q.*[53]

One of his correspondents was the Revd William Dunn Macray, already encountered as the author of the *DNB* article on the Countess of Desmond. Rector of Duckington near Witney, he was also an Oxford don, and called on John Pratt, whose age Lewis doubted, in Oxford:

> On the 2nd of the present month (May), I called on John Pratt, in company with the curate of the parish, in which he lives, with the view of ascertaining, if possible, the evidence by which his assertion respecting his age may be proved. I found him in wonderfully good health, but nearly blind; feeble in his limbs, but with his voice strong and faculties remarkably clear.

His appearance is very venerable, and his countenance pleasing. His chief infirmity appears to be a constant wakefulness, and he complains beside of pains in his head, and of becoming soon confused and dizzy on attempting to think much. He is however, cheerful; and appears to be waiting his appointed time in a spirit of pious trust and hopefulness. He is not, I am glad to be informed, in any actual distress, although poor: one head of a college, and several members of this university, frequently contributing to his relief, and the visitors of the parish affording occasional help. With regard to his age, he gave as the date of his birth the same which is mentioned in Mr Tyerman's pamphlet, viz. 5th March, 1756 ... With reference to the fact, that the entry of his baptism is not found in the register of Grendon under Wood, he says that he was baptised privately when one week old and, since the registers were not kept with scrupulous exactness in the last century, as well as somewhat later, it is probable that the entry may through this cause have been forgotten. He states that he had a family Bible in which the date of his father's birth, as well as of his own, was entered; that it was from this entry that his own knowledge of the date was derived, and that he is certain of the accuracy of his recollection. This Bible he used to carry with him in his wanderings, until it was torn out: he then copied the entries on a paper, which he carried with him in a tin box; but at length, during one of his journeys, the box was lost, and with it was lost all the evidence he had of his age. I forgot to ask him where his first marriage took place, the register of which would of course afford sufficiently proximate proof concurrently with that of the baptism of his eldest son, ... but he incidentally mentioned, in the course of conversation, that the first of *fourteen* Scottish peregrinations was made in the year 1780, eighty-two years ago. It is hardly probable that a self-taught Oxfordshire 'simpler', all of whose travels were made on foot, would be induced to extend his tour to the wilds and moors of Scotland, for the sake of a few rare herbs not to be met with in the rich dells and woods of the South, before he had reached that age which, if Pratt's memory be correct, this year assigns.

It appears from your correspondence, that authenticated instances of as great longevity are by no means unknown; but as Pratt's case has obtained an unusual degree of notice, it may be worth while to endeavour to verify it still more positively. If any of your readers, who may have been interested by the notice of him, should feel disposed to forward any trifling contribution towards increasing his few comforts, or mitigating the burden which his load of years imposes, I shall be happy to be the bearer of their alms when calling on him once more (as I propose to do), to make inquiry about the place and date of his marriage. WD Macray, Magdalen College, Oxford.[54]

Mr Macray was as good as his word and *did* interview Pratt again and informed the readers of *Notes & Queries* that

The fact that both baptismal and marriage registers are not to be found, creates a grave suspicion that Pratt's alleged age does not admit of proof; although his own appearance certainly shows that he has long passed the usual limits of man's longest life. It is observable that in Mr Tyerman's account of him, his first wife (to whom he was married when he was twenty-three years old) is said to have borne the somewhat romantic name of Maria Dellamore. I am informed that the town clerk of Oxford (Mr G Hester) has been also making inquiries upon this subject with a view to publication, and that he does not give credit to Pratt's alleged age.[55]

The most improbable evidence of longevity and its demographical excited by Lewis's paper was a quotation from a letter written in July 1756 by George, Lord Lyttleton, to a certain Mr Bower 'with an Account of a Tour in Wales'. His Lordship was at that time in the vicinity of Festiniog:

Not long ago there died in that neighbourhood an honest Welsh farmer, who was 105 years of age. By his first wife he had thirty children, ten by his second, four by his third, and seven by two concubines. His youngest son was eighty-one years younger than his eldest; and 800 persons, descended from his body, attended his funeral.[56]

Another correspondent, a certain SF Creswell, of The Castle, Tonbridge, Kent, a sociologist before his time, perceived the relevance of class, diet, and housing:

Sir GC Lewis will probably be interested in being informed of the fact, which is undoubted and beyond question, that during the last six or seven years three persons have died in the county of Sussex, all of whom lived to upwards of one hundred years. They belonged to the gentry of the county, were well educated, and were to the last in the habit of mingling more or less in society. In that society, years before they became centenarians, their age was a topic of conversation and remark; any exaggeration as regards age would, therefore, have been easily detected by those who were their contemporaries or a few years their seniors. I believe no Sussex person, who was acquainted with either of these individuals; ever entertained a doubt of their being of the age ascribed to them. Their names were, Mr Trotty, rector of Fairlight; Mrs. Mary Turner, of Ditchling; and Mrs. Constable, of Cowfold.[57]

Cresswell then continues with a practical suggestion to assist Lewis's research:

The question could be sifted if some one, having access to the Registrar General's returns, would pass in your columns a list of persons reputed to be of the age of 100 years and more at the census of 1861. Local friends of *N & Q* could then test the entries; always remembering that family names repeat themselves even simultaneously among brothers and sisters.[58]

The correspondence arising from his paper caused Lewis to modify his thesis, having been supplied by a Mr Cunningham of Edinburgh with an account of two cases of centenarians supported by what he accepted to be authentic evidence. However, he was not yet completely ready to abandon his case:

It will be observed that the case mentioned in my previous article, and the two cases supplied by Mr Cuningham, are all of female lives. I have not hitherto been able to obtain conclusive evidence of a male centenarian.[59]

And so it continued through the summer and interest in Lewis's view continued for some years. Thus, in 1870 there appeared *Life of Thomas Geeran, a Centenarian, with photograph & autograph; being an answer to the late Sir George Cornewall Lewis, on his theory of longevity.*[60] This was followed a year later by *Longevity, with Life, Autograph, and Portrait of Thomas Geeran, a Centenarian.*[61]

Thomas Geeran was an Irishman who died in Brighton in 1871, a reputed centenarian whose life was investigated by Thoms who found there was little substance in the claims of Geeran's 'two credulous biographers'.[62] Mention has already been made of Thoms's own *Human Longevity, its Facts and its Fictions*, which appeared a year later in 1873.

But as far as Lewis was concerned, the credibility of centenarianism was behind him by June 1862. There was a visit to Windsor 'by a special train, with Ld Granville & Lord Stanley, for a Council … The Queen did not speak, or come into the room'.[63] Then there were several sittings at 35 Bryanston Square with Henry Weigall, a young up and coming artist,[64] for a full length portrait which he had promised to give to the Shire Hall at Presteign, as well as work on a second edition of his work on Romance Languages. This latter task, 'with the exception of a list of words in the appendix' occupied him for a week, and then he resumed the composition of the *Dialogue on the Best form of Government*, which he had 'laid aside at the beginning of the session'.[65]

Early in July there was another day trip to Osborne for an interview with the Queen:

> The Queen looks better than when I last saw her, & talked in a natural tone.[66]

There were visits, too, with Theresa, to Battle Abbey in Sussex and Ashridge Park in Hertfordshire. On both occasions the architecture interested him more than the occupants, whose identities are unnamed. Samuel Lewis noted that the gatehouse at Battle was:

> a beautiful specimen of the decorated style of English architecture, is in entire preservation, and many parts of the conventual buildings have been retained in the modern mansion.

The Lewises stayed a weekend at the Abbey, but all that is said is:

> Went with Theresa by train to Battle Abbey where there is a curious gatehouse. Returned on Monday.[67]

The visit to Ashridge fared little better:

> At Ashridge, a large house built by Wyatt about 1808, without beauty and not imposing, considering its great size.[68]

Official duties continued to claim Lewis's reluctant attention even though Parliament was in recess, and in the second week in August the Secretary of State for War:

> Left Kent House by the morning train for Portsmouth, & joined the Duke of Somerset[69] & the other Lords of the Admiralty in the *Osborne*, Admiralty steamer. In the evening we started for Jersey & after a smooth passage across the channel, anchored off St Helier's.[70]

Their cruise of inspection took them on to Guernsey and Alderney and on to Portland, Dartmouth, Plymouth, Falmouth, and the Scilly Islands, where he 'attended morning service in the church at St Mary's'. Then across the Bristol Channel to the Royal Dockyard at Pembroke, founded in 1814:

> where we arrived at 8 o'clock on Monday 16th August. Visited the fortifications and in the afternoon went by train to Newport where I slept.

Now able to travel to New Radnor by train, he was at Harpton next day in time for lunch, and unpacking his books. In what was left of August he completed the transcription of a new edition of his *History of Astronomy* and sent them 'to Dr Holzamer at Prague who has undertaken to translate the work into German', whilst also resuming work on his *Dialogue on Forms of Government*.[71] As August gave way to September he dealt daily with 'Office papers'[72] whilst finding time to continue with the *Dialogue*, to correct the proofs of the new edition of the *Romance Languages*, and to start revising his 'MS on the Belief of the Ancients respecting the state of the soul after death'.[73]

During the Autumn of 1862 in the calm of Radnorshire landscape Lewis contemplated the issues of the American Civil War inasmuch as they affected British politics. The war was now in its second year and in May 1861 Britain had issued a declaration of neutrality, whilst recognizing the southern Confederacy's right to wage war as a sovereign nation. Lewis is considered to have exercised an important influence on British policy towards the United States.[74] At the end of July, the cruiser *Alabama*, launched in the Mersey in the previous May for the Confederates, sailed for the Southern States and was later to cause havoc with Northern shipping. Despite British neutrality, Lord John Russell, as Foreign Secretary, failed to prevent the *Alabama* from sailing, and her depredations subsequently cost the Union the loss of sixty-eight merchant ships before it was itself sunk by a Union warship off the coast of France in 1864. The *Alabama*'s activities also cost the British government over £3,000,000 in compensation. British sentiments tended to be with the Confederates though Abraham Lincoln's proclamation in September 1862 that the slaves in the southern states would be legally free at the beginning of 1863 was well received in Europe. In the same month, September 1863, Russell, despite his failure to act over the *Alabama*, wanted to offer mediation between north and south, and circulated the cabinet with a memorandum containing his views.

A few weeks later, Lewis decided to try out his opinions about the Civil War, which differed from those of Russell, on the Herefordshire farmers, (or was it the four local MPs he could expect to be there, too?) before developing them for Russell and a more sophisticated cabinet audience:

> Went to Hereford by the morning train, & slept at Bodenham's house. I attended the dinner of the Agricultural Society at the Green Dragon. Velters Cornewall in the chair. The 3 County members, Mr King, Ld W Graham, & H Mildmay were present. Also Clifford, member for the City. My health was drunk and I returned thanks. I spoke particularly on the American question.[75]

Next day Lewis returned to Harpton on the morning train and began to write his memorandum 'on the American question'. His composition was interrupted by spending a day at the Quarter Sessions at Presteign, dining with the magistrates afterwards, and perhaps again flying his American kite. On Friday he sent the text to War Office and over the weekend revised the proofs, returning them to London, corrected, on Sunday evening. The following Wednesday he himself returned to London for a cabinet meeting.[76]

The cabinet meeting was not until Friday, so Lewis had Thursday for other matters:

> I received the first sheets of the reprint of my work on the *Origin of the Romance Languages* & returned them to the press. I continued my *Dialogue on Forms of Govt* for a time, then I laid it aside, & examined old letters & documents with a view of making a genealogical summary of the Harpton family. Afterwards I wrote an ironical essay on the application of the Egyptological method to modern history. Soon after nine o'clock I received a written notice that the cabinet for tomorrow is postponed *sine die*.[77]

By the end of the week Lewis was housebound with 'a bad cold' and perhaps not in the best of humours to receive

> a short memorandum from Ld Russell, printed for the Cabinet, commenting in a sore & angry tone upon some passages in my memorandum.[78]

Still confined to Kent House by his cold, on Sunday Lewis

> began to write a paper for the Cabinet on the question of the
> independence of the Southern States.[79]

Monday saw the arrival of Theresa and Alice from Oxford where
they had been staying at Brasenose College at the Principal's lodgings,
and Lewis ventured to the War Office where a memorandum arrived
from Gladstone 'objecting to certain passages in my Memorandum'.
Going out to the office was a mistake and for the rest of the week he
was confined to the house 'by a troublesome cough'. But he put his
time to good use:

> I finished my paper on the Independence of the Southern
> States, which is of considerable length & for which I had to
> make some historical research & to refer to a good many
> books.[80]

He also managed to escape the house to attend, at All Saints,
Knightsbridge, the local parish church, the marriage of Thomas
Villiers Lister, Theresa Lewis's son by her first marriage, to Fanny
Coryton, daughter of William Coryton of Pentillie in Cornwall.
Educated at Harrow and Trinity College Cambridge, Lewis had
taken appropriate interest in Lister's upbringing. It was he, for
example, who took him to Harrow when he entered the school in
1847. He entered the Foreign Office in 1853, as Private Secretary to
his uncle, the Earl of Clarendon, and précis writer to Lord John
Russell. He accompanied Russell to the peace negotiations at Vienna
during the Crimean War in 1855, and the Earl of Clarendon to the
Congress of Paris, and Earl Granville to Russia, both in 1856, and he
was with Clarendon again in Prussia in 1861. He was also Deputy
Lieutenant for Radnorshire, a county in which he never lived.[81]

In his memorandum Lewis argued against British involvement
in arranging an armistice between the American northern and
southern states and his arguments impressed the majority of the
Cabinet to the discomfort of Russell and Gladstone. He began to
receive the usual round of callers voicing their support for his views.
Sir George Grey, Home Secretary, and Milner Gibson, President of
the Board of Trade, were the first and there was a cabinet meeting
to discuss the distress of the Lancashire cotton spinners, deprived of
cotton by the northern blockade.[82] Less stimulating, no doubt, was
the call of duty that after a Saturday morning occupied by work at

the War Office and a Cabinet meeting caused the Secretary of State for the War Department to visit St George's Barracks 'to see cooking apparatus'.[83]

There were consolations, too: the second edition of his *Essay on Romance Languages* and his pamphlet on Egyptology were published, and he sent to the printers the manuscript of his pedigree. After a morning at the office and a meeting at the Horse Guards with the Duke of Cambridge, General Commander-in-Chief of the Army, and the Duke of Newcastle, Secretary of State for the Colonies, he went on to Windsor castle:

> I saw the Queen after dinner & she presented me to Princess Alexandra of Denmark, the intended wife of the Prince of Wales, who has an animated countenance with good features, & a pleasing manner. I also saw Princess Alice. I had a conversation of some length with the Queen, whose manner has become quite natural. The Queen is quite determined that Prince Alfred shall not accept the crown of Greece, for reasons which seem to me sound.[84]

The matter of the crown of Greece was discussed further on Sunday after morning service:

> I had an interview with the Queen before dinner. She has written to the ex-king of Portugal, to sound him as to his willingness to be king of Greece, if England could carry him.[85]

Once again the main interest of the visit was architectural rather than political.

> The Queen has built a Mausoleum for the body of the Duchess of Kent, in Frogmore Gardens, which has cost £30,000. It is completed and has the appearance of a handsome Summer House. She is also building a Mausoleum in the same garden for the body of Prince Albert, which is estimated to cost £60,000 & will probably cost more.[86]

The Duchess of Kent, Queen Victoria's mother, died after a brief illness at Frogmore in Windsor home park in March 1861. At the Queen's resolution a mausoleum was built for her mother at Frogmore and Albert Jenkins Humbert, later to be the architect of Sandringham, designed the building. It took the form of a domed rotunda, and work actually began upon it during the lifetime of the duchess. It was to be joined by a royal mausoleum for Prince Albert, again designed by Humbert with the assistance of Professor Grüner of Dresden, to give the building a suitable Teutonic flavour. The estimate of the cost as reported by Lewis was wildly inaccurate, and eventually came to £200,000. It was not completed until 1871.

On his return to London on Monday morning Lewis was 'at the office' and received the proofs of his pedigree. Lewis's attendance 'at the office' was daily at this time, and obviously affairs of state occupied him, but perhaps others things did, too, which explains the entry in his diary for early December:

> Each day at the office. Wrote the Preface to my Dialogue.[87]

Theresa Lewis was unwell and in early December underwent major surgery for breast cancer which was performed at Kent House:

> Today Mr Caesar Hawking came at 2 o'clock to perform the operation of removing a tumour from Theresa. The operation was performed under chloroform, in the presence of Dr Ferguson. She suffered several paroxysms of pain from time to time during the rest of the day, but the pain abated in the night, & she slept well. My dear wife showed remarkable coolness & courage on this trying occasion.[88]

Lewis, attendance at the office uninterrupted by Theresa's post-operative sufferings, recorded her progress in his diary:

> Thursday 11th December 1862. Theresa suffered little pain today & appeared to be doing well. At office.

> Friday 12th December. Theresa began to feel pains in her feet. The wound gives her little pain. Office.

> Saturday 13th December. Last night & today she suffered severely from pains in the feet & legs. Her biliary system has been completely deranged by the operation & severe gouty pains are the consequence of this derangement. The wound was dressed today for the first time. At the office.

> Sunday 14th December to Thursday 18th December. Theresa's pains became less during this period, & she began to make decided progress towards recovery. At the office each day. Occupied with the revision of my psychological ms.

But despite Theresa's pain and slow progress, Lewis thought there was no cause for alarm and told his brother Gilbert so:

> Theresa has suffered a good deal of pain. There is no symptom to create alarm or even uneasiness, but she has not made much progress.[89]

Caesar Henry Hawking, FRS, appointed Serjeant-Surgeon to the Queen in 1862, is remembered as being both 'eminent and successful' and whose 'opinion was especially valued in difficult cases'. His *Lectures on Tumours* were considered valuable. The physician Robert Ferguson, MD, was a much-respected specialist in gynaecology, whom Lewis had consulted in the case of Isabella Bankes. As an obstetrician, he attended the birth of all of Queen Victoria's children, and his presence at Theresa's operation with Hawking suggests the nature of her tumour. Her recovery was slow, but at the end of the last week in December 1862 Lewis could report

> Theresa is now nearly convalescent. Her progress this week rapid. At the office each day except Christmas day. Working at my psychology.[90]

Theresa lived until November 1865. The Secretary of State for War ended the year 1862, after a weekend at Grove Mill, not at the office, but at the British Museum:

> Left the Grove by a morning train. Called at the British Museum on my way from the Euston Terminus, & had a long conversation with Mr Birch upon the method of interpreting the hieroglyphics. He gave me an intelligible account both of determining the phonetic value of the hieroglyphics, & of the method determining the signification of the sounds.[91]

Similarly the New Year commenced 'at the office' and with the completion of his *Dialogue on the Forms of Government*, and more work on his psychology.[92] In the following week he was dining at the Freemason's Tavern with the Club of the Astronomical Society, with the Astronomer Royal in the chair, proposing his health.[93] It was all very pleasant and there is not a mention of the American War. Perhaps, though, it was mentioned on his visit to Osborne for an audience with the Queen:

> Wednesday 21st January 1863. By the morning train to Osborne, & arrived there about 5 o'clock I had an audience of the Queen, which lasted about two hours. She talked on a variety of subjects. Her mind is less depressed, but is constantly occupied with her loss. She intends to publish some more of the Prince's

papers. I dined with the Royal Family, Princess Louise,[94] Princess Helena[95] … The Queen dines in her own room.

Back from Osborne, it was now Lewis's turn for surgery; troubled by piles, it was time for their treatment:

> Friday 23rd January 1863. Kent House. I staid at home, preparing for the operation of tying some piles which was performed for me on the following day, Saturday 24th January by Mr Barber. I remained in bed for that & the following days. I received the first proofs of my *Dialogue on Forms of Govt.*

> Thursday 29th January 1863. Kent House. Dressed myself, but did not leave my room.

Two days later Lewis received the news of the death of his eldest step-daughter, Thérèse Harcourt, in childbirth.[96] The infant, Lewis Harcourt survived and after a distinguished political career was ennobled as the first Viscount Harcourt in 1917. The choice of the Christian name Lewis was surely not coincidental, and Cornewall Lewis was himself deeply saddened by Thérèse's death:.

> Saturday 31st January 1863. Kent House. This day poor Thérèse died at 2 o'clock She was taken ill on Monday last, with pains in the abdomen & sickness. She gave birth to a child at 8 months on Friday night, after a healthy labour. This event nearly relieved us from all alarm, but she became worse during the night, & had little consciousness at 10 o'clock on Saturday morning. She was mild, intelligent, sensible, & reasonable, of a most affectionate disposition, beloved by all her friends, & was altogether one of the most perfect characters I have ever known. Her age was only 27.

Still recovering from his operation, Lewis remained housebound and was unable to go the funeral of 'poor Thérèse' at Nuneham Courtney. Lady Lewis bore her loss well, as Lewis informed his old friend Mrs Austin:

> I am happy to say that Lady Theresa bears this heavy blow with fortitude, and that her health has not suffered from it, which I as afraid might be the case … I was very sorry at not being able to dine at Senior's, but was unwell and confined to the house for nearly a fortnight.[97]

Back at both office and House Lewis had the consolation of the publication of his *Dialogue on the best form of Government*, which *The*

Times received as 'elegant and candid'.[98] The Army and Navy estimates 'and other important business' kept Lewis at the office and in the House through February and well into March, the Army estimates not being concluded sooner because of 'the present unwillingness of the House to incur expenditure for the military defence of the colonies'.[99] Trelawney thought Lewis made heavy weather of the parliamentary debate:

> Lewis is very superficially informed on military matters. So some of us begin to think. He is industrious & good tempered, & takes censure patiently. But really he is not apt enough for sudden attack & defence of estimates in detail. He is like a 300 pounder in a bog surrounded by sharpshooters who lie concealed in a woody country. There he sticks, every one plying him with small arms; killing his men & horses. Palmerston wants more skirmishers.[100]

It has been described as 'a malign stroke of fate' that Herbert was replaced at the War Office by Lewis.[101] The demanding Florence Nightingale, concerned with the arrangements of her military hospitals, found him a very inadequate match for the Duke of Cambridge, the Army's Commander-in-Chief. She wrote in September 1861 to her helpmate Harriet Martineau:

> The Commdander in Chief rides over the weak and learned Secretary of State as if he were straw. Day rooms, Barrack Inspections, Hospitals, all the Sanitary Improvements, it is the same. Not one will they leave untouched.[102]

Nightingale also thought little of Lewis's powers of administration and considered he did not understand what he was doing.[103]

Cabinet meetings included discussion of the finances of the Prince of Wales in view of his forthcoming marriage. The proposals were generous:

> Discussion about the grant for the Prince of Wales. It was agreed to propose £100,000 for him and £10,000 a year for the princess. His income from the Duchy of Cornwall & its accumulations being reckoned into the £100,000, but £160,000 being deducted for outfit.[104]

The Prince, despite the Queen's anxiety, was popular and when presented to the House, Palmerston's proposal 'was well received & the Resolution carried without a division'.[105] Esteem for the late

Prince Consort was also shown, with a proposed vote of £5,000 for his memorial in South Kensington.[106] Lewis, himself, of course was a committed monarchist, and it was one of the few causes for which he would cheerfully lay aside the calls of both scholarship and politics. So on 7th March he was there

> At the War Office in order to see the procession of the Prince of Wales & Princess Alexandria pass along Pall Mall. Seats were erected, & the office was dressed up for the occasion. There was a great concourse of people, but all orderly & good humoured.[107]

He also offered the hospitality of his vantage point to his old friend Edmund Head and his family;

> If you and Lady Head and Caroline should wish to see the procession of the Prince of Wales on the 7th, there will be places at this office at your disposition, or, if you care to go to Windsor to see the wedding, I can give you a ticket for the antechapel. You need not appear in full dress.[108]

Lewis was at the wedding itself, using the railway for a day return:

> I attended in St George's chapel, & was present at the marriage of the Prince of Wales with the Princess Alexandra. Everybody was pleased with the appearance of the bride. The scene was gorgeous, from the procession of rich dresses. The Queen was in an open logi high up, on one side of the altar. She was in widow's mourning, but wore the blue ribbon of the garter. She stood up and shewed herself without reserve. The royal family bowed & curtsied to her, & she evidently wished to be considered as forming part of the ceremony. This was her first appearance in public since the Prince's death. The day was clear, though cold, & everything passed off without confusion at the illuminations in London.[109]

Well, not quite:

> at night six women were crushed to death by the crowd, all in the City. The City police have been peculiarly inefficient, & the City authorities peculiarly conceited, on the occasion of these festivities.[110]

At the weekend he was back at Windsor, where, besides attending the Queen's private chapel for what he considered to be a good sermon by the Bishop, alluding to the marriage of the Prince of Wales, he 'had another interview with the Queen'.[111] Of what did they speak? Lewis was too loyal a royal servant to have recorded the conversation, but the Queen herself three weeks later told Lady Lewis a little of its content:

> he spoke so kindly of the extraordinary outburst of loyalty, and of my popularity, as he so kindly expressed it.[112]

The week ended with visits to the office and the House where the American Civil War still casting its shadow; he heard an 'excellent speech of Roundell Palmer on the *Alabama* case'.[113] He made his last visit to the office on Monday 30th March 1863.[114] At the end of the week to wrote to his brother Gilbert:

> I intend, if I am able, to go to Harpton on Monday with Theresa, and to stay there until the following Saturday. I am anxious to get some fresh air at Easter, and I think that a complete change may do Theresa good, after so many things to depress her.[115]

Gilbert later recorded that Lewis

> had not passed more than a day at Harpton before he was seized with one of the bilious attacks from which throughout his life he had frequently suffered; congestion of lungs followed. The disorder, at the same time, of two organs which for, many years had been weak and defective, was more than his constitution could withstand. In a few days he breathed his last.[116]

He died at two o'clock on Monday 13th April 1863, the day upon which the House reassembled after its Easter break. Some had already heard the news, borne by the electric telegraph, once denounced by Lewis as 'a most fertile mother of lies'.[117] On the motion of Spencer Walpole,[118] seconded by Palmerston, the House adjourned, but not before Disraeli, like Walpole, a political opponent, had spoken an extempore obituary:

> Sir, until a few minutes ago I was not aware of the calamity which I think I may say has befallen the country. [Hear, hear.] The Queen has lost one of the ablest of her servants, and this House has lost a member who I am sure possessed the universal regard and respect of Hon. gentlemen of both sides. [Hear, hear.] Sir, I never knew a man who combined in so eminent a degree as Sir George Lewis both from acquired and from native power of thought, the faculty upon all public matters, of

arriving at a sound and judicious conclusion. [Hear, hear.] Although he was remarkably free from prejudice and passion, yet the absence of those sentiments which are supposed in general to be necessary to the possession of active power had not upon him the effect which it usually produces, and he was a man who always brought a great organizing faculty and a great power of sustained perseverance to the transaction of public affairs. [Hear, hear.] Sir, I am sure the rising statesmen on both sides may take him as an example that in many particulars may be remembered and followed with advantage, and I am persuaded that his name will never be mentioned in this House without feelings of deep respect, or without unfeigned regret for what may be deemed the untimely loss of a man whom the country could ill spare. [Hear, hear.][119]

As the editor of *Notes & Queries* put it:

The whole proceeding was worthy of the country and worthy of the man.[120]

Lewis's funeral took place on the following Saturday. Never before or since has the diminutive Kington and Leominster Railway carried a more distinguished collection of passengers, which included three earls, one of whom was the Foreign Secretary, another a former Foreign Secretary, and the third Lewis's successor as Secretary of State for War.

The remains of this lamented statesman were on Saturday consigned to their final resting-place among the tombs of his fathers at Old Radnor. The funeral was as unostentatious in character as was the public and private life of the deceased statesman, and had this peculiarity, that all who attended appeared as mourners. Among them were the Earl of Clarendon, Earl Russel, Earl de Grey and Ripon,[121] the Right Hon Pelham Villiers,[122] Mr Vernon Harcourt,[123] Mr Lister,[124] Sir Velters Cornewall, Sir Gilbert Lewis, and Mr Herbert Lewis.[125] About 100 horsemen preceded the hearse containing the body of the deceased, followed by his carriage and those of the distinguished mourners and the gentry of the neighbourhood. The coffin was of massive oak, enclosing a shell, and covered with black cloth, having a brass plate thereon with the following inscription: 'The Right Hon Sir G C Lewis, Bart, died: April 13; 1863, aged 57 years.' The deceased baronet was, however, eight days under that age. The immense concourse of people present testified by their demeanour that their regret for the loss of this estimable statesman was universal and sincere. No landlord was ever more liberal to his tenants than Sir George, and his bene-factions to the neighbourhood was something fabulous, consid-ering his means. Business was suspended in Hereford, Kington, Knighton, Presteign, Radnor, and other towns during the early part of Saturday.[126]

On the Saturday before he died *Notes & Queries* published Lewis's last contribution to that journal, the editor commenting a week later, with characteristic mawkishness 'last Saturday's *N & Q* had scarcely been perused by our Subscribers before the hand which penned it was cold and dead'.[127] His subject, 'The Presidency of Deliberative Assemblies', could not have been more appropriate, nor his style more characteristic.

> In every legislative assembly it is necessary that there should be some established regulation with respect to putting the motions of its individual members to the vote. The invention of a President of the Chamber, whose sole function consists in putting questions and maintaining order, is, however, compara-tively modern.[128]

He then gives a historical survey of how legislative assemblies conducted their affairs, from the practices of ancient Greece and Rome, down to the present Westminster Parliamentary custom:

> The principal functions of the Speaker of the House of Commons were not originally, (as the title of his office indi-cates) what they are at present. The House of Commons were at first a set of delegates summoned by the Crown to negociate with it concerning the payment of taxes. They might take advan-tage of the position of superiority, which they temporarily occu-pied, to remonstrate with the Crown about certain grievances, upon which they were generally agreed.[129]

Lewis's survey embraced the position of the Speaker in the Irish House of Commons, and in Scotland where the three estates sat as one house, there being no separate House of Commons. He concludes with a consideration of the Convocation of the established Church of England:

> The presidency of the Houses of Convocation for the Province of Canterbury bears a close analogy to the presidency of the English Houses of Parliament. The Archbishop, like the Lord Chancellor, is, by virtue of his office, president of the Upper

House; the the Lower House of Convocation elects a president, who is called prolocutor; he … was elected by the Lower House, in order to convey their wishes to the Archbishop and Upper House, and to confer with the body of prelates. He spoke on behalf of the Lower House [prolocutor], and he reported their opinions to the Upper House [referendarius].[130]

And there we have it: Lewis the scholar, Lewis the Statesman, and Lewis the Churchman of the *via media*.

Epilogue

De mortuis nihil nisi bonum: thus the *Standard*, which so berated Lewis in February 1855, saw him in a quite different light in April 1863:

> No speeches were ever heard with more respectful attention, or produced a greater effect upon those who were competent to appreciate their value. As a financier he was trusted and believed in by the great merchants and capitalists of the City, who regarded the brilliant blundering of Mr Gladstone with terror. As a political philosopher he commanded the attention of philosophers and the reverence of statesmen. As an administrator his success was rather perfect than brilliant; he was never caught tripping, and if he was not right in all that he did, at least it was plain that he had done nothing without carefully weighing its consequences, and being prepared to defend it by arguments which, if not conclusive, were at least grave and momentous. Under his guidance the reputation of the Liberals for financial incapacity was exchanged for credit. Under his administration men learned even to respect the Home Office. Sentences were not commuted without reason, or adhered to without reflection; and those who were accustomed to take for granted the unreasonableness of every proceeding of the department, found that they had to do with a man who was neither obstinate nor squeezable; who had reasons for everything that he conceded or refused; who was always consistent, and generally showed even to his censors that he was in the right. As Minister of War he had less opportunity to distinguish himself.
>
> Sir George Cornewall Lewis was a perfectly unselfish statesman; he assumed the post in which his party thought that he could best serve them, without observing that it was the post in which he could do least to promote his own reputation and prepare his elevation to a higher rank. In that post he died; not worn down by labour, but taken from us by the visitation of God,

just when we least expected to lose him. No man was more likely to win the regard of his neighbours than the statesman who, elevated in their esteem by the high rank he held and the great trust devolved upon him, retained the simple, unaffected, somewhat shy and awkward manner of the scholarly student, and the straight forward kindliness of the country gentleman. Perhaps no minister ever had less of the air of a great man, or even of a man of the world. The slouching gait, the uneasy manner, the hesitating speech, all savoured of the closet; and it was easier to recognise in Sir George the author of the *Credibility of Early Roman History* than the Secretary for War and hope of the Liberal party.

Steps were soon taken for his formal commemoration. A few weeks after his death, at the request of 'the gentlemen, freeholders, merchants, bankers, and other inhabitants of the county of Radnor' Henry Thomas of Pencerrig, High Sheriff that year called a meeting at the Shire Hall, Presteign

> for the purpose of enabling all classes to express their regret for the premature loss sustained by the death of the late Sir George Cornewall Lewis, and of providing a monument to his memory.[1]

The meeting was not well attended, but no matter for, as *The Times* assured its readers, 'it comprised all the principal gentlemen in the county and neighbourhood'. These principal gentlemen were identified as Henry Thomas, High Sheriff, Sir John Walsh, the Lord Lieutenant of Radnorshire, Sir John Walsham of Knill Court, Richard Green Price, who succeeded Lewis as MP for the Radnor boroughs, the Revd RL Venables, Chairman of the Radnorshire Quarter Sessions, Captain Walter De Winton of Maesllwch Castle, High Sheriff in 1862, Captain Mynors, of Evancoed, and Captain Trelawney.[2]

Sir John Walsh, seconded by Sir John Walsham, moved the proposition, carried by acclamation that:

> It is the earnest wish of the county of Radnor that some substantial testimonial should be erected to the memory of the late Sir George Cornewall Lewis, in commemoration of his public services and private excellencies.

Richard Green Price, supported by RL Venables, then moved the appointment of the inevitable committee, with power to co-opt, to raise subscriptions. But for what? The Revd John Edmund Cheese[3] suggested the establishment of a county school or a University scholarship, but the meeting was not having that, and seemed to be in favour of something more visibly apparent, preferably in stone. A similar meeting was held in Hereford a week later, and again a committee was set up. This time bronze rather than stone was the choice:

> it shall assume the form of a statue in bronze of the right hon. Gentleman, to be placed in front of the Shire-Hall at Hereford. The work is to be intrusted to Baron Marochetti, who has undertaken its execution for the sum of £1,000.[4]

The Italian-born sculptor, Baron Carlo Marochetti, moved to England from Paris during the 1848 revolution and his work soon found favour with Queen and Prince Consort. He was considered particularly successful in his equestrian statues of the Queen, and the Duke of Wellington and his busts of Thackeray and Landseer were installed in Westminster Abbey. Happily, and perhaps familiar with Lewis's insecure horsemanship, a rather larger than life statue of Lewis standing was chosen. Marochetti became a RA in 1866 and 'his handsome figure and engaging manners rendered him popular with his fashionable patrons in England and on the continent'.[5]

Lady Duff Gordon followed the progress of her nephew's statue with close interest, and in November 1864 she

> saw Archer Clive who had been with Theresa [Lewis's widow] to Marochetti's to see the clay figure done by him for the bronze statue he is to make of Sir George Lewis for the outside of the Hereford Shire Hall and they approved of it![6]

Mrs Austin, the widow of Lewis's close friend John Austin, suggested an epitaph for the stautue's pedestal:

> 'Scholar and Statesman. He did everything for the good of the people; nothing for their applause'.[7]

However, though it enjoyed the approval of Archer Clive and Lady Duff Gordon, it was rejected by the Hereford committee.

In August *The Times* was able to report that

> The bronze statue, from the cast of Baron Marochetti, to the memory of the late Sir GC Lewis, has arrived in Hereford. The 3rd of September is fixed for the inauguration. Lord Palmerston has promised to attend and deliver the inaugural address. The Chancellor of the Exchequer[8] is also expected to be present. While in Herefordshire Lord Palmerston will be the

guest of the Revd Archer Clive, of Whitfield, brother of Mr George Clive, MP.[9]

The Times recorded the statue's progress at Hereford almost blow by blow: its arrival in front of the Shire Hall, the appearance of its base of unpolished Penrhyn granite, the moulded and polished pedestal surmounting it, and the towering 7ft 6ins figure itself, cast in bronze.

> He is represented as standing with his arms folded upon his breast, and the likeness is said to be admirable. The total height of the memorial is 14ft … The statue was erected under the supervision of Mr Chink, county surveyor for Herefordshire, and Baron Marochetti, superintended the raising of the figure on the pedestal. At present the statue is concealed from the public eye by a covering of white cloth, but as already announced in *The Times*, it will be formally unveiled to-morrow [Saturday] by Lord Palmerston. The arrangements for the ceremony are now complete. His Lordship arrives in Hereford to-day from Carnarvon, and will be the guest of the Revd Archer Clive, at Whitfield. On Saturday morning a procession will meet his Lordship on his entrance to the city, and conduct him to the shire-hall, where the inauguration takes place. The procession will consist of the Militia staff and band of music, Volunteer Rifle Corps and band, Odd Fellows' Lodges, and the Mayor and Corporation of Hereford. The ceremony will take place at noon.[10]

The Times in its account of things hints at an underlying tension between the Bishop and the Corporation of Hereford as to which of them should entertain Palmerston to luncheon, and to stop tongues wagging it was explained that:

> his Lordship … will take luncheon with the Bishop of Hereford at the Palace, having already accepted an invitation from Dr Hampden before the invitation of the Corporation reached him.[11]

Lady Duff Gordon happened to be in Herefordshire and went into the city to see Archer Clive's meeting with Palmerston at the railway station. She was, however, disappointed with what she saw:

> I was very glad to see Lord Palmerston again, I quite longed to do so and he is very much aged since I saw him and looks too feeble to be the animated bright speaker that one reads of in the House of Commons.[12]

In the evening Alice Duff Gordon commemorated her cousin by her presence at the ball at the Shire Hall from which she did not return until four in the morning.[13] Next morning Lady Duff Gordon, without Alice,

> went to Hereford for Lord Palmerston to unveil George's statue and to hear him make a speech as for the occasion he was to be received at the entrance to Hereford by the Mayor and Corporation and to be conducted to the Town Hall where they would address him, and leaving it, he was to go outside the building and the ceremony to begin.[14]

But it was all in vain, as far as Lady Duff Gordon was concerned, for as she admitted in the privacy of her diary: 'I cannot stand and I cannot hear'.[15]

There was a season of unveilings, and a week or so later after the Hereford ceremony it was Westminster Abbey's turn. Here Lewis's memorial took the form of a bust by the sculptor Henry Weekes. Again Lewis was keeping good company, for in 1838 it was Weekes who modelled the first bust of the Queen done after her accession, and he was to take a high position as a portrait-sculptor, and his works of this class were thought to have great merit.[16] He was appointed professor of sculpture at the Royal Academy in 1873.

Weekes was commissioned by Robert Lowe, a fellow parliamentarian, but not a close associate of Lewis. Its cost, 215 guineas, was met by 'a circle of Sir George's private friends'. It seems strange to modern standards of discretion that 'private friends' should have made the extent of their generosity so public as to publish it in *The Times*, but Lewis himself was very conscious of the cost of things and usually recorded in his diary whether or not for this or that duty he was being paid. *The Times*, with a waspish taste for detail, went on to explain that the 215 guineas did not include 'the fees of the Dean of Westminster, which are stated to be very considerable for appropriating a space in our national mausoleum'. Nevertheless, it was another 'striking likeness' and 'a beautiful work of art'.

The bust was erected in the western porch of Westminster Abbey, and perhaps an insight to the understanding of Lewis's character held by his subscribing friends is offered by its situation in the abbey and the company it thereby kept, closely adjoining 'the monuments of Sir William Follett, Kemble, and Lieutenant General Sir Eyre Coote'.[17] Was the bust put here to place Lewis amongst those considered his peers? Follett was a former Attorney General, and considered by his biographer to have been 'as nearly perfect as man can be'. Estimations of Kemble were less flattering: 'though not incapable of generosity, he was undoubtedly vain and opinionated'. Coote served with Clive in India and his triumph as at Wanderwash is remembered 'as second only to Plassey in its importance'.

Or what it lack of space? For it could be argued that his memorial was placed amongst those of lesser men. But be that as it may, the inscription had no doubt of his virtues:

> In him eminence as a scholar and as an author large stores of varied knowledge, employed in the advantage and instruction of mankind, and an earnest devotion to literature, unsullied by intolerance or envy, were combined with a gentle and beneficent character, steadfast pursuit of the public good, and the comprehensive wisdom of a statesman.[18]

Still in the Marches towards the end of September Lady Duff Gordon's annual progress had brought her to Harpton itself. Jane Lewis, the new mistress of Harpton, put her donkey chair at her guest's disposal so that she could go over to New Radnor.

> I went in Jane's Donkey Chair to see the memorial that is erected to poor George's memory at New Radnor. It is a pretty kind of Queen Eleanor's Cross, & it is to have inscriptions placed upon it & a medallion of his profile. I liked it.[19]

But when she inspected the finished memorial during the following year's progress she was less certain that she liked it.

> I went with Jane[20] & the Miss Webbs in the car, to see poor George's Memorial at New Radnor. It is very pretty but has faults of course. The basement is not broad and in proportion to the height of the Building, & I don't like the Gargoyles, the jutting out Animals, over the figures, nor do I like the Medallion of George, the whole thing looks too like taking a pinnacle off a Church and putting it on the ground without rhyme or reason.[21]

The season came to an end in November 1864 with 'a very simple but impressive ceremony ... at New Radnor'.[22] The committee constituted at the Presteign meeting in May 1863 received fifty-nine designs in response to its invitation and chose that of John Gibbs, of Oxford. Gibbs was a little known architect with a successful provincial practice. His Banbury Cross is his best known work though the tourist will have seen his Albert memorial at Abingdon and his commemoration of Shakespeare at Stratford on Avon. One W Forsyth was responsible for the considerable amount of sculptured work decorating the memorial.

> It is somewhat after the fashion of the Eleanor Cross, and is built mainly of Box ground stone. It is 77ft. high by 25ft in width at the base, and is octagonal in form. It comprises three distinct stages. On the front of the stage next the base is the following inscription:
>
> Radnorshire
> To her most distinguished Son
> Sir
> George Cornewall Lewis
> Bart.
> Died 1863
>
> Under this inscription there is a medallion portrait, in marble of the late baronet, and on the second stage above it, in four recesses, divided by eight columns, stand, under richly-carved canopies, four allegorical figures, each 6ft high, representing Justice, Truth, Oratory, and Literature. The next stage consists of columns of red Mansfield stone, placed round an octagonal shaft, and decorated with the coats of arms of England, Ireland, Scotland, and Wales, immediately over which are four large griffins grasping the arms of the Lewis family. An ornamental spire springing from this last stage, and having at the top a carved cross with a circle entwined in its centre terminates the structure, the general effect of which will be best conceived by imagining a slender church steeple, richly decorated and grace-fully tapering stage by stage, from a platform ascended by steps at its base to the cross at its summit.[23]

Thus what Lady Duff Gordon saw as a pinnacle off a church put on the ground without rhyme or reason the correspondent of *The Times* saw as 'a slender church steeple, richly decorated and gracefully tapering stage by stage'. The Radnorshire architect, SW Williams, wrote on the inappropriateness of spires for the Radnorshire land-scape, and the debate over the aesthetic appeal of the monument, which *The Times*, ever mindful of its readers' interest in price tags, reported cost £1,000, still continues. Box stone and Mansfield stone were used, but no Radnorshire stone, and the encaustic tiles are not by Godwin of Lugwardine.

The choice of ornament probably represents the taste of the commissioning committee rather than of Lewis himself. The relevance of the statues of Justice and Truth is apparent at once and Lewis's commitment to them both was never doubted by friend or opponent. But no one has ever acclaimed him as an orator, as his generally adoring aunt, Lady Duff Gordon, put it:

> The electric telegraph announced George Lewis as Chancellor of the Exchequer. I don't believe it for he can't speak in the House![24]

It was the scholarly content of what he wrote rather than its elegance of expression which won general approval. Likewise one wonders why the committee chose a design based upon the Eleanor Cross. It is very doubtful whether Eleanor of Castile, who acquired extensive estates with the help of Jewish usurers, and who is associated with the unsubstantiated tradition that she saved Edward I's life by sucking a poisoned wound; would have particularly commended herself to Lewis, who spent so much intellectual energy in freeing Classical history from spurious traditions. Moreover, whilst it is a nice conceit to link Eleanor's Cross at Charing Cross, the centre of London in calculating mileage, with New Radnor, Charing Cross and its attendant hotel were the work of Edward Middleton Barry, son of the more famous Sir Charles Barry, and were not completed until 1865.

It was the committee's original intention to set the memorial on the castle hill, which would have given it a commanding position 100 feet above the road below. However, the discovery of archaeological remains in preparing the site, led to its being abandoned for one by the road at its entrance to New Radnor from Kington. The transposition won the approval of the Bishop of St Davids, Connop Thirlwall:

> I would not have it erected on a lofty summit, conspicuous, indeed, but inaccessible to the general public. It stands on a thoroughfare, at a cross-way, and, thus situated, will remind those who come after us that there are two ways at least in life, and that they who follow that which was trodden by Sir G Lewis, although they may not like him, win for themselves a name in history, will, at all events, secure for themselves that honour which belongs to virtue.[25]

It being Radnorshire at the end of November, it rained continually on the day set for the unveiling of the monument. The original plan of a procession from the Town Hall to a marquee erected close to the monument had to be abandoned. Even the marquee was

> not quite an effectual protection against the heavy rain which fell throughout the afternoon, yet warded it off to such an extent as to prevent those present from being subjected to any serious inconvenience The principal residents in the neighbourhood, including several ladies, occupied seats on a raised platform at one end of the tent.[26]

The still sorrowing Lady Lewis, prevented by 'her feelings and failing health', was not present and it was Sir J Walsh, the Lord-Lieutenant of the county, who presided. Close by him stood the Earl of Clarendon, Lewis's brother-in-law and Lady Lewis's brother; the Revd Sir Gilbert Lewis, Lewis's brother and heir; Richard Green Price, MP; the High Sheriff of Radnorshire, GA Haigh; the Bishop of St Davids; and Vernon Harcourt, Lewis's son-in-law. There followed what by now had become a familiar rehearsal of Lewis's virtues as a scholar, statesman, and administrator, 'as competent to deal with the business of life as with the literature of present or past ages'.

Lister Venables, as chairman of the Building Committee, reported that

> he and his colleagues had completed the work, which they had been appointed to carry into execution and they were ready to hand over the memorial to the subscribers.[27]

Then, following a ritual somewhat akin to that at a wedding, Venables, the bride's father as it were, handed the care of the memorial into the priestly hands of Sir John Walsh, as Lord Lieutenant, who in turn committed it to the Revd Sir Gilbert Lewis, uttering with liturgical dignity:

> acting on the part of the county of Radnor, I place in the hands and under the guardianship of the Lewis family the memorial which I now tender for their acceptance.[28]

Walsh added his personal hope that the memorial would 'be handed down to the latest posterity as a record at once of Sir George Lewis's name, and of our regard and affection for his memory', thereby raising the question for the future as to whom the ownership and responsibility of maintenance and upkeep of the memorial belonged. For those present there was no doubt about the matter: the memorial was a gift to the Lewis family which Gilbert Lewis gladly accepted:

> This memorial which has been offered to me, I accept it with pride, satisfaction, and gratitude, and shall always endeavour to protect and sustain it.[29]

The Earl of Clarendon spoke next. For him the memorial was

> of no ordinary description, whether we regard its artistic beauty, the symmetry of its proportions, or the noble and affectionate sentiment which has led to its erection.[30]

In his opinion it was not only a record of the feelings of those who knew Lewis best, but was also

> an encouragement to others, far and near, to follow the county with which he was so intimately connected, and erected by means of the subscriptions of persons of all classes and of every variety of political opinion, not only does honour to the memory, but reflects the character of a man who never, either in private or public life, made an enemy or lost a friend.[31]

Clarendon felt that in his eulogy personal knowledge and family ties allowed him to speak of aspects of Lewis's character about which others had not the necessary knowledge, *ie* 'the sanctum of domestic life':

> I am better able, perhaps, better than anyone present to say, for during twenty years of the closest fraternal intimacy, every day of which increased my respect and affection for him, I never saw his temper ruffled, never heard him utter an unkind word, and never knew him miss an opportunity to do a kind act. His unvarying good nature, his keen sense of humour, his power of adapting himself to every character and disposition with which he came in contact, made the youngest child feel as much at ease with him as the most intelligent man, and concentrated in him the love of the domestic circle in which he lived.[32]

Lewis's domestic life was indeed a sanctum to which in diaries and letters he makes few references, and when he does, as in the instance of Theresa's 1862 operation, the details are clinical rather than emotional.

The Bishop of St Davids, Connop Thirlwall, followed. Approaching Lewis's equal, at least in matters of scholarship, he was considered to be 'brilliant on paper, but hesitant and remote as a pastor ... more capable of managing the peacocks on his terrace than the clergy of his diocese'.[33] He had resisted Gilbert Lewis's non-residence at Gladestry when the latter, through Palmerston's patronage, became canon residentiary of Worcester in 1856. RL Venables, however, had little time for him, and was all for having his living of Clyro transferred from St Davids to Hereford:

> I have rather less taste for Thirlwall who is a very unsatisfactory man; and with the present humbug that everyone who lives in a Welsh diocese must speak Welsh it is perhaps as well to live in an English diocese.[34]

If there was friction between incumbent and bishop that day at New Radnor, it is unlikely that Connop Thirlwall was aware of it: he was too eccentric for that.[35] But eccentric or not, Thirlwall gave the most enlightening speech of the ceremony, and perhaps the best of all the many obituaries on Lewis. This may have been because he had no personal family or political connections with Lewis:

> For my own part, my acquaintance with Sir G Lewis has never been particularly intimate, although it dates from a period now 30 or 40 years back. It had its foundation in our common studies; its origin was attributable to a publication which I at the time conducted at Cambridge, and the volumes of which were enriched by many most valuable contributions from the pen of the right hon. Baronet.[36]

Lewis, in his classical learning, was in the Bishop's judgement the very best argument in the defence of the study of Greek and Latin in our schools and universities:

> I think I am justified in pointing not only to Sir G Lewis's writings, but also to his life as the best testimony that can be produced, to the value of those studies which some are attempting to deprecate; and I think so for two reasons. When we look upon him in the first place as a great, comprehensive, and profound scholar, as a man who for the variety, range, depth, solidity, and accuracy of his learning has been very rarely equalled, and in the second place as the man of business and the statesman, we cannot fail to perceive, although the connexion between the two characters may not be at once apparent, that his classical studies did not constitute the mere amusement of his leisure hours, but that they were the bases of all his other studies, and that they contributed more than anything else to the nourishment of his mind. In him the statesman was developed out of the scholar. The pursuits of the

scholar never ceased to the end of his life to supply the materials of his political wisdom. There is also another point which renders his testimony to the value of classical studies of the utmost importance, and that is that of all the men who ever lived he was, perhaps, the most thoroughly practical in the bent of his mind. All his studies, however widely they may appear at the first blush to depart from the ordinary business of life, will, on a nearer view, be found to converge to some practical object, and that the highest object of all, the affairs of mankind, the business and welfare of society.[37]

The last speech in this marathon of eloquence was that of Vernon Harcourt, Lewis's son-in-law. Though no doubt sincere in its intent, its undisciplined romanticism emphasized the objective and perceptive content of Thirlwall's appreciation of Lewis, as Vernon-Harcourt proclaimed in the pouring rain:

For me this spot is connected with the dearest and happiest moments of my life. There is not a track on the top of your wild mountains, there is not a sequestered nook in the your remotest valleys which I have not trodden on foot or passed on horseback in the sweet companionship of those who made 'life seem likest to Heaven'. All this is gone. 'The tender grace of a day that is fled' will never return for me. Every spot about this little town speaks to me of 'the touch of a vanished hand and the sound of a voice that is dead'.[38]

To the modern reader one of Lewis's virtues as a parliamentarian seem to have been consistently overlooked in his obituaries, perhaps because in mid-19th-century England it was not seen as virtue. It has been said of Palmerston that he could not remember the name of his unvisited constituency. Be this as it may, Lewis had a home in both his Herefordshire and Radnor constituencies as well as the inevitable town houses. This is interesting because he was very tolerant of his brother's clerical non-residence. He also took an interest in local affairs, be it in rescuing Presteign's John Beddoes School, setting up a county police force, or attending meetings of Radnor Corporation.

It was of course inappropriate for those who eulogized to go on about the other side to Lewis at the inauguration of his memorial. It was not the time, for example, to say that Lewis found it difficult to see much to impress him in his fellow men, even when others thought them distinguished. Thus he dismissed Henry Merewether, the Town Clerk of the City of London, as 'not a man of ability, dull & commonplace'.[39] But the *DNB* writes quite differently of Henry Alworth Merewether:

> It is said by those among the corporation who knew him that the office of town-clerk had never been filled with such dignity as in his time. He appeared on behalf of the corporation in the court of chancery and elsewhere on several occasions, and defended their interests with great learning and ability.

Though never publicly rude or discourteous, Lewis did not maintain the same standards in his private remarks. He often enjoyed the hospitality of Dr Renn Hampden, the Bishop of Hereford, and sat at his table, and slept at the palace when he was electioneering, or attending the meetings of the county Agricultural Society, the diocesan Schools Society, and the Three Choirs Festival.[40] But this did not prevent him from writing to his brother Gilbert:

> I am afraid that Mrs Hampden is an odious woman, & I hear it said that he is not a clever man & did not write his own lectures.[41]

The story about Hampden's lectures was plain gossip for which Lewis had a taste. It will also be recollected how he keenly listened to and recorded fully Lady Langdale's gossip about the circumstances surrounding the birth of William Austin.[42] His tolerance, too, had definite limits, and did not embrace Puseyites and Tractarians, nor did his generosity stretch to either the parish church or the school at Old Radnor, both of which were in sight of Harpton. Indeed, at times his mercenary preoccupation could swamp any attendant spiriruality. Thus he dismissed any possible claim of the deanery of Hereford upon his brother's sense of vocation on purely financial grounds:

> The Deanery of Hereford is not very tempting: £1000 a year with a house in ruins, and the Cathedral to subscribe to.[43]

Similarly, the family living of Monnington on Wye, though of little ecclesiastical consequence, was much to be preferred to the bishopric of Calcutta.[44] Strange sentiments from one whose ancestors included the Silurist Henry Vaughan who 'saw eternity the other night'. There is little spirituality in Lewis and quotations from and references to the Bible are far fewer than those to Roman and Greek authors. It is difficult to imagine him ever singing any of the great Victorian hymns of personal devotion like HF Lyte's *Abide with me*, Charlotte Elliott's *Just as I am, without one plea*, or Cardinal Newman's

Lead, kindly Light, though he might have managed the latter's more objective *Praise to the holiest in the height.*

It is difficult not to see Lewis as mercenary, in his diary he always notes the financial value, or its absence, of appointments and honours offered him. Thus when elected in 1859 by the town council to be Chief Steward of the City and Borough of Hereford he accepts the office, but notes it is honorary.[45] In this respect he was quite different from his father Sir Frankland Lewis who declined, for example, any renumeration for being chairman of the 1843 Commission of Inquiry into the Rebecca Riots.

Above all it was the Andover Workhouse affair and its repercussions which showed Lewis at his worst. It would seem that the workhouse inmates were required to grind human bones into bone meal, but Lewis dismissed it as a matter of 'very small dimensions'. He was happy for Poor Law Inspector Mott to be a scapegoat and a strong instinct for self-preservation allowed him on occasion in his dispute with Ferrand to have difficulty in 'unlocking his memory' in regard to the facts. It could be argued that he behaved unprofessionally with Jenkin Jones and was unduly sensitive about his personal honour in the 1857 episode with Gladstone over the budget.

Though little troubled by the deprivations suffered by the inmates of the Andover Workhouse, the question whether centenarians ever existed occupied his attention for weeks. But as Woodham-Smith observed, Lewis 'was no philanthropist, no reformer'.[46] It would seem that at times he lacked a sense of proportion and sufficient sensitivity to the feelings of others. No doubt he intended to flatter Florence Nightingale's appreciation of the classics when he sent her first a Latin version of 'Hey Diddle Diddle', and then 'Humpty Dumpty' in Greek. But Nightingale was a crusader with no time for trivial pursuits and told Douglas Galton[47] that Lewis would do far better to keep his mind on the War Office.

Lewis knew he was not a great orator, so why did he inflict lengthy and frequent political orations upon the people of New Radnor, the 'smockfrocks and hobnails' of John Merewether? Was it vanity, or was he using them as a means of getting himself reported in the national press?

Connop Thirlwall had an explanation for this less attractive side of Lewis's character. As he saw it, Lewis's love of truth made him intolerant of all forms of error:

his love of truth was the all-pervading principle of his existence, and in him this principle was not of the ordinary type. It was not merely a preference for truth to falsehood, which I hope is common to many of us, but an active love of it, a desire to find it and exhibit it, an impatience, amounting to intolerance, of all forms of error, of everything that was mere show and glitter, of all mock science which usurps the name of true science, and of all mere conjectures and hypotheses which usurp the place of history.[48]

Modem political historians often dwell upon the great prime ministers we never had, and it was inevitable that Lewis should be remembered, especially by his contemporaries, as being within this category. *The Times*, however, went one step further: it was their leader writer's opinion that had Lewis lived, he would have become the leader of a new political party:

He was regarded on all sides as a safe and discreet practical guide, as the man who knew better than any other how to conciliate theory with practice, and to play the part of the Statesman without forgetting the principles of the philosopher. These qualities made him above all men the probable nucleus of some future coalition; the person qualified above beyond all others to draw together discordant parties and interests, and to unite them in the pursuit of the public good, at whatever sacrifice of personal prejudice or predilection.[49]

In this respect the last word, however, must go to Connop Thirlwall, who singled out Lewis as a politician uniquely indifferent to human fame and mortal glory. The glory which surrounded Lewis was quite different:

Sir George Lewis was, if I know anything of his character, of all men the least ambitious of fame or glory. That kind of glory, indeed, which is associated with the roar of cannon and the blare of trumpets he not only did not seek, but would have shunned. There is, however, another kind of glory which, although he did not strive after it, he achieved in a most eminent degree. It is that which consists in the attainment of general love, general confidence, and general admiration.[50]

So much, then, for Lewis the public man. Lewis the private man was indisputably difficult to know. The authors have lived with him in the closest proximity for many years. His Radnorshire landscape has also been theirs and it has changed little in the interim. The main material difference is the disappearance of the railway from New Radnor to Kington and beyond. They have read his letters and his diaries, his contributions to *Notes & Queries*, his writings on Astronomy and Ancient History and his speeches. They have studied portraits of him and his Hereford statue and would certainly recognize him in a crowd. But despite all their best endeavours, they would hesitate to claim they had come to know the private man at all well. The dilemma is illustrated by comparing an entry in his diary with an entry recording the same event in that of his aunt, Lady Duff Gordon. The event was the death in January 1855 of his father Sir Thomas Frankland Lewis who was also Lady Duff Gordon's brother-in-law.

Lady Duff Gordon wrote:

> The 31st of January this year has brought me the sad news of my long loved & respected Brother-in-Law's most unexpected death! Most sad and grievous to me. Age does not accustom one to these heavy losses! Sir Frankland had gone out with several others shooting! … He would have been 75 on the 14th May. His life has been a most fortunate one in every respect. None but the old can know what he has done for the County of Radnor and can fancy the changes wrought in it by him. His loss there is irreparable and in the midst of all our woe poor Ly Lewis ought alone be thought of. She lived but for, & through him so entirely a devoted wife one never saw of any age & I think of her every moment.

> 2nd February 1855. Poor Ly Lewis alone being by his bedside. The account of her was wonderfully good, tho' her grief great and lasting. I can conceive no one more deeply afflicted. He was her only thought, her only admiration and she loses the one only thing she cared for in this world! GC's letter showed how deeply he felt his loss & how stunned he was with the suddenness of the blow.[51]

Caroline Duff Gordon perceives Lewis as weighed down with grief and stunned. The letter he wrote to his aunt has not survived, but the entries in his diary, though referring to his 'poor father's death' are clinically dispassionate and refer mainly to the restoration of his own political career in consequence of his father's death. There is no mention of his step-mother, Lady Lewis, and her grief:

Thursday 1st Febrary 1855. Harpton. It appears from conversations which I had with Dr James and Mr Bennett, the two medical men who attended my father in his last illness, that they consider him to have died of angina pectoris ... the latter afterwards called the cause of death *syncope anginosa.* Today I opened an address offering myself as a candidate for the representation of the Radnorshire boroughs, in my father's place.

Friday 2nd February, Harpton. Wrote letters to the constituents, etc.

Saturday 3rd February. Canvassed Knighton with good success.

Some may think that Lewis showed indecent haste in offering himself as his father's parliamentary successor within a few days of his funeral; others could conclude that it was a case of noblesse oblige whereby private grief had to make way to public duty.

References

Preface
1. Roy Jenkins, Gladstone, London, 1995, p.65.
2. *Ibid.*, p.216.
3. Diaries. Monday 13th June 1859.
4. Jenkins, *op.cit.*, p.231.

Chapter 1: Childhood, education, and early career
1. It was probably leased from a certain Lady Calder, who was perhaps Lady Amelia Calder, wife of Admiral Sir Robert Calder, 1745-1818, and who died mentally deranged.
2. Samuel Lewis, *A Topographical Dictionary of Wales*, London, 1833.
3. Thomas Lloyd, *The Lost Houses of Wales*, 2nd edition, London 1989, p.44.
4. Lewis, The Revd Sir Gilbert Frankland, ed, *Letters of the Right Hon Sir GC Lewis, Bart, to various friends*, London, 1870, p.1.
5. *eg* Diaries: 16.3.1847; 5.8.1847; 6.8.1847; 7.8.1847; 4.9.1847; 5.12.1847; 19.12.1847, suggesting attacks of migraine.
6. Lewis, *op.cit.*, p.1. Robert Southey published an abridged translation of *Amadis de Gaul* in 1803 and of *Palmeirin de Inglaterra* in 1807.
7. Lewis, *op.cit.*, p.1.
8. T Faulkner, *An Historical and Topographical Description of Chelsea*, Vol 2, London, 1829, pp.214, 215.
9. *The Times*, 18th May 1863.
10. He was, however, elected FRS in June 1820 as 'a Gentleman distinguished by his Abilities and Several Attainments, and attached to scientific Pursuits'. He let his fellowship lapse in 1831, but renewed it in 1841. George Cornewall Lewis was never FRS.
11. De Winton Archives. 35/1/40. 20th August 1797. St Aldates, Oxford. William Forster to Walter Wilkins, Maeslough, near Hay.
12. *Ibid.*, 35/1/5. 17th June 1801. Christ Church, Oxford. P Williams to Walter Wilkins, Junior.
13. Eton College Archives. Admissions Register.
14. For example: 'the screwing up and smashing of his desk, the singing of songs in chorus during schooltime, and an occasional fusillade of rotten eggs'. *The Dictonary of National Biography.*
15. *Ibid.*
16. 30th June 1832.
17. GC Lewis to his mother, April 1820. *The Oxford English Dictionary* defines slang in this context as 'the special vocabulary or phraseology of a particular calling or profession; the cant or jargon of a certain class or period'.
18. Lewis, *op.cit.*, p.3. The game, popular at Eton, is a form of hand-tennis in which a ball is struck by the hand against the front wall of a three-sided court. The earliest reference to it is given in the *OED* as occuring in 1636.
19. *Ibid.*
20. Michael Stapleton, *The Cambridge Guide to English Literature*, Cambridge, 1983, p.992.
21. Lewis, *op.cit.*, p.3.
22. *Ibid.*
23. Eton College school lists 1791-1849.
24. *Ibid.*
25. Lewis, *op.cit.*, p.3. The account of the coroner's inquest in *The Times*, April 2nd 1821, reflects the accuracy of Lewis's description of the tragedy.
26. Duff Gordon Archives. ADG 1:3.13th February [1855], Kent House. GC Lewis to GF Lewis. Gilbert entered Eton 25th September 1822, aged 13. Eton College Archives. Admissions Register.
27. Hawtrey, entry in *Dictionary of National Biography*.

28. Duff Gordon Archives. ADG 1:1. 22nd July 1826. GC Lewis to GF Lewis, Mrs Holts, Eton College, Windsor.

29. *ie* Lady Caroline Duff Gordon.

30. Duff Gordon Archives. ADG 1:2. 22nd July 1826. GC Lewis to GF Lewis, Mrs Holts, Eton College, Windsor.

31. *The Standard*, April, 1863.

32. Harpton Papers 3026. Eton College: December 10th, 1823.The Revd Edward Craven Hawtrey to TF Lewis.

33. Cornewall Lewis Diaries: Thursday October 29th 1846. John Ramsay McCulloch, 1789-1864, was Comptroller of the Stationery Office.

34. Harpton Papers C/1450. 1848, 21st June 1848, Eton College, Dr EC Hawtrey to GC Lewis.

35. ET MacDermot, revised by CR Clinker, *History of the Great Western Railway*, Vol 1, 1833-1863, London, 1964, p.97.

36. GC Lewis Diaries, Monday June 13th 1853. Hawtrey had been Provost of Eton since 1852. In July 1846 his visit to Hawtrey at Eton had been a matter of travelling by chaise from the station at Slough. Harpton papers 457 [1846] July 11th July 1846 GC Lewis to Sir TF Lewis.

37. Harpton PapersC/1451. February 5th 1853 GC Lewis to EC Hawtrey.

38. GF Lewis, *op.cit.*, p.6. 13th September 1824. Lausanne. GC Lewis to TF Lewis.

39. *Ibid.*

40. Founded in 1275.

41. Of 1557.

42. Sir Abraham Bradley King, Bart, of Corrard, Co Fermanagh, and Bloomsbury Co. Dublin, was created a baronet in 1821, and died in 1838.

43. GF Lewis, *op.cit.*, p.6. 13th September 1824. Lausanne. GC Lewis to TF Lewis.

44. *Ibid.*

45. He was MP for Fowey until 1830 and a Master in Chancery until 1840, 'when it became apparent that a mental disorder incapacitated him for its duties'.

46. Probably John Nicholas Fazakerley, MP for Peterborough in 1832. He and TF Lewis, as well as other members of the Lewis circle, such as Sir Robert Price of Foxley and Viscount Clive, were members of Grillions Club. He died in 1852.

47. Perhaps Charles Richard Vaughan, 1774-1849, a diplomatist who in February 1823 became British ambassador. In 1825 he was appointed ambassador to the United States.

48. Perhaps Henry Stephen Fox, 1791-1846, another diplomatist.

49. Nowadays the college has over 400 undergraduates and some 150 graduate members.

50. This, and the previous paragraph, leans heavily on Brock, MG, and Curthoys, MC, eds, *The History of the University of Oxford*, Vol VI, Nineteenth-Century Oxford, Part 1, Oxford, 1997, pp.42, 154, and 155.

51. *Ibid.*, p.41.

52. 'The First Public Examination' for the degree of BA, was conducted by Moderators, and Greats was the colloquial name given to the Second, and final, Public Examination.

53. GF Lewis, *op.cit.*, p.9.

54. *The Public Economy of Athens*, in four books; to which is added a dissertation on the silver mines of Laurion. Translated from the German of A. Böckh, 2 vols., John Murray, London, 1828. Second edition, revised, pp.xiii. 688, JW Parker, London, 1842. Lewis met Augustus Böckh, 1785-1867, in Berlin in October 1835, and found him to be 'a middle-aged man, with nothing remarkable in his appearance'. [GF Lewis, *op.cit.*, p.45. October 7th 1835. Berlin. GC Lewis to TF Lewis.]

55. MG Brock, 'The Oxford of Peel and Gladstone, 1800-1833' in Brock, MG, and Curthoys, MC, *op.cit.*, pp.36, 38.

56. *Ibid.*, Christ Church: June 18, 1828. Samuel Smith to GC Lewis. Lewis was elected to a Studentship on 26th June 1828.

57. In 1830 Peacock was a special pleader, and was not called to the bar until 1836. He became a Queen's Counsel in 1850, and was knighted in 1859.

58. Owen Chadwick, *The Victorian Church*, Part One 1829-1859, 3rd edition, London, 1971, p.42.

59. Article on Whately in the *Dictionary of National Biography*.

60. Mullett, CF, ed, *Remarks on the Use and Abuse of Some political terms by George Cornewall Lewis,* Columbia, 1970, pp.14, 15.

61. In 1825 there was a movement in favour of a non-sectarian university in London and in 1828 what is now known as University College London was opened under the ambitious name of the University of London, but it could not confer degrees. King's College was founded and in 1836 the two colleges amalgamated and were incorporated as the University of London, with power to examine, and to award degrees.

62. He married a Miss Sarah Taylor, of Norwich and in June 1821 their only child, Lucie, was born. She married Sir Alexander Cornewall Duff Gordon, 1811-1854. Lady Duff Gordon died in 1869.

63. Duff Gordon Diaries. Sunday 12th August 1855. Hertford Street. George [Cornewall Lewis] talked most comfortably & pleasantly to me, and what really gave me pleasure, he talked with great satisfaction of Alexander as his Secretary.

64. Lewis held Müller in high respect: 'I do not know whether you are acquainted with Ottfried Müller's articles – *Attika, Eleusinia and Pallas*, in Ersch and Gruber's Encyclopädie. They are well worth reading, particularly that on the *Eleusinia*.' GL Lewis, *op.cit.*, p.147. 16th March 1846, Kent House, GC Lewis to George Grote.

65. Sir John Vaughan, 1769-1839, educated at Rugby and Queen's College, Oxford, was created DCL in 1834. Admitted in February 1786, he was called to the bar in 1791, appointed Solicitor-General in 1814, and Attorney-General in 1816. Knighted in 1828 and became a Privy Counsellor in 1831.

66. GF Lewis, *op.cit,* pp.9, 10, July 14th 1831, York. GC Lewis to TF Lewis.

67. *Ibid.*

68. *ie* he was placed in the first class of the Cambridge mathematical tripos.

69. He was knighted in 1834, on being appointed by Peel as Attorney-General, and from 1841-1866 he presided over the Court of Exchequer. Like Lewis, he was a man of parts, and was a Fellow, both of the Society of Antiquaries and of the Geological Society.

70. GF Lewis, *op.cit.* Buckingham House was bought by George III in 1762, and reconstructed by John Nash 1821-36.

71. Banks Archives. MISC 2/1/6. 25th April 1831.

72. Henry Peter Brougham, 1778-1868, first Baron Brougham and Vaux, Lord Chancellor 1830-4.

73. Banks Archives. MISC 1/2/11.

74. GF Lewis, *op.cit.* Perhaps he was anticipating the time he was to be Chancellor of the Exchequer.

75. Harpton Papers 270. April 28th, 1798. The minister, churchwardens, and parishioners of Old Radnor to Ann Hare, thanking her for the present of a clock. See RWD Fenn & JB Sinclair, 'Old Radnor Parish Church', *Transactions of the Radnorshire Society*, LVIII, 1988, pp.85, 86. It replaced a sixteenth century predecessor.

76. Harpton Papers 425. August 16th 1841. Ann Hare to her son Thomas Frankland Lewis.

77. According, that is, to Coneybeare.

78. GF Lewis, *op.cit.*, p.147. Kent House, 16th March, 1846, GC Lewis to George Grote.

79. This was, perhaps, Philipp Carl Buttman, *Ausführliche griechische Sprachlehre*, though why an Oxford fellow had no access to it the work is a mystery. An English version, translated and edited by the Revd JR Fishlake, *A Catalogue of Irregular Greek Verbs, with all the senses extant* had reached its third edition by 1837.

80. *Ibid.*, p.11. December 19th [1831], 17 Henrietta Street. GC Lewis to Edmund Head.

81. Six articles in volume one ['Notice of Knight's 'Nummi Veteres'', pp.122-5; 'Notice of

Aristotle's Œconomic's by Goettling', pp.126-41; 'Iliadus Codex Ægyptiacus', pp.177-87; 'On the Fables of Babrius', pp.280-304; 'The Journal of Education and Vote by Ballot in the Athenian States', pp.420-6, and 679-86], and three in volume 2 ['Dr Arnold on the Spartan Constitution', pp.38-71; 'Misceallaneous Observations III: On English Preterites and Genitives', pp.243-6; 'Miscellaneous Observations II: 'Notice of Micali's History of the Ancient Nation of Italy', pp.689-94].

82. A new edition, with notes and appendix by Sir Richard Kent Wilson, Bart., was published posthumously in 1877.
83. GF Lewis, *op.cit.*, p.33. 23rd July 1834, Glasgow, GC Lewis to EW Head.
84. Weber, M, *Die protestantische Ethik und der 'Geist' des Kapitalismus.* 1904.
85. GF Lewis, *op.cit.*, p.viii.
86. *Ibid.*, p.16. 7th November 1832. Cannes, GC Lewis to EW Head.
87. *Ibid.*, p.24. 20th November 1832. Nice, GC Lewis to GF Lewis.
88. Cited by Woodward, *op.cit.*, p.266 and p.272.
89. 9th October 1832, GC Lewis to TF Lewis. Gf Lewis, *op.cit.*, p.13.
90. He was also prominently connected with the founding of London University, of which for twenty years, 1842-1862, he was vice-chancellor.
91. Webb, *op.cit.*, p.105.
92. *Ibid.*, p.102.
93. *Political Register*, June 10th, 1835.
94. Harpton Papers C/2695. November 12th 1833.
95. William Sturges Bourne, 1769-1845, a Christ Church contemporary of Frankland Lewis, was MP for Bandon, County Cork, 1815-18.
96. GF Lewis, *op.cit.*, p.27. January 1834, TF Lewis to GC Lewis.
97. Maynooth College, County Kildare was a Roman Catholic seminary for the training of priests. That it was the recipient of a government grant caused considerable political controversy.
98. GF Lewis, *op.cit.*, pp.29, 30. Manchester, 2nd February 1834, GC Lewis to TF Lewis.
99. *Ibid.*, p.79. April 27th 1837. Hereford, EW Head to GC Lewis.
100. *The Times*, 18th May 1863.
101. GF Lewis, *op.cit.*, p.79. June 2nd 1837. Malta, GC Lewis to EW Head. In 1839 Lewis published *An Essay on the origin and formation of the Romance Languages: containing an examination of M. Raynouard's theory on the relation of the Italian, Spanish, Provençal, and French, to the Latin.* A second edition followed in 1862. EW Head believed Lewis's book to be the only one in English on the subject.
102. EL Woodward, *The Age of Reform 1815-1870*, Oxford, 1949, p.321.
103. DH Akenson, *The Church of Ireland: Ecclesiastical Reform and Revolution 1800-1885*, Yale, 1971, p.70.
104. GF Lewis, *op.cit.*, pp.35, 36. August 6th 1834. Dublin, GC Lewis to TF Lewis.
105. *Ibid.*, p54. July 15th 1836. London. GC Lewis to EW Head. The Whiteboys were a secret agrarian association formed in 1761 against high rents and tithes. They wore white shirts, the better to distinguish each other by night.
106. *Ibid.*, 31st July 1837. Malta, GC Lewis to EW Head.
107. *Ibid.*, 9th April 1836. London, GC Lewis to EW Head.
108. *Ibid.*, p.37. For an ordered and readable account of this period in the affairs of the Irish Church, see Owen Chadwick, *The Victorian Church*, part one, 1829-1859, 3rd edition, London, 1971, pp 51-60.
109. Archbishop of Dublin.
110. GF Lewis, *op.cit.*, pp.38, 39. GF Lewis to Mrs John Austin.
111. Charles Babbage, *Reflections on the decline of Science on England, and on Some of its Causes*, London, 1830, p.45. See JA Secord, *Controversy in Victorian Geology: The Cambrian-Silurian Dispute*, Princeton, 1986, pp.14-24.
112. Harpton Papers 3654. Nd. In the event *The Silurian System* cost its subscribers eight guineas a copy.

113. It was founded in 1824 as the official organ of the Benthamites, and acquired by Molesworth.
114. GF Lewis, *op.cit.*, p.53. May 13th 1836. 33 Hertford Street, GC Lewis to EW Head.
115. *Ibid.*
116. Founded in 1828, Hayward edited it until 1844, and under his care it was a much respected journal.
117. GF Lewis, *op.cit.*, pp.50, 51. April 9th 1836. London, GC Lewis to EW Head.
118. *Ibid.*, p.53. May 13th 1836. 33 Hertford Street, GC Lewis to EW Head.
119. *Ibid.*, pp55, 56. August 7th 1836. Harpton, GC Lewis to NW Senior.
120. Senior's views on Irish matters had much in common with those of Lewis, *eg* the former's 'Letter to Lord Howick on a Legal Provision for the Irish Poor, Commutation of Tithes, and a Provision for the Irish Roman Catholic Clergy'. 1831.
121. *Ibid.*, p.62. October 8th, 1836. Marseilles, GC Lewis to Mrs TF Lewis.
122. *Ibid.*, p.65. November 5th 1836. Malta, GC Lewis to EW Head.
123. *Ibid.*, p.68. November 8th 1836. Valetta, GC Lewis to TF Lewis.
124. *Ibid.*, p.69. December 6th 1836. GC Lewis to TF Lewis.
125. *Ibid.*
126. *Ibid.*, p.76. April 3rd 1837. Malta, GC Lewis to EW Head.
127. *Ibid.*, p.81. July 15th 1837. Malta, GC Lewis to TF Lewis.
128. *Ibid.*, pp.93, 94. December 13th 1837. Malta. GF Lewis to TF Lewis.
129. *Ibid.*, p.90. October 3rd 1837. Malta. GC Lewis to EW Head.
130. *Ibid.*, p.83. July 31st 1837. Malta. GC Lewis to EW Head.
131. *Ibid.*, p.90. October 3rd 1837. Malta. GC Lewis to EW Head.
132. Harpton Papers C/578. 3rd January 1839, John Walsham to TF Lewis.
133. Harpton Papers C/290. March 5th [1838?], TF Lewis, perhaps to his step-mother Anne Hare.
134. Harpton Papers C/2816. August 10th 1838. GC Lewis to EE Villiers.
135. Harpton papers C/578. 3rd January 1839. John Walsham to TF Lewis.

Chapter 2: Poor Law Commissioner

1. GF Lewis, *op.cit.*, p.115. 11th September 1841. Combe Florey, Sydney Smith to GC Lewis.
2. Harpton Papers. C/1712. 5th July 1841. TF Lewis to GC Lewis.
3. Harpton papers. C/1713 20th July 1841. TF Lewis to GC Lewis.
4. Published in 1841. Sidney and Beatrice Webb, *English Poor Law History*, London, 1929, part II, volume 1, p.166.
5. Sir James Robert George Graham, 1792-1861, became Home Secretary in 1841. Graham's relations, however, with the Lewises were always cordial. See Harpton Papers 411, 19th November 1844, .in which Graham offers TF Lewis his sincere thanks for his very able assistance in the passage of the Welsh Turnpike Bill through Parliament.
6. GF Lewis, *op.cit.*, p.117. March 13th 1842.Chester Street, GC Lewis to TF Lewis.
7. *Ibid.*, Lewis's translation of August Boeckh's *Public Economy of Athens*, originally appeared 1828.
8. GF Lewis, *op.cit.*, p.113. GC Lewis to George Grote. 23rd January 1841.
9. GC Lewis, *Glossary of Provincial Words Used in Herefordshire*, p.v. The incomplete *Collections towards the history and antiquities of Hereford* of the Revd John Duncumb, FSA, 1765-1839, the Herefordshire topographer, were published from 1804-1812.
10. GF Lewis, *op.cit.*, p.17. 7th November 1832, Cannes, GC Lewis to TF Lewis.
11. *Sporting Magazine*, XVIII, 1826, p.213.
12. GC Lewis, *Glossary*, p.7.
13. BG Charles in *Angles and Britons*, Cardiff, 1963, p.96.
14. Mullett, *op.cit.*, p.44.
15. CO Müller's *History of the Literature of Ancient Greece*, 1840-2. The Essay, first published in London in 1846, wore well and was reprinted at Oxford in 1891, with an

Introduction by the distinguished civil servant and British Empire historian, Sir Charles Prestwood Lucas, 1851-1931, and reprinted in Washington and New York in 1901.

16. *Ibid.*, p.113. GC Lewis to George Grote. 23rd January 1841.

17. *Ibid.*. George James Guthrie, 1785-1856, became MRCS in his sixteenth year. He was a distinguished army surgeon in the Napoleonic wars, declined a knighthood, and was several times President of the Royal College of Surgeons.

18. *Crapula*, Latin, a hangover or aftermath.

19. GF Lewis, *op.cit.*, p.113. GC Lewis to George Grote. 23rd January 1841.

20. *Ibid.*, p.128. 11th January 1843. Bilton Hotel, Dublin. GC Lewis to George Grote.

21. *Ibid.*, p.133, 23rd October 1843, Dale Street, Leamington, GC Lewis to E Head. By 1851 Dr Henry Jephson had retired from medicine and he and his wife were living stylishly at Beech Lawn, cared for by their seven servants.

22. Thomas Villiers Lister, b.1832, Marie Theresa Lister, b.1835, and Alice Beatrice Lister, b.1841.

23. GF Lewis, *op.cit.*, p.120. 13th March 1842, Chester Street. GC Lewis to George Grote.

24. Diaries, Sunday, 15th October, 1848.

25. Francis Egerton, first Earl of Ellesmere, 1800-57, statesman and poet. Created earl in 1846. He married Harriet Caroline Greville in 1822.

26. Thomas Hyde Villiers, 1801-1832, politician.

27. Edward Ernest Villiers, 1806-1843.

28. Henry Edward, 4th Lord Holland. He edited his father's *Foreign Reminiscences* which Lewis read with enjoyment: 'If any copy of Lord Holland's *Reminiscences* reaches your province, you will find it worth reading; but it is a gossiping book, and his idolatry of Napoleon is positively puerile, and appears in its true light when the grounds of it come to be stated. I suspect, however, that his account of Marie Antoinette, for which he has been so much abused, is true'. (GF Lewis, *op.cit.*, p.238. March 6th 1851, Kent House. GC Lewis to EW Head.)

29. Lord Holland's brother was Charles Richard Fox, 1796-1873.

30. Duff Gordon Diaries, 9th November 1865.

31. *The Times*, 1st July 1848.

32. Duff Gordon Diaries, 24th July 1857.

33. 'George Cornewall Lewis', *Dictionary of National Biography*, CD-Rom.

34. GF Lewis, *op.cit.*, p.150. 26th January 1847. Kent House. GC Lewis to George Grote.

35. Harpton Papers C/1763. 27th August 1846. TF Lewis to GC Lewis.

36. He was eldest son of the Currer Fothergill Busfeild, and nephew of Walter Ferrand, Esq, MP, of Harden Grange, whose name he assumed on the latter's death.

37. J Horsfall Turner, *Ancient Bingley: or Bingley, Its History and Scenery*, Bingley, 1897, pp.200, 258.

38. London, 1842.

39. *Blackwood's Edinburgh Magazine*, Vol.54, (335) September 1843, pp.407, 8.

40. Charles Mott, *Report from the Poor Law Commissioners ... relative to certain statements concerning the internal management of the Workhouse at Eye, Suffolk*, London, 1838.

41. It was the same with Ferrand, who had already come to the attention of Frankland Lewis, when he was a Poor Law Commissioner, for his support of Richard Oastler, 1789-1861, 'the factory king'. In 1820 Oastler succeeded his father as steward of the extensive Fixby estate, near Huddersfield, of Thomas Thornhill, whilst vigorously agitating for the abolition of slavery and child labour, and opposing Catholic emancipation and the new Poor Law. It was his opposition to the Poor Law at Fixby, which led Frankland Lewis to secure his dismissal by Thornhill in 1838. Unfortunately Oastler owed Thornhill £2,000 and from 1840-44 he languished in the Fleet Prison. His eventual release was partially secured by the endeavours of Ferrand who shared his commitment to achieving the Ten Hour Act.

42. Harpton Papers C/2954 23rd September 1841. GCL to Gilbert, Assistant Poor Law Commissioner.

43. Harpton Papers C/1250 6th October 1841. J Graham to GC Lewis.
44. Harpton Papers 3663. Copy. Poor Law Office, 22nd February 1842. GC Lewis to C Mott.
45. *The Times*, 6th June 1844.
46. Webb, *op.cit.*, p.112, n 2.
47. Harpton Papers C/1251-3 8th-9th October 1841. Sir James Graham to GC Lewis. Sir John Bowring, 1792-1872, friend of Jeremy Bentham, whose works he edited. He was editor of the *Westminster Review*, and contested Blackburn unsuccessfully in 1832. In 1838 at Manchester, with Cobden, he founded the Anti-Corn Law League, and was MP for Bolton 1841-47. Later on, his activities in China incurred Lewis's disapproval. See Lewis, *op.cit.*, p.323.
48. *The Times*, 6th June 1844.
49. *Ibid.*, Copy. Poor Law Office, 19th April 1842.GC Lewis to C Mott.
50. *The Times*, 6th June 1844.
51. *The Times*, 6th July 1842.
52. *The Times*, 6th June 1844.
53. Sir John James Walsham, Bart, 1805-1874, of Knill. He was created a baronet in 1831 and High Sheriff of Radnorshire in 1870. Lewis Diaries: 'Friday September 14th 1855. Harpton. Wrote to Lord Palmerston to propose Pressly as Deputy Chairman of the Inland Revenue Board, & Sir J Walsham as the new Commissioner'.
54. Harpton Papers 3863 nd J Meadows to GC Lewis.
55. *The Times*, 6th July 1842.
56. *The Times*, 6th June 1844.
57. *Ibid.*
58. Harpton Papers 3863.
59. London, 1844.
60. *The Times*, 6th June 1844.
61. Harpton Papers C/3679. Nd. 53 Downing Street, Ardwick Green, Manchester. C Mott to GC Lewis. See also C/3680 and C/3682.
62. *The Times*, 6th June 1844.
63. *The Times*, 27th April 1844.
64. *The Times*, 24th June 1844.
65. *Ibid.*
66. *Ibid.*
67. *Ibid.*
68. PRO M.H. 12/10661. 22nd December, 1837.
69. Parker pleaded ignorance of this. Ian Anstruther, *The Scandal of the Andover Workhouse*, London, 1973, pp.139, 140.
70. Harpton Papers C/1744 19th November 1845.
71. Anstruther, *op.cit.*, pp 148, 9.
72. Author's italics. The *Hereford Times* of Saturday, 10th October 1846. Parker emigrated to South Australia in 1849 where, at the bar, 'as a criminal pleader he especially excelled'. Anstruther, *op.cit.,* p.149.
73. Harpton Papers. C/2193 19th May 1846. Sir Robert Peel to GC Lewis.
74. He was Inspector of the Poor Law Board 1849-50, Secretary to the Board, 1851-59, when he succeeded to the earldom. He was President of the Poor Law Board, 1867-68.
75. Paragraphs 9829ff.
76. The *Hereford Times*, 10th October 1846.
77. Greville, *Memoirs*, vol 2, p.84. 3rd series.
78. Harpton Papers C/1764. 28th August 1846. TF Lewis to GC Lewis.
79. Harpton Papers 457. 11th July 1846 GC Lewis to TF Lewis.
80. George Coode was an Assistant Commissioner 1834-47, 'an able young barrister, afterwards the author of historical and legal reports on the Law of Settlement, etc, of great value'. (Webb, *op.cit.*, p.110, n.1.)

81. *Ibid.*, C/1758. 12th July 1846; C/1760 July 24th 1846; and C/1761 July 24th 1846. TF Lewis to GC Lewis.
82. *Ibid.*, C/1762 25th August 1846. TF Lewis to GC Lewis.
83. Webb, *op.cit.*, p.171, n.1.
84. Diaries; Friday, 2nd October and Saturday, 3rd October 1846.
85. GF Lewis, *op.cit.*, p110. 26th January 1840. Wilton Place: GC Lewis to Sir Edmund Head. Day was the author of *The Claims of the Poor: An Enquiry into the Poor Laws and Surplus Labour, and their Mutual Reaction.*
86. The *Hereford Times*, 10th October 1846.
87. Harpton Papers C/1736 November 1843, TF Lewis to GC Lewis.
88. *Ibid.*, C/1762 25th August 1846. TFL to GCL.
89. *Report and Evidence of House of Commons Committee on the Andover Case*, 1845, Question 22,020. Disraeli, who had been a member of the Committee, asked why 'this monster in human shape was not dismissed'.
90. Webb, *op.cit.*, p.93, n.1; p.113, n.1.
91. *Ibid.*, p.180.
92. GF Lewis, *op.cit.*, p.150. 26th January 1847. Kent House. GC Lewis to George Grote.
93. Webb, *op.cit.*, p.184, citing Bagehot.
94. He was now Lord Lieutenant of Ireland.
95. Lewis Diaries, Wednesday 23rd June 1847.
96. *Ibid.*, Thursday 24th June 1847.
97. GF Lewis, *op.cit.*, p.185. 28th September 1849. Grove Mill house, GC Lewis to E Head. Lewis thought the Health of Towns Act had been so emasculated in Committee 'that its powers will not amount to much in practice'. *Ibid.*
98. Harpton Papers C/1162. 19th August 1846. Sir David Dundas, Middle Temple, to GC Lewis.
99. Harpton Papers C/2669 26th August 1846. John Meadows White, Lincolns Inn Field, to GC Lewis.
100. Harpton Papers 3665 28th Sept 1846. C Mott to Meadows White. Was it from Chadwick he feared a breach of confidentiality?
101. *Ibid.*, 30th September 1846. J Meadows White to C Mott.
102. *Ibid.*, 9th October 1846. J Meadows White to C Mott.
103. Harpton Papers 3669. 20th October 1846. Meadows White to GC Lewis.
104. He was later knighted and served with distinction as a judge in India.
105. Harpton Papers 3672. 26th October 1846. Meadows White to GC Lewis.
106. Harpton Papers 3863. Nd. J Meadows White to GC Lewis.
107. *Ibid.*
108. *Ibid.*
109. *Ibid.*
110. *Ibid.*
111. Harpton Papers. 462. 26th November 1846. On the same day, however, Sir Frederick Thesiger, of the Temple, wrote to Lewis, assuring him that the mode in which the case was being dealt with had given him great satisfaction. Harpton Papers C/2474. 26th November 1846. GC Lewis to TF Lewis.
112. Harpton Papers 3673. 23rd November 1846. Rochdale. C Mott to J Meadows White.
113. Harpton Papers 3674. 5th December 1846. Poor Law Commission. GC Lewis to G Coode.
114. Sir Hugh Owen, 1804-1881, who did much for Welsh secondary and university education. He joined the Poor Law commission in 1836, having impressed Chadwick, he was given a minor clerkship. By 1848 he had risen to be 'Clerk to the Board', in authoritative and confidential relations with his political chiefs. From 1853-1872, when he retired, he was Chief Clerk for Office management, and as such was 'almost the entire department, knowing and controlling every detail; and for twenty years

authoritatively representing the Board in all Parliamentary and other inquiries'. Webb, *op.cit.*,n.1., p.196.

115. Sir John Jervis, 1802-56, was appointed Attorney-General by Lord John Russell in 1846, and became Lord chief Justice of Common Pleas in 1850. He died suddenly in 1856.
116. *The Times,* 18th August 1846.
117. Lewis, it will be recollected, wrote about Pollock's success as a barrister to his father when he was judge's marshal at York in 1831.
118. *The Times*, 29th January 1847.
119. Harpton Papers C/1793 21st November 1847. TF Lewis to GC Lewis.
120. *The Times*, 29th January 1847.
121. Lewis Diaries.
122. Harpton Papers 3675. 25th January 1847. Messrs White & Borrett to J Dobie.
123. *Ibid.*
124. *Ibid.*
125. *The Times*, 29th January, 1847.
126. Harpton Papers 3677. 16th February 1847. Sir John Walsham to GC Lewis.
127. *The Times*, 29th January, 1847.
128. *Ibid.*
129. *Ibid.*
130. Lewis Diaries.
131. *Dictionary of National Biography*.
132. Harpton Papers C/2873. 23rd May 1847. GC Lewis to A Hayward.
133. C/674. 26th May 1847. Sir James Graham to GC Lewis.
134. Lewis Diaries, 23rd July 1847.
135. Lewis Diaries, 27th August 1847.
136. Lewis Diaries, 6th November 1847.
137. Harpton Papers. C/2475 November 10th 1847. Sir Frederick Thesiger to GC Lewis.
138. Lord John Manners, seventh Duke of Rutland, 1818-1906, and fellow politician.
139. GF Lewis, *op.cit.*, p.150. 26th January 1847. Kent House. GC Lewis to George Grote.
140. 'Charles John Vaughan' in the *Dictionary of National Biography* on CD-Rom.
141. Cornewall Lewis Diaries: Friday 15th January 1847. 'Entered into recognisances to prosecute Ferrand. Thursday 28th January 1847. Debate on Ferrand's motion. Saturday March 20th 1847. Received Mr Ferrand's plea'.

Chapter 3: Parliament

1. Cornewall Lewis Diaries. Sunday 9th May 1847.
2. Duff Gordon Diaries. Monday 31st May 1847.
3. Cornewall Lewis Diaries, Saturday 15th May 1847.
4. *Ibid.*, Monday 17th May 1847.
5. *Ibid.*, Monday 25th May; Sunday 30th May, Thursday 3rd June 1847.
6. *Ibid.*, Friday June 4th; Saturday 5th June 1847.
7. GF Lewis, *op.cit.*, p.154. 2nd July 1847, Hereford. GC Lewis to EH Head.
8. Cornewall Lewis Diaries, Wednesday, 28th July, 1847.
9. One of whom was Sir John Taylor Coleridge, 1790-1876. On the King's Bench from 1835, and 'though never great, he was always a sound lawyer'. His religious sympathies were Tractarian and in 1848 he became involved in the controversy over Dr Hampden's appointment as Bishop of Hereford. (*Ibid.*, Thursday, 29th July 1847).
10. Born 1810, he was still Chaplain in 1874, but in 1881 was living at South Bank House, Tupsley.
11. In 1845 Peel increased the government grant to the Roman Catholic seminary at Maynooth from £9,000 to £26,000.
12. Harpton Papers C/843. 8th July 1847. Lewis was canvassing Hereford at the time from his brother's rectory at Monnington on Wye.

13. Harpton Papers C/2837. 19th July 1847. GC Lewis to the Revd JH Barker, Hereford.
14. Harpton Papers C/844. 21st July 1847.
15. GF Lewis, *op.cit.*, p.156. 5th August, 1847. Hereford. GC Lewis to Edmund Head.
16. The Revd Prebendary Francis Haggitt, MA, DD, rector of Nuneham Courtney, near Oxford, and Chaplain to George III.
17. Duff Gordon Diaries, Monday 5th September 1859.
18. GF Lewis, *op.cit.*, p.231.15th September 1850. Grove Mill. GC Lewis to Edmund Head.
19. James Davies of Moor Court, Pembridge, the Kington lawyer and banker.
20. Diaries, Wednesday, 4th August 1847.
21. GF Lewis, *op.cit.*, p.156. 5th August, 1847. Hereford. GC Lewis to Edmund Head.
22. The article appeared in the *Edinburgh Review*, lxxxvii, 1848, p.451, and was reprinted and circulated by the Government when the law of settlement was altered in 1865.
23. Home of Sir Robert Price, Bart, 1786-1857. He was MP for the County of Hereford 1818-1841 and for Hereford City 1845-57.
24. Diaries, Sunday 15th August 1847. He succeeded George Steven Byng, who was Secretary of the Board of Control from 1846 until his ennoblement as the first Viscount Enfield a year later.
25. Sir John Cam Hobhouse, 1786-1869, who was ennobled as the first Baron Broughton, was President of the Board of Control 1835-41 and 1846-52, and is said to have invented the phrase 'His Majesty's Opposition'.
26. Samuel James Loyd, 1796-1883, an influential banker who was created the first Baron Overstone in 1860.
27. GF Lewis, *op.cit.*, p.162, 5th November 1847, Grove Mill House, Watford. GC Lewis to George Grote.
28. 'The Theatre, in Broad Street, is a remarkably small and ill-supported erection. This has been the nursery of many celebrated characters, including Mrs Clive, Mr Powell, Mrs Siddons, the Kembles, and ... Garrick'. (*Lascelles and Co's Directory and Gazetteer of the Counties of Monmouth and Hereford*, Birmingham, 1852, p.23.)
29. GF Lewis, *op.cit.*, p.158, 31st October, 1847, Grove Mill House, Watford: GC Lewis to George Grote.
30. The Hoptons were a well-established Herefordshire family, though originating from Shropshire, and Susanna Hopton, 1627-1709, wife of Richard Hopton, of Canon Frome, achieved an entry the *Dictionary of National Biography* as a devotional writer. The family acquired the advowsons of the prosperous livings of Canon and Bishops Frome, and Stretton Grandison, and they usually filled them with their clerical relations, most of whom displayed a remarkable talent for longevity. Captain John Hopton, of Canon Frome Court, was born in 1810.
31. The Revd William Cooke, MA.
32. Diaries.
33. *Ibid.*, Tuesday 19th October 1847.
34. GF Lewis, *op.cit.*, p.158.
35. *Ibid.*
36. *Ibid.* The book was published as *An Essay on the Influence of Authority in Matters of Opinion*, London, 1849. A second edition was published posthumously in 1875.
37. GF Lewis, *op.cit.*, pp.169-170. 4th March 1848, Kent House, GC Lewis to Mrs Austin.
38. Edward Thornton, 1799-1875, *History of British Empire in India*, 6 volumes, London, 1841-5. By Monday 17th January 1848 he was on volume three (Diaries).
39. Diaries. Thursday 23rd December 1847.
40. *DNB* citing SR Gardiner, *History of England*, iv, p.276.
41. William Leader Maberley, 1798-1885, was Secretary of the General Post Office, 1836-1854, and by his sustained opposition to the reforms proposed by Rowland Hill, it is alleged, caused the loss of some millions of public money.
42. Lord William George Bentinck, 1802-48, was MP for Lynn 1826-1848. He prided himself as a judge of both men and horses, and was in his day the chief man of the turf. He was

a protectionist in the matter of the Corn Laws, but a great believer in religious liberty, arguing that the Roman Catholic priesthood of Ireland should be endowed out of the land; and in December 1847 voted for the admission of Jews into Parliament. This caused him to resign his leadership of the protectionists.

43. Sir Robert Henry Inglis, Bart, 1786-1855, a man 'of many prejudices and no great ability', represented the University of Oxford from 1829-1854. He was opposed to Jewish emancipation.

44. Duff Gordon Archives. ADG 1:6. 25th January 1848. Grove Mill, GC Lewis to his brother GF Lewis.

45. Diaries, Saturday 5th February 1848.

46. Edward Horsman, 1807-1876. Liberal MP for Cockernouth 1836-1852, Stroud 1853-1868, and Liskeard 1869-76.

47. Diaries. Friday 3rd March 1848.

48. *Ibid.* Thomas Babington, Baron Macaulay was unseated in 1847 and from thence devoted himself to literature and history. Charles Austin was an esteemed friend of Lewis, Macaulay, and Henry Hallam. 'His name is often mentioned in memoirs and diaries of the time, and always respectfully, although he never rivalled the conversational supremacy of his contemporaries, Sydney Smith and Macaulay' (*DNB*). Henry Hart Milman, historian and poet, was rector of St Margaret's Westminster and Canon of Westminster Abbey, before becoming Dean of St Paul's in 1849. The king in question was Louis Philippe of France.

49. GF Lewis, *op.cit.*, p.174. 16th April 1848. Kent House. GC Lewis to Edmund Head.

50. Diaries. Monday 10th April 1848.

51. Sir George Grey, 1799-1882, Home Secretary under Russell, 1842-52.

52. John Mitchel, 1815-1875.

53. Diaries. Monday 29th May 1848. Kent House The activities of the Chartists occupy two other entries in the Diaries: Saturday 3rd June 1848:'Chartist meetings in the east of London have continued at intervals during this week. There have likewise been disturbances in the W. Riding & Lancashire. The immediate occasion of these movements has been the conviction of Mitchel'. Monday 12th June 1848: 'The Chartist movement fixed for this day, went off quietly'.

54. Paul Latcham, 'John Allen, Jr. and his Bibliotheca Herefordiensis', p.219, David Whitehead and John Eisel, eds., *A Herefordshire Miscellany*, Hereford, 2000.

55. Diaries. Tuesday 23rd May and Wednesday 24th May.

56. GF Lewis, *op.cit,* pp.175, 176. 20th June 1848. Kent House. GC Lewis to Edmund Head.

57. Diaries. Friday 29th September 1848.

58. *Ibid.*, 4th - 11th October 1848.

59. *Addresses and Speeches of Sir George Cornewall Lewis, relative to the election for the county of Hereford in 1852.* Printed for private distribution: London, 1857.

60. GF Lewis, *op.cit.*, p.204, 6th April 1849, Kent house, GC Lewis to Edmund Head.

61. Diaries, Wednesday 23rd May 1849.

62. GF Lewis, *op.cit.*, p.205. 10th June 1849. Kent House. GC Lewis to Edmund Head.

63. *Ibid.*, p.220. 25th January 1850. Knightsbridge. GC Lewis to Edmund Head.

64. Diaries, Friday 13th October 1848.

65. Auguste Comte, 1798-1857. His six-volume *Cours de philosophie positive* was published 1830-42.

66. GF Lewis, *op.cit.*, p.231.15th September 1850. Grove Mill. GC Lewis to Edmund Head. In May 1851 Lewis told Head that he had read Comte's *Cours de Philosophie* twice, on the recommendation of JS Mill, and thought Head 'would find it worth reading'. (GF Lewis, *op.cit.*, p.246.19th May 1851. Kent House. GC Lewis to Edmund Head.)

67. Diaries. Monday 5th February 1849.

68. *Ibid.*

69. Diaries.

70. Diaries. Saturday 7th April 1849.

71. Diaries. Wednesday 11th April 1849.
72. Diaries. Sunday 13th May 1849. *The Examiner* was a weekly periodical launched in 1808 by the brother John and Leigh Hunt. It dealt with literature and politics. John Forster, 1812-76, became editor in 1847.
73. *The Athenaeum* was an eminent literary and artistic review founded in 1828. It was incorporated in *The Nation and Athenaeum* in 1921, which, in turn, became *The New Statesman* in 1931.
74. GF Lewis, *op.cit.*, pp.207, 208. 10th June 1849. Kent House. GC Lewis to Edmund Head. Milman was now Dean of St Paul's.
75. Diaries. Tuesday 22nd May 1849. Henry Morgan Clifford, 1806-1884, was MP for Hereford 1847-65.
76. Diaries.Wednesday 23rd May 1849.
77. CF Mullett, ed, *Remarks on the Use and Abuse of Some political terms by George Cornewall Lewis*, Columbia, 1970, p..44.
78. Diaries. Saturday 9th June 1849.
79. A reference to the title of the logical writings of Aristotle. 'An instrument of thought or knowledge; a means by which some process of reasoning, discovery, etc., is carried on; *especially* a system of rules or principles of demonstration or investigation', second edition of the *Oxford English Dictionary*.
80. GF Lewis, *op.cit.*, pp.207, 208. 10th June 1849. Kent House. GC Lewis to Edmund Head.
81. Diaries. Saturday 18th August to Monday 20th August 1849.
82. GF Lewis, *op.cit.*, pp.220, 221. 25th January 1850. Knightsbridge. GC Lewis to Edmund Head.
83. Diaries. Wednesday 12th September 1849.
84. Diaries. Wednesday 12th to Monday 17th September 1849.
85. GF Lewis, *op.cit.*, p.117. March 13th 1842. Chester Street, GC Lewis to TF Lewis in Rome.
86. *Ibid.*, pp.209, 210. September 4th, 1849. Garnstone, Herefordshire. GC Lewis to Edmund Head.
87. Diaries. Tuesday 18th September 1849.
88. Diaries. Thursday 20th September 1849.
89. Diaries. Friday 19th October 1849.
90. Diaries. Saturday 20th October 1849.
91. Diaries. Thursday 1st November to Wednesday 7th November 1849.
92. GF Lewis, *op.cit.*, p.217. 27th November 1849. Home Office. GC Lewis to Edmund Head. Sitting for one's portraits was a popular activity at this time with the Lewises: and Frankland Lewis sat for Watts. *Ibid.* and Lady Duff Gordon, who was staying at Harpton, noted that 'Sir Frankland's picture got on famously'. Duff Gordon Diaries, Tuesday 2nd October 1849. George Frederick Watts, 1817-1914: 'For the Duff Gordon ladies Watts at this time painted a portrait of Louisa, Marchioness of Waterford'. *DNB*.
93. Diaries. Tuesday 4th December 1849.
94. Harpton Papers C/1278 15th September 1832. Titley Court. Lady Elizabeth Coffin to GC Lewis.
95. GF Lewis, *op.cit.*, pp.219, 220. 25th January 1850. Knightsbridge. GC Lewis to Edmund Head.
96. *Ibid.*, p.223. 24th April 1850. Kent House. GC Lewis to Edmund Head.
97. John Barrel, 'The Australian Convicts of Radnorshire', *Transactions of the Radnorshire Society*, LX, 1990, p.30.
98. Diaries. Sunday 5th May 1850.
99. *Eg* Diaries. Saturday 18th May 18 and Monday 20th May 1850.
100. GF Lewis, *op.cit.*, p.227. 11th July 1850. London. GC Lewis to Edmund Head.
101. Diaries. Thursday 30th May 1850. Sir Charles Barry, 1795-1886, designed the Houses of Parliament in collaboration with Augustus Pugin, 1812-52. Though the House of Lords was used in 1847, it was not until 1852 that the houses were formally opened by the Queen.

CANAANLANDINGPAGE# REFERENCES

102. *Ibid*. Monday 1st July 1850.
103. Henry Tufnell, 1805-54. MP for Ipswich 1837-38 and for Devonport 1840-54.
104. Sir William Goodenough Hayter, QC, 1792-1878. MP for Wells 1837-65.
105. Edward Pleydell-Bouverie, 1818-1874. MP for Kilmarnock 1844-1874.
106. GF Lewis, *op.cit.*, p.225. 11th July 1850. London. GC Lewis to Edmund Head.
107. *Ibid.,* p.226. 11th July 1850. London. GC Lewis to Edmund Head.
108. Diaries. Thursday 29th August 1850.
109. Diaries. Friday 18th October 1850.
110. GF Lewis, *op.cit.*, p.231. 15th September 1850. Grove Mill. GC Lewis to Edmund Head. Booker, however, did have some connection with Hereford, his father having been rector of Tedstone Delamere for some time.
111. Diaries. Monday 21st and Tuesday 22nd October 1850.
112. *Hereford Times*, 18th October 1851.
113. James Wallace Richard Hall was a Ross on Wye solicitor who, with his partner Henry Minett, acted as solicitors to the Hereford, Ross, and Gloucester Railway Company.
114. J F Vaughan of Courtfield.
115. *Hereford Times*, October 1850.
116. Diaries. Tuesday 5th November 1850.
117. Diaries. Wednesday 4th December 1850.
118. GF Lewis, *op.cit.*, p.232. 28th December 1850. Grove Mill. GC Lewis to Edmund Head.
119. Diaries, Wednesday 30th April and Wednesday 18th June 1851.
120. *Ibid.*, Saturday 26th October 1851.
121. *Hereford Times*,1852.
122. Diaries. *Eg* Monday 18th to Saturday 23rd November 1850.
123. GF Lewis, *op.cit.*, p.234. 28th December 1850. Grove Mill. GC Lewis to Edmund Head.
124. Duff Gordon *Diaries*. Tuesday 12th November 1850.
125. Diaries. Friday 6th December 1850.
126. One wonders how much of Theresa Lewis's book was actually her work. Agnosticism is encouraged by such entries in Lewis's Diary as: 'Saturday 1st February 1851. Kent House. Received today from Clowes the … latter part of Ld Falkland's life, written by Theresa. During the month of January I have corrected the proofs & have worked on the revision of the text in carrying the work thro the press'. *The Times*, when reviewing the three volumes commended Theresa Lewis's 'simplicity and truthfulness'. (*The Times* 23rd July 1852).
127. Founded in 1849 as 'A medium of Inter-communication for Literary Men, Artists, Antiquaries, Genealogists, etc' by the antiquary William John Thoms, 1803-1885.
128. *Notes & Queries*, Vol 2 [33], 15th June 1850, p.35.
129. *Ibid.*, pp.35, 36.
130. Diaries. Saturday 28th June 1851.
131. *The Times*, 19th June 1851.
132. *Ibid.*, Vol 2 [46], 14th September 1850, p.24.
133. *Ibid.*, Vol 2 [49] 5th October 1850, pp.298, 9.
134. *Ibid.*, *Notes & Queries*, Vol 4 [108], November 1851, p.402.
135. *Ibid.*, *Notes & Queries*, Vol 4 [108], November 1851, p.403.
136. GF Lewis, *op.cit.*, p.246. 19th May 1851. Kent House. GC Lewis to Edmund Head.
137. GF Lewis, *op.cit.*, p.241.1st September 1851. Grove Mill. GC Lewis to Edmund Head.
138. Diaries: Thursday 5th August 1852.
139. *Ibid.*, Tuesday 16th May 1854.
140. Diaries. Wednesday 13th, Thursday 14th, and Friday 15th August 1851.
141. JS Mill, *A System of Logic*, 2 Vols, London, 1846. A second edition appeared in 1851.
142. GF Lewis, *op.cit.*, p.246.19th May 1851. Kent House. GC Lewis to Edmund Head. JS Mill, *Essays on some unsettled questions of Political Economy*, London 1844.
143. Unoccupied time.

144. Diaries. Saturday 23rd August 1851.
145. *Ibid*. Monday 15th December 1851.
146. The German historian Barthold Georg Niebuhr, 1776-1831, was Prussian ambassador in Rome 1816-23, and professor of Roman history at Bonn until 1831. His three-volume *History of Rome*, published 1811-32, was important form its critical examination of original sources.
147. *Ibid*. Monday 15th December 1851.
148. Diaries. Saturday 3rd and Monday 5th January 1852.
149. *Ibid*., Saturday 24th January 1852.
150. *Ibid*., Saturday 31st January and Monday 9th February 1852.
151. *Ibid*., Tuesday 24th and Wednesday 25th February 1852.
152. *Ibid*., Monday 1st March to Wednesday 3rd March 1852.
153. GF Lewis, *op.cit*., p.244. 19th May 1851. Kent House. GC Lewis to Edmund Head.
154. *The Times*, 20th October 1851.
155. *Ibid*.
156. *Ibid*.
157. *Ibid*.
158. Diaries. Saturday 18th and Wednesday 22nd October 1851.
159. *The Times*, 21st October 1851.
160. GF Lewis, *op.cit.,* p.248. 21st December 1851. Grove Mill. GC Lewis to Edmund Head.
161. Banks Archives. RWB 6/2. Kent House, Knightsbridge, 22nd February 1852. GC Lewis to Richard Banks.
162. Banks Archives. RWB 6/40 25th February 1852, Copy of letter from Richard Banks to GC Lewis.
163. Harpton Papers. C/814 24th February 1852.
164. Diaries. Friday 5th to Tuesday 9th March 1852.
165. Diaries, Tuesday, March 23rd 1852.
166. *Ibid*., Tuesday, April 6th 1852.
167. Banks Archives.RWB 6/42 Kent House, Knightsbridge, 8th April 1852. GC Lewis to Richard Banks.
168. *Hereford Times*, 18th October 1851.
169. Diaries, Wednesday 7th April to Sunday 11th April 1852.
170. Mention has been made already of Hall and Minett; Hooper was also Town Clerk of Ross.
171. *Alias* the Royal Hotel and Posting House, proprietor James Barrett.
172. Diaries. Tuesday 11th May 1852.
173. Diaries. Sunday 30th May 1852.
174. Diaries. Monday 31st May 1852.
175. Diaries. Tuesday 13th July 1852.
176. *Hereford Times*, July 1852.
177. *Ibid*.
178. Diaries, Friday 16th July 1852.
179. *The Times*, April 23rd 1852.
180. Diaries, Saturday 17th July, and Sunday 17th July 1852.
181. Diaries. Monday 19th and Tuesday 20th July 1852.
182. Duff Gordon *Diaries*. Wednesday 21st July 1852.
183. Diaries. Saturday 24th and Monday 26th July 1852.
184. GF Lewis, *op.cit*., p.254.
185. Those who give their vote solely to one candidate (when one has the right to vote for two or more). (*OED*).
186. Harpton papers C/1132. 24th July 1852. Moor Court. James Davies to GC Lewis.
187. Simpson, *op.cit*., pp.144, 145, quoting Senior's diary, Saturday, 14th August 1852.
188. GF Lewis, *op.cit*., pp.357-359, Harpton, 17th November 1858. GC Lewis to FL Bodenham.

Chapter 4: Editing *The Edinburgh Review*
1. Diaries. 11th January-15th January, and 3'" February 1853.
2. *The Times*, 30th July 1852.
3. GE Cokayne, *The Complete Peerage*, ed. G. White, Gloucester, 1982, V, p.524.
4. Diaries. 6th August 1852.
5. Sheffield Archives, Sheffield City Libraries, Wentworth Woodhouse Muniments, G10/8a, 7th August 1852, Sir George Grey to Earl Fitzwilliam.
6. Ralph Bernal, d.1 854, was a Whig of long parliamentary experience, who lost his seat at Rochester in July 1852, to Edward Horsman, 1807-76, formerly the member for Cockermouth.
7. Diaries, 7th, 9th, and 11th August 1852.
8. *Ibid.*, Friday 13th August 1852.
9. Diaries. Monday, 16th August 1852.
10. John Carr, of York, 1723-1807, Palladian architect.
11. N Pevsner, *The Buildings of England: Yorkshire West Riding*, Harmondsworth, 2nd edition, 1967, p.545. It was built by Carr in 1788.
12. Diaries. Tuesday 17th August 1852.
13. The Revd Mr Strong was a local clergyman.
14. George Davys, 1780-1864, was tutor to the adolescent Queen Victoria and was Bishop of Peterborough 1839-64, where 'he took no active part either in religious controversy or in politics'.
15. George Butler, 1774-1853, was headmaster of Harrow 1805-29, and became dean of Peterborough in 1842.
16. Diaries.
17. *The Times*, 21st August, 1852.
18. *Ibid.*
19. Wentworth Woodhouse Muniments, G10/18, Simpson to Earl Fitzwilliam, 24th August 1852, Sheffield Archives, Sheffield City Libraries.
20. Diaries.
21. *Ibid.* Friday 27th August 1852.
22. Banks Archives. RWB 10/1/41. 30th August 1852. Howey Hall, Esther Crummer to RW Banks.
23. Diaries, 28th and 29th August 1852.
24. Diocesan Board of Education was established in 1849 and enjoyed the enthusiastic support of Richard Dawes, Dean of Hereford, 1850-1867, who shared Lewis's Liberal views.
25. Diaries. Friday 3'" to Monday 6th September 1852.
26. *Ibid.* Wednesday 8th to Thursday 9th September 1852.
27. *Ibid.* Friday 10th September 1852.
28. Diaries, Friday 17th to Saturday 18th September 1852.
29. *Ibid.* Monday 20th to Thursday 30th September 1852.
30. 28th November 1852. GC Lewis to Sir John Graham. Bodleian Library, Oxford. Graham, Bundle 112, on microfilm.
31. *The Times*, 9th December 1852.
32. Diaries. Wednesday 24th November 1852.
33. *The Times*, 9th December 1852.
34. *Ibid.*, 3rd December 1852.
35. *Ibid.*
36. *The Times*, 3rd December 1852.
37. Diaries. Thursday 3rd December 1852.
38. *Ibid.*
39. *The Times*, 9th December 1852.
40. Diaries. Friday 3rd December 1852.
41. *Ibid.* Saturday 4th December 1852.
42. *The Times*, 9th December 1852.

43. Diaries, Monday, 6th December 1852. William Rathbone Greg, 1809-1881, a prominent essayist, who 'discouraged unreasonable expectations' from politics, through Lewis's influence became a Commissioner in the Board of Customs. He was later Comptroller of the Stationery Office.
44. Harpton Papers, C/710, 6th December 1852. Sir James Graham to GC Lewis.
45. Duff Gordon Diaries. Sunday 2nd January 1853.
46. TR Bromund, 'A Complete Fool's Paradise: The attack on the Fitzwilliam Interest in Peterborough 1852', *Parliamentary History*, Autumn, 1992.
47. Thomas Longman, 1804-1879, of the publishing firm founded by Thomas Longman, 1699-1755. Longmans owned the *Edinburgh Review* from 1826.
48. William Empson, 1791-1852, edited the *Edinburgh Review* 1847-52.
49. Diaries.
50. Duff Gordon Diaries. Monday 27th December 1852.
51. GF Lewis, *op.cit.*, p.259. 2nd January 1853. Kent House, GC Lewis to Edmund Head.
52. *Notes & Queries*, 1st January 1853, pp.18, 19.
53. Diaries. Thursday, 20th January -Monday 31st January 1853.
54. Sir Henry Meredyth Jervis White Jervis, 1793-1869, bart, a commander in the Royal Navy. His *History of the Island of Corfu, and of the Republic of the Ionian Islands*, was published London, 1852.
55. Sir John Colborne, 1778-1861, elevated to the peerage in 1839 as Lord Seaton, was Lord High Commissioner of the Ionian Islands 1843-1849.
56. With, for example, his *The Ionian Islands under British Protection*, 1851, and *Mount Athos, Thessaly, and Epiros*, 1852. He was to become the first Governor of Queenstown in 1859, of New Zealand, 1868, Victoria 1873, Mauritius 1879, and Hong Kong in 1883.
57. Harpton Papers, C/2368, 19th January 1853. Deer Park, Honiton. Lord Seaton to GC Lewis.
58. Diaries. Monday 17th January 1853.
59. *Ibid.* Tuesday 18th January 1853: 'K[ent] H[ouse]. Wrote to Ld Seaton about Mr Bowen'.
60. Harpton Papers, C/2368, 19th January 1853. Deer Park, Honiton, Lord Seaton to GC Lewis.
61. *Ibid.* C/2369 22nd January 1853 and C/2370 1st February 1853.
62. *Notes & Queries*, Volume 7 (175) 5th March, 1853, p.241.
63. *Ibid.*, Volume 7 (173) 19th February, 1853, p.182.
64. Diaries. Monday 21st February, Wednesday 23rd to Monday 28th February, and Tuesday 1st March to Sunday 13th March 1853.
65. William Charles Lake, 1817-97, Senior Proctor 1852-53. Educated at Rugby and Balliol, and experienced in academic politics. He was 'a very clever man, with a knowledge of history then unusual'. Fellow of Balliol and later Curator of the Taylor Institution, he was a university reformer. He became dean of Durham in 1869.
66. Thomas Gaisford, 1779-1855, was Regius Professor of Greek at Oxford 1812-1837 when he became Dean of Christ Church. As a Greek scholar he was considered 'scarcely second to anyone of his time'.
67. John Ireland, DD, 1761-1842, dean of Westminster, in 1825 gave £4,000 for the foundation at Oxford of four scholarships, of the value of £30 a year each, 'for the promotion of classical learning and taste'.
68. Diaries. Friday 18th February 1853.
69. Francis Henry Jeune, Master of Pembroke College, Oxford, 1 843-64, and Vice-Chancellor, 1858-62. He was Bishop of Peterborough 1864-68, via the deanery of Lincoln cathedral. He was prominent in the movement for university reform at Oxford.
70. John Conington, 1825-69, educated at Rugby and Magdalen College, Oxford, won an Ireland Scholarship 1844, first Corpus Christi Professor of Latin in 1854, and soon after underwent an evangelical conversion. He was also a university reformer.
71. Arthur Gray Butler, 1831-1909. He was president of the Oxford Union the same year at his election to an Ireland scholarship. He was headmaster of Haileybury 1862-67.

72. William Lambert Newman, 1834-1923, of Balliol, was elected to an Ireland scholarship in 1854.and 'exercised a unique influence on the teaching of history and political philosophy at Oxford'.
73. Diaries. Monday 14th to Saturday 19th March 1853.
74. GF Lewis, *op.cit.,* p.261. 26th March 1853. Kent House, GC Lewis to Edmund Head.
75. Harpton Papers, C/854 1853, 19" February 1853. W Beadon, Otterhead, Honiton to GC Lewis. *Ibid.* C/855 26th February 1853. W Beadon, Otterhead, Honiton to GC Lewis. Diaries. Wednesday 28th February 1853.
76. Diaries. Sunday 20th, Tuesday, 22nd, Wednesday 23rd, Saturday 26th to Monday 28th, Wednesday 30th March, Friday 1st, and Monday 4th April 1853.
77. *The History of Europe from the commencement of the French Revolution in 1789 to the Restoration of the Bourbons*, of the 'intelligent and hardworking, if not brilliant' Sir Archibald Alison, 1792-1867, was immensely successful. Lewis thought it 'trashy', but the *DNB* said of it: 'In truth, the book has been useful as a good business-like summary of an important period of history, whilst the reader can sufficiently discount for the strong prejudices of the author and skip his ambitious reflections upon the currency and political philosophy'. The *Edinburgh Review* article was to be good because of Lewis's input: Diaries, 9th January 1853, 'Wrote notes on the first vol. of Alison's history of Europe since 1815 & sent them to Greg, with a view of an intended article in the next no. of the *Ed. Rev.*'
78. The Revd William John Conybeare, 1815-1857. Some would now think his strictures cruel rather than amusing. Lewis's use of this adjective reflects again his lack of sympathy with anything Welsh.
79. GF Lewis, *op.cit.*, p.261. 26th March 1853. Kent House, GC Lewis to Edmund Head.
80. Duff Gordon Diaries. Thursday 19th May 1853.
81. Treating: 'Regaling, feasting, entertaining; spec. the action of providing a person (wholly or partly at one's own expense) with food or drink at a parliamentary or other election in order totain (or in return for) his vote; bribery or corruption by feasting (illegal in Great Britain since 1854)'. [*OED*] Diaries, Thursday 5th, Saturday 28th May to Tuesday June 7th 1853.
82. Diaries. Friday 22nd April 1853.
83. *Ibid.*, Wednesday 8th June 1853.
84. *Ibid.*, Friday 29th July 1853.
85. Albert Schwegler.
86. Diaries. Tuesday 26th April 1853.
87. *Ibid.*, Friday 22nd July 1853.
88. Thomas Markby, editor, Francis Bacon, *Of the Proficience and Advancement of learning.*
89. *Notes and Queries*, Vol 8, (198 and 199), pp.141-144, and pp.165-167. London 1852.
90. *Ibid.*, p.143.
91. *Notes and Queries*, Vol 8 (208), pp 390-392.
92. Gilbert Lewis married Jane Antrobus in 1845. She was the daughter of Sir Edmund Antrobus, Bart, 1818-1899, of Lower Cheam, Surrey and Amesbury, Wiltshire. He was Liberal MP for East Surrey, 1841-47, and for Wilton, Wiltshire 1855-77.
93. The Hon Edward Turner Boyd Twistleton, 1809-74. Fellow of Balliol, 1830-38, and Liberal lawyer. His elder brother was Lord Saye and Sele, Canon Residentiary and Archdeacon of Hereford.
94. Diaries. Monday 8th - Wednesday 10th August 1853.
95. GL Lewis, *op.cit.*, p.245. 19th May 1851. Kent House. GC Lewis to Edmund Head.
96. Diaries. Friday 9th September 1853. He was staying at Home Lacy.
97. Sir Charles Wood, Bart, 1800-85, first Viscount Halifax. 'Being exceedingly well informed upon Indian questions, he was appointed president of the board of control in the Aberdeen administration on 30th December 1852, and passed an excellent India Act in 1853'. [*DNB*].
98. Diaries. Tuesday 16th August 1853.

99. *Ibid.*, Wednesday 17th August 1853.
100. The Ven R Lane Freer, Prebendary of Hereford and Archdeacon of Hereford 1852-61.
101. The Revd Berkeley Lionel Scudamore Stanhope, Rector of Byford and formerly Fellow of All Souls College, Oxford.
102. Either Thomas Dew of Whitney Court or his son Henry Dew, who was inducted to the family living of Witney on Wye in 1843 and remained there for over half a century.
103. Diaries. Thursday 18th to Thursday 25th August 1853.
104. Alice Lister, Lady Theresa Lewis's second daughter.
105. GF Lewis, *op.cit.*, pp 269, 270. 14th September 1853. Worcester, GC Lewis to Edmund Head.
106. *Ibid.*, p.90. October 3rd 1837. Malta, GC Lewis to EW Head.
107. The King's Head was on the site of the present Market Hall, was closed in 1881 and demolished in 1885.
108. Richard Parry, *The History of Kington*, Kington, 1845, pp.62, 63.
109. Edward Hartopp Grove assumed the name of Cradock in 1849. He was at that time a Canon of Worcester, but he became Principal of Brasenose College in 1853, an office he held until 1886.His wife was Theresa Lewis's sister.
110. The Hon Grantham Munton Yorke, Rector of St Phillip's, Birmingham, 1844-75.
111. Diaries. Friday 16th to Monday 19th September 1853. The building of the Town Hall though commenced in 1832 was barely completed in 1853.
112. GF Lewis, *op.cit.*, pp.269, 270. 14th September 1853. Worcester, GC Lewis to Edmund Head.
113. Henry Richard Vassall Fox, third Baron Holland, 1773-1840, *Memoirs of the Whig Party during my Time*, London, 1852, 2 vols. 'It is written with commendable precision, lucidity, and conciseness, and ... constitutes a first-hand historical authority of great value'. *DNB* entry on Fox.
114. The ambitious John Campbell, 1779-1861, the first Baron Campbell, was Lord Chancellor of Ireland for a few weeks in 1841, became Lord Chief Justice in 1851. He was Lord Chancellor 1859-61.
115. Thomas Babington Macaulay, 1800-59, ennobled in 1857, was a contributor to the *Edinburgh Review* in earlier days, and Longman, its publisher was also his.
116. *DNB* entry for John Campbell.
117. *Ibid.* for Macaulay.
118. GF Lewis, *op.cit.*, p.271. 7th October 1853. Kent House, GC Lewis to Edmund Head.
119. *Eg* Diaries. Friday 21st October 1853: 'Revised an article on French Protestants in England by M Thomas, & corrected the style throughout'.
120. The Revd JH Symons, LLD. A contemporary of Symons was James Price, father of the medical profession in Herefordshire. Appointed Surgeon in the Artillery in 1804, he was also at Corunna, under Sir John Moore, in 1809.
121. We buried him darkly at dead of night,
The sods with our bayonets turning,
By the struggling moonbeam's misty light
And the lanthorn dimly burning.
122. Diaries. Saturday 17th December 1853.
123. *Memorials and Letters of Fox*, London, 4 vols., 1853-4-7.
124. Diaries. Monday 26th to Friday 30th December 1853.
125. *Ibid.*, Wednesday 15th June 1853. The double peace negotiations involved both France and America.
126. William Waiter Legge, 1823-91, was MP for South Staffordshire from 1849 to 1853 when he became 5th Earl of Dartmouth. Diaries. Saturday 26th and Sunday 27th November 1853.
127. Diaries. Wednesday 4th May 1853.
128. *Ibid.* Wednesday 9th and Tuesday 15th November 1853.

129. GF Lewis, *op.cit.*, p.273. 1st December 1853. Kent House, GC Lewis to Edmund Head. The Commission's report, in the writing of which Lewis was prominent, was published in May: 'The City Report has been presented. It has been generally well received by the Liberal press, & scarcely noticed by the Tory newspapers'. Diaries. Monday 6th May 1854.

130. Diaries. Friday, 9th December 1853.

131. *Ibid.*

132. *Ibid.*, Friday, 23rd December 1853.

133. GF Lewis, *op.cit.*, p.273. 1st December 1853. Kent House. GC Lewis to Edmund Head.

134. de Winton Archives 18/2/14. 9th February 1852.

135. GF Lewis, *op.cit.*, pp.275, 276. 4th January 1854. Kent House, GC Lewis to Edmund Head.

136. *Ibid.*, pp.278, 279. 4th March 1854. Kent House. GC Lewis to Edmund Head.

137. Diaries. 9th to 24th February 1854.

138. *Ibid.*, 9th and 10th March 1854.

139. *Ibid.*, Wednesday 15th March 1854. Kent House, GC Lewis to Edmund Head.

140. GF Lewis, *op.cit.*, p.277. 4th March 1854. Kent House, GC Lewis to Edmund Head.

141. *Ibid.*, Thursday 16th to Monday 27th March 1854.

142. *The Life and Letters of Barthold George Niebuhr and Selections from his Minor Writings, and essays on his Character and Influence* by the Chevalier Bunsen and Professors Brandis and Loebell, edited.and translated Susanna Winkworth, 3 vols, 1852. Lewis was no doubt spurred on by the publication of Niebuhr's Lectures on Ancient History in 1853, and his Lectures on Ancient Ethnography in 1854.

143. Mark Pattison, 1813-1884, Fellow and later Rector of Lincoln College, Oxford and contributor in 1860 to the controversial *Essays and Reviews*. In 1850 he was a referee for the Revd James Davies, kinsman of Lewis and translator of his Fables of Babrius.

144. MG Brock and MC Curthoys, eds, *History of the University of Oxford*, Vol VI, part 1, Oxford, 1997, pp.530, 533, citing Pattison, *Memoirs*, pp.84-5.

145. GF Lewis, *op.cit.*, pp.279, 280. 6th June 1854. Kent House. GC Lewis to Edmund Head.

146. Brock and Curthoys, *op.cit.*, p.528.

147. GF Lewis, *op.cit.*, pp.288, 289. 29th December 1854. Kent House, GC Lewis to Edmund Head.

148. GF Lewis, *op.cit.*, p.286. 18th November 1854. Kent House, GC Lewis to Edmund Head.

149. GF Lewis, *op.cit.*, p.281. 6th June 1854. Kent House. GC Lewis to Edmund Head.

150. Diaries Monday 5th and Tuesday 6th June 1854, and GF Lewis, *op.cit.*, pp.279, 280. 6th June 1854. GC Lewis to Edmund Head.

151. Brock and Curthoys, *op.cit.*, p.534.

152. Diaries. Tuesday 8th August to Sunday 13th August 1854. Professor Christian August Brandis, 1790-1867.

153. GF Lewis, *op.cit.*, pp.288, 289. 29th December 1854. Kent House, GC Lewis to Edmund Head.

154. Diaries, Monday 17th June 1854.

155. *Ibid.* Monday 7th August 1854. Alexis de Tocqueville, 1805-1859, French politician, sociologist, and historian, of whom it has been said 'no other 19th-century liberal thinker saw the problems of contemporary democratic society quite as clearly'.

156. Duff Gordon Diaries. Friday 29th September 1854.

157. Diaries. Friday 22nd and Monday 23rd September 1854.

158. Lord Dudley Coutts Stuart, 1803-1854, advocate of the independence of Poland. He died in Stockholm, attempting to persuade the King of Sweden to support the Polish cause.

159. Diaries. Tuesday 21st, Wednesday 22nd, and Thursday 23rd November 1854.

160. Duff Gordon Diaries. Saturday 14th October 1854.

161. Diaries. Wednesday 11th to Monday 22nd October 1854.

162. GF Lewis, *op.cit.*, p.285. 18th November 1854. Kent House, GC Lewis to Edmund Head.

163. *Ibid.*, p.284. 21st September 1854. Kent House, GC Lewis to Edmund Head.
164. *Ibid.*, pp.285, 286. 18th November 1854. Kent House, GC Lewis to Edmund Head.
165. Diaries. Saturday 11th, Monday 20'" November 1854.
166. GF Lewis, *op.cit*, p.287. 29th December 1854. Kent House. GC Lewis to Edmund Head.
167. *Ibid.*, pp.287, 289. 29th December 1854. Kent House, GC Lewis to Edmund Head.
168. Diaries. Monday 8th January 1855. The Revd Whitwell Elwin, 1816-1910, rector of Booton and editor of the *Quarterly Review* 1853-1860.
169. *Ibid.*, Wednesday 10th to Friday 12th January 1855. The Very Revd George Henry Sacheverell Johnson, a broad churchman, fellow of Queen's since 1829 and Professor of Moral Philosophy 1842-1845, he was dean of Wells 1854-1881.
170. *Ibid.*, Tuesday 23rd January 1855.
171. Anne Cornewall, 1779-1872.
172. Robert, Viscount Hereford, d.1855.
173. Sir Velters Comewall, Bart, 1824-68.
174. The Hon Captain [later Admiral] Walter Bourchier Devereux, of Middlewood, Hay on Wye. In December 1867, Lady Duff Gordon, reviewing the past year, wrote in her Diary: 'One of the melancholy things of the year is Walter Devereux continuing quite out of his mind and another is that of our other nephew Velters Cornewall, being in so odd a state of temper or mind that all fear much that his head is going!' He died in a private asylum the following year.
175. Alexander Gordon, son of Lady Duff Gordon, and Lewis's cousin. He was the third baronet, and died from consumption in 1872.
176. James Davies of Moorcourt, 1777-1856, the Kington lawyer and banker.
177. The Revd Henry Fullelove Mogridge, MA, vicar of Old Radnor 1832-66.
178. The Revd George Richard Turner, MA, who became rector of New Radnor in 1855.
179. Diaries. Tuesday 30th January 1855.
180. Duff Gordon Diaries. Friday 2nd February 1855.
181. Edward James, MD, of Castle Hill House, Kington.
182. Mr Bennet received his due reward for faithful service: 'Promised Mr Bennett the lease of Mr Eyre's house, & my support for the situation of medical officer of the N[ew]R[adnor] Union, in the event of Mr Eyre's death. Diaries. Saturday 10th February 1855.
183. Diaries. Thursday 1st February 1855.
184. *Ibid.*
185. Banks Archives MISC 2/1/22.
186. Thomas Lewis Lloyd of Nantgwillt, 1779-1870. He assumed the name of Lloyd in 1824.
187. David Oliver of Rhydoldog, d.1858, was involved with the Kington and Radnorshire Bank with Richard and RW Banks, to whom he was related, and James Davies of Moorcourt. He was High Sheriff in 1842.
188. John Percy Chesment Severn, 1781-1875, of Penybont Hall.
189. William Edwards of Hindwell. He was a Quaker relative of Banks, and a tenant of Lewis. In seconding Lewis's nomination he said that 'he did so with more pleasure from its being his lot to belong to the middle class, a class which he wished to see occupy a more conspicuous part in such assemblies as the present.' *Hereford Times*, 14th February 1855.
190. Diaries. Friday 2nd February to Thursday 8th February 1855.
191. *Hereford Times*, 14th February 1855.
192. *Ibid.*
193. The Harpton bailiff.
194. Diaries. Wednesday 7th and Friday 9th February 1855.
195. *Ibid.*, Monday 12th February to Monday 19th February 1855.
196. GF Lewis, *op.cit.*, p.291. 14th February 1855. Kent House, GC Lewis to WR Greg.

Chapter 5: Back in Parliament

1. Charles Thomas Longley, 1794-1868, was the first Bishop of Ripon, 1836-1856 when he was translated to Durham.
2. The Earl of Ellesmere, 1800-57, a graduate of Christ Church, was the chairman of the Commission.
3. The judge Sir John Taylor Coleridge, 1790-1876.
4. Sir John Wither Awdry, 1795-1878, a retired Indian judge.
5. The Very Revd George Henry Sacheverell Johnson, 1808-1881.
6. Diaries. Tuesday 20th to Friday 23rd February 1855.
7. *Ibid.*, Saturday 24th February 1855.
8. Chancellor of the Exchequer.
9. First Lord of the Admiralty.
10. Secretary for the Colonies.
11. Edward Cardwell, 1813-1886.
12. Thomas Baring, 1799-1873.
13. Diaries. Sunday 25th February 1855.
14. Diary of WE Gladstone, 28th February, 1855, cited by RW Bevan, 'Sir George Cornewall Lewis, A Gladstonian View', *Transactions of the Radnorshire Society*, Vol LVIII, 1988, p.68.
15. Diaries. Monday 26th February 1855. Saw Mr Longman, & requested him to make an arrangement for relieving me of the current number of the *Edinburgh Review*.
16. *Ibid.*, Wednesday 17th May 1848.
17. GF Lewis, *op.cit.*, pp 293, 294. 18th March 1855. Kent House, GC Lewis to Edmund Head.
18. *The Standard*, February 1855.
19. Duff Gordon Diaries. Thursday 1st March 1855.
20. GF Lewis, *op.cit.*, p.302. 27th November 1855. Kent House, GC Lewis to WR Greg.
21. Diaries, Tuesday 6th March 1855.
22. Duff Gordon Diaries. Monday 12th March 1855.
23. Banks Archives. 26th February 1855. Kent House, GC Lewis to James Davies.
24. *Ibid.* RB 8/1/24 27th February 1855. Copy of letter from Richard Banks to George Cornewall Lewis.
25. Duff Gordon Diaries. 'Monday 5th February. An account in the *Galignani* that Mr Robt Mynors is going to stand for the Radnor boroughs in Sir Frankland's place!! [Not true]'. Born in 1809, Mynors was to be High Sheriff for Radnorshire in 1856.
26. Banks Archives. RWB 14/1/8 1st March 1855. Kent House, Sir GC Lewis to Richard Banks.
27. *Ibid.* RB 8/1/39 1st March 1855. Copy of letter from Richard and RW Banks to C Anthony.
28. Duff Gordon Diaries. Monday 12th March 1855.
29. Sir William Swinfield Rossiter Cockburn, bt, 1796-1858, of Downton, New Radnor. Diaries. Sunday 4th March 1855.
30. Diaries. Monday 5th and Tuesday 6th March 1855.
31. *Ibid.*, Sunday 11th March 1855.
32. GF Lewis, *op.cit.*, p.297. 10th June 1855. Kent House. GC Lewis to Edmund Head.
33. Diaries. Friday 26th October 1855. Goldwin Smith, 1823-1910, Oxford reformer, and Professor of Modern History at the university 1858-1866. He was active in the formation of Cornell University and in the academic life of both the USA and Canada.
34. *A History of Ancient Rome*, 2 vols, 1855. It was abridged in 1871 as *The Student's History of Rome to the Establishment of the Empire*.
35. Diaries. Wednesday 12th December 1855.
36. Edward Herbert Bunbury, 1811-1895, author of *A history of ancient geography among the Greeks and Romans, from the earliest ages till the fall of the Roman Empire*, London, 1879.

37. GF Lewis, *op.cit.*, p.312. 13th April 1856. Kent House, GC Lewis to Edmund Head.
38. GF Lewis, *op.cit.*, p.315. 6th July 1856. Kent House, GC Lewis to Edmund Head.
39. *Ibid.*, p.317.
40. Diaries. 19th Monday 1856: 'Letter from Prof Liebreckt at Liége, proposing to translate into German my work on Roman history ... Prof. Liebreckt is chiefly versed in medieval antiquities & has published a translation of Dunlop's *History of Fiction* [John Colin Dunlop, d.1842, *The History of Fiction, being a Critical Account of the most celebrated Prose Works of Fiction from the earliest Greek Romances to the Novels of the present Age*]. He has lately published an edition of extracts of Gervasius [*ie* the chronicler Gervasius Doroborensis, fl. 1188] which he has dedicated to me. My acquaintance with him began, by his sending me a remark on an extract from my work, which he has read in the Athenaeum. This caused me to send him a copy of it, & he has since written to me about it, & has published a notice of it in a German Library Journal'. But once again Lewis was disappointed with the result. Diaries. Wednesday & Thursday 19th & 20th Jan. 1859: 'Kent House. I found the second vol of Liebreckt's translation of my work on Roman History. The notes are much curtailed and the text in parts'.
41. *Ibid.* Wednesday 14th March 1855.
42. GF Lewis, *op.cit.*, pp.293, 294. 18th March 1855. Kent House, GC Lewis to Edmund Head.
43. Diaries. Monday 9th April 1855.
44. Sir Francis Graham Moon, 1796-1871, Lord Mayor of London 1854-55.
45. *The Herald*, April 1855.
46. Diaries. Friday 20th April 1855.
47. GF Lewis, *op.cit.*, pp.294, 295. 10th June 1855. Kent House, GC Lewis to Edmund Head.
48. Duff Gordon Diaries. Friday 18th May 1855.
49. Diaries. Friday 9th June 1855.
50. William Brown, 1784-1864, was MP for South Lancashire 1846-59. An advocate of free trade and decimal coinage, he wrote a pamphlet in the latter's favour in 1854. He was created a baronet in 1863, and is remembered as a generous benefactor to Liverpool.
51. Diaries. Tuesday 12th June 1855.
52. He photographed JMW Turner in 1847.
53. Diaries. Monday 12th November 1855.
54. *Ibid.* Sunday 22nd July 1855.
55. Diaries. Sunday 11th November 1855.
56. *Ibid.* Wednesday 14th and 21st November 1855.
57. Duff Gordon Diaries. Sunday 12th and Tuesday 14th November 1855.
58. Thomas Bradshaw, b.1824, married in 1847 Francis Catherine, only daughter of Henry 14th Viscount Hereford.
59. The Revd Richard Lister Venables of Llysdinam, 1809-1894, vicar of Clyro and chairman of the the Radnorshire Quarter Sessions 1851-1886.
60. Perhaps the wealthy widow, Mrs Sophia Evans of Greenfields, a generous benefactor to Presteign.
61. GF Lewis, *op.cit.*, p.296. 10th June 1855. Kent House, GC Lewis to Edmund Head.
62. *Ibid.*, p.297. 17th August 1856. Downing Street, GC Lewis to Edmund Head.
63. Diaries. Tuesday 11th September 1855.
64. Duff Gordon Diaries. Monday 1st October 1855.
65. Diaries. Monday 1st October 1855.
66. Duff Gordon Diaries. Monday 8th October 1855.
67. WH Howse, *Radnorshire*, Hereford, 1949, p.51.
68. Diaries. Monday 17th September 1855.
69. *Ibid.*, Friday 14th September 1855.
70. *Eg* Diaries. Friday 21st September 1855: 'Harpton. Review. Rode on the Forest with Senior, Therese, [The Revd Wm] Newton, & Turner [Rector of New Radnor]. Fine day, saw the view well. Mr & Mrs Severn [of Penybont Hall] dined'.

71. *Ibid.*, Tuesday 9th October 1855.
72. CJ Robinson, *A History of the Mansions and Manors of Herefordshire*, London, 1872, pp.269, 270.
73. He was MP for the county of Hereford 1858-65.
74. Diaries. Sunday 14th to Thursday 18th October 1855.
75. Duff Gordon Diaries. Sunday 25th November 1855.
76. GF Lewis, *op.cit.*, pp.300-301. 17th October 1855. Downing Street, GC Lewis to Henry Reeve.
77. Diaries. Sunday 23rd December 1855.
78. GF Lewis, *op.cit.*, p309. 28th January 1856. Downing Street, GC Lewis to Edmund Head.
79. Diaries. Saturday 25th January 1856.
80. Diaries. Sunday 16th March 1856.
81. *Ibid.*, Tuesday 18th March 1856.
82. *Ibid.*, Saturday 12th April 1856.
83. *Ibid.*, Tuesday 2nd June 1857.
84. Harpton Papers, C/3208. 15th April 1863. Queen Victoria to Lady Theresa Lewis.
85. *Eg* Diaries. Sunday 4th May 1856.
86. 'There is no member of the House who possesses a more complete stock of easy & complacent assurance. To say the truth, his speeches are very fluent - & sometimes he is facetious. He is never at a loss for a word & his English is that of a cultivated gentleman. He has, too, the great advantages of good looks & a title. He never rises above the forcible feeble', TA Jenkins, ed., *The Parliamentary Diaries of Sir John Trelawny*, 1858-1865, London, 1990, p.56.
87. Diaries. Friday 28th June 1856.
88. *Ibid.* Sunday 1st July 1856.
89. These included the banker Samuel Jones Loyd, 1796-1883, who had been influential in framing the Bank Act of 1844. He was considered to be one of the wealthiest men in England 'whose influence on the financial side of current politics was known to be great'. He was ennobled in 1860 as Baron Overstone.
90. GF Lewis, *op.cit.*, p.317. November 5th 1856. Harpton, GC Lewis to Edmund Head.
91. Diaries. Wednesday 24th to Friday 26th September 1856.
92. Sir Alexander Young Spearman, bart, b.1793. Assistant Secretary of the treasury 1836-40 and Comptroller of the National Debt. He was to be sworn as a Privy Councillor in 1869.
93. Diaries. Sunday 28th September 1856.
94. GF Lewis, *op.cit.*, pp.315, 316. 6th July 1856. Kent House, GC Lewis to Edmund Head.
95. *Ibid.*, p.318. November 5th 1856. Harpton, GC Lewis to Edmund Head.
96. *Ibid.*, p.319. November 5th 1856. Harpton, GC Lewis to Edmund Head.
97. Lord Bateman, 1826-1901, of Shobdon Court. Diaries. Saturday 18th October 1856.
98. Rowland Hill, 1795-1879, well known as the innovator of the penny post, was Secretary to the Post Office 1854-1864.
99. Charles Alexander Saunders, 1795-1864, was secretary and general superintendent of the Great Western Railway 1840-1863.
100. Diaries. Tuesday 1st September 1857.
101. *Ibid.*, Thursday 16th to Friday 17th October 1856.
102. *Ibid.*, Tuesday 28th October 1856.
103. *Ibid.*, Saturday 8th November 1856.
104. WC Maddox, *A History of the Radnorshire Constabulary*, Llandrindod, 1981, p.9.
105. Keith Parker, *A History of Presteigne*, Woonton Almeley, 1997, pp.153, 154.
106. Of Boultibrooke. The Reverend Oliver Ormerod, MA, was rector of Presteign 1841-1880. Richard Green Price was of Norton Manor, and William Stephens was a Presteign solicitor and clerk to the peace.
107. Diaries. Saturday 30th August 1856.
108. *Ibid.*, Wednesday 3rd September 1856.

109. *Ibid.*, Saturday 22nd September 1860.
110. Keith Parker, *op.cit.*, p.154.
111. Diaries. Thursday 4th September 1856.
112. *Ibid.*, Thursday 30th and Friday 31st August 1855.
113. Tomkyn Dew of Whitney Court, JP, DL, MA, patron the of the living, and brother of the Revd Henry Dew, MA, rector of Whitney on Wye. Capt Sir Edwyn Francis Scudamore Stanhope, RN, JP, DL, of Holme Lacy.
114. Capt Daniel Peploe Peploe Webb of Garnstone Castle.
115. Diaries. Thursday 28th and Friday 29th August and Monday 1st September 1856. The Earl of Clarendon was Lady Lewis's brother.
116. Diaries. Saturday 6th September 1856.
117. RW Banks, 'Reminiscences of the Downton Sandstone', *Transactions of the Woolhope Club*, 1892, p.400.
118. Diaries, Saturday 6th to Wednesday 10th September, 1856.
119. Duff Gordon Diaries. Friday 5th October 1855; Diaries. Thursday 18th September 1856.
120. GF Lewis, *op.cit.*, p.317. November 5th 1856. Harpton, GC Lewis to Edmund Head.
121. Diaries. Saturday 13th to Friday 19th December 1856.
122. *Illustrated London News*, 1st January 1848.
123. Diaries. Saturday 20th December 1856 to Thursday 1st January 1857.
124. *Ibid.*, Friday, 2nd to Wednesday 21st January 1857.
125. *Ibid.*, Friday 23rd January 1857.
126. *Ibid.*, Tuesday 27th January 1857.
127. The Duc de Persigny, 1808-72, the French ambassador in London.
128. Count Chreptovich, the first post Crimean War Russian ambassador in London.
129. The Earl of Aberdeen, 1784-1860. Prime Minister 1852-55.
130. George John West, 1791-1869, fifth Earl of De La Warr, was father of the Crimean veteran Charles Richard Sackville-West, 1815-1873, the sixth earl.
131. Diaries. Wednesday 28th January 1857.
132. *Ibid.*, Thursday 29th January 1857.
133. Duff Gordon Diaries. Sunday 1st February 1857.
134. *Ibid.*, Saturday 14th February 1857.
135. Diaries. Saturday 14th February 1857.
136. *Ibid.*, Monday 16th February 1857.
137. *Ibid.*, Friday 20th February 1857.
138. George Clive of Perrystone Court, Herefordshire, 1805-1886. He was Liberal MP for Hereford 1857-69 and 1878-86.
139. Duff Gordon Diary. Sunday 22nd February 1857.
140. James Wilson, Financial Secretary at that time to the Treasury.
141. Diaries. Sunday 22nd and Monday 23rd February 1857.
142. Hansard's *Parliamentary Debates*, 20th February 1857, pp.986-7; Harpton Court Papers C/1672.
143. Duff Gordon Diary. Tuesday 24th February 1857.
144. Richard Cobden, 1804-65, MP at that time for the West Riding of Yorkshire.
145. Diaries. Tuesday 3rd March 1857.
146. Princess Beatrice Mary Victoria Feodore was born on 15th April 1857.
147. Diaries. Wednesday 4th March 1857.
148. Sir Anthony Panizzi, 1797-1879, the Principal Librarian of the British Museum. He thought Lewis should have been elected a Trustee of the Museum in 1856 instead of the Dean of Westminster.
149. *Ibid.*, Friday 20th March 1857.
150. *Ibid.*, Wednesday 25th March 1857.
151. John Adcock Phillips, gentleman, of Presteign. *Ibid.* Saturday 28th March 1857.
152. *Ibid.*, Friday 22nd May 1857.
153. *Ibid.*, Tuesday 24th and. Friday 27th March 1857.

154. *Ibid.*, Thursday 2nd April 1857. The three successful candidates were:
Sir HG Cotterell, Liberal, 3352 votes.
TW Booker Blakemoore, Conservative, 2822 votes.
J King King, Conservative 2771 votes.
155. *Ibid.*, Thursday 23rd April 1857.
156. Harpton Papers. C/919 l857, May 30th 1857. FL Bodenham to GC Lewis.
157. The account was not settled for six months. Harpton papers 3342.
158. Diaries. Monday 13th April and Saturday 2nd May 1857.
159. *Ibid.*, Tuesday 5th May 1857.
160. The Revd Dr David Williams, 1786-1860,was Warden of New College 1840-60 and Vice-Chancellor 1856-8.
161. Diaries. Tuesday 23rd and Wednesday 24th June 1857.
162. *Ibid.*, Saturday 27th, Monday 29th June, Wednesday 8th July 1857.
163. *Ibid.*, Thursday 27th August 1857.
164. GF Lewis, *op.cit.*, pp.324, 325. 3rd September 1857. Harpton, GC Lewis to Edmund Head.
165. Edward John Littleton, first Lord Hatherton, 1791-1863, 'a man of moderate abilities and unimpeachable character'.
166. Diaries. Saturday 4th July 1857.
167. *Ibid.*, Wednesday 8th July 1857.
168. Duff Gordon Diaries. Friday 24th July 1857.
169. *Ibid.*, Sunday 26th to Tuesday 28th July 1857.
170. Diaries. Saturday 1st August 1857.
171. GF Lewis, *op.cit.*, pp.324, 325. 3rd September 1857. Harpton, GC Lewis to Edmund Head.
172. Diaries. Wednesday 5th August 1857.
173. Diaries. Wednesday 12th August 1857. George Douglas Campbell, 1823-1900, was the 8th Duke of Argyll.
174. *Ibid.*, Monday 17th August 1857; Henry Petty-Fitzmaurice, 1780-1863, was the 3rd Marquis of Lansdowne; Granville George Levason Gower, 1815-91, was the 2nd Earl Granville, was prominent in ordering the Great Exhibition and was Chancellor of the University of London, both concerns shared by Lewis; Charles Cavendish Fulke Greville, 1794-1861, was considered to be 'peculiarly well-informed on the most secret transactions of contemporary politics' was assisted by Lewis in his *Policy of England to Ireland*, published in 1845.
175. *Notes & Queries*, Saturday 23rd May 1857.
176. GF Lewis, *op.cit.*, p.325. 2nd October 1857. Downing Street, GC Lewis to Edward Twistleton.
177. *Notes & Queries*, 22nd September 1860, p.240. *Babrii fabulae Æsopeae, cum fabularum deperditarum fragmentis*. Recensuit et breviter illustravit Georgius Cornewall Lewis: Londini, 1846.
178. Diaries. Sunday 14th June 1857.
179. *DNB* article on Lewis.
180. Diaries. Wednesday 2nd February-Wednesday 20th April 1859.
181. *Babrii fabulae Æsopeae*. E codice manuscripto partem secundam nunc primum edidit Georgius Cornewall Lewis. London, 1859.
182. James Davies, *The Fables of Fabrius*. Translated into English verse from the Text of Sir G Cornewall Lewis, London, 1860.
183. Diaries. Wednesday 2nd September 1857.
184. Duff Gordon Diaries. Thursday 24th September 1857.
185. Major JA Whittaker of Newcastle Court.
186. Ruth Bidgood, 'Families of Llanddewi Hall', part V, *Transactions of the Radnorshire Society*, LXI, 1981, p.57, says of the Walsh family: 'They held Downton, then Knill Court, and later Newcastle Court', but gives no details.

187. Edwards, a Quaker and Harpton tenant, was related by marriage both to the Quaker Pease family of successful industrialists of Darlington and to Mrs RW Banks of Ridgebourne.
188. Duff Gordon Archives. Nd. Harpton. GC Lewis to his brother GF Lewis.
189. RCB Oliver, 'The Lewis Family of Downton House, New Radnor: 1758-1858', *Transactions of the Radnorshire Society*, LXI, 1981, p 30.
190. 29th March 1805. Shoreham on Sea, Percival Lewis to Thomas Frankland Lewis, Harpton Court. RCB Oliver, 'The Lewis Family of Downton House, New Radnor: 1758-1858', *Transactions of the Radnorshire Society*, LXI, pp.29, 30.
191. *Ibid.*
192. *Hereford Journal*, 24th October 1821.
193. Oliver, *op.cit.*, p.34.
194. Jonathan Williams, *op.cit.*, p.312.
195. MA Faraday, 'The Radnorshire Hearth Tax Return of 1670'. *Transactions of the Radnorshire Society*, LIX, 1989, p.48.
196. Coincidentally, the Domesday Survey of Herefordshire, 9:13, connects Harpton and Pilleth: 9:13. In Pilleth 2 hides; in Harpton 2 hides; in Middleton 3 hides; in Weston 2 hides. In total 9 hides are waste in the Welsh March. Land for 18 ploughs. There were seven manors; five thanes held them.
197. Harpton Papers, 503. March 28th 1665.
198. *Ibid.*, 631. March 8th 1805.
199. *Archaeologia Cambrensis*, 1847, p.330.
200. *Ibid.*, 1848, p.173.
201. Diaries. 'Friday 7th November 1856. Harpton. Rode to Pilleth & inspected the house'.
202. Harpton Papers. C/927 24th February 1858.
203. Harpton Papers. C/919 30th May 1857; C/920 13th June 1857; C/922 28th June 1857.
204. Harpton Papers. C/925 9th December 1857; C/924 11th December 1857; C/926 11th February 1858; C/931 18th September 1858; C/934 22nd November 1858.

Chapter 6: Party Politics

1. Maddox, *op.cit.*, p.12.
2. *Ibid.*
3. In 1858 Lewis attended on 22nd January; 12th February; 27th March; 8th and 29th May; 12th and 26th June; and 10th July.
4. Diaries. Friday 22nd January 1858.
5. He was to become First Lord of the Admiralty under Palmerston 1859-66.
6. Frederick William Nichols Charles, 1831-1888, Crown Prince of Prussia.
7. Victoria Adelaide Maria Louisa, 1840-1901, Princess Royal.
8. John Bird Sumner, Archbishop of Canterbury 1848-62.
9. Archibald Campbell Tait, Bishop of London 1856-1868 when he was translated to Canterbury.
10. Diaries. Monday 25th January 1858.
11. Diaries. Monday 25th January 1858.
12. *Ibid.*, Wednesday 27th January 1858.
13. Thomas Baring, Conservative member for Huntingdonshire, moved an amendment that it was not at present expedient to legislate for India.
14. Robert Vernon Smith, President of the Board of Control 1855-58.
15. Diaries. Friday 12th February 1858.
16. *Speech ... on the Introduction of the Bill for the better Government of India*, London, 1858
17. Diaries. Saturday 20th February 1858.
18. *Ibid.*, Sunday 21st February 1858.
19. *Ibid.*, Friday 26th February 1858.
20. GF Lewis, *op.cit.*, p.330. 5th February 1858. Kent House, GC Lewis to Edmund Head.

21. *Ibid.*, p.333. 5th May 1858. Rome, Edward Twistleton to GC Lewis.
22. *Ibid.*, p.332. 5th March 1858. Kent House, GC Lewis to Henry Reeve.
23. Diaries. 7th March 1857.
24. Steele, *op.cit.*, p.82.
25. MCM Simpson, *Many Memories of Many People*, London, 1898, pp.143, 145.
26. Diaries. 31st July 1858.
27. Trelawney Diaries, p.32. 25th March 1858.
28. *Ibid.*
29. *Ibid.*, p.59, 22nd July 1858.
30. Diaries. Sunday 13th June 1858. William Vincent, 1739-1815, Dean of Westminster. 'Ancient geography was the subject which Vincent made his chief study' and *The Periplus of the Erythrean Sea* was published in London, 1800-05.
31. Henry Addington, first Viscount Sidmouth, 1757-1844.
32. Lewis's successor as editor of the *Edinburgh Review*.
33. *Notes & Queries*, 3rd July 1858, pp.1-5.
34. *Ibid.*, p.4.
35. *Ibid.*, 17th July 1858, p.57.
36. Andrew Steinmitz, 1816-77, wrote extensively on such esoteric subjects as duelling, the Jesuits, meteorology, and tobacco.
37. *Notes & Queries*, 7th August 1858, pp.101-103.
38. *Ibid.*, p.101.
39. *Ibid.*, 17th July 1858, pp.61-64 and 31st July 1858, pp.81-83.
40. *Ibid.*, p.83. Lewis took the matter further in his 'Supposed Voyages of the Phœnicians in the Northern Seas', *Notes & Queries*, 1st January 1859, p.3.
41. *North British Review*, 1823-1916.
42. Diaries. Tuesday 2nd March 1858.
43. GF Lewis, *op.cit.*, p.333. 3rd May 1858. Kent House, GC Lewis to Edmund Head. Jacob Bryant's, 1715-1804, *A New System or an Analysis of Ancient Mythology* was published London, 1774.
44. Diaries. Thursday 1st April to Monday 12th April 1858.
45. Diaries. Thursday 27th May 1858. He was also, despite his poor delivery, a compulsive speech maker, eg Diaries, Wednesday 23rd June: 'At the British Museum copying Babrius. Then presided over the distribution of prizes at the London University College. Ld Brougham & Grote were present. I made a speech at the end of the proceedings'.
46. Diaries, Sunday 8th August 1858.
47. Diaries. Wednesday 11th and Thursday 12th August 1858.
48. They were later edited by Sir E. Head, Bart, and published posthumously as *Essays on the 'Administrations of Great Britain from 1783 to 1830'*, London, 1864.
49. Duff Gordon Diaries. Wednesday 1st September 1858.
50. Diaries. Thursday 2nd to Saturday 4th December 1858.
51. Napoleon's third sister.
52. Diaries. Tuesday 6th September 1858.
53. Diaries. Thursday 21st October 1858.
54. Diaries. Wednesday 29th September 1858.
55. Diaries. Wednesday 6th to Saturday 9th October 1858.
56. The Hon. Robert Windsor Clive, of Oakley Park, Shropshire.
57. Diaries. Wednesday 18th and Thursday 19th August 1858.
58. WC Maddox, *op.cit.*, p.13.
59. She was the widow of General Sir Loftus William Otway, CB who died in 1854.
60. Jonathan Williams, *op.cit.*, p.270.
61. Diaries. Monday 30th August and Friday 3rd September 1858.
62. Diaries. Wednesday 20th October 1858.
63. Diaries. Saturday 5th November 1858.

64. Diaries. Saturday 13th November. Harpton. Wood only survived to 1862.
65. Diaries. Friday 12th and Monday 22nd November 1858.
66. GF Lewis, *op.cit.*, pp.357-359. 17th November 1858. Harpton, GC Lewis to FL Bodenham. St Martin's feast is on 11th November. Diaries. Sunday 21st November 1858. 'There has been unusually cold weather, much frost with E &NE winds, since the 10th & in Martimas summer. The dahlias were cut off on the 28th October'.
67. Diaries. Friday 1st October 1858.
68. Diaries. Wednesday 20th October 1858.
69. GF Lewis, *op.cit.*, p.359. 21st November 1858, Harpton, GC Lewis to Henry Reeve.
70. 'The Vulture in Italy', *Notes & Queries*, 2nd July 1859, pp.1-4.
71. GF Lewis, *op.cit.*, p.359. 21st November 1858, Harpton, GC Lewis to Henry Reeve.
72. Sir Charles Lyell, FRS, 1797-1875, *Principles of Geology*, London, 1830-33.
73. GF Lewis, *op.cit.*, p.359. 21st November 1858. Harpton, GC Lewis to Henry Reeve.
74. *Ibid.* 'The History and Prospects of Parliamentary Reform', *Edinburgh Review*, No. 219, art. 9.
75. Diaries. Wednesday 24th November 1858.
76. Diaries. Saturday 27th November 1858.
77. *Ibid.*
78. Diaries. Wednesday 15th December 1858.
79. *Ibid.*
80. Diaries. Friday 17th December 1858.
81. Diaries. Sunday 19th December 1858.
82. Diaries. Wednesday 22nd December 1858.
83. Diaries. Thursday 23rd to Monday 27th December 1858.
84. Diaries. Friday 7th to Saturday 15th January 1859.
85. Diaries. Saturday 5th February 1859.
86. Diaries. Saturday 19th February 1859.
87. *Eg* Diaries. Saturday 26th February and Tuesday 5th April 1859.
88. Diaries. Saturday 12th February and Wednesday 16th March 1859.
89. Charles Ross, ed., *Correspondence of Charles, first Marquis Cornwallis*, 3 vols., London, 1859. Diaries. Saturday 5th February to Tuesday 10th March 1859, when he corrected the proofs.
90. 'Tartessus', *Notes and Queries*, 5th March 1859, pp.189-191. There was a certain topicality to this paper because later in the year the cabinet, with Lewis present, discussed at length the possibility of 'a telegraphic cable to Gibraltar'.
91. Modern Cadiz.
92. The river Guadalquivir.
93. Diaries. Wednesday 29th June 1859.
94. Diaries. Thursday 20th January 1859.
95. Diaries. Friday 29th January and Tuesday 1st February 1859.
96. Diaries. Wednesday 2nd February 1859.
97. Diaries. Monday 7th February 1859.
98. Diaries. Tuesday 22nd and Saturday 26th February 1859.
99. Diaries. Sunday 27th February and Tuesday 1st March 1859.
100. Diaries. Thursday 3rd March 1859.
101. Diaries. Tuesday 15th and Tuesday 29th March 1859.
102. Diaries. Thursday 31st March 1859.
103. Diaries. Thursday 21st April 1859.
104. Duff Gordon Diaries. Thursday 21st April 1859.
105. Humphrey Francis Mildmay, of Shoreham Place, Kent, represented Herefordshire 1859- 65.
106. Diaries. Saturday, 30th April 1859.
107. Diaries. Sunday 1st May and Monday 2nd May 1859.

108. Diaries. Sunday 15th May 1859.
109. *Ibid.*
110. Diaries. Friday 20th May 1859.
111. Diaries. Thursday 26th May 1859.
112. Diaries. Monday 30th May 1859.
113. Lewis's brother in law, George William Frederick Villiers, the fourth earl of Clarendon, 1800-70, had been Foreign Secretary under Palmerston 1853-8.
114. Granville George Leveson-Gower, second Earl Granville, 1815-91, had been leader of the Liberals in the House of Lords since 1855. He shared Lewis's interest in the University of London, of which he was Chancellor 1856-91.
115. George Douglas Campbell, eighth Duke of Argyll, 1823-1900. Post Master General in Palmerston's administration.
116. Sir Charles Wood, created Earl Halifax 1866. He was the First lord of the Admiralty 1855-58.
117. Sir George Grey, 1799-1882, was Home Secretary under Palmerston 1855-8.
118. Diaries. Tuesday 31st May and Wednesday 1st June 1859.
119. John Bright, 1811-89. In March 1858 he described Palmerston's ministry as 'the very worst ministry' that he had known and had a substantial part in its downfall. He was an advocate of parliamentary reform, whose opinions were moderated by Russell. Palmerston strongly resented Russell's political liason with Bright.
120. Diaries. Thursday 2nd June 1859.
121. *Ibid.*
122. *Ibid.*
123. *Ibid.*
124. Diaries. Friday 3rd and Saturday 4th June 1859.
125. Diaries. Monday 6th June 1859.
126. The radical John Arthur Roebuck, 1801-79, 'the Diogenes of Bath' was MP for Sheffield in 1859.
127. Trelawney Diaries. Monday, 6th June 1859, pp.81,82.
128. Herman Merivale, 1806-74, Under Secretary of Sate for the Colonies 1848-59, and a frequent contributor to the *Edinburgh Review.*
129. Spencer Compton, Marquis of Hartington, 1833-1908. The speaker, John Evelyn Denison, wrote to the duke of Devonshire that his son possessed 'a power of speaking rarely shown by persons who have had so little practice'.
130. Diaries. Tuesday 7th June 1859.
131. Diaries. Wednesday, 8th to Friday 10th June 1859.
132. Diaries. Saturday 11th June 1859.
133. *Ibid.*
134. Thomas Milner-Gibson, 1806-1884, Liberal MP for Ashton under Lyme.
135. Diaries. Sunday 12th June 1859.
136. *Ibid.*
137. Diaries. Monday 13th June 1859.
138. Diaries.Tuesday 14th June 1859.
139. EL Woodward, *The Age of Reform 1815-1870*, Oxford, 1938, p.166.
140. Spencer Horatio Walpole, 1806-1898. Like Lewis, he was a Trustee of the British Museum.

Chapter 7: Home Secretary

1. Diaries. Thursday 23rd June 1859. James Colquhoun Campbell, 1859-90. Before his preferment to Bangor he was rector of Merthyr Tydfil where he maintained a strong church tradition in a vigorously nonconformist environment. Devoted and able, he had a long innings at Bangor, living in his diocese and administering it with efficiency, despite his English background. Though Lewis had no hand in his appointment, Campbell was the kind of bishop he thought desirable for the established Church in Wales.

2. Cecil Parsons, the Presteign lawyer and banker. He was popular for his successful support of cottagers' rights in 1837, the year in which he was also instrumental in founding the Radnorshire Bank [as opposed to the Kington and Radnorshire Bank]. With Richard Green Price he was active in establishing the Royal Radnor Rifles in 1852 and was county treasurer for a while. He died in 1876, aged 90.

3. Later Sir Richard Green Price, who followed Lewis as MP for the Radnor Boroughs in 1863.

4. Richard Plantagenet Campbell Temple Nugent Brydges Chandos Grenville, 1823-1889, succeeded his father as third Duke of Buckingham and Chandos in 1861. He was a staunch conservative who 'made a laudable effort to pay off his father's debts'.

5. Diaries. Tuesday 28th June 1859.

6. Banks Archives. RB 4/1/14 January 1853, Elizabeth Davies to Richard Banks.

7. Banks Archives. RB 4/1/10 10th December 1852. Elizabeth Davies to Richard Banks.

8. GF Lewis, *op.cit.*, p.372. 1st August 1859. Kent House, GC Lewis to Edmund Head.

9. Trelawny Diaries, Monday 23rd July 1860.

10. Diaries. Wednesday 29th and Thursday 30th June 1859.

11. Prince Alfred, 1844-1900 was created Duke of Edinburgh in 1866.

12. Diaries. Friday 12th August 1859.

13. Diaries. Monday 15th and Tuesday 16th August 1859.

14. Diaries. Thursday 18th August 1859.

15. Diaries. Thursday 25th August 1859.

16. Duff Gordon Diaries. Thursday 25th August 1859.

17. Diaries. Friday 26th August 1859.

18. *The Times*, 5th September 1859.

19. Diaries. Tuesday 30th to Friday 2nd September 1859.

20. *Ibid.*

21. *The Times*, 8th November 1860.

22. Diaries. Saturday 27th August 1859.

23. 'The Lion in Italy' for *Notes & Queries*, 24th September 1859, pp.241, 242.

24. The Revd Dr Edward Daniel Clarke, 1769-1822.

25. His entry in the *DNB*.

26. *Notes and Queries*, 12th January 1850, p.170.

27. His entry in the *DNB*.

28. 'Narrien on a Passage of Strabo', *Notes & Queries,* 1st June 1861.

29. Diaries. Tuesday 27th September 1859. It was of course, 1 am on Wednesday that Lewis arrived at Perth.

30. Sir George Grey, 1812-98, Chancellor of the Duchy of Lancaster.

31. Diaries. Wednesday 28th September.1859.

32. James Duff, 5th earl of Fife, b.1814.

33. Diaries. Thursday 29th September to Saturday 1st October 1859.

34. The Revd Dr Robert Lee, 1804-1868, was Dean of the Chapel Royal in Edinburgh, and first professor of Biblical Criticism in the University of Edinburgh.

35. Diaries. Sunday 2nd October 1859.

36. *Notes & Queries*, Vol 8 2nd Series [196] 1st October 1859, pp.261-3.

37. Sir Charles Beaumont Phipps, 1801-1866. He was in succession equerry to Queen Victoria, and private secretary to the prince consort. He became keeper of the Queen's purse in 1849. His integrity and zeal, it is said, were highly appreciated by both the queen and the prince consort.

38. James Farquarson, died 1862, was lord of the barony of Invercauld. The castle had been the seat of the chiefs of the Farquharson Clan since the early 16th century, but in the late 19th century became the home of Sir Algernon Borthwick, first Baron Glenesk, 1830-1908, who married Alice Lister, Lewis's step-daughter in 1870. It did not acquire its present Scottish baronial appearance until 1874.

39. Diaries. Monday 3rd to Wednesday 5th October 1859.
40. Southampton Palmerston Papers, 104.PP/GC/LE/118. 9th October 1859. Harpton, GC Lewis to Lord Palmerston.
41. Henry Montagu Villiers, bishop of Carlisle, 1856-60, when he was translated to Durham.
42. Diaries. Wednesday 9th November 1859.
43. *The Times*, 10th November, 1859.
44. *Ibid.*
45. Diaries. Monday 14th to Sunday 20th November 1859.
46. William Drogo Montagu, 7th Duke of Manchester, b.1823. His wife, whom he married in 1852, was the Countess Louise Frederice Auguste von Alten of Hanover.
47. Diaries. Thursday 24th November 1859.
48. Diaries. Sunday 6th November 1859.
49. Dr William Smith, 1813-93. He was knighted in 1892.
50. Robert Lowe, 1811-92, ennobled at Viscount Sherbrooke in 1880, and remembered for his reforms in state education. Diaries. Saturday 10th to Monday 12th December 1859.
51. Diaries. Monday 19th December 1859.
52. Diaries. Saturday, 31st December 1859.
53. Diaries. Sunday, 1st January 1860.
54. Diaries, Wednesday 18th to Friday 20th January 1860.
55. Trelawney Diaries, Wednesday 8th February 1860.
56. Diaries, Saturday 11th February to Wednesday 22nd February 1860.
57. GFL, *op.cit.*, pp.376, 377. 12th March 1860. Kent House, GC Lewis to Sir Edmund Head.
58. Diaries. Friday March 16th to Monday March 26th 1860. 'Confined to my room by an attack of influenza'. Also GFL, *op.cit.*, p.378, 24th March, 1860, Kent House, GC Lewis to WR Greg.
59. GFL, *op.cit.*, pp.376, 377, 12th March 1860. Kent House, GC Lewis to Sir Edmund Head.
60. Diaries. Friday, 6th to Saturday 14th April 1860.
61. This is, perhaps, not surprising in view of Lewis's own endeavours to secure a Worcester canonry for his brother Gilbert in 1856.
62. *The Times*, p.12, 21st Februrary 1861.
63. *Ibid.*, p.9, 26th February 1861.
64. *Ibid.*
65. Trelawny Diaries. Tuesday 26th February 1861.
66. Pattison visited Harpton in 1858 and Lewis dined with Jowett at Oxford in 1860.
67. GF Lewis, *op.cit.*, pp.380, 381. 22nd April 1860 and p.381, 382. 27th April 1860. Kent House, GF Lewis to Edward Twistleton.
68. Trelawney Diaries. Tuesday 15th May 1860.
69. Trelawney Diaries, Monday 11th June 1860.
70. *Ibid.*, Wednesday 11th July 1860.
71. GF Lewis, *op.cit.*, pp.383, 384. 23rd July 1860. GC Lewis to Sir Edmund Head.
72. August Boeckh, *Manetho und die Hundssternperiode, ein Beitrag zur Geschichte der Pharaonen*, Berlin, 1845. Manetho was an Egyptian historian of the 3rd C BC.
73. Diaries. Tuesday 25th December to Sunday 30th December 1860. Baron Christian Carl Josias von Bunsen, *Egypt's Place in Universal History: an historical investigation.* Translated from the German by CH Cottrell (with additions by Samuel Birch), 5 vols., London, 1848-67.
74. Sir James South, 1785-1867, had an observatory attached to his Kensington home. A founder of the Royal Astronomical Society, he was its president in 1829.
75. Diaries. Sunday 20th May 1860. George Biddell Airy, 1801-1892, became Astronomer Royal in 1835, FRS in 1836, and KCB in 1872.
76. Diaries. Monday 28th May 1860. The Roman calendar originally consisted of ten months.
77. *Ibid.*, Saturday 23rd June 1860.
78. *The Times*, 25th June 1860.

79. Diaries. Wednesday 17th October 1860.

80. *Ibid.*, Monday 29th April 1861.

81. William Sandys Wright Vaux, 1818-1885, entered the Department of Antiquities of the British Museum in 1841 and in 1861 became the Keeper of Coins and Medals. He was elected FRS in 1868.

82. 'Translations of the Odyssey', *Blackwood's Edinburgh Magazine*, Vol 91, March 1862, p.346.

83. Diaries. Thursday 15th May 1862.

84. *Ibid.*

85. *Ibid.*, Wednesday 18th August to Thursday 25th September 1862.

86. *Suggestions for the Application of the Egyptological Method to Modern History; illustrated by examples*, London, 1862,

87. Diaries. Friday 9th January 1863.

88. University of Southampton Palmerston Papers, PP/GC/LE/168. Nd. War Office. GC Lewis to Lord Palmerston.

89. 'The Pyramids-Who Built them?- and When?', *Blackwood's Edinburgh Magazine*, Vol 94, September 1863, p.364.

90. BM Metzger and MD Coogan, eds, *The Oxford Companion to the Bible*, Oxford, 1993, p.707.

91. Trelawny Diaries. Tuesday 28th August 1860.

92. Duff Gordon Diary. Wednesday 29th August.1860.

93. Diaries. Saturday 22nd September1860.

94. *Ibid.*, Monday 1st October 1861.

95. Harpton Court Papers, 998. 24th March, 1853.

96. Diaries, Thursday 13th December 1860.

97. *Ibid.*, Tuesday 1st January 1861.

98. *Ibid.*, Wednesday 24th April 1861.

99. The dispute was over a piano. Trelawny Diaries, Monday 11th February 1861.

100. Trelawny Diaries. Tuesday 12th February 1861.

101. *The Times*, 12th November 1861, p.9.

102. The Hon Peter Locke King, 1811-1885, represented East Surrey as a Liberal. Trelawny thought him to be 'one of the best members of the House of Commons'.

103. Ralph Bernal Osborne, 1808-1882, MP for Liskeard and political wit.

104. Trelawny Diaries. Wednesday 13th March 1861.

105. Gaythorne Gaythorne-Hardy, 1814-1906, first Earl of Cranbrook, was Conservative MP for Leominster 1856-65, when he ousted Gladstone as the member for the University of Oxford.

106. Sir Richard Malins, QC, 1805-1882, represented Wallingford as a Conservative. He became a judge in 1866.

107. Trelawny Diaries. Wednesday 13th March 1861.

108. *Ibid.*, Wednesday 20th March 1861.

109. *Ibid.*, Wednesday 19th July 1861.

110. GF Lewis, *op.cit.*, p.397. 9th June 1861. Kent House, GC Lewis to Mrs Austin.

111. GF Lewis, *op.cit.*, p.401. 8th September 1861. Harpton, GC Lewis to Sir Edmund Head.

112. GF Lewis, *op.cit.*, p.400. 9th July 1861. Home Office, GC Lewis to his brother the Revd GF Lewis.

113. Jean Baptiste Adolphe Charras, *Histoire de la campagne de 1815. Waterloo*, Brussells, 1857.

114. John Scott, *A Visit to Paris in 1814; being a review of the moral, political, intellectual and social condition of the French Capital*, London, 1815. Scott founded his newspaper, *The Champion*, in 1814, and his writing had the approval of Bishop Heber, Wordsworth, and Thackeray. He died as a result of a duel in 1821.

115. GF Lewis, *op.cit.*, pp.360.361. 7th December 1858. Harpton, GC Lewis to Henry Reeve.

116. *Ibid.*, p.361. 13th December 1858. Harpton, GC Lewis to Henry Reeve.
117. Diaries. Tuesday 9th July 1861.
118. *Ibid.*, Thursday 11th July 1861.
119. Sidney Smith on 16th July 1861, cited by Cecil Woodham-Smith, *Florence Nightingale, 1820-1910*, London, 1950, p.307.
120. *Ibid.*, Monday 29th July 1861.
121. *Ibid.*, Saturday 3rd August 1861. Kent House. 'At the War Office … I sent the first part of my History of Astronomy to the press'.
122. GF Lewis, *op.cit.*, p.401. 8th September 1861. Harpton, GC Lewis to Sir Edmund Head.
123. Diaries. Friday 16th and Saturday 17th August 1861.
124. *Ibid.*, Tuesday 15th October 1861.
125. Duff Gordon Diaries. Monday 7th October 1861.
126. *Ibid.*, Wednesday 9th and Thursday 10th October 1861.
127. RWD Fenn and JB Sinclair, *The Herefordshire Bowmeeting, A Social History*, Kington, 2000, pp.161, 162.
128. Duff Gordon Diaries, Tuesday 15th October 1861.
129. *Ibid.*, Monday 14th October 1861.
130. Diaries. Friday 1st to Friday 8th November 1861.
131. *Ibid.*, Sunday 7th to Saturday 14th December 1861.
132. *Ibid.*, Sunday 15th December 1861.
133. Granville George Levison Gower, second Earl Granville, 1815-1891, Lord President of the Council under Palmerston.
134. Diaries. Tuesday 17th to Thursday 17th December 1861.
135. GF Lewis, *op.cit.*, p.408. 16th December 1861. Kent House, GC Lewis to Henry Reeve.
136. *Ibid.*, Tuesday 24th to Sunday 29th December 1861.

Chapter 8: Lewis the Churchman

1. Delbury Hall, in the Shropshire parish of Diddlebury, and Berrington.
2. BA 1856, MA 1871.
3. The Revd Rhys Bishop, MA, of Corpus Christi College, Cambridge.
4. Christ Church, Oxford, BA 1834, MA 1837, and DD by diploma 1856. Student of Christ Church 1830 to 1838. Ordained 1836, after a year as curate of Deane, Lancashire, became vicar of Kenilworth, Warwickshire in 1837. In 1841 he was presented to wealthy Lord Chancellor's living of St George's, Bloomsbury where he displayed great ability and untiring zeal in the management of this large parish. He was an extreme low churchman, and often enjoyed the support of the dissenters. He was a canon of St. Paul's Cathedral 1847-56. He was no less energetic as Bishop of Carlisle than he had been at Bloomsbury, and in 1860 on his translation to Durham, great things were expected, but these expectations were brought to nothing by his premature death a year later.
5. Owen Chadwick, *The Victorian Church*, part one, 1829-1959, 3rd edition, London, 1971, p.476. See the previous chapter, however, for the controversy over his nepotism.
6. Thomas Musgrave, 1788-1860, educated Trinity College, Cambridge, BA 1810, MA. 1813. Fellow 1812, Professor of Arabic 1821.
7. Sinclair, JB, and Fenn, RWD, 'Kington Orders an Organ', *Transactions of the Woolhope Naturalists' Field Club*, XLVI, 1988, part 1, pp 69-75. Musgrave, though in 1846 now Archbishop of York, donated £10, whereas Sir Thomas Frankland Lewis gave £5.
8. *The Illustrated London News*, 4th October, 1845. The consecration of the new parish church took place at New Radnor on July 31st.
9. Educated privately by the vicar of Warminster, Hampden went up to Oriel College, Oxford, in May 1810 where he took a double first, won the Chancellor's Prize for Latin, and in 1814 was elected a fellow of his college. Broad churchmen, like Thomas Arnold, 1795-1842, later headmaster of Rugby, and Richard Whately, 1787-1863, professor of

Political Economy at Oxford, before becoming Archbishop of Dublin in 1833, were contemporaries and friends. The Tractarians Newman, Keble, and Pusey, were his colleagues. Ordained in 1816, he returned to Oxford in 1829 where in 1833 he became Principal of St Mary Hall which flourished under his direction. He was appointed Professor of Moral Philosophy in 1834, and Regius Professor of Divinity in 1836.

10. Harpton Papers. C/682 30th December 1847.
11. *The Times*, 15th November 1847.
12. Frederick Dolman, 'Great preachers, their homes and households: The Rt Revd John Percival and Mrs Percival', *The Sunday Strand*, 1900, cited in Fenn, RWD, & Sinclair, JB, *The Bishops of Hereford and their Palace*, Hereford, 1990, p.32.
13. *DNB*.
14. Harpton Papers. C/1844 24th March 1850.
15. Diaries. Thursday, 1st November 1855. Harpton. 'We went to Presteign, & attended the reopening of the church, at which the Bishop of Hereford preached a dull ineffective sermon. Afterwards lunched at Mr Omerod's, the rector's, where was the Bishop, Archdeacon Frier, & about 40 people. Mr Omerod proposed the Bishop's health, I proposed Mr Omerod's and he proposed mine'. This judgement of Lewis was later reported by Thomas Mozley, 1806-1893, who said of Hampden 'It mattered not what he talked about, it was all the same, for he made one thing as dull as another'. [Mozley, Thomas, *The Times*, 15th November 1847, *op.cit.*, vol. 1, p.380.]
16. Harpton Papers. C/1430 26th March 1862.
17. Cited by the *DNB*.
18. Nassau William Senior, 1790-1864, political economist, and 'eminently a man of strong common-sense'.
19. GF Lewis, *op.cit.*, p.105. In this Lewis anticpates the judgement of RW Church, *The Oxford Movement*, p.142. 'His mind, which was a speculative one, was not one, in its own order, of the first class. He had not the grasp nor the subtlety necessary for his task. He had a certain power of statement, but little of co-ordination; he seemed not to have had the power of seeing when his ideas were really irreconcilable, and he thought that simply by insisting on his distinctly orthodox statements he not only balanced, but neutralized, and did away with his distinctly unorthodox ones'.
20. *Ibid.*, pp.193, 194.
21. 'A parsonage house and a stable adjoining it and a small garden in front. These premises adjoin the churchyard. Three acres of good pasturage are also attached to the living, lying at a small distance from the town, on the side of the road leading to Kington'.
22. On 22nd July 1829 Francis Merewether, Curate, baptised Sarah daughter of James and Rebecca Evans of New Radnor, Labourer. He also officiated in August, September, and November 1829, and February and April 1830.
23. Obituary notice in the *Hereford Times*. The measures he opposed were those of the Repeal of the Test and Corporation Acts, Catholic Emancipation in 1829, and the Reform Act of 1832. He was one of the two bishops who refused to accept the degrees of the newly founded University of Durham as an adequate academic qualification for holy orders.
24. Baptising, for example, 19th December 1841 and 19th March 1843.
25. Howse, WH, *Radnorshire*, Hereford, 1949, p.77.
26. Chadwick, Owen, *The Victorian Church*, part 1, 1829-1859, London, 1987, p.226.
27. *Ibid.*, p.241.
28. Lewis to his brother Gilbert, 21st December 1847.
29. Cited in *DNB*.
30. Lewis to his brother, Gilbert, 28th December 1847. Thomas Mozley, 1806-1893, was a Tractarian, like his better known elder brother James Bowling Mozley, 1813-1878, the Old Testament scholar and Professor of Divinity at Oxford. After a brief period, 1841-43, as editor, after Newman, of the *British Critic*, a short-lived Tractarian journal, he became in 1844 a regular correspondent of *The Times*. In contrast to Mozley, Julius

REFERENCES

Charles Hare, 1795-1855, was a Broad Churchman who in 1840 became Archdeacon of Lewes. The pamphlet so praised by the *Chronicle* was his *Letter on the Appointment of Dr Hampden to the See of Hereford*, published in 1848. He enjoyed the friendship of the Lewises of Harpton, especially that of Sir Thomas Frankland Lewis.

31. Lewis to Head, 5th January 1848.
32. Lewis to Head, 24th April 1850.
33. Harpton Papers. 998, 24th March 1853.
34. Harpton Papers. 638, 18th May 1845.
35. Lewis to Head, 15th September 1845.
36. Sinclair, JB, and Fenn, RWD, "A most efficient and agreeable coadjutator', The Revd James Banks, alias Davies, MA, 1820-1883', *Transactions of the Radnorshire Society*, LXVI, 1996, p.16.
37. There may have been other reasons that the Trustees were uncertain about the suitability of James Davies to be the headmaster of their school. They may have feared, for example, that he would treat the boys as he once resolved to treat his servants: 'I am determined now to keep a sharp lookout, & put kindness to servants out of my catalogue of virtues'.
38. GF Lewis, *op.cit.*, pp.232,3. 28th December 1850, to Sir Edmund Head, bart.
39. *Ibid.*
40. RG Wilberforce, *Life of Samuel Wilberforce*, vol. 1, p.440.
41. GF Lewis, *op.cit.*, pp.232, 233. 28th December 1850, GC Lewis to Edmund Head.
42. Cardinal Paul Cullen, 1803-1878, became Roman Catholic Bishop of Armagh in 1849, and was translated as Archbishop of Dublin in 1852.
43. 28th December 1850. GC Lewis to Edmund Head.
44. *Ibid.*
45. 2nd July 1847. GC Lewis to Edmund Head.
46. Harpton Papers. C/896.
47. *Ibid.*, C/899.
48. Diaries of Lady Caroline Duff Gordon.
49. There were further extensions in 1860 and 1882. The Roman Catholic Chapel of the Holy Family at Broxwood, with its en suite presbytery, was built by the Cox-Snead family in 1885 for £2,000 and is another illustration of the Roman Catholic presence amongst the Herefordshire gentry.
50. Diaries. Tuesday 13th July 1852.
51. *Hereford Times*, July 1852.
52. GF Lewis, *op.cit.*, p.254.
53. 26th March 1853. GC Lewis to Edmund Head.
54. *Notes & Queries*, Vol iii, 1851, p.118.
55. Kington parish registers, 1859.
56. Diaries. Friday 19th December 1856.
57. *Hereford Times*.
58. Three chancel windows were filled, in his memory, with their blue glass in 1862.
59. Chadwick, *op.cit.*, vol I, p.497.
60. Diaries. Saturday 30th December 1848: 'Went with Theresa to Sir Edmund Antrobus's at Cheam. Slept there ... Sunday 31st December. At Cheam church where Gilbert's little girl was christened. Theresa was godmother for Lady Lewis, Lady Antrobus for Mrs Booth, & I was godfather. The child was christened Mary Anna after her two godmothers. Slept at Cheam. Monday 1st January 1849. Returned to Grove Mill. 8th June 1856'. Lower Cheam, Surrey. Gilbert Lewis to RW Banks: 'I grieve to say I have lost a dear child & have to follow him to his grave tomorrow ...' Banks Archives: RWB 14/1/3.
61. Chadwick, *op.cit.*, p.499.
62. TA Jenkins, ed, *The Parliamentary Diaries of Sir John Trelawny, 1858-65*, London, 1990, p.94.

63. *The Times*, 14th February 1860.
64. *Ibid.*
65. *Ibid.*
66. Diaries. Wednesday, 22nd February 1860.
67. *Essays and Reviews*, London, 1860, p.338.
68. Diaries. Wednesday 17th October 1860.
69. In March 1853, for example, he was involved with Sir Frankland Lewis and George and Gilbert, in raising a mortgage for £6,500. Lewis's widow, Lady Theresa Lewis, who survived her husband two years, died in November 1865, at the principal's lodgings at Brasenose. Dr Cradock shared Lewis's anti-Tractarian feelings.
70. *DNB* entry on Pattison.
71. Henry Bridstow Wilson, 1803-1888, Huntingdonshire. On account of his essay on 'The National Church' he was tried for heresy in 1862 by the Court of Arches, and sentenced, as a clergyman, to a year's suspension, against which he appealed successfully. He was the vicar of Great Staughton.
72. Banks Archives.
73. Banks Archives. GC Lewis to James Davies, 26th February 1855.
74. Harpton Papers. C/1397 6th November 1862.
75. *Ibid.*
76. 6th July 1854. Lewis to Edmund Head.
77. *The Parliamentary Diaries of Sir John Trelawny, 1858-65*, p.130.
78. *Ibid.*
79. *Ibid.*, p.68.
80. The Religious Census of 1851, p.647.
81. 7th September 1858. Lewis to Henry Reeve.
82. Duff Gordon Archives.ADG 1:4. 22nd February 1859. GC Lewis to GF Lewis.
83. Harpton Papers. C/2659 15th July 1859.
84. *The Parliamentary Diaries of Sir John Trelawny, 1858-65*, p.96.
85. Diaries. Wednesday, 19th July 1860.
86. *The Parliamentary Diaries of Sir John Trelawny, 1858-65*, p.202.
87. Diaries. 14th May, 1862.
88. Harpton Papers. C/756.
89. Sir James Harford Jones Brydges, bart, 1808-1891, of Boultibrook, near Presteign. He was the son of Sir Harford Jones Brydges, bart, 17641847, the orientalist and diplomatist.
90. Duff Gordon Archives. 3rd January [1847]. ADG 1:3. Lewis to his brother Gilbert.
91. Banks Archives. RWB 10/1/43 4th November 1852/3.
92. Dawes took great interest in the Blue Coat Schools in Hereford. In 1861 he became master of St. Catherine's Hospital, Ledbury, where during his annual statutory residence of four months he paid much attention to the Ledbury National Schools. In 1864 he was vice-president of the British Association when it met at Bath.
93. Palmerston to Shaftesbury, 29th April 1864, cited in Steele, ED, *Palmerston and Liberalism 1855-1865*, Cambridge, 1991, p.189.
94. In June 1860 he was translated to the see of Durham.
95. Diaries. Thursday July 10th, 1856. 'Ld Palmerston announced to me that he wd confer on Gilbert the canonry of Worcester, vacant by the death of Mr Cook, uncle to Ld Somers, for which I had applied'.
96. Steele, *op.cit.*, p.189.
97. Duff Gordon Archives. Lady Caroline Duff Gordon, Diaries.
98. St John's College, Cambridge, BA 1830, MA 1835.
99. For example, like Gilbert Lewis, he voted for Walsh rather than Wilkins in the 1835 election.
100. Duff Gordon Archives. Diaries of Lady Caroline Duff Gordon, Monday 13th October, 1856.

101. Diaries.

102. A Lord Chancellor's living and worth £368 pa. He stayed there until 1875.

103. Jonathan Williams, *op.cit.*, p.195.

104. *Ibid.*

105. WH Howse, *Radnorshire*, Hereford, 1949, p.76.

106. Diaries. Sunday 1st January 1854.

107. Edward Copleston, Bishop of Llandaff 1828-49, former Provost of Oriel and Noetic was one of those who advised Melbourne to appoint Hampden to the Oxford chair of Divinity in 1836.

108. 29th November 1849. The Home Office, Lewis to Edmund Head: 'the Welshmen clamoured for a Welsh bishop, and Lord John satisfied them very dexterously by giving them an Englishman, formerly head of Lampeter, who understands Welsh'.

109. Conybeare, 'The Church of England in the Mountains', *The Edinburgh Review*, XCVII, no cxcviii, p.348.

110. St David's College, Lampeter was founded in 1827 as a result of the generous efforts of Thomas Burgess, Bishop of St Davids 1803-25, to provide priests for his diocese. Candidates unable to afford Oxford or Cambridge were able to proceed to Lampeter having prepared for the modest demands of the entrance examinations at a local grammar school.

Chapter 9: Sudden Death

1. An anonymous review; 'Sir GC Lewis on the Astronomy of the Ancients', *North British Review*, Vol XXXVI, No 72, p.485f.

2. GC Lewis, *An Historical Survey of the Astronomy of the Ancients*, London, 1862, p.2.

3. *Ibid.*

4. *Saturday Review*, 8th February, 1862, p.162.

5. Lewis was one of the first to use the term.

6. Lewis, *op.cit.*, p.XX.

7. *Ibid.*, p.XX

8. CR Lepsius, *Denkmaeler aus Aegypten und Aethiopien*. Berlin, 1849-59.

9. *ie* a ruler of time.

10. Lewis, *op.cit.*, p.374.

11. Diaries, Wednesday 12th March to Monday 31st March 1862.

12. *Eg* Diaries. Tuesday 1st April to Friday 11th April 1862. See note 17 *supra*.

13. *Fraser's Magazine*, founded in 1830, had Carlyle, Lockhart, Thackeray, Coleridge, and Southey among its early contributors. It was taken over by Longmans in 1863 and ceased to appear in 1882. Its editor in 1862, when Lewis made his contribution, was James Anthony Froude, 1818-94, who became Professor of Modern History at Oxford in 1892.

14. Diaries. Thursday 24th April to Monday 27th April 1862.

15. KO Müller, *History of the literature of Ancient Greece*, Translated from the German MS. by GC Lewis, London, 1840-42.

16. *The Times*, 28th April 1862, Sir G Cornewall Lewis's *Astronomy of the Ancients*.

17. *Ibid.*

18. *Ibid.*

19. *Ibid.* Thursday 1st May 1862.

20. *Ibid.* Wednesday 4th June 1862.

21. Victoria and Albert Museum Internet article 2002.

22. *Ibid.*, citing the *Illustrated London News*. Hereford tired of its famous screen in 1967 and sold it to the Herbert Museum and Art Gallery, Coventry and in 1983 it was given to the Victoria and Albert Museum, where it was fully restored, and is now on view.

23. Duff Gordon Diaries. Saturday 17th September 1864.

24. Diaries. Saturday 3rd May 1862. Philip Henry Stanhope, FRS, 1815-1875, the fifth Earl Stanhope.

25. Entry in the *DNB*.
26. GF Lewis, *op.cit.*, pp.416, 417. 9th May 1862. Somerleaze, Wells. Edward A Freeman to GC Lewis.
27. *Notes & Queries*, 11th April 1863, p.281. Edward A Freeman, *History of federal government from the foundation of the Achaian League to the disruption of the United States*, London, 1863.
28. Sir William Tite, FRS, FSA, 1798-1873.
29. Proceedings of the Society of Antiquaries, Thursday, 15th May, 1862, pp.119,120.
30. *Ibid.*
31. *Ibid.*
32. Diaries. Thursday 15th May 1862.
33. Proceedings of the Society of Antiquaries, 22nd May 1862, p.122.
34. *Ibid.*, 19th June 1862, p.136.
35. GF Lewis, *op.cit.*, p.419. 29th May 1862. GC Lewis to EA Freeman.
36. GF Lewis, *op.cit.*, pp.419, 420. 30th May 1862. Somerleaze, Wells. EA Freeman to GC Lewis.
37. *North British Review*, Vol XXXVI, No 72, p.512. The *North British Review*, a revived quarterly, was edited 1860-63 by the Revd William Garden Blaikie, 1820-99, a Scottish divine of radical sympathies who joined the Free Church of Scotland at the Disruption of 1843. A contributor was Lord Acton, 1834-1912, the Roman Catholic historian. It ceased publication in 1872.
38. *Ibid.* pp.512, 513.
39. GFLewis, *op.cit.*, p.418.
40. *Quarterly Review* for March, 1853, vol. xcii. p.355. The Biblical reference is to Psalm 10:10. 'The days of our years are three score years and ten, and if by reason of strength they be four score years, yet is their strength but labour and sorrow'.
41. Works of William Harvey, M.D, Sydenham Society, 1847, pp.587-592.
42. GF Lewis, *op.cit.*, pp.418, 419. 19th May 1862. Kent House. GC Lewis to Edward Twistleton.
43. The Ven Arthur Blenner-Hassett Rowan, MA, DD, 1800-61 archdeacon of Ardfert, was an energetic Irish antiquarian and anti-Tractarian.
44. Richard Sainthill of Cork 'lover of art and an antiquary'.
45. The Revd William Dunn Macray, MA, 1826-1916, was rector of Duckington near Witney, Oxfordshire for 42 years and contributed some 19 articles to the *Dictionary of National Biography*, one of which was on the Countess of Desmond.
46. Macray in his *DNB* article.
47. Thomas Seccombe, 1866-1923, article in the *DNB* to which he contributed over 700 biographies, as well as to later supplements.
48. *DNB* entry on Parr.
49. Thoms remained editor until 1872 and is considered to have originated the term 'folk lore'.
50. *DNB* entry on Thoms.
51. *DNB* article by Gordon Goodwin who wrote some eleven hundred entries for the dictionary.
52. *Notes & Queries*, April 12th 1862, p.281.
53. *Ibid.*
54. *Notes & Queries*, 7th June 1862, p.453.
55. *Notes & Queries*, 6th September 1862, p.197.
56. George, Lord Lyttelton, *Miscellaneous Works*, ed George Edward Ayscough, 2nd edition, London, 1775, p.718. Ayscough, 'a fool of fashion' and 'a parasite of Lord Lyttleton' was his nephew.
57. *Notes & Queries*, 7th June 1862, p.454.
58. *Ibid.*

59. GC Lewis. *Notes & Queries*, 24th May 1862, p.411.
60. Edited by RH Williams from notes made by HH Copleston, and with an introduction by RT Massy, pp.48, London and Brighton, 1870.
61. *Longevity, with Life, Autograph, and Portrait of Thomas Geeran, a Centenarian*, Brighton. 1871.
62. See the article of Geeran in the *DNB* by the antiquary and historian George Clement Boase, 1828-1897, of Exeter College, Oxford.
63. Diaries. Saturday 7th June 1862.
64. He was 32. He was to paint a portrait of Edward, Prince of Wales in 1865.
65. Diaries, Thursday 10th June to Friday 20th June 1862.
66. Diaries, Wednesday 9th July 1862.
67. Diaries, Saturday 26th July 1862.
68. Diaries, Tuesday 5th to Thursday 7th August 1862.
69. Edward Adolphus Seymour, 12th Duke of Somerset, 1804-85, was First Lord of Admiralty, under Palmerston, and though 'not very popular', was 'an efficient adminsistrator'.
70. Diaries, Saturday 9th August 1863.
71. Diaries, Tuesday 17th August to Wednesday 3rd September 1862.
72. These included 'a letter from the Duke of Cambridge proposing the detailed arrangement for giving military rank to the Prince of Wales on his coming of age & wrote to Ld Palmerston about it'.
73. Diaries, Thursday 4th September to Monday 13th October 1862.
74. ED Steele, *op.cit.*, p.293.
75. Diaries, Tuesday 14th October 1862.
76. Diaries, Wednesday 15th to Wednesday 22nd October 1862.
77. Diaries, Thursday 23rd October 1862.
78. Diaries, Saturday 25th October 1862.
79. Diaries, Sunday 26th October 1862.
80. Diaries, Monday 27th October to Thursday 6th November 1862.
81. He was also Assistant Under–Secretary of State for Foreign Affairs, 1873-1894 and KCMG in 1885.
82. Diaries, Thursday 23rd October and Monday 17th to Thursday 20th November 1862.
83. Diaries, Saturday 15th November 1862.
84. Diaries, Saturday 22nd November 1862. Prince Alfred, Victoria's second son, was 18 in 1862. Palmerston was not opposed to the notion. Eventually the cabinet assented 'to the choice of Prince William of Baden for the throne of Greece' (Diaries, Saturday, 7th March 1863).
85. Diaries, Sunday 23rd November 1862.
86. *Ibid.*
87. Diaries, Wednesday 3rd to Friday 5th December 1862.
88. Diaries, Wednesday 10th December 1862.
89. GF Lewis, *op.cit.*, p.424. 16th December 1862. GC Lewis to his brother GF Lewis.
90. Diaries, Monday 22nd to Saturday 27th December 1862.
91. Diaries, Monday 31st December, 1862.
92. Diaries, Thursday 1st to Tuesday 6th January 1863.
93. Diaries, Friday 9th January 1863.
94. Princess Louise Caroline Alberta, 1848-1939, 'the most beautiful and not the least gifted of the Queen's daughters, and her intelligence and wit made her a favourite with her father'.
95. Princess Helena Augusta Victoria, 1846-1923.
96. Thérèse Lister married Sir George Granville Venables Vernon Harcourt, 1827-1904, Liberal politician, anti-ritualist, and specialist in International Law, particularly in regard to the American Civil War, in 1859. He remarried in 1876.

97. GF Lewis, *op.cit.*, p.427. 8th February 1863. Kent House. GC Lewis to Mrs Austin.
98. *The Times*, 14th April 1863.
99. Diaries, Thursday 26th March 1863.
100. Trelawney, *op.cit.*, Monday 23rd March 1863.
101. Woodham-Smith, *op.cit.*, p.307.
102. *Ibid.*, p.296.
103. *Ibid.*, p.310.
104. Diaries, Saturday, 14th February 1863.
105. Diaries, Thursday 19th February 1863.
106. Diaries, Saturday 21st March 1863.
107. Diaries, Saturday 7th March 1863.
108. GF Lewis, *op.cit.*, pp.430, 431. 26th February 1863. War Office. GC Lewis to Edmund Head.
109. Diaries, Tuesday 10th March 1863.
110. *Ibid.*
111. Diaries, Sunday 15th and Monday 16th March 1863.
112. Theodore Martin, *Life of the Prince Consort,* London, 1875-1880, Vol. 5, page 252, cited by CW Newman, 'Some Contemporary Tributes to Sir George C Lewis', *Transactions of the Radnorshire Society*, XXXIII, 1963, p.55.
113. Diaries, Friday 27th March. Roundell Palmer, first Earl of Selbourne, 1812-1895, Solicitor General in 1863, became Lord Chancellor in 1872. When the *Alabama* dispute was referred to the International Court of Arbitration at Geneva, he appeared as counsel for Great Britain, and 'argued a hopeless case with the utmost patience, tact, and ability'.
114. Diaries, 'KH. At the office'. This is the last entry in his diary.
115. GF Lewis, *op.cit.*, p.431. 4th April 1863. War Office. GC Lewis to his brother GF Lewis.
116. *Ibid.*, p.432.
117. GF Lewis, *op.cit.*, p.273. 1st December 1853. Kent House. GC Lewis to Edmund Head.
118. Spencer Horatio Walpole, 1806-1898, three times Home Secretary, and at Eton with Lewis.
119. *The Times*, 15th April 1863.
120. *Notes & Queries*, 18th April 1863, p.320.
121. George Frederick Samuel Robinson, 1827-1909, succeeded as the second Earl de Grey in 1852. He became Secretary for War in 1863 in succession to Lewis. Gladstone described him as 'a very persistent man with wealth'.
122. Charles Pelham Villiers, 1802-98, grandson of the Earl of Clarendon and President of the Poor Law Board, with a seat in the Cabinet.
123. Son-in-law of Lady Lewis.
124. Thomas Villiers Lister, 1832-1902, son of Lady Lewis and step son of GC Lewis.
125. Herbert Lewis, b. 1846, Lewis's nephew, and son of his brother, Gilbert Frankland Lewis.
126. *The Times*, 20th April 1863.
127. *Notes & Queries*, 18th April 1863, p.320.
128. *Notes & Queries*, 11th April 1863, p.281.
129. *Ibid.*, p.282.
130. *Ibid.*, pp.282,3.

Epilogue

1. *The Times*, 18th May 1863.
2. Whose identity escapes the authors.
3. The Revd John Edmund Cheese, 1827-1879, lived at Castle Weir, Lyonshall, Herefordshire. A Lampeter BA, he was assistant curate of Presteign, before becoming vicar of Bosbury.
4. *The Times*, 13th November 1863.

5. Entry in the *DNB*.
6. Duff Gordon Diaries, Monday 15th February 1864.
7. *Ibid.*, Wednesday March 9th 1864.
8. WE Gladstone.
9. *The Times*, 17th August 1864.
10. *The Times*, 2nd September 1864.
11. *Ibid.*
12. Duff Gordon Diaries, Friday 2nd September 1864.
13. *Ibid.*
14. Duff Gordon Diaries, Saturday 3rd September 1864.
15. *Ibid.*
16. *DNB* entry.
17. *The Times*, 15th September 1864.
18. *Ibid.*
19. Duff Gordon Diaries, Wednesday 21st September 1864.
20. Jane, the wife of the Revd Canon Sir Gilbert Frankland Lewis, who had succeeded to Harpton on the death of his brother.
21. Duff Gordon Diaries, Friday 25th August 1865.
22. *The Times*, 2nd December 1864.
23. *Ibid.*
24. Duff Gordon Diaries,1st March 1855.
25. *Ibid.*
26. *Ibid.*
27. *Ibid.*
28. *Ibid.*
29. *Ibid.*
30. *Ibid.*
31. *Ibid.*
32. *Ibid.*
33. Owen Chadwick, *The Victorian Church*, 3rd edition, London, 1971, Vol I, p.470.
34. Cited by OW Jones, 'Llysdinam and Newbridge', *Brycheiniog*, Vol XX, 1982-83, p.81.
35. Thus Venables and his second wife, Agnes Minna, felt that the bishop's ducks and cat. rather than his peacocks, were his chief concern when they stayed at the palace at Abergwili in August 1869: 'At breakfast 'face, and she heard him murmur "Sweet thing". On looking round to discover the cause, she saw a cat sitting on the window sill. There were more surprises in store: The arrangements for his breakfast were very pecu liar. He had doubles of everything put before him, two small tea-pots, two eggs, two glasses of jam, two toast racks; and seeing there was not quite enough of jam in the second glass to finish his toast, I edged another near him, at which he scowled at me and said: "You have put me quite out. I shall know when I am done", then Thirlwall retreated to his study for the rest of the day and at lunch time she saw a footman carrying a tray with two eggs and the same accessories to the study'. OW Jones, *Rowland Williams, Patriot & Critic*, Llandysul, 1991, p.55.
36. Lewis contributed nine articles to the *Philological Museum*, Cambridge, 1832-3.
37. *Ibid.*
38. *Ibid.*
39. Diaries. Thursday, 12th January, 1854.
40. Cf. Diaries, 31.7..1847; 11-14.9.1849; 16-17.10.1851; 3-4.9.1852, etc.
41. Duff Gordon Archives. ADG 1:6. 25th January, 1848. GC Lewis to Gilbert Lewis. The hearsay reported by Lewis was a resurrection of an earlier rumour that Hampden's lectures were inspired by Joseph Blanco White, 1775-1841, an ex-Roman Catholic priest who had fled from Spain during Napoleon's invasion and was eventually received into the Church of England. He became an honorary member of the Oriel Common Room

when Hampden was a fellow of the college, and a warm friendship grew up between the two men. The suggestion circulating in 1848 that White inspired Hampden's lectures was very damaging because not only did White become an Unitarian, he died in 1841 and so could not support Hampden in refuting the story

42. Diaries. Tuesday 6th September 1858.
43. Banks Archives. RWB 10/1/43 4th November 1852/3.
44. *Ibid.*, p.90. October 3rd 1837. Malta. GC Lewis to EW Head.
45. Diaries. Saturday 5th February 1859. In comparison with his wife, Lewis *was* poor. At her death, for purposes of probate, Lady Lewis's wealth was declared to be under £40,000, whereas that of Lewis was under £20,000.
46. Woodham-Smith, *op.cit.*, p.307.
47. Sir Douglas Strutt Galton, FRS, 1822-1899, in 1858 was a member of the Royal Commission, presided over by Sidney Herbert, on the improvement of the sanitary condition of military barracks and hospitals. In 1861 he was sent with Dr John Sutherland by the War Office into the sanitary condition of the military hospitals and barracks at Gibraltar, Malta, and the Ionian Islands. In 1862 he was a member of the Barrack and Hospital Improvement Committee. See Woodham-Smith, *op.cit.*, p.308.
48. *The Times*, 2nd December 1864.
49. *The Times*, 15th April 1863.
50. *The Times*, 2nd December 1864.
51. Caroline Duff Gordon: Diaries 1855.

Index